Political Construction Sites

POLITICAL CONSTRUCTION SITES

*Nation-building in Russia and
the Post-Soviet States*

Pål Kolstø

University of Oslo

Translated from Norwegian by
Susan Høivik

Westview
PRESS

A Member of the Perseus Books Group

Maps drawn by Trond A. Svensson

Copyright © 2000 by Westview Press, A Member of the Perseus Books Group

Published in 2000 in the United States of America by Westview Press, 5500 Central Avenue, Boulder, Colorado 80301-2877, and in the United Kingdom by Westview Press, 12 Hid's Copse Road, Cumnor Hill, Oxford OX2 9JJ

Find us on the World Wide Web at www.westviewpress.com

Library of Congress Cataloging-in-Publication Data

Kolstø, Pål.
   Political construction sites : nation building in Russia and the Post-Soviet states / Pål Kolstø.
      p.   cm.
   Includes bibliographical references and index.
   ISBN 0-8133-3751-8 (hc) — ISBN 0-8133-3752-6 (pbk.)
   1. Former Soviet republics—Politics and government.   2. Nationalism—former Soviet republics.   3. Ethnicity—Former Soviet republics.   I. Title: Nation building in Russia and the post-Soviet states.   II. Title.

JN6581 .K65   2000
320.947—dc21
                                                                                    99-059717

The paper used in this publication meets the requirements of the American National Standard for Permanence of Paper for Printed Library Materials Z39.48-1984.

10   9   8   7   6   5   4   3   2

CONTENTS

TABLES AND MAPS

Tables

Maps

PREFACE

This book is written for the undergraduate student as well as the general reader. Some chapters and parts of chapters are adapted versions of previously published articles and monographs. These are listed in the bibliography together with other sources; readers who want more detailed analysis than this book provides should consult these works.

This book is part of the research project "Nation-Building and Ethnic Integration in Post-Soviet Societies," financed jointly by the Norwegian Research Council and the Norwegian University Council through the Program for Eastern Europe. Without their support I could not have written this book.

Bente Bergesen, Kristian Gerner, Hans Olav Melberg, Susan Høivik, and the publisher's anonymous reviewer read the manuscript of the whole book, and several colleagues contributed suggestions and corrections to one or more chapters: Aadne Aasland, Helge Blakkisrud, Tor Bukkvoll, Peter Duncan, Germ Jaanmat, Claus Neukirch, Yaacov Ro'i, and Sven Gunnar Simonsen. Their help allowed me to weed out some unfortunate mistakes and inaccuracies and induced me to add some additional perspectives.

Pål Kolstø
Stavanger, Norway, June 1999

1

INTRODUCTION

"When the Soviet Union fell, fifteen new states saw the light of day." At first glance, this statement would appear quite unproblematic. But it cannot stand up to closer scrutiny. A "state" in the full sense of the word does not appear simply because of a political proclamation of independence or international recognition. A true state must have control of its own frontiers, have a monopoly of coercive powers on its own territory, be able to collect taxes and tolls, and so on. To carry out these and other necessary tasks, at least a modicum of administrative apparatus is required, as well as broad societal consensus as to the rules and routines for doing these jobs.

In winter 1991–1992 these preconditions were generally not fulfilled in any of the Soviet successor states of Eurasia. The armed forces on their territories were beyond the control of the new state authorities, as were the levers of economic policy—the joint military command remained in Moscow, together with the state mint and banknote press. Administrations were understaffed, except in Russia, which could take over the old organs of the central Soviet power—so it ended up instead with an outsized central administration. Furthermore, there were no border defense systems between the new states; indeed, state borders were not even marked on the ground.

For these reasons, it is better to say that during the winter of 1991–1992 the *foundations* were laid for the growth of fifteen new states in Eurasia. The establishment of governmental institutions and other attributes of the state is a long-term process that will continue for many years to come. Exactly what forms this process will take, and at what pace, will depend on a series of conditions: economic and geographical factors, the attitudes of other states (especially neighboring ones), the demographic and cultural composition of the population, and the political decisions taken by the elite—to mention only a few of the most important.

In this book, however, I leave aside the economic and institutional aspects and focus instead on some crucial political and cultural aspects of nation-building. If a state is to remain viable in the long term, it is essential that its people believe they have a common identity and a common destiny. They must feel linked together by allegiance to certain shared values, as well as to the same shared symbols and institutions. This need not imply that everyone must feel culturally identical. There may well be pronounced regional differences, differences that can even find institutional expression by means of a federal state structure. But what *is* necessary is broad agreement as to the politicogeographical map of state legitimacy and the principles underlying its structure.

The USSR was officially defined as a "multinational federation." By contrast, the successor states have proclaimed themselves "national states" or "nation-states"—and here a further difficulty arises. This concept, so basic to modern political science and related studies, can have several different meanings. Sometimes it is used simply to apply to all modern states, in contrast to the old dynastic states of the past. The modern state defines its field of responsibility and competence far more broadly than did states in former centuries. It is not enough merely to collect taxes and defend the land against internal and external foes: Today's state also has clear goals and strategies—for improving the lives of its citizens (their standard of living, educational levels, and health conditions); for linking the country together through a tighter infrastructure; and so on.

The national (nation-) state can also be defined by contrast to the empire. An empire is usually understood as a heterogeneous state held together by external means of force, whereas the more homogeneous nation-state is seen as based on the consent of the populace. The empire has subjects; the nation-state has citizens. So what is the glue that holds the nation together? There exist at least two very different views as to what a nation is. Some use a political definition: The nation is simply the sum of all the citizens or inhabitants of that state. In this view the nation is kept together by its common territory, common government authority, and common political history. This has been the dominant understanding in the West and is enshrined, for example, in the name of the world organization: the United *Nations*.

There exists, however, a rival concept that sees the nation as a cultural entity, held together by common language, traditions, folklore, mores, and religion—in short, the ethnic nation. This concept has deep roots in the eastern part of Europe, not least in Russia. One reason was that the multinational empires survived much longer in this part of the world. The state was imperial; the nation was nonstate. Central to the oppositional struggle against the empire was the notion of national autonomy, understood as the right of ethnic groups to organize states of their own.

New States of the Former Soviet Union. Courtesy of Trond A. Svensson.

In ethnically based nation-building, the symbols and traditions of the titular nation become equated with the symbols and traditions of the state: They thereby become the norm for the entire populace.[1] The state authorities will seek to create maximum correspondence between the ethnic and the political "nation"—by means of assimilation, emigration of minorities, or other ways.

By contrast, in civic nation-building the authorities will seek to secure the allegiance of all the inhabitants—without, however, encroaching on their cultural distinctiveness. There is a search for political traditions and symbols common to all ethnic groups, and if necessary these can even be created from scratch. One of the shortcomings of this strategy is the generally weaker emotive power of such supraethnic symbols. They may easily be dismissed as artifacts—which, of course, in one sense they are. Nevertheless, it is quite conceivable that large groups—even the entire populace of a country—may develop a dual set of identities: In political terms, they are proud of being citizens of *their* particular state; in cultural terms, they are proud of being members of their particular ethnic group. In the course of time, a common identity can be built up, centered on the national anthem, the coat of arms, the parliament, and the president. Even though few if any may feel anything special about a newly designed flag, many will come to feel a lump in their throats and tears in their eyes when, to the strains of the national anthem, the top athletes of the nation ascend the winners' block at international sports events.

Successful nation-building need not involve democratization. Democratic and nondemocratic states alike try to gather their populations to form one nation, united in shared symbols and values, but their means and methods vary. In democracies, elections—to the national assembly and to the presidency—are essential elements in nation-building: The president of the country is also *my* president because I helped to vote him into office. And if my candidate lost, well, then, better luck next time.

In nondemocracies it is difficult to achieve a similar kind of identification through the active involvement of citizens. All the same, we should not think that authoritarian and totalitarian regimes always rely solely on force to stay in power. Quite the contrary: Nation-building on the symbolic and ritual level is often particularly intense in precisely such states. Nondemocratic leaders will do their utmost to camouflage their state means of force behind posters with resounding slogans and portraits of the leaders of the country. Impressive patriotic marches may serve to deafen the voices of the opposition. These were conspicuous features of Soviet society, noticed and remarked on by foreign tourists who visited the country during the Communist era.[2]

The Soviet leaders saw it as their goal to create the "new Soviet man."[3] This was *homo sovieticus,* a being who had managed to free himself of all cultural "remnants" *(perezhitki)* of the past and now lived and breathed for the new Soviet values. We have no grounds for dismissing this project as a total failure. Today's Western visitors to the former Soviet Union are often struck by how many people express nostalgia for the good old days before perestroika, when a ruble was a ruble and you knew what the values of your society were. Yet it is also clear that this "Soviet mentality" was never rooted firmly enough in enough people to prevent the state from falling to pieces when perestroika arrived, bringing with it tendencies toward dissolution. The Soviet nation-building project ended up in the dustbin of history—to use the phrase coined by Leon Trotsky.

What about the new projects being launched today? Will they have greater chances of success? Obviously, it is still far too early to offer any decisive answer to that question, but certain tendencies have begun to appear, and in the final chapter I suggest come tentative conclusions.

Nation-Building Versus Ethnic Consolidation

With the exception of Armenia, none of the Soviet successor states is even remotely homogeneous in ethnic terms. The census of 1989—the last one before the breakup of the USSR—found that in all the republics but Armenia, the titular nation constituted 40 to 80 percent of the total populace. In the Ukraine, for example, close to 73 percent of the population were Ukrainians (see Table 1.1). The remainder of the populace in each case was made up of ethnic groups that either belonged to the titular nation of the neighboring republic and had ended up on the "wrong" side of the border when the boundaries were drawn up or had immigrated from other parts of the Soviet Union. Another complicating factor in post-Soviet nation-building is the lack of ethnic consolidation of the titular nations themselves. In many areas there are deep-rooted group allegiances at lower levels—toward the tribe, clan, subethnos, or region. In other cases there may be overarching supranational ties of cultural identity, linked, for example, to language or religion.

Strong subnational identities need not in themselves represent any contradiction to a shared, unifying national identity: A strong national identity can be developed precisely on the basis of pronounced subnational identities. But we should keep in mind that many ethnonationalists see it as their goal to reduce the importance of loyalties that link the individual to entities other than the ethnic group and to develop stronger common traditions linked to shared ethnic customs, language, and so on. This is what we may term "ethnos-building," or ethnic consolidation.

In many states in the former Soviet Union, we can see two processes—nation-building and ethnic consolidation—developing in parallel. One

TABLE 1.1   Language, Religion, and Ethnicity in the Soviet Successor States, 1989 (in percentages)

State	Language of Titular Pop.	Traditional Religion of Titular Pop.	Titular Pop. in Percent of Total Pop.	Largest Minority Group and Percent of Total Pop.	Next Largest Minority Group and Percent of Total Pop.
Russia	Indo-European, East Slavic	Christian, Orthodox	81.5	Tatars, 3.7	Ukrainians, 2.9
Estonia	Finno-Ugric	Christian, Lutheran	61.5	Russians, 30.3	Ukrainians, 3.0
Latvia	Indo-European, Baltic	Christian, Lutheran/ R. C.	51.8	Russians, 34.0	Belarusians, 4.5
Lithuania	Indo-European, Baltic	Christian, R. C.	79.5	Russians, 9.4	Poles, 7.0
Belarus	Indo-European, East Slavic	Christian, Orthodox/ Uniate	77.8	Russians, 13.2	Poles, 4.0
Moldova	Indo-European, Romance	Christian, Orthodox	64.4	Ukrainians, 13.8	Poles, 13.0
Ukraine	Indo-European, East Slavic	Christian, Orthodox/ Uniate	72.7	Russians, 22.1	Jews, 0.9
Georgia	Caucasian	Christian, Orthodox	70.0	Armenians, 7.9	Russians, 6.3
Armenia	Indo-European, sui generis	Christian, Monophysite	93.3	Azeris, 2.5	Kurds, 1.7
Azerbaijan	Turkic	Shi'ite/ Sunni Muslim	82.6	Russians, 5.6	Armenians, 5.5
Turkmenistan	Turkic	Sunni Muslim	71.8	Russians, 9.5	Uzbeks, 8.8
Tajikistan	Iranian	Sunni Muslim	62.2	Uzbeks, 23.3	Russians, 7.6
Uzbekistan	Turkic	Sunni Muslim	71.2	Russians, 8.3	Tajiks, 4.6
Kyrgyzstan	Turkic	Sunni Muslim	52.2	Russians, 21.5	Uzbeks, 12.9
Kazakhstan	Turkic	Sunni Muslim	39.6	Russians, 37.8	Germans, 5.7

SOURCE: Natsional'nyy sostav naseleniya SSSR (The national composition of the population of the USSR) (Moscow: Finansy i Statistika, 1991).

might expect these to be located on two different levels: nation-building on the political and ethnos-building on the cultural level. And yet we often see that the two are intermixed, resulting in a hybrid: ethnic nation-building.

Many of the Central Asian nations are rather recent creations. The boundaries between them have been drawn up by state authorities on the basis of fieldwork carried out by Russian cartographers and ethnographers in the nineteenth and twentieth centuries, often with clearly political motives. The Communists wanted to establish quasi nation-states in Central Asia in order to break down allegiances to such overarching ideologies as Pan-Turkism and the Islamic fellowship *(ummah)*.

After the fall of the Soviet Union, old clan antagonisms began to resurface. In Kyrgyzstan the main conflict is north-south: The Kyrgyz in the southern parts of the country are heavily influenced by Uzbek oasis culture, and Islam is fairly strong, whereas the Kyrgyz of the north are marked more by Russian cultural influence. Southern Kyrgyz were in control during the Communist period, but at present the northerly clans dominate the political life of the country, at the expense of the southerly Kyrgyz and the various national minorities. In Kazakhstan we find a tripartite division of clan patterns between the three large Kazakh "hordes" *(zhuz)*: the Great, Middle, and Small Hordes, who live in the south, the northeast, and the northwest, respectively. The southerly Great Horde currently controls the state apparatus at the expense of both Slavs and the northerly Kazakh groupings.

In neither Kyrgyzstan nor Kazakhstan have clan or regional antagonisms found violent expression. This has, however, been the case in both Tajikistan and Georgia. During the Communist era, the northern Tajiks, centered around the city of Leninabad, dominated in Tajikistan. After the fall of the Soviet Union, the Leninabad leadership found itself challenged by the southern Tajiks. This unleashed a lengthy civil war in which tens of thousands were killed. This conflict had certain ideological aspects, since many of the Tajik leaders from the south and east brandished the banner of Islam, whereas the northerly groups stuck to communism and formed alliances with certain groups from central areas in the country. But when the "Communists" finally emerged victorious, they, too, were hit by rivalries and antagonisms, and the ensuing conflicts saw them split along traditional clan lines. This would indicate that the ideological banners of communism, Islam, and democracy were but thin fig leaves concealing a naked power struggle between clan leaders and regional interests. Most observers would now say that today's "Tajik nation" is a sheer fiction, existing solely in official Tajikistani propaganda.

Georgia has been rent by no less than three bloody civil wars since the breakup of the USSR. In two of these, ethnic Georgians were on one side of the conflict and the national minority groups of Abkhazians and South Ossetians on the other. The third conflict (1992–1993), however, pitted Georgian against Georgian. This was a power struggle marked by fierce personal antagonisms between such figures as former president Zviad

Gamsakhurdia and the current president, Eduard Shevardnadze, but it also had a regional aspect. The Georgian ethnic group is made up of a whole series of subgroups—the mountain Svans, the Kartlis, the west Georgian Mingrelians—with highly disparate self-identities and linguistic norms. Gamsakhurdia was a Mingrelian, and when he was forced out of the capital he found support and refuge in his home area, Mingrelia.

Even in a European nation like Ukraine, the process of ethnic consolidation is far from completed. Both in Galicia in the west and Donetsk in the east, most people consider themselves "Ukrainians"—but what they mean by this term can differ greatly. The Galicians have been subjects of the Habsburgs and of Poland, whereas eastern Ukrainians have been Russian/Soviet subjects for centuries. Both cultural and political identity cannot avoid being marked by such different experiences.

In neighboring Moldova the picture is quite different still: Here, too, is tension between various regional forms of the ethnic Moldovan identity, but the main conflict concerns another issue: the extent to which the "Moldovans" can be said to constitute a separate ethnic group at all. Some Moldovans would say no, that they are in fact Romanians. And so whereas in some states the nation-building project is threatened by subnational and subethnic identities, in Moldova it is the titular nation itself, the Moldovans, who are seen (by a minority) as merely a subethnic group.

Like Tajikistan and Georgia, Moldova has been the scene of civil war in post-Soviet times, although it has assumed somewhat smaller dimensions. In the spring and summer of 1992, the Moldovan authorities in Chişinău fought against separatists from the left (eastern) bank of the Dniester who had proclaimed their own independent Dniester republic. The secessionists won, backed by political and some military support from Russia. Today the Moldovan Dniester Republic remains an independent, lilliputian state lacking international recognition.

The Dniester conflict can be said to occupy an in-between position, between interethnic and intraethnic conflict. To some extent it was a struggle involving Russians and other Slavs on the one (eastern) side of the Dniester against ethnic Moldovans on the other bank of the river—but it was also a showdown between and among various Moldovan groups. The Moldovans living on the eastern side of the Dniester had become more Russified than their ethnic counterparts on the western side. During the Soviet era they enjoyed privileged status, but since independence they have been relegated to the sidelines in the politics of the new country—whose capital, Chişinău, lies to the west of the river.

Topics and Cases

After almost a decade of post-Soviet nation-building, some patterns are emerging. Practically everywhere the titular nation has been placed in the center of the project and given certain prerogatives, implicitly or explicitly. For instance, with a few notable exceptions the language of the titular nation has everywhere been elevated to the status of state language. It would, however, be wrong to claim that the new states of Eurasia are based exclusively on the ethnic principle. Their new state structures embody elements from both the civic and the ethnic model. In the lands of the former Soviet Union, these two nation concepts seem to be living in uneasy cohabitation.

The breakups of Czechoslovakia, Yugoslavia, and the Soviet Union after the fall of communism have provided students of nation-building with an abundance of comparative cases. Not since the decolonization of Africa has the world seen a similar proliferation of new states in one area. The post-Soviet states have all the necessary prerequisites for fruitful comparisons: a large number of similarities but at the same time important differences.

To a surprisingly high degree, the leaders of the new states have chosen different models of nation-building. Up to a point, these variations may be explained by reference to demographic differences, historical experiences, and cultural peculiarities. But in some cases states with very similar cultural and historical preconditions have ended up with strikingly divergent outcomes. Take the case of Ukraine versus Belarus. The Ukrainians as well as the Belarusians are East Slavs, and both ethnic groups have over the centuries been exposed to massive cultural and political pressure from the same two states—Poland to the west and Russia to the east. Even so, we can conclude that Belarusian nation-building today is at the very best an uphill battle; some would call it a complete failure. At the same time, the Ukrainian nation-state is slowly but surely gaining acceptance and maturity.

In this book I look at the ongoing nation-building projects in the Soviet successor states in a comparative perspective, discussing their preconditions, the means employed by the nation-builders, and the goals they are aiming at. I focus on the nationality discourse in the various countries on the one hand and the practical actions taken by the political leaders on the other. Politicians often say one thing and do something quite different. Clues as to what kind of nation the state authorities want to bring about may nevertheless be gleaned from official documents such as declarations of independence, constitutional clauses, and various legal and sublegal texts (laws on national minorities, language, etc.). Whether the authorities have the will and the means to fill their policy declarations with real content is another question. In order to find the answer to that, we must analyze their actual political actions.

Chapters 2 through 5 are thematically structured. Here I take up some aspects and problems of nation-building that are common to most or all of the new states: Chapter 2 deals with the development of nation-building theory in Western research and the applicability of this theory to post-Communist realities in the former Soviet Union. Readers who find such theorizing too heavy can simply skip over this chapter without much danger (unless, of course, they happen to be so unfortunate as to have it as required course reading). Chapter 3 deals with the rewriting of history currently in full swing in all the Soviet successor states. Although the modern theory of nationalism has pointed out that "nations" as we know them today are fairly new as a societal phenomenon, an important part of nationalist self-identity is precisely the feeling that "at least *my* nation is as old as the hills." Thus, most nation-builders do not present their program as nation-*building*; rather, they prefer to see it as a kind of restoration work or perhaps even archeology. The nation has been there all along, at least potentially, and all that is needed is to bring it forth into the open and polish it. For this reason, historians are an indispensable group of craftspeople in the nation-building team. They sift through the available historical material in order to find proof of the nation in past centuries. In relation to the established versions of the historical record, this enterprise is revisionist. The previous historiography was geared toward a legitimation of the existing state—in our case that means the Soviet Union and, prior to that, the czarist empire.

Chapter 4 deals with the role of religion in nation-building. In most parts of Eastern Europe, the cohesion and commonalty of ethnic groups is based on language, with religion playing a subsidiary role. Neighboring groups who profess the same faith may regard themselves as separate nations, citing their linguistic differences as the reason.[4] Even so, in the ongoing nation-building projects of the Soviet successor states religion may play a part. Throughout the world, nationalists comb the cultural landscape in search of construction materials for their respective nation-building projects. Among their discoveries is often "the faith of the ancestors," which they seize upon and utilize—although they may well be nonbelievers themselves. In this way religion is reintroduced into the national identity, not as essence or driving force but as superimposed ideology.

Chapter 5 discusses the millions of Russians and other Russophones living in the non-Russian successor states. In most of the new states, the Russians represent the only cultural tradition that is strong enough to rival, and perhaps even outperform, the culture of the titular nation. Given that the Russians enjoy the express backing of the most powerful post-Soviet state, Russia, they are also politically the most important group. How, then, are the Russian minorities being treated in the non-Russian Soviet successor states? Are they being defined as a part of the new nation, or are they seen as alien elements? What are Russia's interests and priorities on the diaspora issue? And finally, to what extent are the local Russians themselves satisfied or dissatisfied with their new status as national minorities in their respective countries of residence? Do they want to be included in the ongoing nation-building projects, or would they prefer to stay on the sidelines?

Chapters 6 through 10 are geographically structured. In this part of the book, rather than examining all regions or countries in the former Soviet Union, I single out for closer scrutiny six countries I consider particularly interesting: These are Belarus, Moldova, Ukraine, Latvia, Kazakhstan, and Russia.

Belarus is fascinating in that it represents a case of a "dog that did not bark." Ernest Gellner used this expression (from the Sherlock Holmes story "The Hound of the Baskervilles") to describe nationalisms that fizzle out without ever achieving their goals. Expected events that never take place may give the trained detective just as much valuable information as unexpected events that do come to pass.[5] From a theoretical point of view, therefore, bungled nation-building projects may be just as important as the success stories. They remind us that nation-building is not a train on tracks that will reach its destination sooner or later. How and why some of these trains run out of steam or derail may tell us much about the dynamism and mechanisms of nation-building.

Moldova presents us with an intriguing case for precisely the opposite reasons. It represents a nation-building project that seems to have taken off against formidable odds. Prior to the collapse of the Soviet Union, practically all pundits agreed that there was no such thing as a "Moldovan nation." What passed for a Moldovan nation was just one of Joseph Stalin's sinister concoctions, designed to justify his annexation of Bessarabia (that is, Moldova) from Romania during World War II. Stalin reckoned that if a separate Moldovan identity, distinct from the Romanian identity, could be established and accepted, this would complicate the return of this region to Romania. Indeed, the old schemer may have hit upon a shrewd idea. Even while strong cultural elites in today's Moldova are pushing for reunification with Romania, support for this option among the general Moldovan populace is very weak. Most Moldovans, not to mention the members of the ethnic minorities in Moldova, clearly prefer the establishment of a separate, independent Moldovan state. Realization of this fact has given many Romanians, as well as a score of Western nationality experts, a rude awakening. These experts now have to go through their theories anew to try to find out why the Moldovans so obstinately fail to act in accordance with the accepted scheme of things.

As mentioned earlier in this chapter, Ukraine, too, stands in contrast to Belarus, but for reasons other than the Moldovan case. Like the Belarusians, the Ukrainians have historically been exposed to heavy doses of assimilatory pressure from their dominating neighbors to the east, the

Russians. In certain respects this pressure has been even greater in Ukraine than in Belarus. In demographic terms, for instance, Russians are more strongly represented in Ukraine: More than 20 percent of the total Ukrainian population is composed of ethnic Russians (as against 11 percent in Belarus). In addition, millions of Ukrainians in the eastern and southern parts of the country are linguistically and culturally Russified. Probably as much as half of the total population are more familiar with Russian culture and language than with Ukrainian. This is true not least of the urban and political elites.

Nevertheless, Ukrainian nation-building today is imbued by a strong impulse of Ukrainization. Most remarkably, this impulse seems to impact heavily on political leaders elected to high offices in Kiev from the eastern, Russophone provinces—even when they have been elected on a specifically pro-Russian or pro-bicultural ticket. Chapter 9 seeks to provide some explanations for this paradox.

Latvia and Kazakhstan are interesting cases of nation-building since the titular ethnic groups compose only about half of the total populations: currently about 57 percent in Latvia and 50 percent in Kazakhstan, lower than in all other post-Soviet states. In both Latvia and Kazakhstan, most members of the nontitular population seem to be coalescing into a common group with a high level of shared identity as post-Soviet Russophones. This means that both countries are characterized by a notable degree of ethnodemographic bipolarity. In such cases, one would assume, nation-building based on the culture and traditions of the titular group alone would be out of the question. And yet for all practical purposes this is what is taking place. Although the means employed in each of the two states differ somewhat, it seems fair to say that Latvian nation-building is geared toward the Latvianization of the Latvian state, and in Kazakhstan Kazakhization is a desired goal.

But is this at all possible? Is half of the population supposed to be "integrated" into the other half—and if so, what will be the result? Obviously, the answers to these questions will not be the same in both countries. Latvia and Kazakhstan alike are post-Soviet, bicultural states, but they are very different in other respects. Latvia is a small country the size of Ireland, with no more than 2.5 million inhabitants; Kazakhstan covers a territory as large as Western Europe, with a population of more than 18 million. But it is precisely the combination of significant similarities and dissimilarities between the two cases that makes a comparison of Latvia and Kazakhstan a fruitful endeavor.

Finally, I discuss nation-building in Russia. In important respects the contemporary Russian state project differs from nation-building in the fourteen other Soviet successor states. Russia has a continuous existence as an independent state since the Middle Ages but has never been a nation-state. Czarist Russia was an empire in actual fact as well as in self-designation. Whether or not it was also an ethnic empire in which the dominant group, the Russians, enjoyed special rights and privileges is a moot question (though—except with regard to the last decades of its existence, the 1880s to 1917—I would answer in the negative).

In the Communist period, the vast majority of Russians identified with the Soviet Union as their fatherland. This distinguished them from most of the other large nationalities in the country, who tended to feel more attached to the particular republic that bore the name of their group. The challenge facing the nation-builders in Russia today is not how to establish and gain acceptance for a new or newly independent state but how to win support in the population for a drastic truncation of state territory.

In the USSR the Russians made up barely 50 percent of the total population; in today's Russia they constitute no less than 81.5 percent. By dint of this demographic factor, Russia has a far more "Russian" quality than the Soviet Union ever had. Russian nation-builders may therefore be tempted to try to construct a Russian nation-state in an ethnocultural sense. Because, however, Russia—like the USSR—is an ethnically based federation, with separate autonomous territorial units allotted to a large number of minority groups, this will be a risky project indeed, fraught with new state truncation.[6]

Russia has no less than twenty-one ethnically defined republics, one autonomous province *(oblast)*, and ten ethnically defined national districts *(okrugi)*. This federal structure has given the minorities far stronger levers in their struggle for ethnic rights than those the nontitular groups in the other Soviet successor states have at their disposal. This is true even though, taken together, the minorities in Russia make up a smaller share of the total population than in most other former Soviet republics, and they are also divided into a high number of sometimes very small groups. For instance, the largest minorities in Russia, the Tatars and the Ukrainians, make up only 3.7 percent and 2.9 percent of Russia's total population, respectively (see Table 1.1). Moreover, the minorities live scattered over several regions of the country, separated by large areas of compact Russian settlements. They also belong to many different language groups and religions. For these reasons, one might have expected central Russian authorities to have played a successful ethnopolitical game of divide-and-rule. Some attempts at this have indeed been made, but generally speaking the minorities have been more adroit in playing off various groups within the central elites against each other than vice versa. This was particularly true during the constitutional crisis of 1993, when President Boris Yeltsin and the leadership of the Russian parliament confronted each other in a bitter, and eventually bloody, power struggle. During this standoff both the president and his adversaries tried to enlist the support of the non-Russians by holding out the promise of greater self-rule for the autonomous units.

Some republics, however, signaled that they were not content with self-rule in any form: They demanded complete independence. In most cases this demand was apparently set forth primarily to strengthen their bargaining position. Republics such as Tatarstan and Bashkortostan adopted declarations of independence as a tactical ploy to ensure for themselves more profitable agreements with the center than they would otherwise have achieved. In one particular case, however, Chechnya, it soon transpired that the local leadership was deadly serious about independence. The willingness to compromise left much to be desired in both Moscow and in the Chechan capital of Grozny. Indeed, the path of negotiations was hardly traversed at all. The upshot was the deeply tragic Chechen war of 1995–1996. From a nation-building perspective, the Russian military defeat in Chechnya had several important implications. As it sapped the country of badly needed resources, it also seriously impaired the prestige of the central authorities. Worst of all, by fighting against its own citizens the Russian state put into question the very existence of the "Russian nation" in the political sense.

The result of the war seemed to indicate that it was possible for an autonomous Russian unit to break out of the state if its citizens were willing and able to fight for this goal with weapons in hand. But it also showed that the costs of such secession were extremely high. Most potential secessionists in other Russian autonomies will probably regard these costs as prohibitive and be deterred from following in the footsteps of the Chechens.

From 1991–1993 it was widely believed—in Russia as well as among foreign observers—that the Russian Federation might eventually go the same way as the Soviet federation: that is, it might be dissolved into its constituent parts. Chechnya notwithstanding, it seems that the scenario of ever-accelerating fissions has been averted. Many of the autonomous republics in Russia are located in the central regions of the country, surrounded on all sides by Russia proper. Even if they should achieve international recognition as independent countries, practical, geographical circumstances dictate that this would not amount to more than a status comparable to that of the small, landlocked state of Lesotho, heavily dependent on South Africa, which surrounds it on all sides. In addition, in many of these autonomous units the titular nation comprises a relatively modest share of the total population. In several cases, Russians are the largest ethnic group, and they are usually not keen on being separated from Russia.

The debate on the future structure and identity of Russia continues. Several right-wing radical parties, such as the so-called Liberal Democrats headed by Vladimir Zhirinovskiy, are openly revisionist. On the left, the Communist Party, the largest political party in Russia, has repeatedly shown that it is not reconciled to the fact that the Soviet Union has been dissolved. The Communists are strenuously working to establish a renewed union of some kind or another.

Even so, a slow but perceptible identity change seems under way in the Russian population at large, as well as among the elites. More and more people seem to be transferring their political loyalty to the new incarnation of Russian statehood, the Russian Federation. As the memory of the Soviet Union recedes ever further into the past, this new Russian state is likely to be accepted by larger and larger parts of the citizenry. Perhaps Russia may in time become a nation-state, a multiethnic or "multinational" nation-state—for the first time in history.

In 1989 the famous British historian Eric Hobsbawm remarked that it is not implausible to present the history of the nineteenth-century world as one of "nation-building." But toward the end of the twentieth century, he claimed, as state integration through supranational organizations such as the European Union is gaining speed and the countries of the world are becoming increasingly interlinked and interdependent through traffic and trade, the perspective of nation-building is becoming ever more anachronistic. "Is anyone likely to write the world history of the late twentieth and the early twenty-first centuries in such terms? It is most unlikely."[7] I have nevertheless sought to do just that—not the history of the entire world, it is true, but the history of fifteen new states.

2

NATION-BUILDING AND
SOCIAL INTEGRATION THEORY

Nation-Building Theory

The term *nation-building* came into vogue among historically oriented political scientists in the 1950s and 1960s. Its main proponents included such leaders of the American academic community as Karl Deutsch, Charles Tilly, and Reinhard Bendix. Nation-building theory was used primarily to describe the processes of national integration and consolidation that led up to the establishment of the modern nation-state—as distinct from various forms of traditional states, such as feudal and dynastic states, church states, and empires. *Nation-building* is an architectural metaphor that, strictly speaking, implies the existence of consciously acting agents—architects, engineers, carpenters, and the like. As used by political scientists, however, the term covers not only conscious strategies initiated by state leaders but also unplanned societal change.[1] In the apt phrase of Øyvind Østerud, the concept of nation-building became for political science what industrialization was to social economy: an indispensable tool for detecting, describing, and analyzing the macrohistorical and sociological dynamics that have produced the modern state.[2]

The traditional, premodern state was made up of isolated communities with parochial cultures at the "bottom" of society and a distant and aloof state structure at the "top" largely content with collecting taxes and keeping order. Through nation-building these two spheres were brought into more intimate contact with each other. Members of the local communities were drawn upward into the larger society through education and political participation. The state authorities, in turn, expanded their demands and obligations toward the members of society by offering a wide array of services and integrative social networks. The subjects of the monarch were gradually and imperceptibly turned into citizens of the nation-state. Substate cultures and loyalties either vanished or lost their political importance, superseded by loyalties toward the larger entity, the state.

Stein Rokkan's model saw nation-building as consisting of four analytically distinct aspects.[3] In Western Europe these aspects had usually followed each other in more or less the same order. Thus, they could be regarded not only as aspects but also as phases of nation-building. The first phase resulted in economic and cultural unification at the elite level. The second phase brought ever larger sectors of the masses into the state system through conscription into the army, enrollment in compulsory schools, and so on. The burgeoning mass media created channels for direct contact between the central elites and periphery populations and generated a widespread sense of identification with the political system at large. In the third phase, the subject masses were brought into active participation in the workings of the territorial political system. Finally, in the last stage, the administrative apparatus of the state expanded. Public welfare services were established and nationwide policies for the equalization of economic conditions were designed.

In the oldest nation-states of Europe, along the Atlantic rim, the earliest stage of these processes commenced in the Middle Ages and lasted until the French Revolution. Although it is impossible to pinpoint exactly when the entire nation-building process was completed, it certainly went on for several centuries. In the ideal variant, each consecutive phase set in only after the previous one had run its course. This ensured the lowest possible level of social upheavals and disruptions, Rokkan believed.

● ● ●

In the mid-1970s, discussions on nation-building took a new turn. In a seminal article pointedly titled "Nation-Building or Nation-Destroying?" Walker Connor launched a blistering attack on the school of thought associated with Karl Deutsch and his students.[4] Connor noted that the nation-building literature was preoccupied with social cleavages of various kinds—between burghers and peasants, nobles and commoners, elites and masses—but virtually or totally ignored ethnic diversity. This Connor regarded as an inexcusable sin of omission, since, according to his computation, only 9 percent of the states of the world could be regarded as ethnically homogeneous.

Since nation-building in the Deutschian tradition meant assimilation into the larger society and the eradication of ethnic peculiarities, Connor believed that in world history it had produced more nation-destroying than nation-building. But the efficiency of active engineering in nation-building, he held, had generally been greatly exaggerated. Very often it was counterproductive, regularly producing a backlash of ethnic revivalism. Connor maintained that complete assimilation of ethnic minorities had largely failed all over the world, even in that alleged stronghold of consummate nation-building, Western Europe.

Another reason behind the fundamental flaws of nation-building theory Connor found in the terminological confusion caused by the diverse usages of the word *nation*. As he pointed out, this term sometimes is used with reference to cultural groups and peoples and at other times describes political entities (states)—compare, for example, expressions such as *United Nations* and *international politics*. Even more misleading, he felt, was the tendency to use the term *nation* to describe the total population of a particular state without regard for its ethnic composition.

Reserving the term *nation* for ethnic groups only, Connor discarded all objective cultural markers as valid identity demarcations for these units. Neither common language, common religion, nor any other shared cultural reservoir within a group qualified as a genuine sign of nationhood. Any such attempt to objectivize the nation was to mistake the cultural manifestations of a nation for its essence. The true nature of the nation was in every case the sense of common ancestry shared by its members, Connor asserted. The nation is the ultimate extended family. To be sure, hardly ever could a common origin of the members of the nation be proven. In fact, very often it can be established that a nation stems from diverse ethnic sources. The belief in a common genetic origin can therefore usually be shown to be pure myth. Nonetheless, adherence to this myth has remained a sine qua non for every nation, Connor maintained.[5]

Later theoreticians developed Connor's understanding in two different directions. The "modernists"—such as Benedict Anderson, Tom Nairn, Ernest Gellner, and Eric Hobsbawm—strongly underlined the myth aspect of the nation. In a celebrated book title, Benedict Anderson coined the expression "imagined communities" to describe modern nations. The nation is a product of imagination in the sense that the members of the community do not know each other personally and can only imagine themselves to be in communion with each other. But Anderson distanced himself from Gellner and Hobsbawm, who took the "imagination" metaphor one step further, interpreting it in the direction of "invention" and "fabrication." The nation should not be defined as "false consciousness," Anderson insisted. Definitions like that would imply that there are such things as "true communities" that can be juxtaposed to "artificial" nations. "In fact, all communities larger than primordial villages of face-to-face contact (and perhaps even these) are imagined."[6]

At the same time, Anthony Smith, Rasma Karklins, and others developed Connor's themes in another direction, strongly emphasizing the ethnic aspect of the nation. Agreeing with the modernists that "nations" as we know them are recent phenomena, Smith nevertheless insisted that they have a long prehistory, evolving out of ethnic cores. Of the conglomerate of ethnic groups existing in earlier ages, some developed into would-be nations aspiring for nationhood and a state of their own, with a few eventually acquiring it. Why do some groups succeed whereas others fail? Often this must be explained as a result of historical contingencies, a confluence of felicitous circumstances. But it may also be because of the active efforts of determined nationalists, the nation-builders.[7]

Smith and his disciples retained but reemployed the term *nation-building* introduced by the earlier school of thought. In accordance with their "neo-primordialist" understanding of all modern nations as products of age-old ethnic building material, they heavily underlined the cultural, symbolic, and mythmaking aspects of nation-building:

> Even for the most recently created states, ethnic homogeneity and cultural unity are paramount considerations. Even where their societies are genuinely "plural" and there is an ideological commitment to pluralism and cultural toleration, the elites of the new states find themselves compelled, by their own ideals and the logic of the ethnic situation, to forge new myths and symbols of their emergent nations and a new "political culture" of anti-colonialism and the post-colonial (African or Asian) state.[8]

Social Integration Theory

In the liberal tradition of the nineteenth century, we may identify two somewhat divergent views on national integration. One dominant line of thought regarded the cultural and linguistic dissolution of the minorities into "high cultures" as not only historically inevitable but also indisputably beneficial to the minorities themselves. This process was often labeled "assimilation," "acculturation," or "amalgamation" rather than "integration," but no clear distinctions were made among these concepts.

A classic expression of the assimilationist view may be found in John Stuart Mill's *Considerations on Representative Government*:

> Experience proves that it is possible for one nationality to merge and be absorbed in another: and when it was originally an inferior and more backward portion of the human race the absorption is greatly to its advantage. Nobody can suppose that it is not more beneficial to a Breton, or a Basque of French Navarre, to be brought into the current of the ideas and feelings of a highly civilized and cultivated people—to be a member of the French nationality, admitted on equal terms to all the privileges of French citizenship,

sharing the advantages of French protection, and the dignity of French power—than to sulk on his own rocks.[9]

A somewhat different view was taken by Lord Acton. He was more inclined to see cultural diversity as a blessing for the members of society and a safeguard against tyranny: "The presence of different nations under the same sovereignty . . . provides against the servility which flourishes under the shadow of a single authority, by balancing interests, multiplying associations, and giving the subject the restraint and support of a combined opinion."[10] Not unity and uniformity but diversity and harmony ought to reign in society, Acton maintained. But by no means did he regard all cultures as equal or equally worthy of preservation. On the contrary, one of the main reasons people from different cultures ought to be included in the same state was that "inferior races" could thereby be raised, by learning from intellectually superior nationalities: "Exhausted and decaying nations are revived by the contact of a younger vitality. Nations in which the elements of organization and the capacity for government have been lost . . . are restored and educated anew under the discipline of a stronger and less corrupted race."[11]

In fact, Acton was prepared to use such phrases as "the cauldron of the State" in which a "fusion" takes place through which the vigor, the knowledge, and the capacity of one portion of humankind may be communicated to another. Thus, his arguments for a multicultural state lead us toward a surprising result: Under the tutelage of a superior nationality, members of the less-advanced cultures in the state will shed many of their distinctive traits and learn true civilization. Exactly how much will remain of their peculiar identities (to use a modern word that Acton does not employ) remains unclear, but his vision of social integration was not as far removed from John Stuart Mill's as many observers have been led to believe.[12]

Most of what was written on nation-building and integration in the 1960s and 1970s stood in the combined tradition of Mill and Acton. To Karl Deutsch and his disciples, nation-building and national integration were but two sides of the same coin—indeed, simply two ways of describing the same process. A major object of nation-building was to weld the disparate population elements into a congruent whole by forging new loyalties and identities at the national (or state) level at the expense of localism and particularistic identification. Deutsch specified four stages by which he expected this process to take place: (1) open or latent resistance to political amalgamation into a common national state; (2) minimal integration to the point of passive compliance with the orders of such an amalgamated government; (3) deeper political integration to the point of active support for such a common state but with continuing ethnic or cultural group cohesion and diversity; and (4) the coincidence of political amalgamation and integration with the assimilation of all groups to a common language and culture.[13]

Deutsch saw successful assimilation as a prerequisite for upward social mobilization for members of minority cultures. Only those individuals who mastered the language and the cultural code of the dominant group could aspire to achievement. In most of his writings, Deutsch also saw the creation of the homogeneous society, with equal opportunities for all groups, as fully attainable.[14]

Walker Connor took issue with the assimilation theory of Karl Deutsch and his school on two accounts. He did not believe that the eradication of cultural differences in society was necessarily a good thing.[15] And, he questioned the one-to-one relationship between modernization and cultural homogenization:

> The continuous spread of modern communication and transportation facilities, as well as statewide social institutions such as public school systems, can be expected to have a great influence upon programs of assimilation. But can the nature of that influence be predicted? It is a truism that centralized communications and increased contacts help to dissolve regional cultural distinctions within a state such as the United States. Yet, if one is dealing not with minor variations of the same culture, but with two quite distinct and self-differentiating cultures, are not increased contacts between the two apt to increase antagonism.[16]

In later articles Connor dropped the question mark and more and more fiercely insisted that this was indeed the case. Advances in communication and transportation tend to increase cultural awareness among minorities by making their members more conscious of the distinctions that set their own community apart from other groups. Individuals come to identify more and more closely with their own in-groups, contrasting themselves to the immediate surroundings.[17]

This view was accepted and even somewhat sharpened by Arend Lijphart, another pioneer of the new trend in integration theory. Lijphart distinguished between essentially homogeneous societies, where increased contacts are likely to lead to an increase in mutual understanding and further homogenization, and "plural societies," where close contacts are likely to produce strain and hostility. In plural societies segregation among the dominant cultural groups would be preferable to integration, he maintained. "Clear boundaries between the segments of a plural society have the advantage of limiting mutual contacts and consequently of limiting the chances of ever-present potential antagonisms to erupt into actual hostility."[18]

The writings of Lijphart and Connor produced "a minor revolution" in thinking about the processes of national integration, as Anthony Birch put it.[19] It would certainly be wrong to see this as a switch from the assimilationist vision of Mill to the more pluralist vision of Acton: Their "revolution" was far more radical than that. Whereas Acton remained a firm believer in the blessings of cross-cultural intercourse, and for that very reason extolled the multinational state as an unqualified good, Connor and especially Lijphart not only accepted but relished the abundance of plural states. They were skeptical about the possibility and indeed the desirability of assimilation.

On the issue of assimilation, Ernest Gellner took a stance in between the two positions sketched above. Himself a Central European thoroughly integrated into British academe, he shared the conviction of the early liberals that full assimilation of cultural minorities was highly desirable, but he was somewhat more pessimistic about its feasibility. Gellner identified what he called "entropy resistance" as a major obstacle to successful assimilation and, by the same token, to the social mobilization of minorities. By *entropy* Gellner meant the inherent tendency of modern industrial society to erase social and regional barriers, creating a homogeneous, equalized society. The territorial and work units of industrial societies are basically ad hoc, he pointed out: "Membership is fluid, has a great turnover, and does not generally engage or commit the loyalty and identity of members. In brief, the old structures are dissipated and largely replaced by an internally random and fluid totality, within which there is not much (certainly when compared with the preceding agrarian society) by way of genuine substructures."[20]

Yet some group attributes, Gellner maintained, have a marked tendency not to become evenly dispersed throughout society over time. Very often these entropy-resistant, ineradicable traits are of a physical nature, such as black skin—or, to stick to Gellner's more surrealistic variant, blue pigmentation. Whenever a high number of persons of blue complexion are located near the bottom of the social ladder, color may become an easily detectable identity marker checking the upward social drift of all blue people. A convenient tool for social stigmatization and oppression of the have-nots has thus been found.

So far, it would seem that Gellner's theory of entropy resistance would belong to the research of racial discrimination rather than to the study of ethnocultural integration. Gellner went on to claim, however, that "some deeply engrained religious-cultural habits possess a vigor and tenacity which can virtually equal those which are rooted in our genetic constitution. . . . An identification with one of two rival local cultures [may be] so firm as to be comparable to some physical characteristic."[21] Thus, whereas Connor and those who agreed with him saw the impediments to smooth cultural assimilation as stemming from the very logic of modernization itself, Gellner located these hindrances in traits and characteristics usually borne by only some members in society.

Applicability to Non-Western Societies

The classical theory of nation-building was an endeavor to understand the evolution of Western states. Inevitably, it reflected Western realities. Nevertheless, its proponents maintained that the theory was applicable also to the study of non-Western societies. This belief was based in part on a linear perception of history that was not always made explicit: All societies were, by the inner logic of human development, bound to pass through the same stages. In addition, most nation-building theorists believed that Western society was really a better society to live in. If they were not compelled by the forces of history to emulate the West, the leaders of non-Western states ought to do so—for their own sake and the sake of their populations.

In fact, contrast with the outside world was from the very beginning part and parcel of the endeavor. It was certainly not fortuitous that this theory developed in the 1960s. The increased interest in the genesis of states came as a response to the flurry of new state-making in the wake of decolonization in Africa. Nation-building theorists wanted to underline that "states" could mean very many different things in different settings and that one should not too readily equate these new, hastily created political contraptions with the sturdy, time-tested nation-states of old.[22] At the very most, these new members of the international community should be viewed as nation-states in the making only. A fair number of the contemporary nation-building projects, it was assumed, would never succeed.[23] Such unfortunates would either sink back into nonexistence or remain internationally recognized states devoid of any national character.

Rokkan remarked that the one distinguishing factor that set nation-building in the new states off from the "old" processes was the time factor. Developments that in Western Europe had lasted for centuries now had to be telescoped into decades. Under such circumstances the various phases could hardly be kept apart but would overlap or even run parallel. This, in his opinion, would produce "fundamentally different conditions." The risks of wrong turns and discontinuities would multiply. Likewise, the element of conscious social engineering in the nation-building process would increase. Nevertheless, Rokkan felt that the new states could learn from European experience, "more from the smaller countries than from the large, more from the multiculturally consociational polities than from the homogeneous dynastic states, more from the European latecomers than from the old established nations."[24]

The assumptions that informed the nation-building debate in the post-colonial era of the 1960s and 1970s have a bearing also upon the debate on nation-building in the post-Communist world of the 1990s and beyond. Once again we see the state authorities and scholars in today's newly independent countries employing the categories and terminology of Western political science to describe—and prescribe—social processes in their own countries, while their Western colleagues hasten to remind them that similarities in terminology easily may obscure significant differences in substance.

Nations and Nation-Building in Eastern Europe

As I pointed out in Chapter 1, the key term *nation* may have two very different meanings: as a community of a state and as a community of culture—the civic nation versus the ethnic nation. In the former case, the nation will be coterminous with the population of a (nation-) state; in the latter case, it may be both larger and smaller than the population in the state in which it resides.

In Eastern Europe—east of the Elbe—the ethnic understanding of the nation has deep roots, whereas the civic concept has tended to have very few adherents.[25] There are probably two important, interrelated reasons for this. First, in the West the bourgeoisie was the main motor behind the civic nation-state and civic national consciousness, whereas in Eastern Europe the national bourgeoisie has traditionally been conspicuously absent.[26] Trade and commerce were not regarded as prestigious occupations and tended to be relegated to outsiders. As a result, the thin stratum of bourgeoisie that could be found was very often of foreign stock—diaspora groups of Jews, Armenians, Germans, and Greeks. Such groups were frequently vilified as unnational leeches on the national body.

In addition, the imperial, dynastic state held its ground much longer in Eastern Europe than along the Atlantic rim. Both the Habsburg and the Romanov empires collapsed only as a result of the cataclysm of World War I. The appellation and identity of these two states were in principle unrelated to the nations that were politically dominant, the Germans and the Russians. Both states represented cultural and ethnic patchworks—in the Habsburg domains Germans made up less than 25 percent of the total population in the nineteenth century.[27] The Russian census of 1897 listed 146 nationalities; the largest of them, the Russians, constituted only 45 percent.[28] In the Habsburg as well as the Romanov empires, local privilege and customary law held sway in many regions to the very end.

The cultural and territorial heterogeneity of the East European empires was not a result of their size only. It also reflected the fact that their rulers were far less energetic and systematic nation-builders than were their Western counterparts.[29] As long as internal peace was retained and taxes paid, they were basically uninterested in the inner life of the various linguistic and religious groups of the state. Left to their own devices, these communities could over time develop strong national identities based on their cultural particularities. As long as the state was imperial, the nation could remain cultural and nonstate.

In Russia the ethnic understanding of the nation was reinforced rather than weakened after the Bolshevik takeover.[30] As early as 1903, Lenin's party declared the right of all nations to self-determination, *nations* here being unequivocally identified with the (major) ethnic groups of the empire. As soon as Communist power had been consolidated, however, the promised right to secede from the state became so heavily circumscribed as to be rendered totally unattainable. Instead, national homelands in the form of Union republics and autonomous republics were instituted as kind of substitute nation-states. These territorial units were given the name and, up to a point, the cultural imprint of the dominant ethnic group, the so-called titular nations.

The 1920s and early 1930s saw a vigorous policy of promoting (often this meant creating) new elites among these groups.[31] This is usually referred to as *korenizatsiya,* or "nativization," but one leading Western expert on Soviet nationality policies prefers to call it the Soviet policy of "nation-building."[32]

In most respects the USSR was a strictly unitary state in which the powers of the center were formidable. Throughout most of Soviet history, the federal element in the state structure was largely dismissed as a mere sham. In the final years of Leonid Brezhnev's regime, however, the ethnically based federation became imbued with a certain degree of real content. Although this trend fell short of a complete return to the *korenizatsiya* period, federalism did become an important fact of Soviet life.[33]

The republics of the Soviet Union were strange halfway houses between civic and ethnic units. In the two-layer Union legislature, they were represented in the Chamber of Nationalities. Deputies to this chamber were chosen not only from among the titular nationalities but from among all residents of the republic. In some cases only a minority of the deputies from a certain autonomous formation actually belonged to the titular group. As far as these deputies had any political clout at all, they were expected to represent the interests of the territorial unit, not of the titular ethnic group.

To the other chamber of the Supreme Soviet, the Chamber of the Union, delegates were chosen according to the territorial principle, and ethnicity played no role. The real organs of power—the Politburo, the Secretariat of the Central Committee, the KGB, and the armed forces—

were also formally ethnically neutral, but in reality ethnic Russians (and to some extent other East Slavs) were clearly overrepresented.[34]

Thus, not only the Union republics but also the very Union itself was a curious hybrid of ethnic and civic state: On the one hand, it was a multinational state based on a nonethnic ideology (Soviet Marxism); on the other, an ethnic empire based on the power dominance of the largest nation, the Russians. This duality gave rise to a perennial debate on the nature of Soviet nationality policy—"internationalism or Russification?"[35]

Russian culture, especially the Russian language, certainly enjoyed a privileged position and was forced on the non-Russians as well. Nonetheless, it should be borne in mind that the autonomous formations did in fact give the various titular groups some special rights within their respective territories. Indeed, whatever privileges and protection the non-Russians enjoyed in the Soviet Union (primarily in the fields of culture, education, and language policy), they enjoyed *only* within "their" republics. Members of the nationality living in other parts of the Union had no special rights, even if they should happen to dwell in a compact ethnic community. Such diaspora groups were more exposed to assimilation than the core group. The important lesson the Soviet nationalities' elites drew from this arrangement was that protection of minority rights "necessarily" takes the form of territorial arrangements. Nonterritorial schemes of minority protection were something they had no experience with. The Austro-Marxist idea of cultural (nonterritorial) autonomy had been rejected by the future people's commissar of nationalities, Joseph Stalin, as early as 1913 and remained a dead issue.[36]

At the same time, Soviet authorities did nothing to create ethnically pure Union republics in the demographic sense. The many ethnic groups had for centuries been living heavily intermingled with each other, and considerable interrepublican migration in the Soviet period further complicated the ethnic map.[37] This is the dual legacy that the new states of Eurasia have to come to grips with today as they embark upon their various nation-building projects: on the one hand, an exclusionary concept that equates the nation with the ethnic group; on the other hand, a medley of disparate ethnic groups living on the territory of the state.

Applicability to Post-Communist Realities

Throughout the former Soviet Union, the new leaders have proclaimed their states as national states or "nation-states." As Rogers Brubaker has suggested, they might perhaps more appropriately be called "nationalizing states." They are ethnically heterogeneous, "yet conceived as nation-states, whose dominant elites promote (to varying degrees) the

language, culture, demographic position, economic flourishing, or political hegemony of the nominally state-bearing nation."[38]

The distinction between nation-states and "nationalizing states" is analytically useful but is one of stages and degrees rather than qualitative
differences. As Anthony Smith has argued, even the oldest nation-states
in Western Europe, such as France, seem to have evolved out of ethnic
cores.[39] Moreover, the forging of a national identity is, in a sense, a never-
ending process: Thus, all nation-states are also nationalizing states. In
Ernest Renan's celebrated expression, the nation is constituted and reconstituted in "a daily referendum."[40] Like a house that has to be kept up
and repaired continuously once it has been constructed, nation-building
in nationalizing states gradually shades into what we might call nation
maintenance.

Even so, nation-building in newly independent states does not necessarily have to repeat the experiences of Western Europe or end up with
the same architectural solutions. Although there is hardly any question of
whether the leaders of the post-Soviet states will pursue a policy of
nation-building (they have repeatedly said that they will), we will need
to find out *what kind* of nation-building this is supposed to be.

Brubaker has suggested a tripartite typology of alternative nation-
building models in the nationalizing states in the new Europe:

1. the model of the civic state, the state of and for its citizens, irrespective of ethnicity
2. the model of the bi- or multinational state, as the state of and for
   two or more ethnocultural core nations
3. the hybrid model of minority rights in which the state is understood as a national but not a nationalizing state. Members of minority groups are guaranteed not only equal rights as citizens and
   are thus protected, in principle, against differentialist nationalizing practices but also certain specific minority rights, notably in
   the domain of language and education, and are thus protected, in
   principle, against assimilationist nationalizing practices.[41]

In the civic state, ethnicity and ethnic nationality have no place,
whereas in the bi- or multinational state they have major public signifi-
cance. In the former case, the constituent units of the polity are individuals, in the latter ethnonational groups. The third model draws on elements from both.

Another typology, overlapping with Brubaker's, has been suggested by
Alexander Motyl.[42] Although his typology is particularly geared toward
the Ukrainian situation, in principle it is applicable to all post-Soviet

states. Motyl contrasts two types of ethnic nation-building—exclusive and inclusive—with a political/territorial model that for all practical purposes is identical with Brubaker's civic model. The exclusive variant, which is based on the linguistic, religious, and cultural traditions of the titular nation only, has relatively few adherents in the former Soviet Union, Motyl notes with relief. Its disruptive potential may therefore easily be exaggerated. The real temptation for contemporary post-Soviet nation-builders, he believes, is the inclusive model. This model is not necessarily inconsistent with a state-based national idea, but it nevertheless views the ethnically defined titular nation as the cornerstone of state-building. What Motyl strongly advocates is the political, nonethnic model of nation-building.

Jack Snyder has remarked that civic nationalism normally appears in well-institutionalized democracies.[43] Ethnic nationalism, in contrast, appears in an institutional vacuum. Therefore, it predominates when institutions collapse, when existing institutions are not fulfilling people's basic needs, and when satisfactory alternative structures are not readily available. This, Snyder believes, is the main reason ethnic nationalism has been so prominent after the collapse of the Soviet state.

In the new states of Eurasia, strong, smoothly functioning state organs are certainly a scarce commodity. The establishment of such institutions will inevitably be a protracted process. Nevertheless, they are slowly coming into existence. According to Snyder, then, the time factor should work in favor of civic nationalism. The new state leaders will gradually feel that they have the necessary tools and the political security they need to implement a color-blind and culturally neutral variety of nation-building. Brubaker, however, disagrees. He recognizes that since the civic model has a certain international legitimacy, civic principles have been incorporated into some constitutional texts and are being evoked in some public declarations:

> But these civic principles remain external. It is hard to imagine a civic self-understanding coming to prevail given the pervasively institutionalized understandings of nationality as fundamentally ethnocultural rather than political, as sharply distinct from citizenship, and as grounding claims to "ownership" of polities (which, after all, were expressly constructed as the polities of and for their eponymous ethnocultural nations).[44]

It is not difficult to find evidence in support of Brubaker's conclusion. What follows is a random selection of quotations from post-Soviet academics.

In April 1994 a Kazakh law professor tried to define the difference between "national" (*natsional'nyy*) sovereignty and "popular" (*narodnyy*) sovereignty. He concluded that "in character" Kazakhstan is a national state of the Kazakh nation, but "in content" it is a democratic, law-governed state. These two aspects, in his view, do not contradict each other: "To my mind, a national state stems from the fulfillment of a nation's right to self-determination. In our case, this means the Kazakh nation, as the indigenous nation which has an historical and unalienable right to fulfill its right to self-determination on its own territory."[45] The ethnic understanding of the nation is here unmistakable.

In 1997 a Latvian professor of sociology reminded his readers that a national state is not the same as a monoethnic state—that, in fact, an absolute monoethnic society does not exist anywhere. Therefore, he believed, Latvia could become a national state. "The idea of the national state is that it ensures the security of the ethnic nation in the long run," he concluded.[46]

The ethnocentrism of the statements quoted above are perhaps not representative of the whole spectrum of the nation-building debate in their respective countries. Yet this kind of thinking may be found as well among post-Soviet scholars who represent liberal traditions clearly oriented toward the West and Western values. The prominent scholar and former Estonian minister of nationalities Klara Hallik asked, "Is it possible to combine the idea of a nation state with the integration of the non-citizens and democratic perspectives of the state?"[47] Hallik's question, too, is based on an ethnic understanding of the nation. She explicitly stated that "restored national statehood must guarantee the ethnic security of the Estonian nation." The "Estonian nation" is here equated with the ethnic Estonians.

In her question Hallik linked the concept of the nation-state directly to the issue of integration, as did the pioneers of classical nation-building theory. But the way she posed the question would probably have made little sense to them. The early nation-building theorists, as we have seen, *defined* nation-building as the inclusion of parochial, culturally anomalous groups into the greater polity. Reinhard Bendix, for one, saw the extension of citizenship to members of ever-larger groups as the very hallmark of successful nation-building.[48] It is clear that the key concepts of the debate have undergone significant transmutations since they were first formulated. These transmutations we must keep in mind when we turn to today's nation-building strategies in the former Soviet republics.

3

DISCOVERING THE CENTURIES-OLD STATE TRADITION

In his *Considerations on Representative Government* (1861), John Stuart Mill noted that people may experience a feeling of belonging to the same nation for various reasons. In some cases, it may be due to family bonds and common ancestors; in other cases to a common language or religion. "But the strongest of all is identity of political antecedents; the possession of a national history, and consequent community of recollections; collective pride and humiliation, pleasure and regret, connected with the same incidents of the past."[1]

But it is debatable to what extent shared humiliations and sorrow can contribute toward uniting a group of people to become a nation. In some instances this may indeed happen, as we see from the Serbs, who even today commemorate their defeat at the hands of the Ottoman forces on the plains of Kosovo in 1389. In most cases, however, far more important is collective pride in connection with glorious events. And the most glorious of all, so it would seem, is to have an ancient history as a separate state. That is why it becomes necessary to link the nation to one or more earlier state formations defined as nation-states or as forerunners of a particular nation-state.

One case in point is Norwegian nation-building in the nineteenth century. Historians within what came to be called the "Norwegian historical school"—Rudolf Keyser, P. A. Munch, and others—could trace a separate Norwegian identity all the way back to the days of the Vikings. They interpreted the nation-building that took place on Norwegian territory during the Middle Ages as a Norwegian nation-state. And this nation-state was, in turn, linked with the modern-day Norwegian nation-building project that emerged after 1814 when Norway was ceded from Denmark and entered into a personal union with Sweden. All this was seen as varying guises of one and the same idea of the state—the Norwegian state—which had been interrupted by the centuries spent under Danish rule.[2]

It was the poet Henrik Wergeland (1808–1845) who gave these ideas their most explicit and popularized expression. Wergeland drew on the metaphor of a broken ring: one half being the era of Norwegian greatness in the Middle Ages and the other Norway after the 1814 Eidsvoll constitutional convention. By simply excising the intervening "400-year night" of Danish rule, one would be able to see "*our* Norway and the Norway of the past as two interrupted halves of a ring, halves that fit together perfectly, with the interim period merely being the impure solder, interposed between the two genuine components."[3] Similar types of silversmithing are actively practiced throughout the former Soviet republics today.

In the nineteenth century, a distinction was drawn in Europe between what were termed "historical" and "ahistorical" nations. "Historical" nations were those that had existed as separate states in the past, whether or not they continued to do so. The "ahistorical" states were those that lacked a political history of their own. This distinction was relevant for the way in which one regarded the future prospects of the various nations: The historical ones were entitled to reestablish their state if they happened to have lost it. The prime example of such a nation was the Poles. The ahistorical nations, however, should abandon all thoughts of political independence. They were rather to be seen as "ethnographic material," as mere building blocks in the nation-building projects of other, stronger peoples. Even radical thinkers like Karl Marx and Friedrich Engels thought along these lines and employed this terminology.[4]

Very few—if indeed any—of the titular nations in the successor states to the Soviet Union were considered "historical" in the 1800s. Now that they have received their "own" status as separate states, however, most of them are managing to rediscover a political past, a state tradition, to dust off and burnish. For some, this golden age lies buried in the far, far distant past; for others it may be of considerably more recent vintage.

The Baltics

Not every earlier state formation is equally well suited as raw material for a modern nation-building project. Some such states may be seen as instances of foreign rule and thus highly unnational. For example, between about 1290 and 1561 there existed a relatively firm state formation in the Baltics, Livonia. The Livonian state covered most of present-day Latvia and Estonia, but in neither of these countries is there now any feeling that this was the forerunner, the ancestor, of today's state. The reason is simple: The ruling class in Livonia was German-speaking estate owners, and they remained so after the region was conquered by the Swedes in the seventeenth century and by the Russians in the eighteenth century. The Latvian- and Estonian-speaking populations lived in serfdom, with no political rights.

When the Livonia state collapsed, its territory was conquered by various neighboring great powers: first Poland-Lithuania, then Sweden (after 1629), and finally the Russian empire (with the Peace of Nystad in 1721). These periods are not seen as preincarnations of today's independent Baltic states. True, the years with Sweden appear in a somewhat rosier glow than the others. The Swedish kings sought to restrict the power of the German-Baltic aristocracy and indirectly made conditions for the Estonian and Latvian peasantry somewhat better.[5] All the same, Sweden's redoubtable Gustav Adolf has not been elevated to the status of trailbreaker for Latvian or Estonian independence.

The first independent Latvian and Estonian states did not arise until early in the twentieth century, as a result of the defeat of the czarist regime and World War I. Today it is *these* states that in every respect—historical, national, legal—are seen as the precursors of the states that gained their independence in 1991. In fact, it is a matter not so much of precursors as of one and the same state. This is a state that saw its existence broken off by the Soviet occupation of 1940 but has now been resurrected. Today's Estonian and Latvian authorities insistently deny that their countries are to be reckoned among the Soviet successor states. In distinction to all the other former Soviet republics, they have not established their political independence: They have *re*established it. Nor did they seek any portion of the Soviet "inheritance" when the affairs of the deceased Soviet estate were being settled. And this view has become totally accepted in the international community.

Estonian and Latvian representations of the Soviet period may seem reminiscent of Wergeland and his views on Norway's years under the Danish crown: This was a period in the life of the people that brought them nothing good, only harm and suffering. It can—indeed, it *must*—be excised resolutely, preferably leaving no trace behind. But among the undeniable traces of the Soviet Union in the Baltic we find today hundreds of thousands of human beings who moved there in the Communist years. Whereas Latvians and Estonians can rid themselves of the rusting remnants of deserted Soviet military bases by simply heaving them all on the scrap heap, getting rid of the human material in the "impure solder" is quite another matter. And this is one of the most serious political, social, and moral issues confronting these states today.

The third Baltic state, Lithuania, was an independent nation-state in the interwar years and thus enjoys the same position in international law as Estonia and Latvia. In historical terms, however, the Lithuanian nation-building project has a different, more distant starting point. The twenty-year period of independence in the interwar period is not all that today's national-builders in Lithuania have to conjure with. Whereas the northern Baltic territories were conquered by Teutonic knightly orders in the 1200s, the Baltic peoples further to the south managed to hold their own. They defeated the Teutonic Knights in several major battles in the 1200s and 1300s, the final, decisive one being that of Tannenberg (Grünewald) in 1410. It is from these battles that the primary emblem of the Grand Duchy of Lithuania has its motif: the white knight.[6]

The Lithuanian dukes not only retained control over the traditional areas of Lithuania, but they also expanded their territory considerably in the 1300s, until the Lithuanian state extended all the way to the shores of the Black Sea. For a time, Lithuania was among the largest states in Europe in land area. This was a very loose feudal state, characterized by a weak central power and a high degree of cultural and linguistic diversity. Although the ruling house and most the people in the north spoke the Lithuanian language, these "Lithuanians" were definitely in the minority in terms of the overall population.

In 1385 Grand Duke Jagiello of Lithuania married a Polish princess in order to cement a strategic alliance against the Baltic/Teutonic forces. After this move, Poland-Lithuania remained a dual monarchy for over 200 years; in 1569 the personal union was deepened to become a real union and a single state. It was the Polish cultural element that became dominant, with most of the Lithuanian upper class gradually becoming Polonized as the political center of gravity moved westward.

Today Lithuania's past as a medieval great power is an important part of what Lithuanian children learn at school. Whereas most Western scholars point out that this was a premodern, dynastic, and multicultural state, Lithuanians themselves experience it as a Lithuanian national state.[7] The interwar Lithuanian state was a restoration of their old, medieval state, much as the present-day Lithuanian republic is a restoration of the interwar state.[8]

This Lithuanian approach has also found its way into some of the Western literature. A Danish researcher team inquires, "Why are the Baltic countries so different after independence?" and finds much of the answer in their differing historical backgrounds: "The most decisive difference is probably that Lithuania is the only one of the three with a long history as an independent national state, one that only recently came under foreign (Russian) dominion."[9] This should at best be seen as a highly compressed and simplified explanation. But that Lithuanians themselves construe their history in this way is clearly important in explaining why Lithuania is in some important respects different from the other two Baltic states today.

Ukraine

The Ukrainian declaration of independence of 24 August 1991 proclaims that the Ukrainians have "a thousand-year tradition of state-building."[10] And indeed, if we go back 1,000 years we find on the territory of what is today Ukraine a relatively firm state formation called Rus', with Kiev as the capital city, ruled by the legendary Kiev prince Vladimir the Great. Whether it was a *Ukrainian* state is quite another question.

This grand duchy was a very loosely organized entity. The lords of the various towns enjoyed a high degree of local power, whereas the ruler of the city of Kiev was recognized as a grand duke with a certain suzerainty over the others. When gradual dissolution of this state formation set in during the 1200s, the demographic and political center of gravity among East Slavs began to move to the deep taiga forests to the northeast, toward the upper course of the Volga. This process gained momentum when the Mongol hordes came in 1240, as their mounted forces found the terrain forbiddingly difficult. Taking as its starting point what had been a minor town in this area, Moscow, a new realm arose among the East Slavs, the Grand Duchy of Muscovy, which also called itself Rus' and in the 1700s was to become the Russian empire.

Muscovy differed from Kiev in many respects. Customs and lifestyles were influenced by the Finnish groups that were settled in the area when the Slavs arrived; there were strong cultural impulses from the Mongolians as well—witness the fact that the Muscovite ruler, unlike that of Kiev, demanded absolute power over his realm. Yet there were also three important bonds linking the new Muscovite state to that of Kiev: The people had the same religion (Orthodox Christianity) and largely the same language (Old East Slavonic), and the Muscovite rulers were the direct descendants of a branch of the Kiev ruling family, the Ryurik dynasty.

Thus, Russian historians have always considered the Kievan state as being the direct precursor of the Muscovite empire. All accounts of the history of Russia have commenced with the 800s—and not the 1100s, which was when Moscow started to emerge. From a Russian nation-building perspective, this had one clear advantage: It made the Russian nation a good 300 years older than it otherwise would have been. In the Soviet Union—which was officially a multi- or supranational state—this view was perpetuated. And so, to take one example, almost all celebrations marking the millennium of the Russian Church in 1988 were held in Moscow, even though the great St. Vladimir—the baptizer of the Russian lands—had in fact been a grand duke of Kiev. (Incidentally, according to the Ukrainians, he should be known not as "Vladimir" but "Volodymyr," since that was his name in the Ukrainian language.)

Western historians have generally accepted the Russian time perspective. True enough, certain émigré Ukrainian historians have always maintained that this was a theft of the history of the Ukrainian people, but most of their Western colleagues have brushed these objections aside, dismissing them as rather pathetic manifestations of Ukrainian nationalism. In their view, whether or not Kievan Rus' was "Ukrainian" or "Russian" is a totally anachronistic way of posing the question, since at the time of Kievan Rus' there had not yet been any ethnic differentiation between those two groups of East Slavs.[11] Historians have argued and disagreed about the character and origin of Kievan Rus', but this has been quite a different discussion, a question of whether the empire was founded by the Slavs themselves or by Scandinavian Vikings.

Now that Ukraine has become an independent state, the tug-of-war as to who are the bearers of the legacy of Kievan Rus' has entered a new phase. Whereas the Russians maintain their view, the Ukrainian authorities have quite simply *proclaimed* that Kievan Rus' was Ukrainian. And this is the view presented in Ukrainian schoolbooks.[12] Here there is little room for compromise, even though some of the main towns of Kievan Rus'—like Novgorod and Pskov—actually lie within the borders of today's Russia.

This Ukrainian view of history may at times also assume a directly anti-Russian tone, as when schoolbooks feature drawings that show how "the Muscovites plundered Kiev in 1169." The episode in question was one of the countless feuds involving various branches of the Ryurik family; on this occasion it was the Muscovy duke Andrey Bogolyubskiy who was on the warpath. Incidentally, the Ukrainian word for *Muscovite* used in the schoolbook, *moskal'*, has now taken on a second meaning in addition to the historical one: It has become a derogatory term for Russians in general. A Russian in Donetsk in eastern Ukraine showed me this particular textbook as an example of meaningless attacks on the Russian people in Ukrainian historiography.

It can seem, however, as if the Ukrainians themselves feel they are on shaky ground in seeking to expropriate the entire Kievan state for use as a construction site for the Ukrainian project of nation-building. Very often, when it is maintained that the Ukrainians have a centuries-old state tradition, what is being referred to is not Kievan Rus' but the Ukrainian Cossacks. In the 1400s and 1500s, these Cossacks settled along the middle course of the Dnieper in the southernmost reaches of what was then the Polish-Lithuanian commonwealth. Here they established a belt of more or less autonomous communities, the most important of which was Sich, with its main base on an island in the Dnieper, to the south of the Porogi rapids.

In today's Ukraine the Cossacks are represented as ethnic Ukrainians.[13] In fact they were of more mixed origin: Over the centuries fugitive serfs had intermingled with the peoples of the plains. From the latter the Cossacks adopted many traditions and customs, not least their military skills and their abilities on horseback. All the same, they were not nomads but tillers of the soil, like most other Ukrainian peasants. Unlike the Tatars and Nogai to the south, they were not Muslim but Christian. Furthermore, unlike the Poles, they were Orthodox, not Roman Catholic. Taken together, these features provided the basis for the development of a separate Cossack identity.[14]

The Cossacks swore fealty to the Polish king but retained an autonomous position within the Rzeczpospolita Polska—the Polish Commonwealth—and could, for instance, carry on their own diplomatic correspondence. To the Poles, they served as a buffer against the Tatars, but the Poles frequently came into open conflict with the Cossacks. The most important Cossack uprising against the Polish king took place in 1648, when the hetman Bohdan Khmel'nytskyy undertook a series of victorious campaigns far to the north and west in the country, not stopping until he came to Lwow (Lvov in Russian; L'viv in Ukrainian). For a time, his forces represented a threat to the entire Polish state.

For six years, the Sich community was not only autonomous but in practice totally independent. In 1654, however, Khmel'nytskyy realized that he needed an ally in order to stand against the Poles and thus concluded a pact with the Russian czar, Aleksey Mikhaylovich, in Pereyaslav. Today this agreement is interpreted quite differently in Ukraine and in Russia. According to the Ukrainians, this was merely a temporary tactical alliance; Russian and Soviet historiographers, however, hail it as the reunification of the Ukrainian and Russian lands. In 1954 Nikita Khrushchev celebrated the 300th anniversary of this agreement by transferring to the Ukrainian Soviet Socialist Republic jurisdiction over the Crimean peninsula, which until then had been under the Russian SSR.

For almost a century and a half after the Pereyaslav union, the Ukrainian Cossacks retained a degree of autonomy within the Russian state, although they also rose up against their new lords. The most famous of these rebellions was under the hetman Ivan Mazepa in 1708. Mazepa joined with Charles XII of Sweden against Peter the Great of Russia in the Great Northern War. In 1709, however, the Swedes were defeated in the battle of Poltava. In Russian historiography Mazepa has been represented as the archtraitor incarnate; today he is celebrated as a freedom fighter in Ukraine.

In 1775 Russia's Catherine the Great decided she had had enough of the unruly Cossacks. She dissolved what was left of their autonomous communities and removed some Cossacks to the Kuban area east of the Black Sea; others were resettled in Ottoman-controlled areas in the Balkans. Although this meant the end of the Ukrainian Cossacks, they lived on in memory, not least in the literary works of Nikolay Gogol and Ukraine's national poet, Taras Shevchenko.

With perestroika, tales of the Cossacks resurfaced, circulated by Ukrainian nationalists in western Ukraine—which may seem a bit ironic, since there had never been any Cossacks in that area.[15] The explanation was probably that many other issues vital to the western Ukrainians, such as the struggle for the Ukrainian Catholic Church and against the Russian language, could have split the Ukrainian people rather than uniting them, whereas the Cossack issue had the potential to provide a rallying point for the eastern parts of the country.

Cossack society came to be depicted as decidedly democratic and egal-itarian; indeed, the Cossacks were even held to have produced the first democratic constitution in Europe.[16] At one point Ukrainian military journals featured articles on how Cossack battle techniques could be put to use in the military doctrine of the new Ukraine. The national anthem praised the Ukrainian people as the literal descendants of the Cossacks—a rather dubious claim, since the great majority of the Cossack popula-tion had left the country after 1775.

Today the Ukrainian Cossacks have been "resurrected," with several divisions around the country. Their main headquarters is located on Bohdan Khmel'nytskyy Street in Kiev, but when I paid a visit in 1994, the premises were almost deserted. The new hetman said that the Cossacks felt they had again been forgotten; support—both financial and moral—had withered after Ukraine regained its independence. The Cossacks had done their job, and now they were no longer needed.

In fact, the modern Ukrainian state has not two but three or four, and perhaps five or six, precursors, depending on how one approaches the question. The fall of the czarist empire saw the establishment of several short-lived Ukrainian republics that partly overlapped and partly suc-ceeded one another. One of these was led by a former general under the czar, Pavlo Skoropadskyy, whose right-wing regime (April–December 1918) collaborated with the Germans, who occupied most of Ukraine during World War I. Skoropadskyy assumed the title of hetman and maintained that he was of Cossack blood.

The other republics of 1917–1919, Tsentral'na Rada (the Ukrainian Cen-tral Council) and the Directorate, were national socialist in character. The

president of the former was Mykhaylo Khrushevskyy, the leading contemporary Ukrainian historian. It was he who first developed the thesis
that there was no organic link between the Kievan state and that of
Muscovy. Khrushevskyy was responsible for designing the new national
coat of arms with the trident, a heraldic symbol harking back to the days
of Kievan Rus'. The trident was reintroduced into the Ukrainian coat of
arms after 1991, thereby binding together two historical threads—one
going back to 1918 and one to the early Middle Ages.

These short-lived Ukrainian state formations were established while
the Red Bolsheviks and White Russian troops were fighting a civil war—
largely on Ukrainian territory. Neither the Reds nor the Whites were willing to grant political independence to Ukraine; for that matter, exactly
how many Ukrainians were aspiring to a separate Ukrainian state is hard
to say. In eastern Ukraine there was a strong guerrilla movement during
the civil war under the leadership of Nestor Makhno, fighting against
both the Whites and the Communists. But Makhno was an anarchist and
agrarian populist rather than a Ukrainian nationalist. His goal was not so
much to free Ukraine from Russia as it was to free the countryside from
the tyranny of the towns and cities.

The years of World War II saw yet another attempt at establishing a
Ukrainian national state, this time in western Ukraine (Galicia), where an
independent Ukrainian state was proclaimed. Galicia had never been
part of the Russian empire but had been annexed by the Soviet Union
after the signing of the pact between German foreign minister Joachim
von Ribbentrop and Soviet foreign minister Vyacheslav Molotov in 1939.
The Ukrainian Insurgent Army (UPA) put up steadfast resistance against
the Soviet forces, at times working together with the Germans in an attempt to achieve its goal of a separate Ukrainian state.

The Germans may well have appreciated that the Ukrainians wanted
to fight against the Bolsheviks, but they were less enthusiastic about the
idea of a separate Ukrainian state, and in June 1941 they jailed the leader
of the Ukrainian nationalist organization, Stepan Bandera. In hindsight
we can see that this was in fact the best thing the Nazis could have done
for the cause of Ukrainian nationalism, since this made it appear far less
of a brownshirt movement. In Soviet Ukraine, however, Bandera was
always branded the archvillain, and many eastern Ukrainians saw no
reason for celebration in 1990–1991 when western Ukrainians began to
commemorate him as a hero. Millions of Ukrainians have a parent or
grandparent who died in the fight against Hitler's Germany and those
they regard as collaborators and traitors to their own country. Soviet
veterans in the cities of eastern Ukraine have continued to celebrate the
victory in World War II with mass gatherings on 9 May every year. On
these occasions I imagine that the Ukrainian police are grateful for the

many hundreds of intervening kilometers between eastern Ukraine and the city of L'viv to the west, where UPA veterans march, demanding the right to receive war pensions. If these two demonstrations took place in the same town, bloodshed could easily ensue. And on such days one may begin to wonder whether there is in fact any hope for the Ukrainian nation-building project.

It is safer to focus on the tragic side, on those occasions where all have had to confront the same foe. The greatest Ukrainian catastrophe of modern times is undoubtedly the forced collectivization of agriculture that took place in the 1930s and was followed by devastating famine. Millions of Ukrainians died as a result, and many today maintain that the forced collectivization was intended not as a (totally unsuccessful) measure for improving agricultural production but rather as a conscious effort to eradicate the Ukrainian people. True, collectivization was carried out throughout the entire Soviet Union, with catastrophic results everywhere—but in Ukraine the crimes committed by Stalin are seen as reflecting his particular animus toward the Ukrainian people. A film depicting the famine of the 1930s in this light was shown on Ukrainian television immediately prior to the referendum on Ukrainian independence of 1 December 1991. Many largely attribute to the film the result of the plebiscite: a 90 percent vote in favor of independence.[17]

Belarus

The Belarusian constitution of 1994 states that modern Belarusians pride themselves on having a "centuries-long history of the development of Belarusian statehood."[18] This claim is of course somewhat more modest than the Ukrainian claim of a tradition 1,000 years old. All the same, it came as a surprise to most observers, who had tended to believe that the first attempts at establishing a separate Belarusian state had taken place in the twentieth century. The nation-builders of Belarus, however, maintain that they have had a (perhaps considerable) share in two of the earlier state formations presented in this chapter: Kievan Rus' and the Grand Duchy of Lithuania.[19]

Two of the constituent principalities within Kievan Rus', Polotsk and Turov, lay in what is today the territory of Belarus. When Ukrainian historians complain that the Russians have stolen their ancient history by making Kievan Rus' into a Russian state, Belarusian nationalists react by accusing the Ukrainians of a similar historical theft. They maintain that the local rulers of Polotsk and Turov had always retained a high degree of independence in relations with Kiev and cared little about the perpetual squabbles as to who was to title himself the "grand duke of Kiev." Furthermore, the populations of Polotsk and Turov did not belong to the same East Slavic tribes as those living further south in Kievan Rus'. As a German historian has remarked, "Thus, Polotsk and the neighboring principalities became an argument against the claim that it is only now that the Belarusians have a state of their own."[20]

It is from the Kievan era that Belarusian nation-builders have taken their first national martyr as well. Princess Rahnieda of Polotsk was abducted by Duke Vladimir (Volodymyr) the Great, who then forced her to marry him after he had killed her father and her brothers. Later in life the same Vladimir was to become a pious man, indeed a candidate for sainthood. To Belarusian nationalists, however, his abduction of their princess stands as a symbol of the sufferings of an assaulted, raped nation.

After the Mongol invaders had crushed Kievan Rus' in the 1240s, Polotsk and Turov gradually became part of the Grand Duchy of Lithuania, which as it expanded southeasterly in the 1300s received more and more Slavic subjects—proto-Belarusians but also proto-Ukrainians and probably proto-Russians as well. It did not take long before the Slavic-speaking subjects outnumbered the Lithuanian-speaking ones. As administrative language for his vast realm the grand duke therefore opted for an early variant of Belarusian, even though he himself and his court spoke Lithuanian. It is thus not surprising that Belarusians consider it misleading to represent this as a purely Lithuanian realm, as is often done. In fact the full name was not the "Grand Duchy of Lithuania" but the "Grand Duchy of Lithuania, Rus', and Samogitia." Samogitia was an area in the northwest of the grand duchy, whereas Rus' designated the East Slavic areas. It is this part of the official title that Belarusians have seized upon to prove their centuries-long state tradition. When the grand duchy sought to defend itself against attacks from the Teutonic knightly orders in the fourteenth and fifteenth centuries, Belarusian nobles were also there. The Belarusian coat of arms, which was adopted in 1991, the so-called Pohonia ("Pursuit" in Belarusian), has the same motif as the white knight of the Lithuanians and has its origins in the same battles of medieval days.

When Lithuania ended up in the personal union with Poland in 1385, the Lithuanian ruling classes, and gradually all Lithuanian-speaking subjects, converted to Roman Catholicism. The Belarusians, however, kept their Orthodox faith, thereby gradually becoming a cultural-religious minority group. For a long time, however, this had scant consequences, as in both Lithuania and Poland religious tolerance was high.

With the establishment of the Polish-Lithuanian union in 1569, Lithuania retained a certain degree of autonomy, with its own state institutions, its own army, and certain established privileges. Until 1696 the language of administration remained Old Belarusian, which in the course of the 1500s had developed into a literary language. The Belarusian humanist

Frančišak Skaryna translated the Bible into Old Belarusian between 1517–1519, so it can be argued that the Belarusians not only have a tradition of statehood but are an old cultural nation as well.

But Belarusian fortunes took an abrupt downturn after the 1600s. When Poland was divided in 1772, 1793, and 1795, almost all of the Belarusian areas were ceded to the Russian empire. In the wake of these political upheavals, Belarus was left as an even more undeveloped peripheral province than it had been under Poland. Only the peasantry spoke Belarusian, which was no longer accounted a "proper" language. Russian linguistic scholars viewed it as a plebeian form of Russian; it was inconceivable that this should be used as the medium of instruction in the schools, for instance. Officially, (Great) Russian, Ukrainian, and Belarusian were merely three variants of the same language—Russian—not three different languages.

The first to attempt to (re)establish a separate Belarusian identity were the revolutionary socialists and populists who fought together with the Polish rebels in the uprising of 1863. There existed no organized movement for Belarusian independence, however, and when an independent, democratic Belarusian republic was proclaimed in Minsk in March 1918, this should be seen basically as an effort to spare the country from the consequences of the Bolshevik seizure of power in Russia. An elaborate version of Pohonia was drawn as the new coat of arms. In the nationalist historiography of Belarus, the republic is seen as proof of the Belarusians' will and ability to form a state of their own in modern times.[21]

But this republic was short-lived: It existed less than one year, and then the Bolsheviks were back. The Belarusian Soviet Socialist Republic was established in January 1919, initially encompassing only the easternmost portions of today's Belarus. The state of Poland, born after World War I, gained control over the westerly portions. In "their" Belarusian areas, the Poles pursued a harsh Polonization policy—and in return the Bolshevik regime went to the opposite extreme and promoted a vigorous Belorussification of "its" territories. Belarusian was introduced as the language of administration and the schools, even in places where the population scarcely understood a word of the language and definitely preferred Russian.

Ironically enough, Belarusian had not yet been codified as a modern written language. In all haste, language-builders in Minsk set about turning out Belarusian grammar compendia and dictionaries. Where the language lacked terms for modern concepts and phenomena, new ones were manufactured, preferably not on the basis of Russian. Thus, pupils frequently found themselves memorizing words unfamiliar even to their teachers. According to one Western historian, some of these Belarusian "enlighteners" were killed by irate peasants who would have no truck with all this unnatural nonsense.[22]

Then, from the early 1930s, an abrupt end was put to the Belarusian cultural experiment in the Soviet Union. Russian was reintroduced in most schools, and it was only among some of the peasantry and some of the cultural intelligentsia that the Belarusian language was still spoken.

Thus, it came about that when the Soviet Union was dissolved the Belarusians had the status of a separate national group and indeed their own republic, which had even been a member of the United Nations since 1948. And yet they scarcely had any culture to call their own, beyond a rather anemic official "folklorism" complete with "national" costumes and "national" songs alien to most of them.

It was from this point of departure that Belarusian historians in the early 1990s set about revising their national history. Not only did it emerge as anti-Soviet, but it was to a considerable extent anti-Russian as well. "National identity was defined primarily in contrast to that of Greater Russia. The Belarusians' new version of their national history would have to be first and foremost a non-Russian one."[23]

Moldova

Like the Ukrainian declaration of independence, the Moldovan declaration, adopted three days later, on 27 August 1991, claimed a centuries-long tradition of statehood. Independence was proclaimed "in recognition of the thousand-year history of our people and our unbroken state tradition within the historical and ethnic boundaries of our nation."[24] These somewhat vague formulations indicated that the Moldovan nation-builders sought to legitimize the new state in both ethnic and historical terms. This "unbroken state tradition" was, however, not so immediately apparent, unless the Moldovans latched on to the Romanian state tradition. And that was probably exactly what the Moldovan authorities at the time wished to do.

Moldova, or Moldavia, is one of the three main historical regions of Romania, the other two being Wallachia and Transylvania. Over the centuries Moldavia has been situated on the border between the Russian and the Turkish-Ottoman empires, tossed back and forth between these two great powers. The area known to history as Moldavia is considerably larger than the independent Moldovan state of today, which is composed mainly of the easternmost portions of the historical territory, the remainder of which lies in Romania.

Eastern Moldova is often termed Bessarabia, a name that was not commonly used before the beginning of the nineteenth century and that has nothing to do with Arabia; it is derived instead from the Romanian nobility, the house of Basarab. Bessarabia denotes the lands between the rivers Dniester, Danube, and Prut, the latter being a tributary of the

Danube. The main portion of Bessarabia comprises the core of today's Moldova. From the tenth century up until the middle of the twelfth century, the territories of Bessarabia were part of Kievan Rus'. With the collapse of this realm, Bessarabia gradually came under the expanding Lithuanian grand duchy.

Somewhat further to the south and west there emerged the proto-Romanian principalities of Wallachia and Moldavia, later also known as the Danubian Principalities. The Moldovans and the Wallachians spoke a language related to Vulgar Latin, unlike their Slavic neighbors, although they shared the same Orthodox faith. These states were characterized by a considerable degree of Slavic cultural influence; for instance, in the principality of Moldavia, the administrative and liturgical language was Old Church Slavonic, written with the Cyrillic alphabet.

The territory of the Moldavian princes was gradually expanded; in 1367 they gained control over Bessarabia as well. By that time the Ottomans had begun their march northward into the Balkans, conquering one area after another. Moldavia's resistance was led by their prince Stefan the Great (Stefan cel mare, 1457–1504), who managed to ensure the independence of the principality and even expanded it somewhat. Today he is one of the great heroes of Moldovan (and Romanian) history, and the main street of Chişinău now bears his name. During the Soviet era, the street was called Lenin Prospect; prior to that, it had been named after Czar Alexander I, who conquered the area.

All the same, shortly after the death of Stefan, Moldavia became a vassal state of the Ottomans. In 1538 the most famous of all the Ottoman sultans, Süleyman the Magnificent, conquered most of Bessarabia as well, and the Dniester became the outermost border of the Ottoman Empire. The lands to the east of the river had long been nearly uninhabited. The steppes north of the Black Sea were harried by fierce horsemen, and few peasants dared to settle there.

In the course of the 1700s, Russian influence over the Danubian Principalities became steadily stronger. Following one of the countless Russo-Turkish wars, both Moldova and Wallachia became de facto protectorates of Russia under the terms of the Treaty of Küchük-Kainarji in 1774. Then in 1812, during the Napoleonic Wars, Bessarabia became part of the Russian empire. It was only much later that the nation-state of Romania was established, when Wallachia and the remainder of Moldova merged into one state under one monarch. This was a gradual process between 1859 and 1881.

Romanian nationalists had never come to terms with the loss of Bessarabia. Together with other "unredeemed" areas with Romanian-speaking populations—Transylvania to the west, Bukovina to the north, Dobrudja to the south—Bessarabia was part of what they called (and still call) Romania Mare, or Greater Romania. Today most of these territories have been "redeemed," with the exception of some smaller areas lying in Ukraine as well as the lands of the state of Moldova.

During the Russian Revolution in 1919, the Romanians took the opportunity to annex Bessarabia. For the Moldovans, this meant that they were reunited with their ethnic group—not, however, that this brought many improvements. Today many older Moldovans complain that the Russian administrators and estate owners in the interwar years were merely replaced by rather arrogant administrators from Bucharest. Still, there is no reason to believe that the Moldovans wished a return to Russia, or to the USSR, as it then was known.

But the rulers in Moscow had no intention of accepting the loss of Bessarabia. The first signal of plans for reconquest came in 1924, when the Moldavian Autonomous Soviet Socialist Republic (MASSR) was established on the left (eastern) bank of the Dniester as a separate administrative area within the Ukrainian Soviet Socialist Republic. This area is also known as Transnistria—the land on the "other" side of the Dniester as seen from Bucharest. Transnistria had never been part of the Romanian state and was populated mainly by Ukrainians and other Slavic groups, though with a considerable Moldovan/Romanian minority. Moscow's intention behind demarcating this as a separate autonomous area under the name of "Moldavia" was fairly obvious: for use as a platform from which to regain control of Bessarabia. And this was what happened during World War II.

In the secret additional protocol to the 1939 Ribbentrop-Molotov pact, Bessarabia is mentioned as belonging to the Soviet sphere of influence; one year later Moscow forced Romania to cede the area. When the Romanians joined with the Axis powers during the war, they briefly regained control of Bessarabia again, even marching well into Ukraine before they were halted. But when 1945 came, the Soviet flag was once again flying over Chişinău—or Kishinev, as Russians called the town.

The next step was the establishment of a Moldavian Soviet Socialist Republic (MSSR), formed by joining half of the MASSR together with most of Bessarabia. The southernmost areas by the Black Sea, with considerable Ukrainian and Bulgarian populations, were not made part of the MSSR but went instead to Ukraine, the UkSSR.

After World War II, Romania turned Communist, becoming a "socialist brotherly country" of the USSR. All the same, nearly all contact between Romania and Moldavia was broken off. In the Soviet Union it was forbidden to write the Moldavian/Romanian language with the Latin alphabet (as the Romanians do); the Moldovans were now to use the Cyrillic alphabet.

The historiography of Soviet Moldavia emphasized the Slavic cultural influence and the close historical ties to Russia.[25] These ties are undoubtedly both many and strong, but the Soviet regime exaggerated them out of all proportion. Soviet linguistics, for example, maintained that as much as 40 percent of the vocabulary of Moldavian consists of Slavic loanwords.[26] More than most other non-Russian republics, Moldavia was administered by bureaucrats sent from Moscow—including two party bosses who were later to make their careers in the Kremlin: Leonid Brezhnev and Konstantin Chernenko.

Almost all of the borders of the Moldavian Soviet Republic were brand-new. Its territory overlapped with the historical lands of Bessarabia, with certain additions and subtractions. Many have seen in this a classical instance of the divide-and-rule tactics of Stalin, who deliberately set borders so as to interweave a whole series of political and ethnic conflicts to play ethnic groups off against each other. For example, the MSSR was given a sizable Slavic minority with the inclusion of the strip of land east of the Dniester.

Yet this cannot be the entire explanation. Moldavia would have received a large Slavic population no matter what, since even more Russians and Ukrainians live to the west of the river. Throughout the Soviet Union, the various ethnic groups lived so intermingled and admixed that constructing "ethnically pure" units would have been an impossibility. In fact, a U.S. scholar has maintained that in the Soviet Union a great many boundaries were drawn up precisely with the aim of creating republics that were as ethnically homogeneous as possible.[27] It may well be that this was the case with Moldavia as well.

At any rate these new borders are clearly an important reason Moldova has not been reunited with Romania after the disintegration of the Soviet Union. The Moldovan Popular Front, so instrumental in the 1989–1991 struggle for independence, pressured for such reunification, insisting that *all* of Moldova, not just the areas that were historically Romanian, should be part of a reunited Romania. The map of Romania Mare displayed in the front's Chişinău headquarters includes the Dniester region as well, as I noticed on a visit in September 1992.

Unification with Romania was not something the Dniester population was ready to accept. Historical experience had left its scars: During the Romanian occupation in World War II, the soldiers of Marshal Ion Antonescu had spread fear and terror throughout Transnistria. And so from the top hat of history, Dniestrian leaders conjured up a separate Dniestrian statehood: the Moldovan Autonomous Soviet Republic of 1924, the MASSR. In September 1990 they resurrected the MASSR within the areas under their control, christening it the Dniester Moldavian

Soviet Socialist Republic (DMSSR). (When the Soviet Union was dissolved the following year, the *Socialist* and *Soviet* were dropped, leaving the name DMR; in Russian, PMR) Nor was that all: They had at their disposal the physical means to defend their independence when Moldovan forces attempted to regain the territory in spring 1992.

Thus, rather than having their cake and eating it, too, reunification enthusiasts in the Moldovan Popular Front ended up with nothing: Moldova and Romania are still two separate states, with Moldova currently de facto split in two. History had given the reunificationists an appetite for more than they managed to swallow. In 1992–1993 they were forced to the edges of the political stage in Chişinău, to be replaced by Moldovan nationalists who concentrated instead on building a civic Moldovan nation-state.

Kazakhstan

After the dissolution of the USSR, Kazakhstan was the last of the Union republics to proclaim its independence, on 16 December 1991. That Kazakhstan was last past the post indicates that the desire for political independence was not as pronounced, for various reasons. The country is linked to Russia through strong economic, structural, and not least demographic ties. About half of the country's approximately 18 million inhabitants are either Russians or Russian-speaking Ukrainians, Belarusians, and Germans. As of 1990 at most 40 percent of the total population were ethnic Kazakhs. But once independence was a fact, the Kazakhs were determined to make the most of it. Here, too, a nation-building process was inaugurated, and a new national history was written.

Kazakhstan declared itself an independent nation-state. What was less clear was *whose* nation was meant. On the one hand, it was to be the country of all its inhabitants; on the other, it was the state of the ethnic Kazakhs in a special sense. Ever since independence, there have been signs pointing in various directions: now an ethnic nation concept, now a political one.[28] All the same, a clear tendency seems to be emerging, with the Kazakhstani state increasingly presented as the culmination of what is seen as the uninterrupted 500-year-old state tradition of the Kazakh people. At a semiofficial conference on the development of Kazakhstan's statehood held in the capital city of Almaty in April 1996, it was claimed that the Kazakh khanate, created in the mid-1400s, was "the first nation-state in Central Asia established by a people who still exists."[29]

What sort of state was this khanate, then? The Kazakhs have traditionally been a nomadic people, and there exist few written sources on their earliest history. Russian archeologists and historians of the nineteenth century carried out a major job in collecting and systematizing the available material, and it is largely to their work that today's Kazakh historians must turn in their attempts to rewrite the history of their nation. But the notion of a Kazakh nation-state tracing back to the 1400s does not appear in the nineteenth-century Russian scholarship. That has been added more recently.

The Kazakh khanate was established as a loose federation of various tribes with diverging ethnic backgrounds. Its core area lay to the south of Lake Balkhash and along the rivers Chu and Talas in what is today southern Kazakhstan. The Kazakhs migrated with their herds and had no towns or cities as such. The ruler himself, the khan, lived in a traditional nomad's tent, a yurt. Any territorial control was highly rudimentary, as was the khan's control of his subjects. He also had very limited powers of taxation. Indeed, when an American scholar ventured to refer to this khanate as a "state," this was immediately countered by a colleague who held that the concept of "state" is highly misleading for such a community.[30]

Gradually the Kazakh tribes went further north on their migrations, toward the rivers Irtysh and Ural, in search of good pasturelands for their herds. As a result of this territorial spread, plus internal rivalries in the ruling family, the khanate was split into three *zhuz* in the mid-1500s: the Great Horde, the Middle Horde, and the Small Horde. In some periods all three were led by the same khan, whereas at other times each had its own leader. In either case the khans and the Kazakh nobility had very little power. The individual tribes and the extended families enjoyed autonomy in all internal matters.

In the early 1700s, the Kazakhs were threatened by the Mongol Jungars who had by then established a mighty and warlike khanate in southern Siberia. In hopes of withstanding this danger, the two northernmost *zhuz*, the Small and Middle Hordes, sought protection under the Russian state. This protection came in the form of agreements concluded in 1731 and 1740, respectively. Parallel to the Ukrainian-Russian disagreement over the Pereyaslav Treaty of 1654, Kazakhs and Russians today see these agreements in very different terms. The Russians take them as proof that the Kazakhs voluntarily submitted to the Russian imperial power, whereas for the Kazakhs this was merely a matter of a short-term tactical alliance.

In support of their view, Kazakh historians point out how a whole series of Kazakh rebellions took place in the ensuing decades. This they see as an expression of national opposition to the foreign yoke. Russian historians, however, tend to consider this a natural reaction to the desperation felt by Kazakhs whenever they were unable to find enough areas to graze their herds.

Kazakh tribal society was marked by internal feuds. In bad years the tribes would often trespass on each other's territories, stealing animals and plundering trade caravans. In order to keep them under control, the Russian authorities erected fortresses throughout the steppes, manned largely by Cossacks. And when hunger and poverty intensified, several of the Kazakh tribes were allowed new grazing lands on Russian territory west of the Ural River. It was here that the Inner *Zhuz* was established in 1801.

In the 1820s the northernmost khanates were dissolved and the Kazakh areas placed under regular Russian rule. The Russian statesman Mikhail Speranskiy prepared a new set of administrative regulations for what was called the Kirgiz steppe. (At that time, and for the next 100 years, the Kazakhs were referred to as Kirgiz. Later the term *Kirgiz*, or *Kyrgyz*, was reserved for a kindred ethnic group living to the south of the Kazakhs.) Several major Kazakh revolts against the Russian regime were put down in the 1830s and 1840s. The most important of these was led by Kenisary Qasimov, who in Soviet times was depicted as the greatest of all villains in the history of the Kazakhs, rebel and traitor par excellence, almost the counterpart to the Ukrainians' Mazepa. Today, however, he has been allocated quite a different role, as the great freedom hero of Kazakhstan.[31] His grandfather, Ablay Khan, who concluded the first voluntary pact with the Russians, is also still held in high esteem as a great statesman of the Kazakh nation.

In the 1860s the southern *zhuz*, the Great Horde, was conquered by czarist Russia. Toward the end of that century, hundreds of thousands of land-starved Russian peasants migrated into Kazakh territory, settling down in the best areas. The Kazakh nomads had always traveled over vast areas with their animals; now when they returned to a traditional grazing area, they often found that it had been taken over by Russian newcomers.

By the outbreak of World War I, Kazakhstan had over 1 million Slavic inhabitants. Kazakh bitterness peaked in 1916, culminating in a major revolt when the czar tried to conscript Central Asians for (noncombatant) military service. The revolt began as an apparently spontaneous uprising in several different places, among Kazakhs as well as among Kyrgyz and Uzbeks. The rebels plundered and killed thousands of Slavic settler families, to which the soldiers of the czar responded by killing even more Central Asians. Hundreds of thousands of Kazakhs and Kyrgyz then fled over the border to China. The uprising of 1916 is today one of the greatest traumas in the historical consciousness of the Kazakhs. Under the Soviet Union, more were to come.

Toward the end of the nineteenth century, some of the Kazakh elite had become strongly influenced by Russian culture and lifestyles. They left their traditional yurts, built Russian-style houses, started to cultivate crops, and sent their sons off to Russia to be schooled. This was to lay the foundations for the emergence of a thin layer of Kazakh intelligentsia. During the 1917 Russian Revolution, a group of Western-oriented Kazakh intellectuals proclaimed an autonomous Kazakh state, Alash Orda, which supported the Provisional Russian Government against the Bolsheviks.

It was, however, the Bolsheviks who won the civil war. In 1920 they established a "Kirgiz" (read: Kazakh) Autonomous Republic within the Russian Federal Soviet Republic. Initially this administrative entity included only the northern part of today's Kazakhstan (together with a narrow strip of the southern Urals and southern Siberia in what is today the Russian Federation). In 1924 and 1925, however, the territory was more than doubled when the provinces of Syr Darya and Semirech'e to the south were added on. And finally, when Stalin's new constitution was adopted in 1936, Kazakhstan was elevated to the highest level in the hierarchy of autonomous units within the Soviet system. The area was now proclaimed a separate constituent republic, outside the Russian Federation (but of course very much within the USSR), under the name "Kazakh Soviet Socialist Republic."

Not only the outer boundaries of the Kazakh republic but also its administrative center seemed always on the move—almost as if the whole affair were a nomad camp. To begin with, the capital of the republic was located far to the north, in Orenburg, which today lies in Russia. In 1924 it was moved to Kzyl Orda in the southwest, and then finally found a relatively permanent home in Alma-Ata in the southeast in 1929. In recent years, however, the capital has once again taken up the wanderer's staff and has now pitched camp in Astana, in the north of the country.

Nor is that all. These capitals have also changed names at least once—Russian and Soviet names at one point, Kazakh at another. For a while during the Soviet era, Orenburg was rechristened Chkalov in honor of the first Russian transpolar pilot; Kzyl Orda was the Soviet name for the ancient oasis town of Aq Mechet, known as Perovsk under the czars; Alma-Ata, founded in 1855 by Russian Cossacks as the garrison town of Vernyy, has now been renamed Almaty. Finally, Astana is the latest name for Akmola, known as Akmolinsk under the czars, rechristened Tselinograd ("the city of the virgin soil") under Khrushchev, and once again called Akmola in the first years after independence. Akmola (Aq Mola), however, means "white grave," and present-day Kazakhstani statebuilders decided that the name had too negative a ring to it. In spring 1998, therefore, they changed the name of the city once more, this time to Astana, which means simply "capital."

All these peregrinations of capitals and nomenclature may well have left the reader confused. But they should be seen as telling reflections of the highly complex, ambiguous, and composite politicocultural nature of the Republic of Kazakhstan.

Forced collectivization under Stalin hit the Kazakhs hard. In the 1930s most of them were still nomads or seminomads, so it was extremely difficult for them to adapt to the new system of collective farms, which required a settled, agriculturist lifestyle. Their traditional source of livelihood was ruined. At least 1 million Kazakhs died, and others escaped to China and Mongolia. The Kazakhs had probably the greatest demographic loss relative to the size of the population of any Soviet people in the 1930s. This also meant that Kazakh opposition to Soviet power was broken. With time the Kazakhs were to become more Russified and more closely integrated into Soviet society than any of the other peoples of Soviet Central Asia.

During and immediately prior to World War II, over 1 million Koreans, Germans, Poles, Chechens, and several other ethnic groups were forcibly relocated to Kazakhstan from various other parts of the USSR. In the late 1950s, Khrushchev instigated a massive campaign for putting the so-called virgin soil of north Kazakhstan to the plow. Any Kazakh leaders who happened to oppose this policy were simply removed. Hundreds of thousands of Russians and Ukrainians moved into the republic. As a result of all these demographic changes, the proportion of Kazakhs in the total population of Kazakhstan had fallen to approximately 30 percent by 1959, whereas Russians accounted for 42 percent. In no other Soviet republic was the titular group so outnumbered. But the Kazakhs had a far more rapid reproductive rate than the European groups; by the time of the 1989 census the former had regained their status as the largest single ethnic group, although still under the 40 percent mark.

Throughout the postwar period, Russians and other Slavic groups dominated the economic and political life of Kazakhstan; for instance, Leonid Brezhnev was first secretary of the Communist Party of Kazakhstan from 1954 to 1959. But under the leadership of his Kazakh successor, Dinmukhamed Kunayev, more and more high positions in the republic and party apparatus were filled by ethnic Kazakhs. Indeed, Western scholars often touted Kazakhs in Kazakhstan as a striking example of a titular nation that had managed to put their mark on "their" Union republic, far above and beyond what their actual demographic weight would have led one to expect.[32]

The Kunayev regime was not only a nationalizing one; it was also corrupt. In an attempt to rectify matters, Mikhail Gorbachev, then general secretary of the Communist Party in the Soviet Union, had Kunayev removed in 1986, replacing him with an ethnic Russian who had never before set foot in the republic. This was taken as a clear infringement on the unwritten laws regulating relations between the ethnic groups in the Soviet Union and as an unpardonable insult to the Kazakh people. Masses gathered in the streets of Alma-Ata in protest, and when the police went to counterattack at least three persons were killed. This was the first but not the last time that Gorbachev's lack of flair in nationalities issues was to have violent consequences.

Today the memory of the December massacre has become an important part of the national Kazakh state mythology. It is presented as proof of the Kazakh desire for political independence and at the same time given "global importance" as (allegedly) the "first blow against the totalitarian Soviet system," the initial pebble that precipitated the landslide.[33] Kazakhstan gained its political independence, it is proclaimed, not as a result of external events and pressures but as the inevitable outcome of the Kazakh people's deep yearning for freedom.

•   •   •

The new national histories that are being written throughout the former Soviet republics focus on a whole series of events and individuals never mentioned during Communist times. Soviet historiography simply removed all persons who had fallen from grace, even central figures in important events of the past. The strategy was to act as if they had never existed at all—the classic example being the omission of Trotsky from virtually all accounts of the 1917 October Revolution, which he had in fact led. Even photographs in which he figured were often retouched.

In the new states of the former Soviet Union there are other Trotskys—historical actors whom the Communists transformed into nonpersons. Precisely because it was so selective, Soviet historiography presents ample opportunities for those who now seek to write new, national histories. And because the Soviet versions serve to inspire so little confidence, any alternative versions may well appear all the more reliable.

But nation-building historiography is more than merely filling in the blanks left by the official Soviet versions. As Ernest Renan once remarked, creating a national history is as much a matter of collective forgetting as of collective remembering.[34] Not everything in the history of a nation is equally suitable as construction material in a nation-building project. The new versions of "history" are occasionally characterized by suppression of facts and "memory shifts." The Latvians, for example, would prefer to present the Soviet regime as something forced upon them by the ethnic Russians, so the Communist era is often referred to as *krievu laiki*, the "Russian times." What is thereby *not* mentioned is that communism is an international ideology rooted in that same Western Europe that they so much want to be part of. That also means forgetting how Lenin's propaganda was well received in the factories of Riga among Russian and Latvian workers alike. In the Red Army there was a separate Latvian elite division, the Latvian Rifle Company. In November 1919, when the regime of Lenin was about to break down during the civil war, Petrograd was defended by precisely these Latvians. During the Soviet period, the Latvian Rifles had their own museum in the center of Riga. The museum still stands, now rechristened the Museum of the Occupation—and the "occupation" in question is that of the Soviet era. Many of the old objects on display have been retained, whereas the descriptive accompanying text has been conveniently altered.

Modern Ukrainian history texts may praise Khmel'nytskyy and his struggle in the national cause, but they touch very lightly on the extensive anti-Jewish pogroms that followed in the wake of the Cossacks. Ukrainian nation-builders are also doing what they can to limit the damages of Bandera's collaboration with the Nazis during World War II. If there is no way of hushing up this interlude completely, then relegating it to the footnotes of history may be the answer—likewise for the case of the SS Galicia division recruited among west Ukrainians. A complicating factor, however, is that some Ukrainian nationalists have no desire to "forget" these persons and organizations but in fact take pride in them. In similar fashion, certain Moldovan nationalists have sought to make a hero of Marshal Antonescu and want to erect a statue of him in the center of Chişinău. Others, however, have realized that it is precisely such attitudes that make it difficult to get the entire population of the country to join hands in the shared project of building a nation.

The historiographical disputes within and among the Soviet successor states are often conducted in the same uncompromising, dogmatic spirit and one-sidedness that once characterized Soviet ideology. This, as Soviet Marxists were prone to say, is "hardly a coincidence." As Mark von Hagen has pointed out, often the very same historians who control the rewriting of the national history today ruled supreme in the good old Communist days. Sometimes they even occupy the same offices they used to, except the nameplate now reads "professor of Ukrainian history" or "professor of Lithuanian history" rather than "professor of the Communist Party of the Soviet Union."[35]

4

NATION, STATE, AND RELIGION

By around 1990 the Soviet version of Marxism had run its course. At the time, it was expected that religion would fill the vacuum left behind by the demise of Soviet ideology. To some extent these expectations were in fact fulfilled, at least for a while. There was a certain renaissance within the churches; some people did find faith and took part in religious services. Opinion polls conducted in Russia and the other Soviet republics indicated that between a quarter and half of the population affirmed their belief in a god, depending on how the questions were formulated and which groups were in focus.[1] Among nonbelievers as well there was considerable respect for religion. Two Russian researchers found in 1991 that 46 percent of the Russian population identified themselves with the Orthodox faith, even though only some 29 percent considered themselves to be believers.[2]

Believers can be many different things, however. A study undertaken among ethnic Russians in five former Soviet republics in spring 1993 distinguished between two types of believers: practicing and nonpracticing.[3] The results of the survey are shown in Table 4.1. From the table we note relatively sizable regional variations. The greatest share of believers is found among Russians living in Latvia, whereas their ethnic counterparts in neighboring Estonia go to church far less often. On average no more than about one-fourth to one-third of those who termed themselves believers said that they practiced their faith. Compared with many Western countries, these figures are relatively high but still not high enough for us to speak of any extensive religious reawakening in the former Soviet Union.

Nationalism was a stronger force of upheaval. When perestroika introduced currents of liberalization, ethnic identities became politicized.

TABLE 4.1   Religion Among Russians, 1993 (in percentages)

	Russia	*Kazakhstan*	*Estonia*	*Latvia*	*Ukraine*
Practicing believers	9.7	10.4	7.9	18.0	17.1
Nonpracticing believers	31.9	34.8	30.3	33.1	35.2
Nonbelievers but respect believers	37.9	29.9	41.5	1.5	33.4
Consider religion harmful	0.9	1.1	3.7	0.9	0.7

SOURCE: David D. Laitin, *Identity in Formation: The Russian-Speaking Populations in the Near Abroad* (Ithaca, N.Y.: Cornell University Press, 1998), 319.

Hundreds of thousands, even millions, of people thronged the streets, demanding national independence for their republics. And yet, can we set up religious and national identity against each other? Is it not often the case that religion is an integral part of national consciousness and that this linkage is particularly close precisely in the case of Eastern Europe? This may well be so, but that does not mean that religion is the basic element in the national self-understanding of Eastern Europeans. Even in Yugoslavia this is not necessarily the case, although the most obvious cultural difference separating Croats, Serbs, and Bosnians, who speak largely the same language, is that they identify with different creeds: Roman Catholicism, Orthodoxy, Islam. Under Tito, however, Yugoslav society became highly secularized. Croats and Serbs clung to their identities, but usually as former Catholics or as people whose parents or grandparents had been Orthodox believers. This was perhaps most clearly the case with the Bosnian Muslims, who in 1971 for the first time were allowed to register themselves as Muslims, with *Muslim* as a national category.[4] This was at a time when *Muslim* for most people was no longer operative as a religious category.[5] For this reason, I believe, it is wrong to see the wars in Croatia and Bosnia as wars of religion. The religious reawakening that has in fact taken place in the former Yugoslavia in recent years has come as a *reaction* to the wars and bloodbaths rather than what brought them on in the first place. These are wars caused first and foremost by political factors.

Historically speaking, national identity in many countries has been connected to one specific religion. The Peace of Westphalia of 1648, which marked the end of the Thirty Years' War, established for the countries covered by the agreement the principle *cuius regio, eius religio*—as the ruler, so the religion.[6] Basically, this linked the choice of religion to the ruling house and the state, not to the nation. As the states of Europe gradually evolved into nation-states, the religion of the ruler also became the religion of the nation—as, for instance, in Norway and the other Scandinavian countries.

In many countries religion has long been an important national marker because other markers have been weak or totally lacking. For example, in Ireland by the time the revolt against the British got under way during the nineteenth century, most of the people had stopped speaking Gaelic and had adopted English, the language of the occupying forces. The solid Irish opposition was based on many factors, not least that the Irish were devoutly Catholic, as opposed to the preponderantly Protestant English. This rigid demarcation between the two faiths served to maintain and strengthen the ethnic boundary, as can be clearly seen in Northern Ireland today.

Similarly, the concept of Polishness has been very much linked to the Roman Catholic faith, as a kind of substitute for the Polish state that disappeared in the late 1700s. In the absence of political boundaries around the nation, religious differences served as an important shield to protect the specifically Polish identity: The Prussians were Lutheran Protestants; the Russians were Orthodox (and the Habsburgs, in contrast, were coreligionists of the Poles). The cultural boundary between the Poles and their powerful neighbors to the east and west was a dual one—religious and linguistic—as well as being linked to memories of the eradicated Polish state. All the same, both sides—the administrators of the czar and of the Prussians alike—sought to assimilate "their" Poles. According to one prominent Poland expert, the historian Norman Davies, the Prussianization of the Poles might have been as successful as the Anglicization of Wales (under way during the same period) if only Otto von Bismarck had left the Poles free to follow their own religion. Bismarck's Kulturkampf against the Catholic Church—which was, incidentally, not directed specifically against the Poles, although it hit them with particular force—served to remind them that they were different from the German Lutherans. It was the religious factor that made them into Poles.[7]

Whenever nationalists find that neighboring nations from whom they want to distance themselves happen to profess a different religion from the traditional creed of their own group, they avidly seize upon this cultural contrast and elevate it to the status of an essential, constitutive element of the cultural landscape. Conversely, if the group they want to be dissociated from professes the *same* faith as their own, they are likely to downplay religious differences and concentrate on other contrasts instead. A good case in point is Lithuanian nationalism. From 1569 and right up to the dismemberment of the Polish state in the 1790s, Poles and Lithuanians lived in the same state. In Rzeczpospolita Polska Polish culture dominated and the Lithuanian upper class underwent heavy Polonization. Lithuanian nationalists of the nineteenth and twentieth centuries wishing to revive, or create, a Lithuanian national identity gave high priority to rolling back Polish cultural influence in the Lithuanian lands. This goal, however, was impeded by the fact that the Poles, like the Lithuanians, are Roman Catholics. Hence, Lithuanian nationalists as a rule were anticlerical or even antireligious. Their approach was to brand the priests as unnational agents of Polish cultural hegemony.[8]

After World War II, however, the situation changed dramatically. Lithuanian nationalists were confronted not by Polish cultural domination but by Soviet communism. The Moscow Communists were atheists and were also in the popular understanding associated with the Orthodox Russian nation. All at once, then, the Catholic faith became a rallying point of Lithuanian national consolidation. Under perestroika the reopening of the Vilnius cathedral was seen not only as an important religious event but also as a milestone in the struggle for the reestablishment of Lithuanian national independence.

In spite of the nationalist use the Catholic faith has been put to over the centuries, Roman Catholicism is and remains a universalist and not a national faith. Its message therefore inevitably suffers some distortion whenever it gets harnessed to a nationalist cause. In this respect the position of the Orthodox Church is somewhat different. Although it, too, has a universal message, it lacks the unified, worldwide ecclesiastical structure of the Church of Rome. The Orthodox world is divided into a network of independent territorial churches, most of which are associated with one particular nation. Thus, there are separate Serbian, Bulgarian, Romanian, and Greek Orthodox Churches. The leaders of these churches, the patriarchs, reside within the corresponding nation-states of Bulgaria, Romania, Greece, and so on, and the churches are generally regarded as an attribute to the respective nations.

The Moscow patriarch is intimately identified with one particular nation, that of the Russians. Indeed, the official name of the institution he heads is the "Russian Orthodox Church." Even so, in the czarist and Communist periods the Moscow patriarchate was hardly a "national" church in the same sense as the cases mentioned above. Several larger and smaller ethnic groups in the Soviet Union were traditionally Orthodox—Moldovans, Georgians, Belarusians, and Ukrainians, to mention only the largest ones. In the course of the twentieth century, Ukrainian nationalists made several attempts to establish a separate Ukrainian Orthodox Church. Time and again they were rebuffed and forced back into the Russian fold, but with the advent of perestroika the struggle for Ukrainian ecclesiastical independence was renewed. In other parts of the former Soviet Union as well, religious national assertiveness among the Orthodox faithful has emerged.

Russia

Throughout their more than 1,000-year history, the Russian Orthodox Church and the Russian nation have become intermingled and interwoven. St. Basil's Cathedral in Red Square has become one of the best-known symbols of Russia and of all that is Russian. Orthodoxy was introduced among the East Slavs by Grand Duke Vladimir of Kiev in the late 900s. To begin with, Christianity was the religion of the rulers and their retinue, taking root only gradually in the villages. (Once established there, however, it was to prove very hard to eradicate, as the Bolsheviks later discovered.) During the Kiev period, the Russian Church was headed by a metropolitan appointed by Constantinople, usually a Greek. Back then there was no question of a national Russian Church and far less so of a nationalistic one. This changed with the Mongol invasions of the 1240s. Contact with Constantinople was broken, and the weak state entity held together by the Kievan princes finally crumbled. Under the Tatar yoke, Orthodoxy was to become the most important cultural marker, distinguishing the Russians from their Mongol (Tatar) conquerors. The latter chose to adopt Islam rather than Christianity.

Throughout the Middle Ages and onward, Orthodoxy became increasingly central to the national identity of the Russian people. In the absence of any broader political entity, the Church emerged as the most important all-Russian institution. The Russian peasant gradually began to call himself *krestyanin*—a word for "peasant" that is derived from the word for "Christian." Until well into the nineteenth century, it was also common for Russians to present themselves not by saying, "I am a Russian" but with the words, "*Ya pravoslavnyy*"—"I am an Orthodox believer."

Throughout Russian history two developmental trends have run parallel, reinforcing each other. On the one hand, there was the convergence of the Russian national and religious identities; on the other, the state and the Church came closer and closer together on both the institutional and the ideological levels. In 1448 the Russian Church broke away from Constantinople, five years before the city was to fall to the Ottomans. Constantinople had been the throne of the Orthodox world, the "New Rome"; soon voices came to be heard in Russia proclaiming Moscow as the third (and final) Rome. This idea has later been seen as an expression of Russian national-religious messianism. Even though the notion of Moscow as the third Rome probably had scant import when originally formulated, it was later to gain prominence when it resurfaced among Russian nationalist thinkers of the nineteenth century.

In the Russia of the 1500s, men of the cloth exerted considerable influence in the realm of secular politics. In 1589 the Russian metropolitan was titled "patriarch," and under Czar Mikhail Romanov (from 1613) he functioned as coregent.[9] In the second half of the 1600s, however, the power of the Church became weakened through a wrenching internal struggle, the great Raskol, which led to a break with the so-called Old Believers. At the same time, there was a harsh power struggle between the czar and the patriarch, from which the former emerged triumphant. Also after this, Church and state continued in close partnership, but from then on with the state dominant.

In the early 1700s, Peter the Great abolished the patriarchate and organized the Russian Church as a state-run department. In the 1830s the ideology of the czarist powers was expressed in terms of a trinity: autocracy, Orthodoxy, and "nationality" *(narodnost)*. At about the same time, a group of Russian thinkers formulated a program for a religious Russian nationalism, the so-called Slavophile movement. The label itself is actually somewhat misleading, as the Slavophiles were more concerned with the Orthodox faith than with the "Slavic" element as the basic factor of Russianness. The Slavophiles were to exert considerable influence on the shaping of Russian nationalism, perhaps more so in the twentieth century than in their own times.

During the 1917 October Revolution, the Russian Church seized the opportunity to reestablish the patriarchate. The Bolsheviks had no desire to legitimize their power on the basis of Orthodoxy, and the intimate historical linkage between state and Church was broken. But Stalin retained complete control over the Church, formalizing this power during World War II by establishing the Council for the Affairs of the Russian Orthodox Church. In 1965 the council was merged with another body to form the Council for Religious Affairs—not that the control was weakened, however.

When Soviet power crumbled away under perestroika, the stage would seem to have been set for the triumphal reentry of the Russian Orthodox Church as national and state church alike. Mikhail Gorbachev was engaged in a desperate search for support in his struggle to renew Soviet society, and when the Russian Church was celebrating its 1,000-year anniversary, he made repeated attempts to ingratiate himself with Church leaders.[10] The Orthodox prelates, however, remained skeptical of the new reformer in the Kremlin, whom they saw as far too Western-oriented. When they finally began to involve themselves in the public debate, it was frequently with a message akin to that of Gorbachev's political foes, the conservative Communists and the Russian nationalists.

Although Communists and nationalists are often placed at opposing poles of the political spectrum, on the extreme left and right flanks, these two factions began to draw nearer and nearer after the events of 1990–1991, entering into what have been termed "red-brown" alliances. A great many of the antireformist organizations that came into being had one or more Orthodox priests and bishops in their upper ranks. One of these was Russkiy Sobor, under the leadership of a former KGB general, Aleksandr Sterligov. His movement held one of its first meetings in the Danilov monastery, headquarters of the Moscow patriarchate, with Patriarch Aleksiy and several other high-ranking clergymen in attendance. Although the prelates insisted that they were not engaged in politics, such public appearances were taken as a clear statement of political convictions.[11]

The meeting at Danilov monastery took place while Boris Yeltsin was involved in an intense power struggle with the Russian parliament, the Supreme Soviet, where Communists and the "red-browns" dominated. This conflict peaked in October 1993 when tanks encircled the parliamentary building. In a desperate last-minute attempt at conciliation, Patriarch Aleksiy was asked to mediate. The mediation failed—or rather, it never got off the ground. All the same, this indicates that the Russian Church, despite its various controversial moves of recent years, was still seen as a national, Pan-Russian institution, indeed perhaps the only one that at that time enjoyed at least a modicum of respect from all sides.

Yeltsin himself had a certain amount of success in attempting to use the Church as a legitimizing factor. When Yeltsin was installed as Russian president in summer 1991, the patriarch was in attendance and bestowed his benediction upon the new president. As political officers gradually disappeared from the military, they were in many units replaced by field chaplains. Several Church feast days were proclaimed public holidays. The new Russian constitution states explicitly that Russia is a "secular" state where no religion may be the state religion (article 14). Still, many observers have viewed the moves made by the Orthodox Church as intended in precisely that direction. This has worried and irritated many Russians, not least among the Muslim population.[12]

In June 1997 the new national assembly, the Duma, passed a bill on religion, the preamble of which makes special mention of the role of the Russian Orthodox Church in the history of Russia. This bill defines four religions—Islam, Judaism, Buddhism, and Orthodoxy—as the "traditional religions" of Russia, giving them several special rights not granted to other creeds. The bill was greeted with heavy criticism from abroad, particularly from the Vatican and Washington. American missionaries had been engaged in extensive evangelizing throughout Russia; with the passage of the religion bill, they feared that their activities would be banned. Indeed, Patriarch Aleksiy expressly condemned "proselytizing activity" in Russia, saying that it should be forbidden since it "lures people away from the faith of their forefathers."[13] Initially, Yeltsin used his presidential veto to stop the bill from becoming law, sending it back to the legislative assembly. At this, a series of Communist Party leaders denounced what they saw as Yeltsin's "anti-Russian" policy on religion.[14]

In September, however, Yeltsin made a volte-face and signed the controversial law. In the meantime the law had undergone certain changes, but its basic thrust remained the same.

After the fall of communism, the Moscow patriarchate's most serious rival in Russia has been not Protestant missionaries but a Church that is both Russian and Orthodox—the Russian Orthodox Church Abroad (Russkaya Pravoslavnaya Tserkov' za Rubezhem). This is one of several Russian religious communities that flourished in émigré circles during the Soviet period. Highly pro-czarist and anti-Communist, the Russian Orthodox Church Abroad considers itself the sole true carrier of Russian Orthodoxy. It has accused the Moscow patriarchate of a sin it sees as worse than heresy: active collaboration with those who sought to eradicate the faith in Russia. It has issued a list of ultimate conditions for reconciliation: The Moscow patriarchate must seek to atone for having bowed to the godless Bolsheviks; the last czar, Nicolas II, is to be canonized; and there is to be no ecumenical collaboration with other denominations or church communities. Since the Moscow patriarchate has refused to meet these demands, the Orthodox believers of Russia today are split into two irreconcilable camps along dividing lines that are purely political.[15]

Orthodox Territorial Churches and Phyletism

The two developmental trends in the history of the Russian Church briefly sketched above—fusion between the national and the religious and between state and Church—were complex. The Russian state was an empire, not a nation-state, whereas the Russian Church was at the same time supposed to serve both as state church and as national church. Its official name, "Russkaya Tserkov'," reflected links to the Russian nation and not the Russian state (in that case it would have been "Rossiyskaya tserkov'"). Orthodoxy was the national religion of not only the Russians but also a whole series of other peoples living in Russia. All of these, regardless of ethnic identity, were members of the Russian Church and subjects of the Moscow patriarchate.

According to a view widely held within the Orthodox world, each and every Orthodox people should have its own autonomous church. Not only Orthodoxy as religion but also the Church as institution is seen as an attribute of the nation. This was clearly shown in the discord attendant on the establishment of the Macedonian Church in Yugoslavia in the 1960s. An important motive behind the demand for a separate church was the struggle for recognition of Macedonia as a separate nation. Macedonia has long been a bone of contention between Bulgaria and Serbia: The former has maintained that the Macedonians are western

Bulgarians, whereas the Serbs have insisted that they are southern Serbs. More and more Macedonians have come to feel that they are neither: They are, quite simply, Macedonians. When Tito, for his own political reasons, acceded to the Macedonian demands in 1967, loud protests came from the Serbian patriarchate.[16]

In order to counter the threat of nationalistically inspired schisms, the multinational Orthodox patriarchates have, ever since the end of the nineteenth century, stressed that in the strict legal sense of the term the various Orthodox communities are neither national churches nor state churches but territorial churches (in Russian, *pomestnye tserkvi*). Ancient Church principles decree that there is never to be more than one Orthodox bishop for each area.[17] Attempts to identify the Church with a single ethnic group are in fact considered heresy and condemned as phyletism (a term derived from the Greek for "tribe," *phyle*).[18]

The first charges of phyletism had come from Greek theologians in 1872, when Orthodox Bulgarians sought to establish their own Bulgarian Church. At that time the Orthodox congregations in Bulgaria belonged to the dioceses of the patriarch of Constantinople, and religious life in Bulgaria was exposed to massive Greek influence. All the higher clergy were Greek, and the liturgy was in Greek—even in the villages where the Bulgarian-speaking inhabitants understood not a word of the language. For the Bulgarians, then, it became vital to establish their own Bulgarian Orthodox Church, as they had in fact had during the Middle Ages. But the Greeks would have none of this. That the Bulgarians finally did manage to get their way was thanks to support from the holders of political power in the country—the Muslim Ottomans, who in 1870 established a separate Bulgarian exarchate.[19] This led to a bitter break with the patriarch of Constantinople, which was not healed until 1945.

With the Bulgarian schism came a flood tide of theological, legal, and political tracts studied throughout the Orthodox world. Today the Greek view of phyletism has been accepted in principle by most of the major Orthodox national churches and is supported not least by those who have ethnic minorities among their members and who fear new schisms—the Moscow patriarchate, for example.[20] At the same time, the ethnonational principle is also strong in practice. For instance, nearly all Orthodox Christian groups in the United States have their own church communities, even though they all live on the same territory and are citizens of the same state.[21] The only Orthodox congregation in the United States to be organized on an explicitly nonethnic basis is the Orthodox Church of America. All references to ethnic affiliation have been avoided in order to make this a territorial church, open to Orthodox believers of all nations. The Orthodox Church of America has been granted independent status by the patriarch of Moscow but is not recognized by the patriarch of Constantinople. This issue is one among many points of dis-agreement between the two most powerful institutions in the Orthodox world.[22]

There exists no higher Pan-Orthodox body to adjudicate in such ques-tions of church law. The individual Orthodox patriarchates are totally au-tonomous in all internal and external matters of the Church. To put this in Orthodox terminology, each is to be seen as autocephalous, as having its own head. Should the religious communities within one territory so desire, they may request the autocephalous Church leadership to grant them self-rule in the form of their own autocephaly or merely as internal self-rule, autonomy.[23] In several cases such requests have been granted, and the break has taken place without complications. But there are even more examples of local congregations that have broken off without offi-cial approval. In this way countless schisms have erupted throughout the Orthodox world, generally as a result of altered political circumstances.

The main rule is that state and territorial Church go together. When a territory breaks loose from another state and achieves status as a separate nation-state, then the church in this new state has, according to the Or-thodox line of thought, the right to have its status upgraded. Whether this will result in total, autocephalous independence or merely internal autonomy for the community in question will depend on various factors. Size is one of them: Small minority congregations are often granted only autonomous status, and indeed often request nothing more. Yet the Mother Church may be unwilling to grant full autocephalous status to new national churches even when the political and demographic circum-stances would seem to indicate that solution. This has several times been the reaction of the Moscow patriarchate during this century.

The Orthodox Church in the Baltics

In the Baltic republics, almost all Orthodox believers are immigrants from other parts of the former Soviet Union. Ethnic Lithuanians are nearly 100 percent Roman Catholic, whereas ethnic Estonians are almost as strongly Protestant Lutheran. Latvians, befitting their "middle" loca-tion, are split between a Lutheran majority and a Roman Catholic minor-ity. In addition, other Western denominations have established congre-gations in the Baltics in recent years—Baptists, Seventh-Day Adventists, Pentecostals, and others. Most of these new converts have come from the non-Baltic minorities.[24]

This means that religious dividing lines overlay the ethnic divides and reinforce them, or—to put it differently—they represent one aspect of these. Samuel Huntington maintains that the cultural boundary between the Baltic republics and Russia constitutes one of the fundamental fault lines between the great civilizations of the world, in this case between the Western and the Orthodox. Such fault lines, according to Huntington, have emerged as the result of a series of factors: history, language, culture, tradition, and most important of all, religion. In his view the borderlines of civilizations are not only real, but they are basic. Throughout the centuries they have unleashed "the most protracted and most violent conflicts."[25]

Many Baltic scholars draw on Huntington's analysis for support of their own view that the Baltic area is part of Europe, whereas Russia is not.[26] At the same time, it is clear that the political situation in the Baltics today can hardly be said to provide backing for Huntington's thesis. Even if both Estonia and Latvia have been marked by deep conflicts between the titular populations and the Russians, these conflicts have been basically nonviolent, and religion has scarcely featured in them at all. The reason for the latter is probably the low level of religious fervor in general throughout the area. When Lutheranism was introduced in the Baltics, it came as the religion of the German upper class. Even though German pastors managed to convert the Baltic peasants to Protestantism, the new creed never struck particularly deep roots among the Estonians and Latvians, who continued to regard it as a form of German cultural imperialism.

There has, however, been one case in the Baltics of a sharp religious conflict with ethnic overtones. Among the ethnic Estonians, there exists a small Orthodox minority, some 15,000 persons in all. This is a figure far lower than the number of Orthodox believers among the Russians and other Slavic groupings in Estonia, but this Estonian Orthodox group feels it has the backing of the Estonian state in case of disagreements between them and the Orthodox Slavs in the country.

During the interwar years, while Estonia was independent, this Estonian Orthodox Church had no wish to be under the Moscow patriarchate, which it saw as the extended arm of the Soviet state. Instead, it decided to recognize the patriarch of Constantinople as its spiritual leader. When Estonia was forced into the USSR after World War II, the Estonian Orthodox Church continued to exist among the Estonian exile congregations, whereas its buildings in the Estonian Soviet Socialist Republic were taken over by the Russian Orthodox Church.

Today both the Moscow patriarchate and the exile Church claim status as *the* Estonian Orthodox Church in Estonia.[27] In 1992 Moscow granted autonomy, but not autocephaly, to the Estonian Orthodox Church (together with the Latvian Orthodox Church), but then in February 1996 the patriarch of Constantinople declared that the Orthodox believers of Estonia lay under *his* purview. Thereby the disagreement was elevated to become a confrontation between the two most powerful prelates in the

Orthodox world. At the same time, Moscow accused the secular Estonian authorities of interfering on the Estonian/Greek side. In March 1996 a protest march through the streets of Tallinn drew over 10,000 Russian Orthodox participants. But in May that same year a settlement was reached when Constantinople and Moscow agreed that believers in each congregation should have the right to decide the patriarchate to which they owed allegiance.[28]

Orthodox National Churches

The religious situation in Ukraine, Belarus, Georgia, and Moldova differs from that in the Baltic republics in that nearly all believers belonging to the titular nations in these states are Orthodox Christians. Here, then, we might assume that the stage was set for the emergence of new national churches, as in fact did happen with the establishment of the new nation-states in the Balkans. In fact, however, the Moscow patriarchate has not granted autocephalous standing to any new churches in these former Soviet republics. To the contrary, Patriarch Aleksiy has stated, "The canonical territory of the Moscow Patriarchate includes not only Russia, but Ukraine, Belarus, Moldova, the countries of the Baltics, Azerbaijan, Kazakhstan, and Central Asia. . . . One cannot form fifteen local Orthodox churches in a country that has been divided into fifteen sovereign states."[29]

Patriarch Aleksiy did not include Georgia on this list, as the Georgian Orthodox Church enjoyed autocephalous status throughout the entire Communist era and still does. That was in itself a break with the principle of one state, one territorial Church, since Georgia was, of course, a part of the Soviet Union. The official reason given was that the Georgian Church was an ancient institution, dating back to the fourth century A.D., and thus considerably older than the Russian Orthodox Church.

Belarus

Belarus lies on the borderline between Orthodoxy and Catholicism in Europe. When its territories were joined to the Polish-Lithuanian grand duchy, the upper classes generally converted to Roman Catholicism, whereas the peasants retained their Orthodox faith. In 1596, during the Counterreformation, a church council was held in Brest, and a large proportion of the Orthodox clergy of Poland-Lithuania declared that they recognized the pope in Rome as their spiritual and religious leader. Those congregations that united with Rome were allowed to keep their traditional Orthodox liturgy and practices. This was the beginning of the Catholic Church of the Eastern Rite, also known as the Uniate Church.

Belarusians tend to call it the Belarusian Catholic Church, Ukrainians the Ukrainian Catholic Church. In addition the Roman Catholic Church (Western rite) continued and continues to exist in both countries, with its congregation drawn primarily from the ranks of ethnic Poles.

When, as a result of the three partitions of Poland (1772–1795), Belarus ended up under the Russian empire, it became usual to apply religious criteria in dividing up the population of the area: All Roman Catholics were counted as Poles regardless of which language they spoke, and all Orthodox believers were Russians. Those belonging to the Uniate Church were seen as a kind of residual group, neither Poles nor Russians; they were primarily peasants and looked down upon by the others.[30] They comprised about four-fifths of the population.

In 1839 the 1596 Brest Union was condemned by a Uniate synod meeting in Polotsk, following heavy pressure from the Russian authorities, and the Uniate Church of Belarus was merged with the Russian Orthodox Church. It was not until 1905 that the Uniate Church could operate freely once more, but by then membership had sunk drastically. In an opinion survey conducted in 1992 in Belarus, 72 percent of the respondents said that they were Orthodox, 6 percent Roman Catholic, and only 1 percent Uniate.[31]

The Belarusian Orthodox Church was granted autonomous status in 1991, but it still recognizes Patriarch Aleksiy II of Moscow as its spiritual leader. The liturgical language is Old Church Slavonic, with Russian pronunciation. In sermons and official correspondence, the Belarusian Orthodox leaders generally use Russian, as in fact do many of the faithful. There does not appear to be any opposition to the Church's pro-Russian orientation among the lay congregation.

Moldova

Not only the Moldovans/Romanians but also most ethnic minorities in Moldova have traditionally belonged to the Orthodox Church. This applies both to the Slavs—Russians, Ukrainians, Belarusians, Bulgarians, and Serbs—and to the Turkish-speaking Gagauz in the south. Thus, there is scant basis for any religious conflicts between the titular population and the minorities in Moldova. A considerable cultural lowest common denominator exists among the various ethnic groups in this country.

Since Moldova gained its independence, no demands seem to have been put forward for a separate, autocephalous Moldovan Orthodox Church. The Orthodox Church of Moldova is still under the Moscow patriarchate, although it was granted autonomous status in October 1992. And yet all the same, the Moldovan Orthodox Church has been plagued by ethnically based strife. A small group of Ukrainians in Moldova has chosen to place itself under the Ukrainian Autocephalous Orthodox Church in Kiev.[32] More serious is that some believers in Moldova, considering themselves to be ethnic Romanians, do not wish to be under Moscow but direct their allegiance to the patriarch in Bucharest instead. In December 1992 a group of Moldovan priests, led by Bishop Petru, formally recognized the Romanian patriarch as their religious leader. This breakaway body, which terms itself the Bessarabian Church, has repeatedly sought official recognition from the authorities. For five years, the Moldovan state authorities refused, but then in August 1997 the Moldovan Court of Appeals ruled that the government would have to grant its approval—on which the Council of Europe had also insisted, citing the principle of freedom of religion.[33] Instead of a single national church for all Moldovans regardless of ethnic background, the Orthodox Moldovan congregation finds itself with three different structures, each community with its own seat in a neighboring capital: Moscow, Kiev, and Bucharest.

Ukraine

The religious landscape of Ukraine differs considerably from that of Belarus and Moldova. Church politics in Ukraine have been highly turbulent in recent years, and national motives have occupied a central position. Throughout this century, powerful forces within the Ukrainian Orthodox Church have been unwilling to recognize the spiritual authority of Moscow. As soon as political liberalization under perestroika made it possible, an autocephalous Ukrainian Church was established—or reestablished—in August 1989. Links were immediately formed with the Ukrainian Autocephalous Orthodox Church (UAOC) in exile, which had been in existence ever since the early 1920s. As a countermove, five months later the Moscow patriarchate bestowed on the Russian Orthodox Church in Ukraine a new name as well as autonomous status. It was to be called the "Ukrainian Orthodox Church," while remaining under the Moscow patriarchate. Since then, a whole series of new rifts and reunifications have brought about the situation of today: There are three bodies all claiming to be *the* Ukrainian Orthodox Church. In addition there is a strong Ukrainian Catholic (Uniate) Church in western Ukraine.

The strong politicization of religious life in Ukraine is first and foremost a reflection of Ukrainian nationalism. Whereas national identity in Belarus and Moldova has been weak and uncertain, the Ukrainian identity is more firmly rooted, at least in the central and western parts of the country.

Historically speaking, Ukrainian nationalism has been linked more to the Ukrainian Catholic (Uniate) Church than to the (Russian) Orthodox Church. One reason is that the Uniate Church had been based in those portions of Ukraine that had never been part of the Russian empire—

Galicia and Transcarpathia in the far west. These areas belonged to the Habsburg empire until World War I; in the interwar period they were given to Poland and Czechoslovakia, respectively. Here the political pre-conditions for the growth of a separate Ukrainian identity were far more favorable than in the Russian-controlled areas to the east.

After World War II, eastern Galicia and Transcarpathia were made part of the Soviet Union. In connection with his crusade against west Ukrainian nationalism, Stalin demanded in 1946 that the Ukrainian Catholic Church be placed under the Moscow patriarchate. It was now claimed that the 1596 Council of Brest, at which this church had been established, had acted against the will of the Ukrainian people.[34] Now, this is of course quite possible, but just as the Danish and Norwegian populations have long since come to terms with Lutheranism and adopted it as their religion even though it was originally forced upon them—and likewise with England and Anglicanism and a whole series of other similar cases—a great many west Ukrainians had over the years developed a firm sense of identity linked with the new faith. That is why the Lvov/L'viv Council of 1946 was every bit as much an infringement of the rights of the believers as the Brest Council may have been 350 years earlier.

The Ukrainian Catholic Church remained forbidden throughout the Soviet era but continued to exist as an underground community and abroad. It then reemerged from its catacombs during perestroika, demanding the return of church buildings that were now at the disposal of the Orthodox Church. In some cases this led to bitter conflicts, but in the course of 1991–1992 most of the specific disagreements were solved.[35]

Although the Ukrainian Catholic Church identifies strongly with the national Ukrainian cause, only a minority of the total population of Ukraine are adherents, even among the nationalists. This church is a minority community with backing in only one of the many regions of Ukraine. That is why it has not been able, in the long run, to serve as a unifying symbol for the entire Ukrainian nation. Most of the country's new political leaders today, and indeed most of the population at large, belong (at least formally) to the Orthodox Church. A 1992 survey showed that about 50 percent of the population considered themselves "believers"; of these, approximately three-quarters were Orthodox and only about 17 percent Uniate.[36]

This is a card that Moscow has attempted to play to the full in its struggle with the Ukrainian Catholics. At the June 1990 Council of the Russian Orthodox Church, Metropolitan Filaret of Kiev and Galicia claimed:

> The protagonists of Uniatism are seeking to present their community as a national Ukrainian movement. In reality, however, it is, as it has always been, a tool for disrupting the spiritual unity of the Ukrainian people. It is a tool for wresting Galicia not only from Moscow but also from Kiev. We ap-

peal to all who wish Ukraine's national rebirth: you must realize that *unio* [the Uniate Church] represents a serious threat to the unity of the Ukrainian nation.[37]

In this way the Moscow patriarchy tried—quite blatantly—to court the Ukrainian nationalists, who by this time were beginning to form a powerful movement. But this was a game over which the patriarchate lacked control, because within Orthodoxy there also exists a Ukrainian national/nationalistic alternative to the Russian-dominated Moscow patriarchate: the Ukrainian Autocephalous Orthodox Church. Originally established in 1921, the UAOC had been forcibly dissolved by the Bolsheviks in the 1930s (but as I pointed out above, had continued to exist in exile). During World War II it had reemerged in the German-controlled areas of Ukraine, only to be forcibly dissolved once again after the war.

The UAOC sees itself as the true successor to the Orthodox Church in Kievan Rus'. In legal terms, however, its position is very weak, since the ordination of its first bishops in the 1920s did not follow the accepted canonical rules of apostolic succession. That is why the UAOC has never been recognized by any Orthodox Church in any other country. This matter was put right when the Church was reestablished in 1942, and since then it has continued to exist in the West—among other things, as the community of the Ukrainian diaspora in the United States. The exile church was headed by the nonagenarian metropolitan Mstyslav Skrypnik. He had been active in the Ukrainian national movement of the 1920s and thus personified the strong ties between Ukrainian nationalism and the Ukrainian Autocephalous Orthodox Church. In June 1990 the ninety-two-year-old émigré prelate was elected patriarch of the UAOC at a synod held in Kiev.

Riding on a wave of national enthusiasm, the UAOC soon had between 1,000 and 2,000 congregations, most of them in western Ukraine, that is, in the same area where the Ukrainian Catholic Church is strong. Many west Ukrainians have now turned to the UAOC instead of the Uniate Church of their parents and grandparents. The reasons for this are probably many. In the more than fifty years that have passed since Stalin placed the Uniate Church under the Moscow patriarchate, some of its members have found an Orthodox identity—or, perhaps more correctly, they have rediscovered the Orthodox identity that their ancestors had prior to 1596. This applies especially to west Ukrainian priests who have studied theology in Moscow or Leningrad. At the same time, these west Ukrainians were nationalistic enough to realize that they no longer wished to remain under the Moscow patriarchate. For them, the UAOC was the solution. Indeed, many Ukrainian nationalists became convinced that this church was *more* truly Ukrainian than the Ukrainian Catholic

(Uniate) Church. After all, they now recalled, their Ukrainian Cossack forebears of the 1500s and 1600s had been Orthodox, whereas *unio* was something that had been forced upon them by the hated Poles.

Additionally, it was clear that some priests in Galicia had managed to compromise themselves rather thoroughly by collaborating with the Soviet authorities, including the KGB. Fearing a welcome that was at most lukewarm if they returned to the Uniate Church, some of their number turned to the UAOC. As a result, the UAOC ended up with a leadership comprising a remarkable mixture of nationalists and opportunists, former dissidents and former collaborators.[38]

Elsewhere in Ukraine many priests had had uncomfortably close relations with the Soviet authorities as well. Most prominent among the Communist fellow travelers in the leadership of the Ukrainian Orthodox Church was Filaret (Denysenko), the Kiev metropolitan of the Moscow patriarchate. In spring 1992 articles appeared in the Moscow press documenting that Filaret had been a prominent KGB informer operating under the code name "Antonov." In addition came the first open reports of his rather unusual private life. Like all the other top clergy within the Orthodox Church, Filaret was an ordained monk, but he had both a mistress and several children. The Russian Church leadership saw no other alternative: Filaret would have to go. In summer 1992 he was officially defrocked.[39]

Filaret, however, was not willing to accept this. That same autumn he broke with the Moscow patriarchate, together with a group of Ukrainian bishops, and formed a separate autocephalous Ukrainian Orthodox Church in which he was elected patriarch. Like the UAOC, this new body—the Ukrainian-Orthodox Church–Kiev Patriarchate—has not been recognized by Orthodox ecclesiastical bodies anywhere else in the world. But support was forthcoming from Ukraine's new political leadership. Ukrainian president Leonid Kravchuk resolutely and actively involved himself in the internal religious struggles in his country. Like Filaret, Kravchuk became a sudden convert to the cause of Ukrainian nationalism in the early 1990s on rather opportunistic grounds. He was quick to see the advantages in a pure Ukrainian Orthodox Church that could have close links to the Ukrainian political authorities without being in any way dependent on Moscow.

And thus, in addition to the small Uniate Church, there came to be three Orthodox churches in Ukraine: the UAOC, the autonomous Ukrainian Orthodox Church (under the Moscow patriarchate), and finally Filaret's Ukrainian-Orthodox Church–Kiev Patriarchate. For the Ukrainian state authorities, the best solution would be a single national Ukrainian Orthodox Church that could present a unified front against the Moscow-dominated autonomous church, which was still by far the largest of the three. In June 1992 a merger synod between the UAOC and Filaret's community was in fact convened. Patriarch Mstyslav was proclaimed head of this united Ukrainian church, and Filaret was to be his deputy.[40] But Patriarch Mstyslav soon disavowed this merger, and after his death in June 1993 quite a few Autocephalists wished to remain true to his last wish. They broke away from Filaret's community and reestablished the Ukrainian Autocephalous Orthodox Church under the leadership of Patriarch Dmitriy (Yaremu). Within the Kiev patriarchate, Mstyslav was replaced by Patriarch Vladimir (Romanyuk); however, when Vladimir died only two years later, Filaret was elected his successor.

In this brief survey, I have been able to sketch out only a few of the main features of Ukrainian church history after 1989. It is a history full of confusing details.[41] What, then, can we conclude? For one thing, in Ukraine, too, it has not proven possible to realize the Orthodox principle of one people, one church—not because of any *lack* of an Orthodox nationalist church but because there are simply too many of them.

Georgia

Nationalism is strong in Georgia, and a separate, national Orthodox Georgian Church has existed ever since the fourth century A.D. During Soviet times the Georgians were also the only nation to be allowed to retain their own autocephalous church, led by their own *patriarch katholikos*.

Thus, of all the Orthodox areas of the former Soviet Union today, Georgia has probably come the closest to realizing the principle of one people, one church. All the same, historically speaking there have not been strong links between Georgian nationalism and the Georgian Church. Quite the contrary: The nationalist intelligentsia of Georgia have traditionally been highly anticlerical, if not directly atheistic. To them, the Georgian Church was too acquiescent to the Russian and Soviet authorities. A commonly held view has been that "the Russians—if not the Soviets—are gloomy religious mystics: we Georgians are bright, rational thinkers with traditions from the Middle Ages."[42] This attitude would seem to have changed somewhat in recent years. The country's first non-Communist president, Zviad Gamsakhurdia, was both a thoroughgoing nationalist and a fervent Orthodox believer; even the current president, Eduard Shevardnadze, formerly prominent in the upper echelons of the Soviet Party elite, was baptized into the Georgian Church in 1991.

At the same time, the Georgian Church has placed its full weight behind what it sees as the cause of Georgian nationalism. This is a two-pronged nationalism: one prong directed against Russia and the Russians, the other against the many national minorities in Georgia. Two of these groups, the South Ossetians and the Abkhazians, had their own autonomous territories in the Soviet period. Their autonomous status, always a thorn in the side of Georgian nationalists, was revoked by the new Georgian national assembly in 1991. In both Abkhazia and South Ossetia, civil war broke out in 1992 between the titular population and the Georgians. In these struggles the Georgian Church has come out uncompromisingly on the Georgian side. Then in 1993 civil war erupted within the Georgian population itself, between adherents of Gamsakhurdia and those supporting Shevardnadze. Patriarch Ilya II stepped into the breach by declaring that any Georgian to lift a weapon against a compatriot would be excommunicated. But he was speaking in a strictly ethnic sense of fellow Georgians, not Abkhazians or Ossetians.

Some of the population of Georgia are Muslim, but the fighting in Georgia has not had the character of religious warfare. Among the Georgians and the Ossetians, there are Muslim minorities; while the Abkhazians are divided almost evenly between Muslims and Orthodox. Georgian-speaking Muslims are sometimes seen as a distinct ethnic group known as Ajars. Since 1921 they have had their own autonomous area, Ajaria, in the southwestern corner of the country. This is in fact the only autonomous area still recognized by the authorities in Tbilisi. The Georgian Orthodox Church, however, does not recognize the Ajars as a separate group; in the eyes of the Georgian prelates they are lapsed Georgians.

•　•　•

There can be no doubt that the principle of autonomous national churches is firmly embedded in Orthodox Church law and in general Orthodox thought. Although all this principle actually says is that there is to be one and only one bishopric for each geographical area, in practice the concept of an Orthodox National Church has become closely linked with ethnicity. The case of Macedonia reflects a view widespread in the Orthodox world, that a nation is not recognized as truly independent until it also has an independent church of its own. Thus, an autonomous—preferably also autocephalous—church becomes an attribute of the nation and an important goal in the national struggle. At the same time, church nationalism in Ukraine is countered in Moscow with accusations of phyletism. The unspoken premise underlying this line of argument is that the Ukrainians are not a separate nation. Russian nationalist thought sees the Ukrainians as one of several subgroups under the Pan-Russian "nation."

In only one case do we find almost perfect realization of the principle of one church, one nation in the former Soviet Union: Armenia. Ethnic Armenians make up well over 90 percent of the total population of the country. The Armenian Apostolic Church is one of the oldest in the world, dating to the fourth century A.D. It professes Monophysitism: that Jesus had but one, divine nature—a teaching contradictory to the more widespread Christian belief that he was both true God and true man.[43]

Ever since the ruling of the Council of Chalcedon in 451, the Armenian Church has been isolated from neighboring religious communities. In the course of more than 1,500 years, it has developed into a purely national church that the Armenians share with no others, led by its own *katholikos*. Moreover, the closest of their neighbors—the Turks and the Azeri—are Muslim nations. During World War I, the Armenians living in Turkey were subjected to a genocide that has left deep scars in the collective Armenian psyche. This historical enmity has contributed to strengthening the national religious consciousness of the Armenian people.

Islam and Nation-Building in Central Asia

In six states of the former Soviet Union—Kazakhstan, Uzbekistan, Kyrgyzstan, Tajikistan, Turkmenistan, and Azerbaijan—Islam is the traditional religion of the titular group. To some extent the new power holders in these countries have begun utilizing Islam in their nation-building: They have used Islamic symbols and Islamic rhetoric to bolster their power and create legitimacy for the new order.

These regimes are highly authoritarian, in part downright dictatorial, and thus can hardly be said to rest on support garnered through democratic elections. For precisely these reasons, the new leaders have realized the necessity of finding alternative sources of legitimacy. The most important of these are nationalism and the discovery of a glorious and honorable national history, but Islam as well is administered in small, carefully controlled doses. Mosques are erected, *medreses* (theological seminaries) are opened, and official events often include a decorative touch of Islamic ceremony. In Azerbaijan the situation is complicated by the fact that the country is home to Muslims of both the Shi'ite (two-thirds of the population) and Sunni (one-third) branches.[44] Divisions between these two are at least as pronounced as between the various Christian denominations, making it more difficult for Azerbaijani nation-builders to employ Islam and its symbols as construction materials than it is for their counterparts elsewhere in the former Soviet south.

In Uzbekistan and Turkmenistan, the regimes have been flirting openly with Islam. In 1992 Uzbekistan's president Karimov (whose first name happens to be "Islam") was sworn into office with his hand on a copy of the Quran. In the same year he made the pilgrimage (hajj) to Mecca, as did the president of Turkmenistan, Saparmurad Niyazov. The daily prayer recited by all the clergy of Turkmenistan asks Allah to "protect independent Turkmenistan and bring luck to our beloved

Motherland and our honorable President, Saparmurad Turkmenbashi, in all his intentions."[45]

But not even here is the relationship between nation and Islam without contradictions. As a tool for nation-building, Islam can prove itself a double-edged sword. First, with one single exception (Kyrgyzstan's Askar Akayev), the heads of state of all six Central Asian republics are old Communist bosses in new guise. Until only a few years ago, they all condemned religion in general, and Islam in particular, as sheer superstition and an opiate of the people. It may seem less than convincing when they now appear as zealous converts. Political rivals with a cleaner religious slate may well do better if the true faith is what counts.

Second, Islam links its adherents in the universal fellowship (the *ummah*) of all those who follow Islam, the path of submission. Any exploitation of Islam (as of Christianity) for nationalistic purposes will therefore run counter to an important Muslim tradition. Indeed, an Islamic identity will often compete with a national identity based on language, ethnic culture, and territory. Islam links the Tajik, the Turkmen, and the Uzbek together with Muslims both inside and outside the former Soviet Union. Thus, religion acts to weaken the cultural contrasts to neighboring peoples—but these contrasts are precisely what have to be cultivated in order to establish a separate national identity. Leaders in Central Asia nevertheless make active use of Islam, and therein lies the double paradox: nonbeliever heads of state employing a religious and nonnationalistic ideology in their attempts to build a nation.

In Communist times Islamic identity was one of the most important factors that set the people of Central Asia apart from the Russians and the other Europeans in the Soviet state. Leaders in the Kremlin were clearly worried lest religion function as a strategy of mobilization against communism—which was, after all, originally a European ideology and which could easily be seen as alien in Central Asia. It is commonly agreed that a major reason the Soviet state divided the population of Central Asia into five "national" (read: ethnic) categories was to counteract and split the religiocultural homogeneity of the region.

To a great extent this strategy was successful. Many of the ethnic categories allocated to the Central Asians were seen in the 1920s as artificial and random. In order to "tidy up" the ethnic confusion in the region, smaller ethnic groups were simply merged with larger ones. New ethnic boundaries were established, often bisecting traditionally mixed populations, like the Tajik-Uzbek double culture. This culture, often called Sart, predominated in many towns of the area. Although Tajik and Uzbek are mutually incomprehensible languages, related to Persian and to Turkish, respectively, in the oases most people were equally at home in both tongues. Now those who were living in what became the Uzbek Soviet republic were registered as plain Uzbeks. Today, some two or three generations later, these choices have become internalized. Tajik and Uzbek have become separate and in some cases rival identities.[46] The same can be said of the Kazakh and Kyrgyz identities, which represent a historical continuum as well.[47]

The secular ethnic categories have clearly lessened the importance of Islam as an identity marker, without, however, erasing it totally. As long as the context was Central Asia versus Moscow, Islamic identity could be reactivated. Yet this was not necessarily a religious identity in the strict sense; often it had a more general cultural character. The antireligious campaigns of the Communists hit the Muslims as hard as they did the Christians, and not without some success. The people of Central Asia did become more secularized than their neighbors in Iran, Afghanistan, and Pakistan. The five pillars of Islam were not regularly practiced. As to the hajj, restrictions on travel obviously were a major hindrance. But even those religious duties which the individual can perform privately, like the giving of alms or daily prayers, were perhaps honored more in the breach than in the observance. Likewise, even in the towns very few women wore the veil (women in the countryside never did). At least moderate consumption of alcohol was not unusual.

All the same, by far the majority of Central Asians would see themselves as Muslims and would not agree that they had lapsed in their faith. The main events in life—birth, the transition to the adult world, marriage, and death—all were celebrated according to Islamic tradition, often by Communist Party members as well.[48] To the Kremlin, these "remnants of the past" were an irritation, and as late as in 1985–1986 Gorbachev instigated yet another campaign against them. Moscow found it difficult to understand that such rituals were not necessarily connected with "religious conviction" or "personal faith." Indeed, expressions like those, taken from the Christian conceptual universe, have little meaning in Islamic society, where religion, cultural traditions, and social structures are interwoven to form a nearly seamless whole. Furthermore, it could often be difficult to determine just where local tribal traditions ended and Islamic ritual began.

But there were (and still are) some important regional distinctions among former Soviet Muslims as far as religion is concerned. The Kazakhs and Kyrgyz turned to Islam far later than the peoples of the oases to the south. They had remained nomads until well into the twentieth century, and a great many pre-Islamic practices and beliefs became intermingled with "true" Islam in their religious practice. In the late 1700s, Catherine the Great of Russia had concluded that the only way to "civilize" the nomads was to make "proper" Muslims of them. To that end, she sent Tatar Islamic missionaries from Kazan to proselytize among them, but even then the Kazakhs and Kyrgyz continued in their rather lax attitudes to the faith.

Later these two groups were to be exposed to considerable cultural influence from Russia, far more so than the other Islamic peoples of Central Asia. From the end of the nineteenth century and right up until the 1970s, millions of Russians, Ukrainians, and other Europeans moved to the Kazakh steppes and the Kyrgyz mountain valleys. The native populations were by no means assimilated, but they still felt the influence of the culture and lifestyles of their new neighbors. This weakened their already loose ties to Islam.

Among the traditionally settled, nonnomadic people further south, Islam had a much stronger position. Here Islamic influence dates back to the first centuries of the faith. A whole series of Muslim learned and holy men are linked with this area and its many pilgrimage destinations: holy groves and oases, tombs and mosques. Not only official Islam but also the "parallel" or "underground" Islam has deep roots here, especially the various Sufi orders, with their secret or semisecret societies. Sufi mysticism frequently sees a different, more spiritual meaning in the Quran than does official Islam. At times Sufis have been persecuted as heretics. Sufi orders are found throughout the Muslim world; one of the most widespread in Central Asia, Qadiriya, was established in Baghdad in the twelfth century. Another important order, Naqshbandiya, emerged in Central Asia itself in the 1300s.

Although Sufi orders tend to be primarily mystical and inward-looking, in some situations Sufism can find militant expression. Naqshbandiya became important in the northern Caucasus as a driving force in the struggles of the mountain peoples against Russian colonialism in the nineteenth and twentieth centuries. As Sufism is not dependent on a system of clergy, mosques, and other fixed points, it has proven exceedingly difficult for the central authorities to control. Indeed, it has often seemed that the more the Soviet authorities put pressure to bear on official Islam, the more strongly did parallel Islam thrive and blossom.[49]

There have been speculations as to whether parallel Islam might, after the collapse of Soviet power, develop into a militant Islamist movement that would work for a total Islamization of society, as is not unknown from, for instance, the Middle East and Afghanistan. A great many Russian observers as well as some Western experts have been much preoccupied with such a scenario. In particular, it has been maintained that Islam has a considerable potential in the poorest and most overpopulated parts of Central Asia, as in Tajikistan and the Fergana Valley of Uzbekistan and south Kyrgyzstan. Here social need and religious fanaticism could easily become an explosive mixture. In addition to Sufism, this scenario has also been linked to the spread of Wahhabism, a strict reform movement within Sunni Islam that emerged in the 1700s and is now the state religion of Saudi Arabia. In other Muslim countries, however, Wahhabism stands in opposition to the official clergy.

In June 1990 the Islamic Renaissance Party (IRP) was formed as part of the new party flora under perestroika. The IRP had branches in several Soviet republics and was not linked to any particular nationality or nation. It was, however, especially strong in Tajikistan and Uzbekistan, not least in the Fergana Valley. In both these republics, the IRP emerged as a kind of rival to the secular national democratic opposition movements formed during that period, such as Birlik (Unity) and Erk (Strength) in Uzbekistan and Rastokhez (Rebirth) in Tajikistan.

The Communist leadership of Uzbekistan found that it was easier to discredit the IRP than the national democratic opposition and effectively banned it. It seems likely that the party still maintains a secret network, but the harsh regime of president Islam Karimov has managed to keep it under control.

Karimov's colleague in neighboring Tajikistan, Rakhmon Nabiev, was less fortunate. When riots broke out in the capital, Dushanbe, in February 1990, claiming over twenty lives, islamist slogans had been shouted. Thus, when the Tajik branch of IRP was established later in the year it was immediately banned. Then, in October 1991, after the failed August coup attempt in Moscow, the Tajik IRP was briefly legalized.

In April 1992 Nabiev was forced to form a "national government of reconciliation," which meant including eight ministers from the opposition (including the religious opposition). Hard battles continued, however, in the southern provinces and at times in the capital. After an attack on the presidential palace, Nabiev tried to flee but was stopped at the airport and forced to renounce the presidency on 7 September 1992. This unleashed a full civil war that swept the country throughout autumn 1992 and winter 1993. In the end the Communists managed to regain control of the capital and the northern provinces, and the Islamists escaped into the Pamirs or over the border to Afghanistan. From here the opposition struggle was led by, among other figures, the prominent Muslim religious leader Qadi Akbar Turajonzoda. A series of raids were launched into Tajikistan, and the civil war continued, albeit at a lower level of intensity, until the Communist regime and the opposition joined in a treaty of reconciliation in summer 1997.[50] By then the war had claimed at least 50,000 lives.

Tajikistan is often cited as proof that political Islam represents a real threat in the former Soviet Union.[51] Experts on that republic, however, point out that the Tajik civil war has highly complex causes. Clan and regional loyalty have always been strong in Tajikistan. The lines of ideological conflict separating Communists, Islamists, and democrats tend to coincide with lines of traditional regional conflicts. The Communists are especially strong in the northern province of Leninabad (Khojent) and in Kulyab, whereas the Islamists have their strength in the southern and eastern regions. Leninabad is the only part of the country with any degree of industrialization, and its leaders dominated Tajik politics during the Soviet era. Rakhmon Nabiev came from Leninabad and represented this province more than he ever represented Communist ideology as such. Similarly, Islam has tended to provide an ideological canopy for regional and political interests.[52]

Far from promoting nation-building, religion in Tajikistan has been one factor among several that have prevented any consolidation of the Tajik nation. The authoritarian regimes of neighboring countries seem honestly afraid that their own states may be torn asunder by similar conflicts. In March 1993 Uzbekistan took the drastic step of intervening in the Tajik civil war on the side of the Communists, and the Uzbek air force bombed positions held by the Tajik opposition.

At the same time, leaders in both Uzbekistan and Turkmenistan employ the Tajik tragedy actively and cynically in their own nation-building projects. The message is clear: We must use all available means, including the most authoritarian ones, to prevent a breakdown of state power in our midst. All opposition must be suppressed and a strict rein kept on religion. In other words, while the Central Asian leaders erect mosques and open new *medrese*s with the one hand, they use the other hand to throttle all spontaneous religious activity.

In Kazakhstan and Kyrgyzstan, the political leaders are perhaps more fortunate than are their colleagues elsewhere in Central Asia. In these two countries, Islam does not represent any political power, whether real or potential. Even among those who would term themselves believing Muslims, religion is rarely more than a Friday affair. Thus, President Akayev in Kyrgyzstan and President Nursultan Nazarbayev in Kazakhstan are free to administer Islam in doses as large as they see fit in their respective nation-building projects, without having to fear an uncontrolled Islamization of society. Theirs is not the predicament of the sorcerer's apprentice of fable—he who managed to get the cauldron to boil but not to stop again: In the Kazakh and Kyrgyz cauldron, the religious brew seems likely to remain well below the boiling point. As of 1996 the number of Muslim congregations in Kazakhstan was under the 600 mark. This, it is true, is a sharp increase from the forty-four that existed in 1989, but it is still very low compared with the situation in, for instance, Uzbekistan, where there were already 5,000 actively functioning mosques in 1993.[53]

A survey taken in Kazakhstan in 1996 showed that approximately 40 percent of the population considered themselves to be "believers," 4.4 percent were atheists, and almost 60 percent said that they were agnostics.[54]

These are the figures for all religious and ethnic groupings. Among the titular population, the ethnic Kazakhs, the share of believers was 47 percent, with 30.8 percent considering themselves agnostics. It was only among the Uzbek minority in the country—most of whom live in the southern areas near the Uzbek border—that religious involvement was markedly above average: As many as 75.8 percent replied that they counted themselves as "believers."

The pollsters who conducted this survey had believed that there might be a certain danger of Islamic fundamentalism in the southernmost parts of the country, where a few nonregistered, illegal Islamic schools had begun to sprout up. "Still, in our opinion," they wrote, "there is no broad basis for such ideas in Kazakhstan. . . . The official Muslim clergy is loyal to the state and does not transgress the boundaries of acceptable religious activity."[55]

During the Soviet era, all of Central Asia lay under the Spiritual Directorate of the Muslims of Central Asia and Kazakhstan, led by a mufti based in the Uzbek capital of Tashkent. Non-Uzbek Muslims today complain that ethnic Uzbeks had too much influence; for instance, not a single Kazakh was ever appointed mufti. In January 1990 the Kazakhs therefore established their own spiritual directorate for Kazakhstan, with headquarters in Almaty. With this decision the Kazakh state leadership killed two birds with one stone: They gained better control over the development of Islam in the country and, by having a separate Kazakh mufti, signaled the sovereignty of the republic.[56]

Although Nazarbayev may not be threatened by any Islamic opposition, he does face another problem that the other Central Asian leaders do not have: Many among the population of Kazakhstan are not Muslim but Christian; even if they do not practice their faith, they are Christian in their cultural identification. Russians, Ukrainians, and Belarusians are Orthodox, whereas most of the Germans are Protestant. In the other Central Asian states as well, most Europeans are Christians or former Christians, but there they tend to be such tiny minorities that their religion does not play any role in terms of nation-building. By contrast, in Kazakhstan the central authorities must take into consideration the sensibilities of Muslims and Christians alike. No Islamic holy days have been declared national holidays, and when the mufti graces state occasions with his presence, the Russian Orthodox archbishop of Almaty is almost always in attendance as well.[57]

As we have seen, since 1989 the Moscow patriarchate has granted autonomous status to the churches in a whole series of Soviet successor states. One might perhaps expect a similar solution to have been chosen for the Orthodox Church in Kazakhstan, which has, after all, more adherents than either the Estonian or the Moldovan Orthodox Churches.

But this has not been the case. One reason would seem to be that in Kazakhstan the Orthodox Church is not seen as a national entity, since of the titular nation—the Kazakhs—only a minuscule number are Orthodox believers. Yet the Orthodox diocese in Almaty was split in 1991, so that there now exist three separate Orthodox dioceses in Kazakhstan: one in Almaty, one in Shymkent to the south, and one in Uralsk in the northwest.[58]

There were undoubtedly sound practical reasons for this tripartite division: Kazakhstan is spread over a vast territory five times the size of France, and it is very difficult to maintain contact between north and south. The political leadership in Kazakhstan is, however, worried lest a separate Russian Orthodox diocese in the north become the pawn of forces within the Russian population who want total secession from Kazakhstan and incorporation into Russia.[59]

There can be no doubt that there do exist such nationalist forces among the Russian-speaking inhabitants of Kazakhstan, although it is less certain how much grassroots backing they actually have. But it does seem clear that they enjoy support from some of the Russian clergy in the country.

Orthodoxy Versus Islam

As in Georgia, there are two dominant religions in Kazakhstan: Islam and Orthodoxy. When we consider the situation in terms of the relationship between nation and religion, we can note a highly important difference between the two countries: In Georgia religious boundaries and national boundaries cross and intersect each other at various points. This serves to weaken the cultural split between the titular nation on the one hand and the various national minorities on the other. In Kazakhstan, however, religious boundaries basically follow ethnic divisions, thereby strengthening the bipolarization of society.

Other factors make Kazakhstan a strongly bicultural society. The Kazakh people have Asiatic facial features, whereas the Russians are "European" in appearance. It is usually a simple matter to identify at a glance who belongs to which ethnic group. Moreover, Kazakhs and Russians have traditionally had different lifestyles; whereas the Kazakhs have been nomadic herdspeople, the Russians have been either agriculturists, industrial workers, or members of the technical intelligentsia. The two groups also live in different geographical areas: Russians predominate in the northern provinces, whereas Kazakhs are in the majority in the south. Taken together, this means that the borderline between the Slavo-Orthodox north and the Muslim-Asiatic south becomes what Samuel Huntington has seen as a major fault line of civilizations.

And yet Kazakhstan has not experienced anything like the conditions of civil war that ravaged Georgia and Moldova. Some violent incidents have occurred, but on a far different scale. This is in fact rather remarkable when we recall that the religiocultural threshold between the ethnic groups is much higher in Kazakhstan than in Moldova or Georgia. Thus, in my opinion, Huntington is mistaken when he maintains that the dominant conflict lines in the modern world will follow religious fault lines. We will have to search for other explanatory models if we are to understand the social and political unrest in the former Soviet Union.

5

INTEGRATION OR ALIENATION? RUSSIANS IN THE FORMER SOVIET REPUBLICS

In the outskirts of the core area of Russian settlements, Russians have been living intermingled with other ethnic groups for centuries. But it was only toward the second half of the nineteenth century that large-scale migration of Russians to the peripheries of the czarist empire commenced. To a large extent, this migration was triggered by the societal changes usually referred to as "modernization." Together with the Jews, the Russians were the first ethnic group in the empire to be affected by these changes. More and more Russians received education, moved to the cities, and acquired a modern lifestyle. Infant mortality was significantly reduced, leading to high population growth. This demographic pressure was alleviated to a degree by migration to the outlying non-Russian regions of the empire.[1]

This Russian migration consisted partly of peasants in search of new land to till, but increasingly the Russian migrants moved to the new industrial towns and cities that were growing rapidly at the time—Riga, Baku, Yuzovka (Donetsk), and others. The local populations in these areas—Latvians, Ukrainians, Azeris, and so on—were generally less motivated and less qualified for work in the new factories. As millions of new Russians joined the first waves of migrants after the Russian Revolution, they also settled overwhelmingly in urban areas. All over the Soviet Union, towns and cities acquired an unmistakably Russian look, whereas the surrounding countryside kept its traditional lifestyle.

In the Soviet era, ever more new ethnic groups in the USSR were drawn into the modernization process. Even so, a kind of ethnic division of labor continued to function in many places. During the first two five-year plans in the 1930s in particular, when the country underwent head-long industrialization, veritable torrents of Russian migrants flooded the non-Russian republics. Between 1926 and 1939, the number of Russians living outside of the Russian Soviet Federated Socialist Republic (RSFSR) rose from 5.1 million to 9.3 million, almost a doubling in thirteen years.[2]

Some of these Russian migrants no doubt returned to the Russian core area after a while, but many of them remained in their new homes, got married, raised children who felt at home there, and generally settled down. By the time of the last Soviet census in 1989, the size of this Russian "diaspora" had reached 25 million, or approximately 17 percent of all Russians in the Soviet Union. And then, when the Soviet unitary state collapsed, these people were no longer an internal but an external diaspora.[3]

On numerous occasions Russian politicians have pointed to the existence of these 25 million Russians as a source of great concern. Indeed, taken together they represent by far the largest minority created by the breakup of the Soviet Union. Given that they enjoy the express backing of the most powerful post-Soviet state, Russia, they are also politically the most important group. It is not, however, a foregone conclusion that the Russian diaspora issue will lead to political pandemonium. Whether or not this will happen depends primarily on three factors: the attitudes and actions of the state authorities and titular nations in the new states, the political course taken by the Russian Federation, and finally, the behavior of the Russian minorities themselves. As these three variables interact, they may lead to either the integration or alienation of the Russians in their new homelands.[4]

Political leaders in Russia are often accused of exploiting the Russian diaspora issue for ulterior purposes.[5] But in Moscow assertions are heard that state leaders in the "near abroad" frequently flash the diaspora card in order to extort economic concessions from Russia. Whenever Russia demands that these states pay their substantial arrears for Russian oil and gas deliveries, their leaders complain that such demands will lead to economic hardships that, they claim, will hit the Russian minority particularly hard.[6]

Caught in the middle of these exchanges of mutual recriminations are the people of the Russian diaspora, who have unwittingly become pawns in a political chess game of influence and power in the former Soviet Union. But the Russian minority communities are not necessarily mute and easy to manipulate. Many of them are well-educated people quite capable of articulating their own desiderata and fighting for their realization.

How, then, are the Russian minorities being treated in the non-Russian Soviet successor states? Are they being defined as a part of the new nations, or are they seen as alien elements? Have the state authorities in the new non-Russian nation-states been willing to make any adjustments or concessions in their policy toward the Russian diaspora? What are Russia's interests and priorities on the diaspora issue? May the notion that these people constitute a kind of Russian diaspora in itself complicate the national consolidation of the neighboring countries? And finally, to what extent are the local Russians themselves satisfied or dissatisfied with their new status as national minorities in their respective countries of residence? Do they want to be included in the ongoing nation-building projects, or would they prefer to stay on the sidelines?

Not One Diaspora, but Fourteen

The new Russian diaspora communities are far from homogeneous. Any talk of "a" or "the" new Russian diaspora in the singular is highly misleading. It would probably be more fruitful to see them as fourteen different diasporas, each with its own peculiar characteristics. The qualities of each community are influenced by many different factors, such as their size (absolute and relative to the total population in the state), ethnic cohesion, social composition, cultural distinctiveness (the cultural contrast to the dominant ethnic environment), compactness of their settlements, and rootedness in the area.[7]

For the sake of convenience, the homelands of the Russian diaspora communities may be divided into five categories: the Slavic states, the Baltics, Moldova, Transcaucasia, southwestern Central Asia, and northeastern Central Asia (Kazakhstan-Kyrgyzstan). Some 12.5 million diaspora Russians, or roughly half of the total, are living in the Slavic states of Ukraine and Belarus (see Table 5.1). In this region the cultural distance between the Russians and the titular nations is very short. With the partial exception of western Ukraine, hardly any Russians here have a feeling of living in an alien cultural milieu at all.[8] In such a situation, serious ethnic conflicts are not likely to arise.

In the Baltic states, important parts of the indigenous population claim that a yawning chasm separates their own culture from Russian culture, though the Russians themselves more often underline the common elements of Europeanness, Christian faith, and so on that unite them.[9] Since the incorporation of the Baltic states into the USSR during World War II, the influx of Russians and other Russophones to the area has been dramatically steep. In the course of four decades, the share of the titular nation in the total population dropped from 90 percent to 60 percent in Estonia and from 75 percent to 52 percent in Latvia. Many Balts feel that this demographic development is undermining the very basis of their separate cultures, and they are determined to roll back Russian influence. The Russians, however, are already so numerous and so entrenched in

TABLE 5.1   Russians in the Soviet Successor States, 1989

Republic	In Thousands	In Percentage of Total Pop. in Republic	In Percentage of Nontitular Pop. in Republic	Percentage of Russians Living in Urban Settlements
Russia	119,866	81.5	–	77
Estonia	475	30.3	78.8	92
Latvia	906	34.0	70.7	85
Lithuania	344	9.4	45.8	90
Belarus	1,342	13.2	59.5	87
Moldova	562	13.0	36.4	86
Ukraine	11,356	22.1	80.8	88
Georgia	341	6.3	21.1	86
Armenia	52	1.6	23.0	85
Azerbaijan	392	5.6	32.2	95
Turkmenistan	334	9.5	33.7	97
Tajikistan	388	7.6	20.2	94
Uzbekistan	1,653	8.3	29.1	95
Kyrgyzstan	917	21.5	45.1	70
Kazakhstan	6,228	37.8	62.6	77

SOURCES: *Natsional'nyy sostav naseleniya SSSR* (The national composition of the population of the USSR) (Moscow: Finansy i Statistika, 1991); Y. V. Arutyunyan, ed., *Russkie. Etnosotsiologicheskie ocherki* (The Russians: Ethnosociological sketches) (Moscow: Nauka, 1992), 25.

society that this would be a formidable task that could be accomplished only by exceptional measures, if at all. Only in Lithuania is the share of the Russians so low (around 9 percent) that they are not perceived as a serious challenge by the titular nation.

Moldova is one of very few former Soviet republics where Russians do not constitute the largest ethnic minority. At approximately 13 percent of the population, they were slightly outnumbered by Ukrainians (at 14 percent) in the last Soviet census, in 1989. In many parts of the former Soviet Union, the majority of the Ukrainians are so linguistically and culturally Russified that it would make little sense to treat them as a separate category. Although this may be true to some extent in Moldova as well, relatively many Ukrainians in this country have nevertheless retained an identity of their own, by dint of their high numbers and the proximity to the Ukrainian state.

In the secessionist Dniester republic in the eastern part of Moldova, the share of ethnic Russians is larger than in the country as a whole, 24 percent. But even here, in 1989 they constituted only the third largest ethnic group, after the Moldovans (40 percent) and Ukrainians (26 percent). It is therefore highly misleading to speak about the Dniester population as "the Russians." And as a matter of fact, far more Russians in Moldova live to the west of the Dniester than to the east—400,000 as against 160,000.

In Transcaucasia and the southern tier of Central Asia, Russian demographic penetration has historically been weak. In the 1989 census, the Russian share of the total population in all of these republics was below 10 percent (in Armenia as low as 1.6 percent); since that time, Russian communities in much of the region have been further depleted by out-migration. The Russian populace has been almost exclusively clustered in the larger towns and cities, particularly in the capitals, whereas the countryside has been dominated by the locals. The cultural contrast between the Russians and the indigenous population is significant.

In Kazakhstan and to some degree also in Kyrgyzstan, the ethnodemographic situation is rather different from other parts of Central Asia. On the Kazakh steppe and in the Kyrgyz valleys, Russian peasants have been tilling the soil for generations. These are the only republics where rural dwellers made up substantial parts of the local Russian groups (23 percent and 30 percent, respectively). At the same time, the Russian presence in urban areas is also very large. The 1 million Russophones in Kyrgyzstan made up 23 percent of the total population, and the 7.8 million Russophones in Kazakhstan constituted 47 percent in 1989. The vast majority of Kazakhstani Russians live in the northernmost parts of the country.

Although there are large varieties *among* the various Russian diaspora communities, there are also of course significant differences *within* each group. As pointed out above, some members of these communities have been living outside the ethnic Russian core area for generations, whereas others are recent immigrants. These newcomers are typically less able or willing to adapt to the alien ethnic environment. Their command of the titular language is usually poorer. The language proficiency among the Russian diaspora is influenced as well by such factors as the complexity of the various languages and the number of native speakers they meet in daily life but even more, it seems, by such intangibles as the prestige the various languages carry.[10] In the Soviet Union, European languages with long literary traditions obviously had higher status than Asian languages with recently established literary standards. Thus, for example, in the 1989 census 37 percent of Russians in Lithuania said that they were fluent in Lithuanian, whereas only 2.3 percent of Russians in Turkmenistan claimed fluency in Turkmen, even though the Russian share of the total population in the two republics was the same (9.5 percent).

Language, Culture, and Education

All over the former Soviet Union, language disputes have been in the forefront of the ethnic controversies. Between 1988–1991 practically all non-Russian Soviet successor states proclaimed the language of the titular nationality as the official state language. Most of them also passed timetables for the gradual expansion of the use of this language in official administration and education at the expense of Russian. There are, however, enormous differences in the vigor with which these language policies are being pursued and also as regards the consequences that implementation will have for the Russian populace. In countries where the Russians constitute small minorities, such as in Lithuania and Transcaucasia, the Russian language will most likely not be able to hold its position under any circumstances. In these regions the Russians will inevitably have to learn the new state language to avoid being confined to a cultural ghetto. In Central Asia the situation is somewhat different. Since the indigenous languages lack terminology for many modern items and concepts, the indigenous populations in many capacities use Russian. It has therefore been speculated that Russian will be retained as a lingua franca, as has the erstwhile colonial language in many former English and French colonies.[11]

In countries where the Russians compose very large minorities, the Russian language may be able to hold its ground even if it is denied any official status. It is being supported by Russian cultural facilities such as television, radio, newspapers, and so on that are fully able to compete with the corresponding media of the local cultures. In Moldova, Belarus, Ukraine, and Kazakhstan, not only Russians but also many members of the titular population often turn to Russian-language media for information. (Almost the entire educated public in the former Soviet Union is well versed in Russian.) The largest television channel by far in the former Soviet Union is ORT (formerly Ostankino) in Moscow, which continues to function as a Russian-language network throughout the Commonwealth of Independent States (CIS), just as it did in Soviet times.

In Latvia and Estonia, the Russophones are numerous enough to be able to form self-contained Russian-language communities. In order to prevent this from happening, the authorities in both countries have passed exacting language laws.[12] Nonspeakers of the state language who fail to pass specified language tests risk being fired from or not being hired to jobs for which they are otherwise qualified.

In the constitutions and language laws of a few countries—Kazakhstan, Moldova, and Ukraine—Russian has been granted official status as the language of interethnic communication. It is far from clear, however, what this implies in practical terms. Certainly, whenever two persons of different nationalities meet on the street, they will converse in the language that is most convenient to them, without regard for legal regulations.

In most new states, the number of Russian-medium schools is steadily decreasing. To some extent this is a natural process, reflecting the priorities of the parents. In Soviet times many non-Russians sent their children to Russian schools since fluency in that language opened the gates to a career in society. In most of the new states, this has changed, and today social advancement is often linked to proficiency in the new state language. But Russians frequently complain that Russian-language schools now have to run day and night shifts with overfilled classes. To the degree that this is really the case, such schools are clearly being closed down faster than their pupils are abandoning them.

Citizenship and Political Representation

In the new states in Eurasia, with two exceptions, the Russians and all other ethnic minorities have been granted automatic citizenship rights. The exceptions are Estonia and Latvia, which regard only citizens of interwar Estonia and Latvia and their descendants as the original body politic. All other permanent citizens must apply for citizenship on a par with recent immigrants and must fulfill relatively stringent criteria regarding residence, proficiency in the state language, and so on. The official reason for these decisions is legal and constitutional: The Baltic states were occupied by the Soviet Union in 1940; all those who have settled in the country since that time are in principle illegal immigrants.

The legal aspects of these conflicts are highly complex. Many Western experts and international lawyers point out that the Russians moved to the Baltic states in good faith, not crossing any international borders, in search of a livelihood.[13] Nevertheless, the principles upon which the Latvian and Estonian citizenship policy is based have largely been recognized by the international community, although some international organizations and nongovernmental organizations (NGOs) for human rights have been strongly critical of particular aspects.[14] In any case there can be no doubt that the underlying motivation behind the inflexible Latvian and Estonian position on the citizenship issue is a deeply felt concern about the countries' ethnodemographic makeup: The citizenship laws are intended to safeguard the indigenous culture by marginalizing the Russophones politically. And it seems to be working. In the Estonian parliament elected in September 1992, 100 percent of the members were ethnic Estonians.

If noncitizens in Estonia and Latvia are being denied basic political rights, it is often pointed out that these countries adhere more closely to international standards of human rights than do the authorities in most other Soviet successor states. It is, however, very difficult to draw a definite dividing line between political and human rights. In both Estonia and Latvia, Russian noncitizens are certainly deprived of more than just the right to vote or stand for election in national elections. They are, for instance, denied the right to hold certain positions and conduct certain kinds of business.[15]

It is important to note that in some states where the Russians do enjoy full voting rights they are not automatically guaranteed political representation in proportion to their share of the total population. In many new states, the titular nationality is to an increasing degree monopolizing political positions and top administrative jobs. This tendency is most pronounced in Central Asia and reflects the traditional clan structure of these societies.[16] Access to power is gained through tightly knit kinship networks from which Europeans are excluded. These traditional networks were not disrupted under the Soviet system; on the contrary, in many places they thrived and blossomed. The Brezhnev regime largely accepted that political power in the Asian republics remained concentrated in the hands of the titular nationality, as long as the local leadership did not challenge the power structures in Moscow.[17]

Obviously, if both cultural groups in a bicultural society vote more or less en bloc for their own candidates, this voting pattern will secure a solid overrepresentation of the largest group in all elected organs.[18] Any such tendencies will be further reinforced by the introduction of a majoritarian rather than a proportional system, as is the case in most former Soviet republics. In addition, there are strong indications that correct election procedures are frequently violated. The Kazakhstani electoral commissions tend to strike from the local ballots any potential candidates who represent the interests of the Slavic community, particularly if they lean toward Russian nationalist positions.[19] Elsewhere in Central Asia, as in Tajikistan, Uzbekistan, and Turkmenistan, political elections today are just as pro forma as they were in Soviet times.

On the basis of the citizenship laws alone, it might seem that the preconditions for political participation of the minorities should be better in Central Asia than in the Baltics, but things may develop differently. Political democracy in Estonia and Latvia is indeed limited to one part of the population only—the citizens—but within these narrow confines it functions more or less in accordance with generally accepted norms. Requirements for naturalization are stringent, but they nevertheless allow for the gradual inclusion of noncitizens into the body politic over the next decades. Since the official rules are being followed, the minorities have an incentive to make use of the possibilities for political participation that are opened up to them. The Estonian national elections in 1995 saw the number of Russophone members of parliament (MPs) increase from zero to seven. As new generations of noncitizens become naturalized, this figure may continue to rise. In local elections in Estonia (but not in Latvia), permanent residents without citizenship are allowed to vote. In the 1993 local Estonian elections, minorities turned up at the polls in greater numbers than did the Estonians. In the 1998 Saeima (the new national assembly in Latvia), the nontitulars for the first time achieved a representation more or less in accordance with the shares of the total population: ten Russians, four Poles, two Jews, one Lithuanian, one Livian, and one Roma (Gypsy).

Employment, Promotion, and Economy

In most non-Russian Soviet successor states, Russians are overrepresented in the intelligentsia, particularly in the technical intelligentsia.[20] They often occupy leading positions in the economy—not necessarily due to any ethnically motivated recruitment policy in Soviet times but by dint of their high qualifications. In the cultural and political fields, however, Russians were clearly underrepresented already in the Brezhnev era, and this tendency has been further strengthened in recent years. In many new states, particularly in Transcaucasia and Central Asia, Russians are gradually being squeezed out of technical professions as well. The Russians seem to resent this kind of discrimination more than political marginalization, as it hits them where it hurts most—in professional opportunities, income levels, and standards of living.

In the Baltics the "locals" are gradually monopolizing entire sectors of the labor market, particularly jobs in the state bureaucracy. In these countries, however, the effects of this tendency as concerns the employment of Russians are to some extent being offset by the new opportunities opening up in the private business sector. Indeed, the Russians are believed to be in the forefront among the new entrepreneurs in the budding market economy, partly, perhaps, as a result of their marginalization in other fields.[21]

Yet Russians have also been greatly overrepresented in heavy industry formerly controlled by the Soviet ministries. This industry suffered a severe crunch when the economic ties among the Soviet republics were broken. Typical recession areas are the heavily Russian-populated eastern part of Estonia and the Russophone Donbass area in Ukraine. In these regions ethnic controversies have been strongly intertwined with the economic issue. The economic misery of the local Russians, however, should not necessarily be seen as a result of any deliberate anti-Russian policy on the part of the state but more often as an unfortunate side effect of its economic policy.

Street-Level Discrimination

In many of the new states, serious ethnic pogroms were reported in the late 1980s and early 1990s. With one or two exceptions, however, the ethnic frenzy was directed not against the Russians but against smaller underdog groups without deep historical roots in the area—Armenians, Meskhetian Turks, and so on.[22] In Tajikistan and Azerbaijan, full-scale ethnic warfare also broke out within and among indigenous ethnic groups. Although the Russians were not directly involved in this violence, their houses and property—as well as their faith in the future— were often destroyed by it. As a result, all over the Asian parts of the former Soviet Union the Russian communities have been drastically reduced through massive out-migration.[23]

Even when no blood is shed, many Russians fear the local mobs. It is difficult to assess the validity and gravity of the reported cases of anti-Russian popular harassment, but ethnic tension has clearly been on the rise in many places. In Kyrgyzstan the situation has been aggravated by the decision to abolish the Soviet *propiska* system, which under communism made it very difficult to change one's place of residence without official permission. As a result of the new freedom, thousands of jobless Kyrgyz youths have been descending on the capital, blaming the Russians when, as often happens, they fail to find employment there.

Russia's Policy on the Diaspora Issue

The 1992 Russian citizenship law gives all former Soviet citizens the right to take up Russian citizenship even while they continue to live in one of the other successor states.[24] This right was originally set to expire on 1 February 1995, but it has since been extended several times. As of spring 1997, approximately 4 percent of all diaspora Russians—1 million—had procured Russian passports.[25] Latvia and (especially) Estonia have disproportionately many citizens of Russia in their population—hardly surprising, as it is so difficult for postwar immigrants to these countries to acquire Estonian or Latvian citizenship. If the alternative is statelessness, many local Russophones prefer Russian citizenship. As of March 1997, no less than 120,000 Russians in Estonia—out of a total of half a million— had taken up Russian citizenship.[26] These people are entitled to vote in Russian elections, and many who have done so (not that many do) have preferred antiliberal parties. In 1993 a majority of them supported Vladimir Zhirinovskiy; the Russian Communist Party was the preferred party of Russian citizens in Estonia and Latvia in the Russian parliamentary election in December 1995.

By dint of their choice of citizenship, these Russians are defined out of the Estonian (or Latvian) nation-building project and are instead included in the Russian one. Many Baltic politicians have indicated that this is the best possible solution to a difficult problem: As these Russians hold such extremist political views, it would have been impossible to integrate them into the Estonian or Latvian nation in any case. It may be argued, however, that the causation here actually runs in the opposite direction: In many cases the Russians in Estonia and Latvia may instead have been pushed into the embrace of Russian imperialists and nationalists by the exclusivist tendency in Estonian and Latvian nation-building. A Danish political scientist, Mette Skak, believes that the Estonian and Latvian authorities, with their restrictive citizenship policies, have been "shooting themselves in the foot."[27]

The Russian constitution proclaims that Russian citizens abroad are to enjoy the protection and patronage of the Russian state.[28] In reality, in its policy toward the new Russian diaspora the Russian authorities make few distinctions between those Russians abroad who hold Russian passports and those who do not. They believe that they have a responsibility to offer protection to everyone who in some sense or another feels attached to Russia through cultural identification, birth, or ethnicity. It has been extremely difficult, however, for these authorities to find unambiguous and clear criteria by which to delimit the diaspora population. This is reflected in a vacillating terminology. Russian state authorities try as much as possible to avoid the expression *Russian (russkaya) diaspora*. This term might easily be regarded as an expression of Russian ethnocentric nationalism and as discrimination against members of other ethnic groups in the former Soviet Union whose "historical homelands" today are a part of the Russian Federation, such as, for instance, Tatars and Bashkirs.

At times Yeltsin and his staff have ended up with a hybrid expression: *etnicheskie rossiyane*, which literally means "ethnic citizens of Russia." This term includes both an ethnic and a territorial aspect. The most common word, however, is *sootechestvenniki*, "compatriots." A law on "the state policy of the Russian Federation with regard to *sootechestvenniki* living abroad" includes in its definition of *sootechestvenniki* "all citizens of the USSR who live in states that at one time were part of the USSR, whether or not they have citizenship in this state or are stateless persons."[29] The law further includes all descendants of these former Soviet citizens, with the exception of those who belong to the titular nation in the state they are living. This is a broad definition indeed, and it is based on the idea that Russia is the continuator state of the USSR (see Chapter 10).

Policy toward these *sootechestvenniki* soon after 1991 became an important topic in Russian politics.[30] Politicians on the extreme right and extreme left issued thinly veiled threats to state leaders in the other Soviet successor states who dared to discriminate against the Russian part of their populations. The right to decide what amounted to discrimination they reserved for themselves. A special organization, the Congress of Russian Communities (CRC, or KRO in Russian), was established in

Moscow in spring 1993 as a diaspora pressure group; it soon adopted a maximalist line.[31]

In the first few years after the dissolution of the Soviet Union, the Russian Foreign Ministry was primarily interested in integrating Russia into international and Western organizational structures. Relations with the other former Soviet republics were relegated to the back burner. To the extent that Russian authorities tried to influence the minority policy of the neighboring countries, they preferred to do so through the mediation of international organizations such as the UN, the Organization for Security and Cooperation in Europe (OSCE), or the Council of Baltic Sea States.

Even so, already in 1990–1991 the Yeltsin administration had taken several important steps to ensure that the rights of the Russians in the former Soviet republics would not be trampled upon should the unitary Soviet state disintegrate. In January 1991, while Soviet tanks were wreaking havoc in Vilnius and Riga, President Yeltsin hastily convened a meeting with the presidents of Latvia and Estonia in Tallinn and signed bilateral agreements with these two countries. This act demonstrated active and vital Russian support to the Baltic independence struggle at a critical moment. These agreements stipulated among other things that the Baltic Russians should be allowed to choose freely of which state they wanted to be citizens. Subsequent Estonian and Latvian citizenship legislation has ignored if not the letter then certainly the spirit of these agreements, even though they were immediately ratified by the Estonian and Latvian parliaments.[32] The Russian Supreme Soviet ratified the Estonian-Russian agreement in 1992 but never the Latvian-Russian agreement, which thus did not acquire legal force.

Estonian and Latvian citizenship legislation was one important factor that contributed to a hardening of the official Russian attitude on the diaspora issue. Another was the Moldovan civil war in summer 1992 (see Chapter 7). By autumn 1992 Russia was increasingly seeking to influence internal political developments in the so-called near abroad through bilateral pressure.

Some elements of the hard-line rhetoric of Russian nationalists on the issue were now adopted by more moderate politicians. A much-publicized memorandum authored by the deputy director of the Institute of Europe in the Russian Academy of Sciences in 1992 suggested that Russia ought to make full use of the circumstance that millions of Russians live on the territory of the neighboring state in order to promote Russia's interests vis-à-vis these states.[33] Several centrally placed politicians in the executive branch, among them presidential adviser Sergey Stankevich and Vice President Aleksandr Rutskoy, were regarded as "statists." Stankevich openly accused the Foreign Ministry of passivity and compliance on the diaspora issue.[34]

Foreign Minister Andrey Kozyrev was pressured to adopt an increas- ingly menacing rhetoric. In a well-known statement in April 1995, he did not exclude the possibility of using military force to protect Russians in the near abroad, a comment received with consternation in the neighbor- ing countries.[35] When Yevgeniy Primakov replaced Kozyrev as foreign minister in December 1995, this new assertive policy line was basically retained. But the bellicosity of Russian policy toward the former Soviet republics on issues related to the diaspora has usually been restricted to the verbal level. Russia has no doubt had the necessary means to exert much harsher pressure on its neighbors than it has in fact done. Several scholars regard moderation as a key characteristic of Russian diaspora politics.[36]

Russian military units have indeed been actively involved in several conflicts in the post-Soviet Eurasian space. Often this has been seen as ev- idence of the destabilizing potential of the Russian diaspora issue in Rus- sian politics.[37] Most of these interventions, however, have taken place in areas where relatively few Russians are living, such as Abkhazia and Tajikistan, and interests other than diaspora protection, primarily related to economy and state security, seem to have been at stake for Russia.[38]

An important document, "The Main Directions of the State Policy of the Russian Federation Toward Compatriots Living Abroad," was adopted by the Russian government in August 1994.[39] A top priority of the Russian government, according to this document, is to prevent a mass influx of compatriots from the near abroad to Russia, since it is believed this would have a disruptive effect on the Russian economy, as well as being difficult for the migrants themselves. In order to achieve this goal, Russia will do its utmost to promote the voluntary integration of these compatriots into the political, social, and economic life of the newly inde- pendent states. Russians ought to adapt to the local culture while retain- ing their specific cultural identity, the Russian government stated. Al- though this program would seem to be compatible with the minority policy pursued by most Soviet successor states, the Russian authorities apparently have doubts about the willingness of the other states to work together toward this aim. The iron fist in the velvet glove is revealed in the following sentence: "Questions of financial, economic, social, and military-political cooperation between Russia and the individual states will be linked to the concrete policy they pursue regarding the rights and interests of Russians [*rossiyane*] living on their territory." But the docu- ment goes on to assert that harsh measures against delinquent states "will be executed only after a serious situational analysis, taking into consider- ation the interests of the people they are intended to defend."

There is indeed broad consensus among Russian politicians across ide- ological dividing lines that Russia has a moral obligation and a political right to protect the rights of all ethnic Russians and other Russophones in the near abroad. There is also a strong general feeling that these rights are frequently violated. Disagreements among various Russian politicians primarily concern the means that could and should be employed to uphold Russophones' rights. Whereas liberals advocate diplomatic pressure and multilateral initiatives coordinated through international organizations, hard-liners prefer direct unilateral actions such as economic sanctions and military coercion.

There is, then, a certain tension between means and aims in Russian diaspora policy. The explicit readiness of the Russian state to stand as defender of the Russophone minorities in the neighboring states may well complicate the desired integration of these minorities into their new homelands. To the degree that Russia is becoming involved in the domestic affairs of the former Soviet republics, this involvement may—almost irrespective of motives and causes—induce local Russians to direct their loyalty and identity not toward their country of residence but toward Russia.

Reactions and Demands of the Russian Minorities

To the Russians in the former Soviet republics, the breakup of the unitary Soviet state entailed severe mental adjustments.[40] From being members of a majority culture in a superpower, they were practically overnight turned into national minorities in small nationalizing states. Those who have reacted to their ordeal and discomfort by migrating to Russia leave the arena of diaspora politics—and also the purview of this book. I instead focus on those who remain.

Far from all who stayed behind have been actively fighting for their group interests as Russians. Only a fraction have joined the various Russian cultural centers, societies, organizations, and political parties that have sprung up after the fall of the Soviet Union.[41] In part this may be seen as a legacy of the Soviet era. Under communism the Russians relied on the state structures to facilitate their social and cultural needs, and most people took them for granted. To be sure, the services offered by these structures were often very rudimentary, but independent social initiatives from below were ruled out under any circumstances. This situation certainly affected the attitudes of all ethnic groups in the Soviet Union, not only the Russians; even so, it is striking to what degree Armenian, German, Ukrainian, and other cultural centers got established long before the Russians began to organize. It seems clear that groups accustomed to a minority status have found it easier to adjust to the new political realities than the formerly dominant nation.

Many Russians evidently also fear that political mobilization under Russian banners may be counterproductive and trigger a backlash of aggressive nationalism among the locals. This sentiment is particularly strong in countries where the state authorities are seen as less nationalistic than the indigenous political opposition. In almost all states in Central Asia and Transcaucasia, a majority among the Russians regard the present regimes as a bulwark against Islamism and nationalism and seem to have no intention of doing anything that could rock the boats of the often very authoritarian indigenous leaders.

Furthermore, the politically and socially active parts of the Russian diaspora communities do not express identical demands. Rival organizations have emerged that are bitterly divided on basic issues. The major fault lines here follow the same cleavages as Russian politics in Russia, with Russian "democrats" pitted against Russian red-browns. The antiliberals in the new states often insist on forming "pure" Russian organizations, excluding other Russophone groups (such as, for instance, the Jews), whereas democrats are more in favor of broad alliances, including even members of the titular nationality who want to fight for human rights issues. Personal animosities among local Russian leaders can also lead to organizational fragmentation.

Restitution and Secession

The red-brown solution to the Russian diaspora problem is usually a very simple one: Life was much better in Soviet times, so the unitary state should be restored. That is why Russian antidemocrats, in Russia and in the other new states, often show scant enthusiasm for small incremental steps toward the improvement of their lot. They reason, logically enough, that if only the USSR could be reestablished, there would no longer be any Russian diaspora problem.[42]

As an alternative to, or a first step toward, wholesale restitution of the USSR, the transfer of compact Russian territories to the Russian Federation is sometimes suggested. Such demands have been set forth by certain (often very small) groups in eastern Estonia, eastern Ukraine, northern Kazakhstan, eastern Moldova, and Crimea. Separatism, it should be noted, is not the exclusive slogan of reactionaries. In the Crimea the campaign for territorial transfer has been supported by groups that would loathe being lumped together with Communists or red-brown nationalists.

It goes without saying that restitution and separatism are anathema to the state authorities in all of the new states. Attempts to press for such demands are fraught with the threat of bloodshed and war and could easily lead to the same spiral of violence as has harried former Yugoslavia. Many if not most of the other demands set forth by Russian activists in the Soviet successor states, in contrast, may find their solution within the framework of the new state system. Roughly speaking, these demands may be divided into three categories: favoritism, nonfavoritism, and bipolarism. Although these demands often contradict each other, they do not necessarily amount to inner inconsistencies in the political programs of the Russian diaspora communities, since they usually are set forth by different groups in different situations.

Favoritism

Some of the demands of the Russian diaspora involve various special rights in society. One such demand is territorial autonomy for certain Russian-dominated areas. In post-Soviet political discourse, this demand is often—deliberately or unwittingly—confused with separatism; in principle, however, this is a very different matter, as it does not challenge the territorial and political integrity of the state.[43] Such autonomy schemes range from administrative autonomy with greater control of the local budget, via free economic zones, to political sovereignty within the framework of a federated or confederate state.

Other pleas for special treatment have been directed not toward the state authorities in the country of residence but toward the Russian Federation. Russia is exhorted to grant a kind of "most-favored status" to Russian businesses in the area, such as special customs tariffs on import and export, so as to help the Russian communities survive economically.[44] Any such positive discrimination of Russians in other states on the basis of ethnicity might easily make them more vulnerable to negative discrimination from the side of the local population or state authorities, on the same basis.[45] Although Russia has not adopted any special trade regulations for the diaspora communities, the law on *soochesteven-niki* abroad does mention that the Russian Federation will "encourage cooperation between Russian firms and firms in foreign countries in which the majority of the employees are *soochestevenniki*."[46] Unless such encouragement is followed up by financial stimuli, however, it is unlikely to have much effect.

Nonfavoritism

The most urgent and universal Russian appeal, however, is that *no* ethnic groups in the state should be given any kind of favored or privileged position. In official documents and practical politics, no distinctions should be made between the titular nationality and other ethnic groups.[47] All permanent residents, irrespective of ethnicity, should be recognized as making up the nation. For instance, when the Ukrainian law on national minorities was under preparation in 1992, Russian activists insisted that the very term *national minorities* was inapplicable and harmful to Ukraine. All major ethnic groups in Ukraine should be considered indigenous. The law should therefore simply be called the "law on the peoples of Ukraine."[48] During the same year Russians in Kyrgyzstan fought fiercely to have a reference to the ethnic Kyrgyz nation deleted from the preamble to the new constitution, arguing that such a reference would hamper the consolidation of a unified political nation, the people of Kyrgyzstan.[49]

Although these particular campaigns in Ukraine and Kyrgyzstan were unsuccessful, Ukraine nevertheless is one of the Soviet successor states where the ideal of a nonethnic, civic nation-state has dominated the nation-building discourse. Developments in that direction may be registered elsewhere as well. For instance, in Moldova an exclusive and ethnic concept of the nation was discarded after the 1992 civil war, in an attempt to bring the Dniester separatists back into the fold.

Bipolarity

A fourth strand of Russian diaspora thinking involves what one could call bipolar models. The starting point is that a number of the non-Russian Soviet successor states are, strictly speaking, bicultural rather than multicultural. The overwhelming majority of the population belong to one of two main linguistic cultures: the indigenous culture or the Russophone culture. The cultural situation in such countries cannot be described as one big, indigenous monolith surrounded by a motley mosaic of minority cultures, the Russians point out. One of these nontitular cultures, the Russophone culture, is far more prominent than the others. If any languages are to enjoy a special status in the state, such a treatment ought to be accorded to both the titular language and to the most common nontitular language, Russian.

Most activists of the indigenous ethnic groups usually reject out of hand any demands for two official languages.[50] They point out that it will deprive the Russians of any incentive to learn the titular language and will perpetuate the language situation that prevailed in the Soviet Union. It is in fact probably utopian to expect full reciprocal bilingualism, in which all members of society are fluent in both their native tongue and the language of the other cultural group. In many areas, however, the introduction of two state languages may lead to a situation in which most people in each language group have a passive command of the other tongue; they are able to understand the language of their interlocutor even if they do not speak it.[51] Such passive bilingualism can be said to exist among the three Scandinavian peoples and mutatis mutandis could also probably function among the likewise similar Russian, Ukrainian, and Belarusian languages in Ukraine and Belarus.[52]

In Kazakhstan, where the population is not only ethnically but also geographically bifurcated, two state languages would in time probably lead to two distinct cultural zones: Everyone living in the south, whether Kazakh or Russian, would have to know the Kazakh language, whereas all denizens of the north would necessarily be fluent in Russian.

In some cases demands for Russian as an official language are being met. In an attempt to stem the out-migration of Russians from Kyrgyzstan, President Askar Akayev in June 1994 announced that Russian was henceforth to have the status of official language in regions predominantly populated by Russian speakers, as well as in "vital areas of the national economy." Following a referendum in Belarus in May 1995, Russian was introduced in that country as a state language on a par with Belarusian. In Estonia and Latvia, however, frequent amendments to the language laws tend to place increasingly stringent demands on the Russian populace to learn the titular language—fast and well.

In addition to two state languages, Russian diaspora activists also often demand the right to obtain two citizenships: of the Russian Federation and of the state of residence. Appeals for two state languages and dual citizenship are often pronounced in the same breath as twin issues, but in reality they are qualitatively different.[53] Although the introduction of two state languages does not necessarily jeopardize the consolidation of a unified political nation, dual citizenship does. Dual citizenship may too easily imply divided allegiances. If dual citizenship should be granted to hundreds of thousands, perhaps millions, of Russians in the former Soviet republics, their political loyalty in a crisis situation would surely be open to question.

What the introduction of dual citizenship would mean in legal or actual terms is far from clear. Dozens of states in the world allow for dual citizenship, but the schemes differ from one another.[54] The most liberal regimes will usually be found in states with a relatively homogeneous population at home and a large number of members from the same ethnic group abroad, as is the case for Hungary.[55] Most countries in the former Soviet Union have flatly rejected dual citizenship. A system of dual citizenship was, however, included in a bilateral treaty concluded between Russia and Turkmenistan in 1993. Turkmen president Saparmurad Niyazov evidently believed that the (energy-based) economy of his country was strong enough, the number of Russians in Turkmenistan so small, and the distance to Russia so large that he would be able to withstand any Russian attempts to use this clause to turn his country into a Russian protectorate.

According to many observers, Belarus and Tajikistan, in contrast, are already Russian protectorates for all intents and purposes. The present leadership in these countries favors tight integration with Russia, economically and otherwise, and would probably not have anything against a dual citizenship arrangement. A Russian-Tajikistani treaty on dual citizenship signed in 1995, however, was never ratified by the Russian Duma, and none of the Russian-Belarusian agreements concluded since 1995 include any practical provision for such a system. This may indicate that Russian authorities are perhaps not quite as interested in a dual-citizenship regime as they profess to be.

Any agreement between two countries that gives to all citizens of both countries unlimited right to obtain dual citizenship may have detrimental economic and demographic consequences for the economically stronger country. Russia will probably try to avoid an agreement that could give all citizens of poor and war-torn Tajikistan an automatic right to move to Russia and search for jobs there. In the British Commonwealth, a very liberal regime for migration between Commowealth member countries led to a flood of job-seeking immigrants in the 1960s and 1970s. Primarily for that reason this regime was scrapped in 1981.

A compromise solution on the dual-citizenship issue that may possibly set a precedent for other bilateral arrangements is found in the Russian-Kazakhstani agreement concluded in January 1995. Although it does not allow for dual citizenship, it guarantees almost automatic citizenship in the new state of residence for persons moving from the one state to the other. Similar simplified citizenship procedures also govern Kyrgyzstani-Russian relations.

The New Russian Diaspora— an Identity of Its Own?

The degree to which the post-Soviet Russian minorities will be integrated into their new homelands is intimately linked to the question of what kind of collective identity each will develop. In recent years many scholars have pointed out that the category "Russian" is very broad indeed.[56] The self-understanding of the czarist state was not based on cultural Russianness; indeed, according to many knowledgeable observers, the self-understanding of most Russians as well has historically been linked more to territory and state than to culture and ethnicity. One of the reasons for this is that prerevolutionary Russia never got a chance to develop into a nation-state but passed directly from a patchwork of small principalities in the fourteenth and fifteenth centuries to a multinational empire from the sixteenth century onward. As this state continued to expand, it acquired more and more non-Russian subjects.

Historically speaking, the Russian nation has been open to the assimilation of non-Russians. As long as they adopted the Orthodox faith and learned the Russian language, members of other cultures were accepted as Russians without reservation. Only toward the end of the nineteenth century did this inclusive attitude begin to change. As competition for prestigious jobs in the czarist state apparatus and in commerce began to increase, "genuine" Russians tried to define their rivals on the job market out of the nation, branding them as "aliens," as Germans, Jews, Tatars, and so on—anything but Russians.[57]

Although the Russian nation has thus traditionally been poorly demarcated vis-à-vis other ethnic groups, it is also characterized by rather strong cultural variations within.[58] Russians who live in the core area of Russian settlement—in northwestern and central Russia—meet with mostly fellow Russians in their daily lives. By contrast, Russians in the outskirts of this area will have more frequent contact with members of other ethnic groups as well. There has been some disagreement within the scholarly community as to the effects these contacts have had on Russian mentality and self-understanding. Some believe that such cross-cultural encounters have strengthened the ethnic identity of the periphery Russians, since identity, as a rule, is developed through a process of contrast: "us" versus "them."[59] Russians living in the periphery of the Russian lands inevitably realize that their way of life is different from that of other groups and consequently develop a high degree of consciousness about their own ethnicity. Those Russians who are rarely exposed to other ethnic cultures, in contrast, have scant need to emphasize, and also few opportunities to discover, their Russianness.

To be sure, Russians, like any other individuals, may develop a plethora of cultural identities besides the ethnic one. They may see themselves as Slavs, Europeans, Orthodox Christians, even Soviets, depending on the context. An individual may also be strongly attached to a particular town, region, or neighborhood. A common Russian word for "home district" is *rodina,* which may also be translated as "motherland" or "the country in which I was born." Sometimes Russians distinguish between the "little *rodina,*" referring to the local or regional attachment, and "greater *Rodina,*" meaning the country.

Many diaspora Russians readily acknowledge that although they continue to see themselves as distinctly Russian, their lifestyles and cultural preferences have been strongly influenced by the titular ethnic group in the country where they live. In countries where the cultural distance between the Russians and the titular nation is narrow, as in Slavic and Orthodox regions, strict identity boundaries are difficult to maintain; in areas where cultural contrasts between the Russians and the locals are more marked, the identity boundary will more easily be clearly demarcated. This is particularly true of the Muslim countries in the former Soviet Union. There we find extremely few marriages among Russians and members of the titular population.

At the same time, in these bifurcated societies certain other ethnocultural processes may be observed. Individuals belonging to non-Russian minorities who live in the same areas as the diaspora Russians often adopt a distinctly Russian lifestyle and are frequently seen—by themselves and others—as a part of the "Russian" group. This is true not only of kindred groups such as Ukrainians and Belarusians but also of many Germans, Poles, and Jews in the Soviet successor states. What pulls them toward the Russians is, on the one hand, an awareness of being somehow different from the country's titular ethnic group, and, on the other hand, an attachment to the Russian language and to Soviet values.

Soviet values is admittedly a vague term, and necessarily so. Rather than involving adherence to Communist ideology, it is often linked to a nostalgia for what is perceived as having been a predictable, stable society. If the "new man" of Soviet propaganda ever existed, it was among these Russophone groups in the non-Russian republics. Life in the diaspora has functioned as a relentless melting pot in which particular ethnic cultures are to a large degree dissolved. This does not, however, mean that the non-Russians are absorbed into the Russian diaspora culture without leaving any trace. They contribute their shares to a common, distinct Russophone diaspora identity into which the local Russians as well are socialized. These processes increase the cultural distance between the Russians in Russia and their coethnics in the other Soviet successor states.[60]

Quite a few of the Russians who have left Central Asia and "returned" to Russia—"returned" must be enclosed in quotation marks since many of them had never actually lived in Russia before—complain that the reception they have been given by the local Russians has been less than cordial. To their immense surprise, they find themselves referred to as "the Tajiks," "the Uzbeks," and so on, as if they belonged to the titular ethnic group in the country they just left. Put off by such labels, some of them retaliate by telling their new neighbors that Russians where they come from have a far higher ethical code than the Russians in Russia: They drink less, don't beat their spouses, and keep their marriage vows. It goes without saying that such altercations hardly contribute to good neighborly relations between newcomers and old-timers in Russia.

In some cases Russian refugees from Central Asia soon decide that they have had enough of life in Russia. In 1993 a spokesperson of the Russians of Kyrgyzstan wrote: "Many have already returned, at a considerable economic loss. It is indeed very difficult to adapt to new circumstances when you have a radically different mentality. More often than not, those who think that they have arrived in their historical homeland find that they are regarded as aliens."[61]

In 1996 and 1997, I coordinated a research team that conducted large-scale surveys in Latvia and Kazakhstan.[62] We tried to find out what kind of cultural and political identities the Russians and other Russophone inhabitants in these two countries were developing. Our assumption was that if these identities are strongly linked to Russia, this will complicate their integration into their present country of residence. Conversely, to the extent that their identities draw strength from local sources, this will make it easier to include the Russians into the ongoing nation-building of Latvia and Kazakhstan (provided, of course, that this is what the political authorities in these two countries actually want to achieve).

The answers we got indicated that no uniform identity has crystallized among the Russophones in either country. We found that some Russophones are primarily oriented toward Russia, both politically and culturally, but others are more strongly attached to their present country of residence. In Kazakhstan approximately 40 percent of the Russians indicated Kazakhstan as their homeland, whereas slightly more than one-third still felt attached primarily to the USSR (see Table 5.2). Only 10–13 percent of the Russophones regarded Russia as their homeland. The latter, somewhat surprising piece of evidence must be rather encouraging news for the Kazakhstani nation-builders.

As time goes by and the Soviet era recedes into the past, probably fewer and fewer Russians in Kazakhstan will cling to the memory of the lost Soviet state. They will then most likely identify with either Russia or Kazakhstan. Which of these options will they choose? The political allegiance of Russians in Kazakhstan seems to have been moving away from this new state over the last years. Although 5 percent of them in our survey indicated that they had earlier been opposed to the establishment of an independent Kazakhstani state but were now in favor of it, as many as 12 percent confided that they had previously supported Kazakhstani statehood but had now turned against it.

TABLE 5.2   "Which Country Do You Regard as Your Homeland?" Kazakhstan, 1996 (in percentages)

	Russians (N = 409)	Ukrainians (N = 48)	Other Europeans (N = 31)
Kazakhstan	39.9	27.7	32.3
USSR	35.7	45.8	32.3
Kazakh SSR	9.5	6.3	6.5
Russia	13.0	6.3	9.7
Another country	0.2	12.5	16.1
I have no homeland	1.5	–	–
Don't know	0.2	2.1	3.2

SOURCE: Pål Kolstø, ed., *Nation-Building and Ethnic Integration in Post-Soviet Societies: An Investigation of Latvia and Kazakstan* (Boulder, Colo.: Westview, 1999), 239.

TABLE 5.3 "Which Country Do You Regard as Your Homeland?" Latvia, 1997 (in percentages)

	Russians (N = 297)	Ukrainians (N = 16)	Belarusians (N = 43)
USSR	17.8	18.8	17.8
Latvian SSR	21.5	6.3	11.1
Latvia	41.1	12.5	37.8
Russia	11.4	6.3	2.2
Another country	1.0	50.0	17.8
I have no homeland	2.4	0.0	6.7
Don't know	4.7	6.3	6.7

SOURCE: Pål Kolstø, ed., *Nation-Building and Ethnic Integration in Post-Soviet Societies: An Investigation of Latvia and Kazakstan* (Boulder, Colo.: Westview, 1999), 239.

In Latvia considerably fewer Russophones in our survey clung to the Soviet Union as the homeland compared to Kazakhstan: less than 20 percent (see Table 5.3). At the same time, their support for the new nation-state was more or less on the same level as in Kazakhstan: 40 percent. Once again we found that identification with Russia was low.

Next we asked respondents whether they regarded the local Russians as being in any way different from Russians in Russia. In Kazakhstan the answers were evenly divided between yes and no. This was roughly true of all ethnic groups—Russians, non-Russian Europeans, and Kazakhs (see Table 5.4). When asked to flesh out this difference, respondents from all groups in Kazakhstan were inclined to invest the local Russians with more positive character traits than they were willing to grant Russians in general: The local Russians were regarded as more hospitable and industrious, more cultured and tolerant than Russians in Russia itself.

TABLE 5.4 "Do Russians in Kazakhstan Differ from Russians in Russia?" 1996 (by respondents' ethnicity, in percentages)

	Kazakhs (N = 376)	Russians (N = 409)	Ukrainians (N = 48)	Germans (N = 41)	Other Europeans (N = 31)
Significantly	31.6	27.9	22.9	29.3	32.3
Somewhat	17.3	21.3	29.2	19.5	25.8
No	26.9	33.0	25.0	19.5	25.8
Don't know	24.2	17.8	22.9	31.7	16.1

SOURCE: Pål Kolstø, ed., *Nation-Building and Ethnic Integration in Post-Soviet Societies: An Investigation of Latvia and Kazakstan* (Boulder, Colo.: Westview, 1999), 260.

Integration or Alienation?

TABLE 5.5 "Do Russians in Latvia Differ from Russians in Russia?" 1997 (by respondents' ethnicity, in percentages)

	Latvians (N = 549)	Russians (N = 296)	Lithuanians (N = 23)	Ukrainians (N = 16)	Belarusians (N = 45)
Significantl	35.2	41.6	34.8	25.0	24.4
Somewhat	34.8	35.1	30.4	50.0	37.8
No	8.7	11.1	4.3	25.0	22.2
Don't know	21.3	12.2	30.4	0.0	15.6

SOURCE: Pål Kolstø, ed., *Nation-Building and Ethnic Integration in Post-Soviet Societies: An Investigation of Latvia and Kazakstan* (Boulder, Colo.: Westview, 1999), 260.

In Latvia we found a much stronger tendency than in Kazakhstan to see the local Russians as different from the core group of Russians. Among all ethnic groups in Latvia, between 65 and 75 percent answered yes to the question whether the two groups of Russians differed (see Table 5.5). When we asked respondents in Latvia what exactly this difference consisted of, we found much more disagreement than in Kazakhstan. Russians in Latvia and Russians in Kazakhstan have very similar self-perceptions: They all believe that they are a better lot than the Russians in Russia. But few ethnic Latvians would agree with them. On the contrary, they gave Russians in Latvia a low score on "cultured" and a high score on "being easily drawn into conflicts." The results of our surveys seemed to indicate that ethnic Kazakhs tend to welcome the local Russians into a common nation-building endeavor, whereas the ethnic Latvians to a much higher degree want to keep the Russians out.

•   •   •

During perestroika non-Russians in the republics time and again mobilized hundreds of thousands of participants at demonstrations and other mass manifestations in the struggle for independence. The diaspora Russians have never been able to match this high level of activism—neither then, nor later. But given that these communities possess well-educated elites, their political torpor will not necessarily last. It is of crucial importance that if and when the Russians in the near abroad shake off their lethargy, their activity is channeled into constructive nation-building in their states of residence. And in order for this to happen, these Russians must feel convinced that they, too, have a role to play in the new states.

6

NATION-BUILDING IN TWO BICULTURAL STATES: LATVIA AND KAZAKHSTAN

Of all the states of the former Soviet Union, it is in Latvia and in Kazakhstan that the titular nation represents the lowest share of the total population: as of 1999 approximately 57 percent in Latvia and 50 percent in Kazakhstan. In such a situation, it is difficult to see how the "national" (Latvian, Kazakh) culture can serve as a binding or consolidating element in the project of nation-building. Quite the contrary: Any ethnic-based nation-building could easily act to reinforce the existing dividing lines between members of the titular group and "outsiders." And yet in both these states nation-building would seem to be following the same general post-Soviet pattern: The traditions and symbols of the titular nations form the basis, whereas the remainder of the population, no matter how large a part it may be, gets treated as ethnic "minorities."

In Chapter 5 I argued that many minority groups in the Soviet successor states are in the process of developing a common identity based on the Russian language and shared experiences from the Soviet era. If that analysis is correct, then it would make more sense to treat Latvia and Kazakhstan as bicultural rather than multicultural states. In that conception the language of the titular nation can be seen as representing the one cultural pole in society and Russian-language culture the other.

One authority on nationalism, Donald L. Horowitz, has claimed that states with few but large ethnic groups will be particularly susceptible to serious ethnic conflict. Such states have what he has termed a "centrally focused ethnic system." Often what the groups fight to control is the central power of the state itself: "When conflict occurs, the center has little latitude to placate groups without antagonizing others. Conflict is not easily compartmentalized, and problems cannot be dealt with one at a time; they involve the whole state."[1] Recent events in Rwanda and Burundi have provided horrifying examples of precisely this.

Moreover, states with many small ethnic groups may experience riots and other forms of ethnic unrest, but in such cases, says Horowitz, ethnic tensions will not threaten the very existence of the state. Instead, the state power may be able to stand over and above the individual groups, acting as a kind of conciliatory judge and peacemaker.

If Horowitz's analysis is correct, we should expect a high degree of ethnic unrest in Latvia and Kazakhstan. Nor is there any doubt that ethnic tensions have played a considerable role in the politics of both countries since independence. All the same, in Latvia there has not been one single instance of ethnically motivated violence after the final break with the Soviet Union. Kazakhstan has also been characterized by a relatively high degree of ethnic stability, at least compared with the situation elsewhere in Central Asia. True, there have been signs of ethnic violence in some of the provinces, but in only one case—the so-called December massacre in 1986 (see Chapter 3)—have the conflict lines in Kazakhstan followed the division between the titular nation and the Russophones.

How, then, can we best explain the absence of ethnic violence in Latvia and in Kazakhstan? Might it be that Horowitz's general theory is flawed? Or perhaps his theory is correct, but I am mistaken in viewing Latvia and Kazakhstan as bicultural states. A third possibility could be that both Horowitz's theory and my description are correct, but that the authorities in the two countries have pursued a policy that has managed to stifle any incipient violence.

Latvia

Construction Materials for the Latvian House

In both Latvia and Kazakhstan, sociocultural structures do not necessarily follow strict ethnic categories. There can be a high degree of community among several ethnic groups, and the converse: There can also be sharp identity borderlines and rival loyalties within one and the same group and within the titular nation.

Among the ethnic Latvians, we can identify two cultural subgroups: the Latgalians and the Russian Latvians. The latter refers to those ethnic Latvians who lived in the Soviet Union in the interwar years and returned to Latvia after World War II. Many of them are the descendants of peasants who had migrated to Russia prior to World War I looking for work or land to farm. Others were inspired by ideological motives to move to Soviet Russia during the Communist period. The Russian Latvians, with their generally fluent Russian as well as Latvian, often easily made careers in the Soviet Latvian (and sometimes all-Soviet) political elite, which in turn did not endear them to the average Latvian. Even those Russian Latvians who were not politically active were frequently seen as potential or actual minions of the Soviet forces of occupation.[2]

The term *Latgalian* is applied to the ethnic Latvian populace of the province of Latgale. Located in southeastern Latvia, Latgale has a political and cultural history different from that of the rest of the country. Whereas the three other provinces—Kurzeme, Zemgale, and Vidzeme—were long under German-Swedish rule and thus became marked by German culture, Latgale remained under Polish-Lithuanian rule until 1772, when it was ceded to the Russian empire.

Most Latvians are Lutherans and generally quite secularized. By contrast, the Latgalians tend to be Roman Catholic, and many of them practice their faith. The Latgalian dialect, with its own written norm, is to some extent used as the liturgical language in Latvian Catholic churches. But the differences between Latgalian and standard Latvian are not particularly great. It would be quite erroneous to speak of a distinct Latgalian nationalism, as all Latgalians view themselves as Latvians. Nor are there any census statistics to indicate how many Latvians consider themselves to be Latgalians.

The Latgalians have had scant opportunities for political influence. For one thing, they are too few, even in the province of Latgale, where Russophones dominate. In the largest town of Latgale, Daugavpils, less than 15 percent of the populace are Latvians (including Latgalians). In the interwar period, Jews were the main element; today Russians and Belarusians are in the majority.

There is much to indicate that Russian Latvians and Latgalians are increasingly becoming assimilated into the common Latvian ethnic group, especially among the younger generation. The political authorities in the country, for their part, have favored and indeed promoted such an ethnic consolidation of the titular nation. "Latvian," they hold, should be as unified and unambiguous a category as possible. At the same time, the authorities have adopted a series of regulations obviously aimed at *splitting* the Russophones into smaller groupings with less political potential. The clearest instance of this is the decision to maintain the Soviet-era official registration of ethnic affiliation. This registration is compulsory and objective—that is, it does not reflect the individual's subjective experience of identity.

108

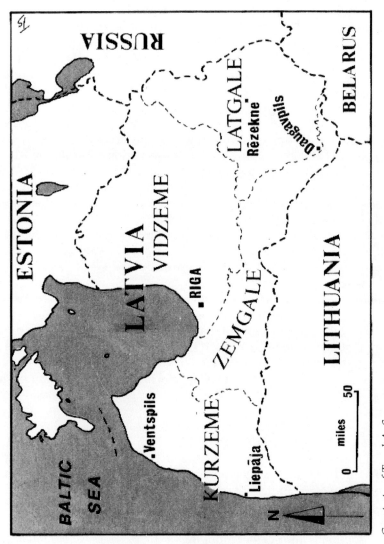

Courtesy of Trond A. Svensson

True enough, according to the Law on Cultural Autonomy for National and Ethnic Groups, adopted in Latvia in March 1991, immediately prior to independence, individuals were to be allowed to determine their ethnicity on the basis of self-experienced identity. But the provisions of this law were never accepted by the Directorate of Citizenship and Immigration. This office issued directives stating that nationality in passports and other identification papers was always to be registered on the basis of family background and not subjective experience.[3] As justification, the directorate stated, "The demographic situation of the country is discouraging. What is needed is a whole series of measures aimed at protecting the Latvian nation."[4] This statement implicitly includes two important principles: The bureaucracy can ignore the law, and the primary duty of the state is to serve the interests of the titular nation (as the bureaucracy defines these interests)—not the interests of the entire population. Three years later the Law on Cultural Autonomy was amended to bring it into line with the registration principles practiced by the Directorate of Citizenship and Immigration.

Beyond any doubt this official division of Latvia's population into ethnic groups is in many cases artificial. Seen in terms of language, the great majority of non-Latvians in the country do function as one single group. Most minority-group members speak Russian far better than they do their supposedly native tongue, which in many cases they do not know at all. Only a few, small minority groups are more at home in their own language than in Russian, and that applies to those with historical roots in the Baltic region—Estonians, Lithuanians, and Roma (Gypsies). Census data from 1989 present a three-part picture: There are the Latvians, the Russophones, and the Baltic minorities (see Table 6.1).

But even though most minorities in Latvia speak Russian as their everyday language, they may well maintain their own strong identities as Ukrainians, Belarusians, Poles, or Jews. Even people who speak the same language may consider themselves different in sociocultural terms, as is the case in Northern Ireland. There would seem nothing, however, to indicate that there exist similar strong contradictions within the Russian-speaking groups of Latvia. Instead, the contrary is true: There is every reason to say that any ethnosocial tensions among them are very low indeed.

A common method for estimating so-called social distance between groups is to start with the prevalence of mixed marriages. Opinion surveys often ask, "How would you feel if your son or daughter married a black/Jew/Catholic/Turk?" One difficulty with such surveys is that people may not always answer truthfully, perhaps afraid to reveal their prejudices. It may be better to rely on actual marriage statistics, although that, too, is not without problems. If there happens to be only one Jewish

TABLE 6.1   Language in Latvia, by Ethnicity, 1989 (in percentages)

		Regard as Native Language			Know Another Language Fluently			
	N in 1,000s	Traditional Language of Group	Latvian	Russian	Traditional Language of Group	Latvian	Russian	Other
Latvians	1,388	97.4	–	2.6	1.3	–	65.7	0.4
Russians	906	98.8	1.1	–	0.7	21.1	–	1.8
Belarusians	120	32.2	2.5	64.8	11.6	15.6	29.7	1.6
Ukrainians	92	49.5	0.9	49.4	14.7	8.9	43.8	1.2
Poles	60	27.3	14.7	54.2	–	22.8	33.8	15.2
Jews	23	22.5	2.0	74.9	4.4[a]	27.0	17.5	28.5
Tatars	5	46.7	0.6	51.6	11.3	6.6	44.6	5.7
Germans	4	34.0	12.4	53.0	n.a.	16.4	36.1	3.9
Total, Russian-speaking	1,120							
Lithuanian	34	63.9	23.8	11.9	9.6	40.3	36.0	0.3
Romany	7	84.7	10.2	4.8	3.4	52.3	28.6	0.8
Estonians	3	50.3	25.1	24.2	12.2	28.7	40.1	1.7
Livians	>1	37.0	62.2	n.a	17.0	27.4	31.1	4.0
Total, Baltic minorities	45							

[a]The traditional language of Jews in Latvia is Yiddish.

SOURCE: Natsional'nyy sostav naseleniya SSSR (The national composition of the population of the USSR) (Moscow: Finansy i Statistika, 1991).

(or Turkish or whatever) family in the neighborhood, then, statistically speaking, that drastically lowers the chances that the son or daughter of the house will find a marriage partner among his or her own ethnic group. Just who one finally marries will, of course, depend on who it is one actually meets. Among minority groups, mixed marriage will often be a virtue of necessity. But there are also many examples where small cultural groups force endogamy (marriage within the group) upon their members so as to prevent the group from becoming assimilated into the mainstream culture.

During the Soviet era, figures for mixed marriages in Latvia were clearly above the overall USSR average: around 30 percent. This need not mean that the registrars' offices throughout the republic functioned as massive melting pots where all the ethnic groups were mixed together. Instead, we can glimpse the contours of *two* cultural melting pots: one Latvian and one Russophone (see Table 6.2).

Among ethnic Latvians approximately 20 percent married someone outside their own group. This is a considerably lower share than the case among most of the other large ethnic groups in the country. Perhaps most

TABLE 6.2   Marriages Registered in Latvia, by Ethnicity, 1978 and 1988

Ethnic Group	Year	Mixed Marriages, Men	Mixed Marriages, Women	Number Who Got Married	Percent Marrying Outside Own Group
Latvians	1978	2,321	2,473	23,358	20.5
	1988	2,339	2,400	23,681	19.9
Russians	1978	3,329	3,376	19,177	35.0
	1988	3,396	3,467	18,357	37.4
Ukrainians	1978	977	688	1,929	86.3
	1988	1,049	935	2,340	84.8
Belarusians	1978	1,050	1,268	2,790	83.1
	1988	1,058	1,139	2,591	84.8

SOURCE: "Data on Ethnic Intermarriages," *Journal of Soviet Nationalities* 1, 1 (1990): 160–174.

noteworthy is that the number of mixed marriages involving Latvians actually *decreased* between 1978 and 1988, even though the share of Latvians in the total population of the country also fell during the same period. We may note the opposite tendency among the Russians of Latvia: 1.5 times more Russians than Latvians married outside their own ethnic group, and from 1978 to 1988 there was a 2.4 percent increase. As to the Ukrainians and Belarusians living in Latvia, over 80 percent of marriages in those same years were mixed, usually involving Russians or other Russophone peoples.[5] (No statistics are available on the smaller ethnic groups.)

Thus, both marriage statistics and language statistics indicate that the Russophones of Latvia constitute a community of their own, marked by a high degree of shared identity. The sociocultural division in the country is further strengthened by the fact that the two groups—Russophones and Latvians—tend to live in different areas. The former live mainly in the larger towns and cities, often in specific sections of town or suburbs. In the countryside the Latvians are clearly predominant. One reason for this geocultural split is occupational: Latvians tend to work in agriculture, whereas Russians and other Russophones are often found in industry, in both blue- and white-collar jobs.

Latvian State-Building: Laying the Foundations

In 1988 the Latvian Popular Front was established along the same lines as the popular fronts of Estonia and Lithuania. During the first years, the front fought for democratization and greater autonomy for Latvia within the framework of the unitary Soviet state, but demands gradually escalated to include full political independence. This became a mass movement that gathered almost the entire political spectrum among ethnic Latvians, from former Communists to right-wing nationalists. As a countermovement, some Russian-speaking circles formed an "international front," or "interfront." This movement sought to keep the Soviet Union together but never achieved anything like the support given to the Latvian Popular Front.

Although the interfront was primarily a Russophone movement, some of its leaders were in fact ethnic Latvians. Similarly, the popular front numbered quite a few Russians and other non-Latvians among its membership. As Gorbachev became increasingly unpopular, more and more non-Latvians joined in the demand for independence. This tendency got a powerful boost in January 1991 after the bloody events in Vilnius and Riga. One week after Soviet military divisions entered Vilnius, fighting erupted in Riga as well. Forces from the Soviet Ministry of the Interior attacked buildings that were defended by Latvian police units. Among the six persons killed in the skirmish were one Belarusian and one Russian policeman, both fighting on the Latvian side.

Six weeks later the Latvian authorities organized a nonbinding referendum on independence. Turnout was 80 percent; of these, 73 percent voted for independence. We have no exact figures on how the various ethnic groups voted. But the ballots were prepared in two versions, one in Latvian and the other in Russian, and Western election observers noted that at least 60 percent of those who used the Russian-language ballots supported independence.[6]

Many of the Russophone inhabitants of Latvia probably had economic motives for supporting the demand for independence. For one thing, they expected to be able to have a higher standard of living outside the Soviet Union. Furthermore, they had also been given to believe that they would enjoy full civic rights in an independent Latvian state. As pointed out in Chapter 5, the bilateral Russian-Latvian treaty of January 1991 had among its provisions that the entire population of Latvia would be free to choose which state they wished to be citizens of, Russia or Latvia. True, there were nationalistic Latvian movements that held that citizenship in a post-Communist Latvia should be restricted to those who had been citizens of the Latvian state in the interwar years and their direct descendants. This was a major issue for organizations like the Latvian Citizens' Committee and the Movement for National Independence in Latvia (MNIL, or LNNK in Latvian). Far more inclusive attitudes were expressed by most leaders in the Latvian Popular Front, however.[7] When everyone living in Latvia was asked to participate in the March referendum on independence, this was in itself a signal that all—including the Russophone immigrants—were considered part of the Latvian "nation" in the political sense of the term.[8] And with the actual advent of independence in August 1991, many observers envisaged a development toward a nonethnic, "civic"-type nation-building in Latvia.[9]

The political climate soon changed, however. Major disagreement erupted concerning the proposed Latvian citizenship bill: For one thing, controversy arose over the question of who had the right to adopt it. Latvian nationalists held that the current national assembly, the Supreme Soviet of Latvia, was illegitimate and represented the Soviet forces of occupation. In fact, this body had been elected in a fairly democratic manner in March 1990, during the days of perestroika. It was dominated by the popular front, but there were also Soviet-loyal Russians among the representatives.

In November 1991 the Latvian Supreme Soviet adopted a declaration stating that all those who had been citizens of the Latvian state during the interwar years, as well as their direct descendants, were automatically to be considered citizens of the new, independent Republic of Latvia. What status the other inhabitants were to have was a question to be decided by the new national assembly, the Saeima. And this assembly was to be elected by citizens of Latvia and only by them.

In order to determine who was entitled to citizenship, a comprehensive registration campaign was implemented in 1992–1993. Each individual was required to present documents proving his or her affiliation to the interwar Latvian state. Those who had lost their papers were often quite helpless. Western human rights organizations found proof of many serious clerical errors committed by the Directorate for Citizenship and Immigration, as well as cases where existing rules and regulations were deliberately ignored.[10] Most of these cases concerned Russophones, but even some ethnic Latvians were refused citizenship on irrelevant grounds. Still, it was always obvious that the Latvians would be heavily overrepresented among "citizens," no matter how the rules were followed.

With voter rolls prepared on the basis of the new Register of Residents, elections to the Fifth Saeima were held in June 1993. (It was called the "fifth" because there had been four Saeimas in the interwar years.) Whereas some 30 percent of the total population were ethnic Russians, they represented only some 16 percent of the citizens, that is, those entitled to vote. And conversely, although only some 55 percent of the total population were ethnic Latvians, they made up over 78 percent of those entitled to vote. This could not but be reflected in the composition of the new national assembly (see Table 6.3).

As can be seen from Table 6.3, Latvians were overrepresented in the national assembly, not only in relation to the total population but also in relation to the number of registered voters, the electorate. This tendency

TABLE 6.3   Ethnic Representation in the Latvian National Assembly (as a percentage of electorate and of number of representatives)

Supreme Soviet of Latvia, March 1990		
	Latvians	*Russians*	*Others*
Population	52.7	34.3	13
Electorate	52.7	34.3	13
Representatives	69.5	22.5	8

Fifth Saeima, June 1993		
	Latvians	*Russians*	*Others*
Population	54.0	33.8	12.2
Electorate	78.6	16.3	5.1
Representatives	88	6	6

Sixth Saeima, June 1995		
	Latvians	*Russians*	*Others*
Population	56.0	32.0	12.0
Electorate	79.3	15.9	4.8
Representatives	90	6	4

SOURCE: Pål Kolstø, ed., *Nation-Building and Ethnic Integration in Post-Soviet Societies: An Investigation of Latvia and Kazakstan* (Boulder, Colo.: Westview, 1999), 101.

was noticeable as early as 1990, at a time when all those living in Latvia were equally entitled to vote. This would indicate that there were other social or psychological mechanisms that acted to reduce the political representation of the Russophone groups: The formal restrictions imposed by the later citizenship law cannot be the full explanation.

There is reason to believe that at the time of the 1990 elections Russophone voters were not particularly concerned about the ethnic background of the various candidates. Many non-Latvians voted for Latvian candidates who represented the popular front because the front was seen as being anti-Communist and prodemocracy.[11] By 1993, however, ethnic issues ranked high on the political agenda in Latvia, and the candidates' ethnic background had now become a far more salient factor. All the same, the Russophones failed to achieve representation in the Saeima reflecting their share of the total population. One reason may be that many Russians, even those with Latvian citizenship, had begun to get used to the idea of "Latvia as the Latvians' national state." "Politics is for the titular population."[12]

In autumn 1993 the Saeima began its deliberations on the citizenship bill. All the Latvian-dominated parties agreed on the need for strict requirements for naturalization: At least ten years' residence in the country, good knowledge of Latvian history, and written proof that the candidate fulfilled the language law's strictest requirements as to fluency in Latvian. In addition, several parties held that even persons meeting all these requirements should not automatically be entitled to Latvian citizenship. If too many non-Latvians were to be naturalized at the same time, that could entail the risk of weakening the ethnic Latvian character of the Latvian nation-state. For that reason, they argued, the government should have the right to introduce maximum annual quotas for naturalization on the basis of the demographic and economic development of the country.

In November 1993 a citizenship law with provisions for such a quota system was adopted, but in Latvia a law must be passed three times before it can enter into force. Criticism of this new law was immediately forthcoming from the Council of Europe and the Conference on Security and Cooperation in Europe (CSCE), and before it was passed for the third time it had been amended on several points. The quota principle remained, however, and the Latvian president, Güntis Ulmanis, refused to sign the law for precisely that reason. And so it was returned once gain to the Saeima, where further amendments were introduced before it was finally adopted in July 1994. By this time the quota system had been replaced by a system of "windows" that would be opened to various groups at various times. Initially, only persons married to Latvian citizens were eligible for naturalization. This also applied to ethnic Latvians without citizenship papers, persons who had held permanent residence permits in Latvia in the interwar years, and some other very small groups. Then in 1997 all permanent residents over the age of twenty-five were allowed to apply for citizenship, with the proviso that they must have been born in Latvia. Not until the year 2003 would the quota system be abandoned.

Ethnic Nation-Building with Citizenship as a Tool

Seen in formal terms, the Latvian law on citizenship was not ethnically discriminatory. It was based on the principle of strict legal continuity between the interwar Latvian republic and that of today. This concept of continuity was why it was decided to adopt the constitution of the interwar period rather than making a new one, to cite one example. Yet as we have seen, Latvia did not choose to reintroduce the interwar citizenship law, which had been very liberal. Obviously, there were purely ethnopolitical reasons for deciding to adopt a totally new law instead. With amendments introduced in March 1995, these considerations found explicit expression in the text of the law. There it was stipulated that all ethnic Latvians not already citizens could receive their citizenship papers, without having to wait in line and without having to fulfill any formal requirements as to linguistic competence, years of residence, and the like.

A whole series of Latvian laws adopted in recent years serve as tools in an ethnocentric kind of nation-building. Especially central here is the language law. It was adopted in its original form in October 1988 but underwent radical changes in March 1992. In the first version, Russophone residents were guaranteed various important rights. For one, in correspondence with public offices it was to be up to the private individual to choose the language in which the correspondence was to be conducted. The new version of the law reversed this: Now it was to be up to the official in question to decide whether to respond in a language other than the state tongue. With the 1992 amendments, it also became forbidden for private firms to use anything but the state language in their business correspondence and in the minutes of their internal meetings, even in cases where all employees were Russophones.

In 1992 the State Language Inspectorate was established to ensure compliance with the new version of the Latvian language law. By 1994 the inspectorate had sixteen full-time employees as well as several hundred volunteers. It is empowered to impose fines of up to $150 for breaches of the language law—a considerable sum in a country where the average monthly wage in 1993 was $80. In the course of the first two years, approximately 1,000 fines were levied, to a total value of more than $40,000.[13]

Since 1992 almost all members of the workforce who did not graduate from a Latvian-medium school have been required to take a language test to document sufficient knowledge of the language to perform their jobs. The various occupational groups are divided into three categories according to the degree of fluency considered necessary. By the end of 1995, some 250,000 persons had been tested.[14] Although many have failed these tests, few have lost their jobs, but there have been some cases of mass notice being given.[15] The most important effect of the law seems to be that no one is hired for a job unless the language requirement is met. This is enforced with special rigor in the most prestigious positions.

Scant data are available on the ethnic backgrounds of those in top-level positions within the Latvian state apparatus. In January 1994, however, it became known that of the country's 152 judges, 142 were ethnic Latvians. Similarly, no Russian has ever been appointed minister in a Latvian government. The Norwegian political scientist Anton Steen has written: "Russians are almost non-existent in top state bureaucracy and in the judiciary. . . . The inclusion of Russians into the elite structure is seen by the elites as a real threat to national culture and independence."[16]

The Latvian House: Two-Family,
Semidetached or Latvian Bungalow?

There exists no official Latvian nation-building ideology; however, various statements made by leading Latvian politicians can give some indications as to the goals that have been set.

Many right-wing politicians maintain that Latvia cannot become a national state until the share of ethnic Latvians in the total population approaches at least 75 percent, as it was in the interwar period.[17] As pointed out in Chapter 5, in the Soviet period the immigration of Russians to Latvia and Estonia was particularly massive. At the same time, more than 100,000 Latvians were deported to Siberia and other parts of the Soviet Union during the 1940s. Coming on top of several other catastrophes in the twentieth century, such as the population losses in the two world wars, these events made many Latvians extremely sensitive to demographic issues. Once Latvia regained political independence, they were determined to redress what they saw as artificially created ethnodemographic imbalances.

Some extremists want to have all Soviet emigrants expelled through so-called decolonization and deoccupation in order to reach this target. A spokesperson for the Directorate of Citizenship and Immigration said in 1993, "At all times the Department has emphasized and we want to reiterate that sooner or later all of these 700,000 inhabitants will have to leave Latvia."[18] Valdis Birkavs, later Latvian prime minister and foreign minister, did not agree with this goal but opined that the Latvian state should actively support "voluntary repatriation" as well as "free emigration to a third country."[19]

A great many of the Russian-speaking population have in fact followed this appeal. Over 53,000 persons left Latvia in 1992, almost all of them Russophones. Since that time the stream of emigrants has lessened each year; by 1995 the demographic loss due to emigration was down to about 10,000. Among all of Latvia's ethnic minorities, however, there was more emigration than immigration, whereas there was a weak degree of positive immigration for ethnic Latvians.

In the course of seven years, the share of ethnic Latvians in the total population has risen by 6.5 percentage points (see Table 6.4). That is still far from the 75 percent/25 percent target—if such a goal can in fact ever be achieved. Latvia's nation-builders will thus have to accept that for the foreseeable future Russophones will continue to represent a sizable share of the population. What sort of relationship, then, should there be between the two groups?

In 1992–1993 the concepts of "one-community state" and "two-community state" appeared in the nation-building debate in Latvia. It

TABLE 6.4   Changes in Ethnic Composition of Latvia, 1989–1996 (in percentages)

	1989	1992	1994	1996
Latvians	52.7	53.1	54.8	57.2
Russians	34.4	34.3	33.4	30.7
Belarusians	4.5	4.5	4.1	4.3
Ukrainians	3.5	3.4	3.1	2.8
Poles	2.3	2.3	2.2	2.6
Lithuanians	1.3	1.3	1.3	1.4

SOURCE: Aina Antane and Boris Tsilevich, "Nation-Building and Ethnic Integration in Latvia," in Pål Kolstø, ed., *Nation-Building and Ethnic Integration in Post-Soviet Societies: An Investigation of Latvia and Kazakstan* (Boulder, Colo.: Westview, 1999), 70.

was maintained that various Russophone organizations were working to create a Latvian state where the larger language groups could live, each in its own sociocultural space, with as little mutual influence as possible. In other words, the "Latvian house" ought to be a two-family semi, preferably with a solid firewall between the two units. This idea, however, was unacceptable to the Latvian nation-builders, who then began to promulgate the concept of a "one-community state." For example, the quota arrangement in the first version of the citizenship law was explicitly justified in terms of the wish to "develop Latvia as a national, one-community state."[20]

Will the Russophones in Latvia agree to inclusion in Latvian society on the premises drawn up by the Latvian nation-building elite? No clear tendencies can be seen today. It is otherwise widely held that minority groups would like to be integrated into the political and social structures yet at the same time resist any comprehensive cultural integration or assimilation. But the figures from Latvia may indicate that many Russophones hold rather different attitudes. Although the signs are far from easy to interpret, it would seem that many are more interested in cultural and linguistic integration into Latvian society than in political integration into the Latvian state.

When the Law on Citizenship entered into force in February 1995, only a fraction of the many potential applicants actually made use of the possibility to become naturalized citizens when their turn came. As of fall 1998, more than 120,000 individuals had had their "windows" opened, but fewer than 10,000 had received citizenship.[21] This came as a great surprise to most observers, since opinion polls had indicated that the large majority of stateless residents in Latvia desired citizenship.

Why, then, has naturalization proceeded so slowly? Several explanations have been launched. Many have pointed out that a Russian living in Latvia could experience various difficulties if he or she were granted Latvian citizenship. For instance, a visa would be required to visit Russia, noncitizens are exempt from military service in the Latvian army, and so on. More likely, however, is that psychological factors are at least as important for most people: A great many noncitizens felt that the conditions for obtaining Latvian citizenship were both unreasonable and unfair.

One of the most important requirements involves fluency in the Latvian language. One might think that this would be the major obstacle for Russophones, but in fact that is not always the case. Studies have shown that more Russians in Latvia than in, for example, Estonia or Ukraine are willing to learn the language of the titular nation.[22] More and more Russians are sending their children to Latvian-medium schools: Over 18 percent did so in 1997 as against less than 3 percent one generation earlier (see Table 6.5).[23]

If these tendencies continue, a considerable share of the non-Latvian population may, in the course of a few decades, become assimilated—linguistically and eventually perhaps also in terms of self-identity. Still, the passport regulations requiring official registration of ethnic affiliation on the basis of family background act as a strong barrier against this. In addition, Latvian school authorities have been seeking to prevent too many Russophone children from enrolling in Latvian-medium schools, arguing that with too many Russian pupils in a Latvian school class, assimilation will go in the "wrong" direction: The Latvian children will imitate their Russian classmates in language and behavior, not the other way round.[24] In June 1996 the minister of education issued reassurances that "under no circumstances . . . will we accept a mechanical mixture of Latvian children and children of other nationalities in the same school or the same class."[25] Just what was meant by "me-

TABLE 6.5   Choice of School in Latvia, 1997 (in percentages)

In Which Language . . .	. . . Were You Taught at School?			. . . Are Your Children Taught at School?[a]		
	Latvians	Russians	Others	Latvians	Russians	Others
Russian	14.0	96.6	67.7	8.7	81.2	70.0
Latvian	84.4	2.7	15.7	89.9	18.3	21.8
Other language	1.6	0.7	16.3	1.4	0.5	8.2

[a] Some respondents had more than one child, and if their children were enrolled in different kinds of schools, they checked more than one answer. The figures, therefore, do not add up to 100 percent.

SOURCE: Pål Kolstø, ed., *Nation-Building and Ethnic Integration in Post-Soviet Societies: An Investigation of Latvia and Kazakstan* (Boulder, Colo.: Westview, 1999), 249.

chanical" is not clear; it almost seems as if the word was used to stress that such mixing is seen as a definite evil. Although the Latvian authorities have categorically rejected a nation model based on the concept of the two-community state, they actively contribute, through their school policy, to the perpetuation of two separate cultural communities in the country.

In political and cultural terms, then, we may note a marginalization of the non-Latvian population. In socioeconomic terms, however, no such marginalization seems evident. The Latvian authorities have, it is true, adopted a whole series of restrictions as to the type of economic activity permissible for noncitizens, but most of these regulations have proven to be largely of curiosity value.[26] Whereas the Russians have few opportunities for improving their societal status qua group, they do have considerable possibilities for making careers within private enterprise. As long as there exist alternative social ladders that well-qualified and ambitious Russians can climb, it is less frustrating that career possibilities within the state apparatus are in practice closed to them.

There is another feature of Latvian society that appears to function as an important safety valve for frustrations in the Russophone community. Noncitizens in Latvia may be deprived of some basic political rights, but their nonpolitical, individual human rights are respected. Latvia's firm desire to join first the Council of Europe and then the European Union (EU) and the North Atlantic Treaty Organization (NATO) is a strong contributory factor here. Several all-European organizations, among them the OSCE, have permanent representation in Riga and follow closely the political and legal developments in the country. The OSCE high commissioner on national minorities, Max van der Stoel, has sent many letters to the Latvian foreign minister with proposals on how to ensure better conditions for noncitizens. The possibility of appealing to the courts if other means of obtaining one's rights fail also functions as a social lightning rod. These are conditions that most of the Russian-speaking population in Latvia seem to have accepted—although the depths of their pockets may conceal clenched fists.

Even so, the citizenship issue remained highly contentious in Latvia. Nationalistic Latvian parties in the Saeima regarded the citizenship law as far too liberal and actively worked to get it changed, whereas Russophone activists were pushing for greater liberalism.[27] A spark was enough to ignite the tinderbox. Such a spark was provided by a demonstration of mainly Russophone pensioners in Riga in March 1998. The angry crowd protested a sudden hike in the electricity bill that cut deep into their already meager pensions. Losing control of the situation, the Latvian police used rubber batons to disperse the protesters. Footage of the event on Russian television created an uproar in Moscow and led to a boycott of Latvian goods in many Russian shops. The entire issue of the plight of the Russophones in Latvia was torn wide open.[28]

Several parties in the Latvian coalition government threatened to withdraw unless the citizenship law was softened. In the upshot an amended law was pushed through the Saeima in June that removed the naturalization windows and simplified language tests for persons sixty-five years or older. Although it did not meet the OSCE recommendation that all children born in Latvia should be granted automatic citizenship, the new law was unacceptable to the nationalist Fatherland and Freedom Party. As a leading member of the coalition government, this party was in fact responsible for the law, but party activists started to collect signatures to force a referendum on its repeal.[29] As more than 220,000 signatures were collected, far more than required by law, the referendum was held on 3 October. Not only the relationship to Russia but also the prospect of Latvia's eventual entry into the EU was at stake. The amendments, however, were accepted by 53 percent of those who voted and so remained in force. The referendum results nevertheless confirmed the deep divisions in the Latvian population on the citizenship issue.

Kazakhstan

Kazakhstan is in many ways very different from Latvia. What makes comparisons interesting, however, is the sociocultural bipolarity that characterizes both countries. As mentioned, nation-building in most of the states of the former USSR has been based on the language and culture of the titular group. What, then, of those states where the titular nation makes up no more than half the total population? How is it at all possible to conceive of ethnic integration in culturally bipolar states? Is the one half of the population to be integrated into the other half? Or are the "nontitulars" to be integrated into certain common social and political structures only? Or should one think rather of a process of mutual cultural influence?

Our 1996–1997 research project sought to find answers to these questions.[30] On the cultural level, we found considerable differences between Latvian and Kazakhstani nation-building: Whereas the Latvians have made some headway in "Latvianizing" the country linguistically and culturally, in Kazakhstan there has been no success in making the language and culture of the titular group into a shared national culture for all the population. In the political sphere, however, we can note clear and indeed remarkable similarities between the two nation-building projects: Despite their numerically weak starting point, the elites of the titular nations in both countries have managed to establish themselves as the politically preponderant force, almost absolutely so.

Courtesy of Trond A. Svensson

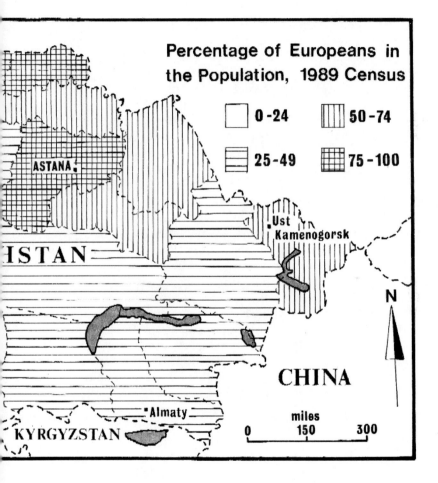

Percentage of Europeans in the Population, 1989 Census

0-24   50-74
25-49   75-100

Construction Materials for the Kazakhstani House

Kazakhstan is perhaps even more split along bipolar lines than is Latvia. In terms of most common criteria, the sociocultural gap between the titular nation and the Russophone population is enormous. The Kazakhs are Turkic-speaking Muslims, many of whom were nomads until well into the twentieth century. By contrast, the Russophone groups came as farmers and belonged to the Christian cultural sphere. Kazakhs and Europeans usually live in separate geographical areas. The titular group is preponderant in the countryside, whereas the Russians tend to cluster together in the larger towns and cities. For example, the last Soviet census showed that Russians composed nearly 60 percent of the population of the capital city, Alma-Ata, whereas the Kazakhs accounted for only 22 percent.

Statistics on marriage and language in Kazakhstan paint a picture of a tripartite culture: On the one side are the Kazakhs; on the other the non-titulars, who can be divided into two categories: Russophones and local minorities. As in Latvia this latter category comprises some smaller minority groups with historical roots in the region: Uzbeks, Kyrgyz, Uighurs, and so on. These local minorities are, like the Kazakhs, Muslim and Turkic-speaking; however, there is little intermingling with the titular population.[31] In any case these groups are all very small.

In choosing a marriage partner, the Kazakhs stick to their own ethnic group far more than do the Latvians: Only some 4 percent of the Kazakhs live in mixed marriages. The local minorities tend to be strictly endogamous: Among the Uzbek minority in the south of the country only 12 percent of the marriages are mixed. By contrast, among the Slavic groups in Kazakhstan we find no social or psychological barriers to mixed marriage. The Ukrainians and Belarusians are particularly exogamous: Nearly 90 percent find their partner outside their own ethnic group. Since the Asian groups are so endogamous, this means in practice that the Europeans nearly always marry other Europeans. A Kazakh research report from 1994 noted that "today there is often no other difference between a Ukrainian, a Belarusian, a Pole and a Russian than the nationality written in their passports."[32] Table 6.6 indicates the pattern of marriage by ethnicity in Kazakhstan.

At the same time as there are reasons to downplay the identity differences among the Russophone groups, many Kazakhstan experts would hold that within the Kazakh ethnic group itself there are considerable differences not visible in any statistics. The historical *zhuz* loyalties (described in Chapter 3) are still of great importance. The Great Horde dominates Kazakhstani politics: The largest city and former capital, Almaty (formerly Alma-Ata), lies within the territory of the Great Horde, and President Nazarbayev comes from this group.[33]

TABLE 6.6   Marriages Registered in Kazakhstan, by Ethnicity, 1978 and 1988

Ethnic Group	Year	Mixed Marriages, Men	Mixed Marriages, Women	Number Who Got Married	Percent Marrying Outside Own Group
Kazakhs	1978	2,837	1,573	95,876	4.6
	1988	2,975	2,422	138,537	3.9
Russians	1978	14,346	16,177	130,865	23.3
	1988	12,692	15,893	115,121	25.7
Ukrainians	1978	7,740	7,615	20,335	75.5
	1988	7,482	7,383	18,379	80.9
Belarusians	1978	1,612	1,830	4,076	84.4
	1988	1,851	1,712	3,777	94.3
Uzbeks	1978	409	275	5,462	12.5
	1988	526	419	7,443	12.8
Tatars	1978	1,701	1,896	5,957	60.4
	1988	2,183	2,332	6,483	69.6

SOURCE: "Data on Ethnic Intermarriages," *Journal of Soviet Nationalities* 1, 1 (1990): 160–174.

Little research has been done on subnational identities among Kazakhs, and much of the conventional wisdom is based on assumptions and vague generalizations. At least one expert has opined that the Kazakh nation does represent a consolidated entity with a high degree of shared identity and loyalty; she warns against ascribing too much political importance to the *zhuz* identities.[34] What does seem clear is that any dividing lines and rivalries that may exist within the Kazakhs as a group do not lessen the fundamental contrast in the political and societal life of Kazakhstan: There the line goes between the Kazakhs on the one side and the Russophones on the other.

The 1989 census shows that the Russians in Kazakhstan were less proficient in the language of the titular nation than was the case for Russians in any of the other Soviet republics: Less than 1 percent said that they could speak the Kazakh language fluently. For some of the other Russophone (Slavic) groups, the figures were even lower: less than 0.5 percent for the Belarusians, for instance. For most Europeans living in Kazakhstan, the local language is a closed book. Yet even among the Turkic-speaking groups, fluency in Kazakh was generally very low. Next to Belarus and Kyrgyzstan, Kazakhstan was probably the Union republic where the language of the titular group had the weakest footing. In public administration Russian is clearly predominant, and in many areas specialist terminology in Kazakh is nonexistent.

This does not mean, however, that the various ethnic groups in Kazakhstan live in separate linguistic universes of their own, with no

TABLE 6.7 Language in Kazakhstan, by Ethnicity, 1996 (in percentages)

		Regard as Native Language			*Know Another Language Fluently*			
	N in 1,000s	*Traditional Languages of Group*	*Kazakh*	*Russian*	*Traditional Languages of Group*	*Kazakh*	*Russian*	*Other*
Kazakhs	6,535	98.6	–	1.4	0.2	-	62.8	0.2
Russians	6,228	99.9	0	–	0	0.9	–	0.7
Germans	958	54.4	0.1	45.4	–	0.6	50.6	0.7
Ukrainians	896	36.6	>0.1	63.3	5.8	0.6	32.3	0.7
Belarusians	183	34.5	>0.1	65.3	6.0	0.4	31.8	1.4
Koreans	103	51.7	0.3	48.0	–	1.0	47.0	1.9
Poles	60	12.2	>0.1	76.4	–	0.4	19.8	50.0
Total, Russian-speaking	8,423							
Uzbeks	332	95.6	1.3	2.8	0.3	4.6	52.1	0.3
Tatars	327	68.9	3.4	27.3	3.2	3.2	64.3	0.7
Uighurs	185	95.1	1.5	3.1	–	9.1	62.0	0.5
Azeris	90	87.1	0.5	10.4	0.9	5.7	64.7	1.5
Total, Turkic-speaking	934							

SOURCE: Pål Kolstø, ed., *Nation-Building and Ethnic Integration in Post-Soviet Societies: An Investigation of Latvia and Kazakstan* (Boulder, Colo.: Westview, 1999), 31.

possibilities for intercommunication. This we can see from the figures on proficiency in Russian (see Table 6.7). Among the Kazakhs nearly two-thirds say that they are fluent in Russian. With the possible exception of the most remote village settlements, it is possible to make yourself understood in Russian everywhere in Kazakhstan.

In recent years there have been signs that far more ethnic Kazakhs are in fact Russian-speaking than had been thought to be the case. Of the 98.6 percent in the latest census who gave Kazakh as their native tongue, many seem to have done so because any other response would have been an insult to the culture of their ancestors. Some scholars think that as many as 30 percent of all Kazakhs cannot express themselves properly in the Kazakh language.[35]

Kazakhstan: A Common Multinational State and a Kazakh National State

Kazakhstan, like Ukraine and Belarus, lies in the shadow of Russia. In terms of geography, climate, and demography, northern Kazakhstan is in fact an extension of Russia's Ural Mountains and the steppes of Siberia.

At the same time, the region is physically separated from the southern areas of the country by vast, nearly uninhabited expanses of desert and semidesert. In six of the northerly counties, Russophones compose between 70 and 80 percent of the population. Russian nationalists in both Russia and Kazakhstan have maintained that these areas must be allowed to join with Russia, of which they are already a part in terms of culture, geography, and economy.

This is something that Kazakhstan's political leaders are determined to prevent. Thus, they make frequent reference to Kazakhstan as the shared state of all the inhabitants, not just the national state of the Kazakhs. And yet there is no denying that Kazakhstan is also seen in a special sense as the national state of the ethnic Kazakhs. This in turn means powerful built-in tension between an ethnic and a supraethnic model in the Kazakhstani nation-building project.

President Nazarbayev has long sought to avoid having to choose between these two models, maintaining that Kazakhstan can be both at the same time. In a speech to the Kazakh language association Kazak Tili in November 1992, he declared, "The sovereignty of Kazakhstan is in many ways special. First and foremost it is a unique synthesis of the [ethnic] Kazakh people's sovereignty, on the one hand, and the sovereignty of the entire population of Kazakhstan as an ethnopolitical fellowship, on the other."[36] What Nazarbayev spoke of as a "synthesis" has, however, been seen as an internal contradiction by most observers.[37] It also seems clear that the balance between the two elements in the Kazakhstani nation concept has not been stable. Although the signals are rarely unambiguous, it would appear that the supraethnic aspect has gradually been pushed into the background.

In the years immediately after 1991, Nazarbayev used to stress heavily the shared, citizenship-based aspects in Kazakhstan. For example, at a conference held in May 1993 he said:

> There are a great many states in the world, some of them very wealthy indeed, which consist of even more nations and nationalities than we have in Kazakhstan. In these countries patriotism is particularly well developed. For instance, the national anthem is played and the flag unfurled at the start of each schoolday or when a jury or higher official is sworn in, as well as on many other occasions.[38]

Statements like these are expressions of political nation-building in its pure form. It was doubtless the United States that Nazarbayev had in mind on this occasion. But despite the patriotic Pan-Kazakhstani rhetoric, several specific political decisions of those early years were marked by a different line of thought. Hundreds of Slavic-sounding place-names and street names were replaced by Kazakh names, even in areas with a preponderance of Slavs.[39] The Kazakhstani constitution that was adopted in 1993 gave to ethnic Kazakhs living outside the country the right to dual citizenship, without bestowing the same right on ethnic Russians living in Kazakhstan.[40]

The constitution of 1993 opened with the words, "We, the people of Kazakhstan"—clearly a supranational entity. Then, however, the very first article went on to declare that Kazakhstan was to be "the Kazakh people's form of statehood," so the ethnic-based concept of nation-building had managed to sneak its way in again. Russian activists maintained that the terms *people of Kazakhstan* and *Kazakh people* must be seen as synonymous: The Russian-speaking inhabitants had thereby been made invisible in the constitution.[41] This was in fact not quite correct, but when the new constitution of 1995 was written, the reference to "the Kazakh people's statehood" was nevertheless omitted. Instead, the formulation was, "We, the people of Kazakhstan, united by a common historical fate, have created a statehood on the ancient land of the ethnic Kazakhs."[42]

In this way it would seem that the authorities in Kazakhstan had taken an important step away from ethnically based nation-building. All the same, many observers interpreted the reference to "the ancient land of the Kazakhs" as an expression of ethnocentric nation-building.[43]

Scholarly publications in Kazakhstan that take up ideas around the nation-building question have generally been characterized by the ethnic line of thought.[44] For example, in an August 1995 article a professor at the state university of Kazakhstan discussed the theme of "interethnic integration in Kazakhstan."[45] She expressed the hope that all the people of Kazakhstan would gradually develop a shared identity and mentality as "Kazakhstanis" and as the "Kazakhstani people." The main obstacle to this was, in her opinion, the attitudes prevailing among the Russian portion of the population. They have not understood that, after independence, the two largest ethnic groups have in effect changed places:

> From being in a subordinate position, the Kazakh ethnos has become the titular nation. Because the state has gained its independence, the Kazakh ethnos has been able to redress the historical injustice that had been committed. The Kazakh people have regained their ancient right to their historical fatherland, to their lands and their language, their customs and traditions. From being "little brother," the Kazakhs have become the leading ethnos, the native nation.

At the same time, the Russians had been reduced in status, from "big brother" to a "regular ethnos, or more correctly: they have become yet another ethnic group."[46]

No Linguistic or Cultural Integration

At times the Kazakh nation-builders have given the impression of attempting to push back the Russian language in favor of the tongue of the titular nation, as has been the case in practically all the other Soviet successor states. At other times the linguistic Kazakhization campaigns look like sheer grandstanding, not seriously meant. Be this as it may, one thing seems certain: To date these campaigns have met with little success.

In 1989 Kazakhstan's parliament adopted a new language law, making the Kazakh tongue the state language. At that time similar laws were being passed in most of the other Soviet republics. In fact, Kazakhstan's law stood out as perhaps the most liberal. Russian was defined as "the language of interethnic communication"; furthermore, according to the law, no one could be discriminated against on the basis of lack of proficiency in the state language. Only one year later, however, an action program was adopted for a gradual transition to the use of the Kazakh language in all public administration. Within ten years all regions—including those with a clear preponderance of Russophones—were to become fully bilingual.[47]

Studies undertaken in 1992 showed that the number of Russians who maintained that they spoke Kazakh fluently had doubled since 1989. But because the starting point had been so low, this made little practical difference: Their share had risen from 1 percent to 2 percent. The new constitution adopted in 1995 strengthened the official position of the Russian language. From being "the language of interethnic communication" it was now defined as an "official" language with a status "on a level with the state language."

In 1996, however, signs in the new "Concept for the Language Policy of the Republic of Kazakhstan" pointed in various directions. Although it stated that Russian could still be used to the full in all social functions, the document also presented several models for functional linguistic development. According to the "optimal model," use of the state language should be made compulsory in all official connections and official correspondence. Communications from all public offices should be in the state language only.[48] As we have seen, this has been the main rule in Latvia since 1992. And if this principle were to be introduced in Kazakhstan, interpreters and translators would soon have their hands full.

Many Russophone Kazakhstanis were concerned about the new language law that was to replace that of 1989. When it was formally adopted in summer 1997, however, it proved to be just as toothless as its predecessor. The law commences by declaring that every citizen of Kazakhstan has the duty to learn the state language: "This is absolutely necessary for the consolidation of the people of Kazakhstan." But it also states that Russian can still be used in all organs of the state and in local administration.[49]

Our own survey taken in 1996 showed that almost no non-Kazakhs have begun sending their offspring to Kazakh schools: Among the Russians in Kazakhstan over 98 percent of the parents have their children in Russian-medium schools.[50] The share of non-Russian minority children being taught in Russian has risen by over 6 percentage points, to 89 percent, whereas only some 5 percent have Kazakh as the medium of instruction (see Table 6.8). As long as no career paths have been closed for those not fluent in the state language, there seems no reason to assume that more will do so. That is why Kazakh nationalists have urged the adoption of a list specifying occupational categories where proficiency in Kazakh must be considered a precondition for employment.

Although there may not be signs of any language shift among the minorities of Kazakhstan comparable to that which we noted in Latvia, there has been a certain transition to Kazakh among ethnic Kazakhs. Those in Kazakh circles feel the considerable pressure of linguistic Kazakhification. Ethnic Kazakhs are expected at least to be able to express themselves acceptably well in Kazakh, even if they continue to use Russian for everyday communication. Those who do not know their native tongue risk being branded as *mankurt*—an expression from a novel by the Kyrgyz author Chingiz Aytmatov meaning "an identity-less individual."

Some Russophone Kazakhs have started sending their youngsters to Kazakh-medium schools in the hopes that the school can provide them with skills in Kazakh that they themselves lack. Our survey found that the share of Kazakh children attending Kazakh-medium schools had increased from 57 percent in the previous generation to some 66 percent today. If this tendency strengthens, the result may be that Kazakhstan be-

TABLE 6.8   Choice of School in Kazakhstan, 1996 (in percentages)

In what Language . . .	. . . Were You Taught at School?			. . . Are Your Children Taught at School?[a]		
	Kazakhs (N = 369)	Russians (N = 408)	Others (N = 213)	Kazakhs (N = 232)	Russians (N = 280)	Others (N = 131)
Russian	42.5	99.0	83.1	40.1	98.2	89.3
Kazakh	57.7	0.7	2.8	66.4	3.2	5.3
Other language	0.5	1.5	15.5	0.9	0.7	6.1

[a] Some respondents had more than one child, and if their children were enrolled in different kinds of schools, they checked more than one answer. The figures, therefore, do not add up to 100 percent.

SOURCE: Pål Kolstø, ed., *Nation-Building and Ethnic Integration in Post-Soviet Societies: An Investigation of Latvia and Kazakhstan* (Boulder, Colo.: Westview, 1999), 247.

comes *more* culturally bipolar, not less—with two linguistic universes: Russian and Kazakh.

But it is not certain that this linguistic Kazakhification among Kazakhs will continue. Compared with Russian-medium schools, the Kazakh schools are generally poorly equipped and understaffed. In many subjects no proper textbooks exist in Kazakh, nor are there qualified teachers. The newspapers have printed several letters from furious parents who have discovered that not even in the Kazakh-medium schools are their offspring being instructed in proper Kazakh—or in much of anything else, for that matter.[51] Despite all the efforts of the custodians of the Kazakh language, the state language may end up the loser in the battle against Russian in the independent Republic of Kazakhstan.

Political Marginalization

The main reason the pressure on the Russians of Kazakhstan to learn Kazakh has been so intermittent and mild is that the Kazakh political and financial elite rarely have a good command of the language themselves. It is almost only the cultural elite, and those who have left the villages and countryside for the towns, who have been exerting pressure for stricter enforcement of the language law. If the language policies of Kazakhstan were to be changed along the lines of those of Latvia, this would give these groups a clear competitive edge over the Russified "town Kazakhs"—which is, of course, precisely why the latter have fiercely resisted linguistic Kazakhification in terms of practical policy while pretending to go along with it.

The Russophones of Kazakhstan need not fear cultural marginalization, but they have every reason to expect that they may become just as politically marginalized as the Russophones in Latvia. Even today it is clear that they are being pressed out of most positions of power in Kazakhstani society. This is quite remarkable for several reasons. First, the titular population is even weaker in numbers in Kazakhstan than in Latvia. Second, alternative career routes outside the state apparatus are less in evidence in Kazakhstani society. Since independence, Kazakhstan has seen a much slower economic development than have the Baltics. Even though there has been a certain degree of transition to a market economy, this has moved far more slowly and has not specifically benefited the Russophones. And finally, in Latvia the restrictive citizenship law is the most important instrument for ensuring ethnic Latvians political control of their republic. In Kazakhstan, in contrast, all permanent residents have been granted full civil rights and thus should be able to put their candidates in place through the normal electoral process. And yet even in Kazakhstan the titular population has managed to attain a high degree of political preponderance. How has this been possible?

Even under Brezhnev the titular population of Kazakhstan was over-represented in top administrative positions and political posts. Since independence, this political imbalance has increased greatly. As of 1994 a full 60 percent of the seats in Kazakhstan's Supreme Soviet were held by ethnic Kazakhs, whereas the Russian share was down to 28 percent. A similar picture can be seen in the new national assembly that was introduced under the 1995 constitution: In the first elections to the new upper chamber, the Senate, twenty-six Kazakhs and twelve Russians were in part elected, in part appointed. And in the lower chamber, the Mazhilis, forty-two Kazakhs, nineteen Russians, and five representatives from other ethnic groups took their seats.[52]

The 1995 constitution gives to the Kazakhstani presidency a great deal of power. The president appoints the government, can dissolve the national assembly, and can issue decrees with legal force. The national assembly has correspondingly little power, so the distribution of mandates noted here does not necessarily provide a realistic picture of the influence enjoyed by the various ethnic groups in the political life of Kazakhstan. The decisive factor is what ethnic policy is pursued by the president and what groups are represented among the president's advisers.

Western and Kazakhstani analysts alike have tended to view the president and the presidential apparatus as less nationalistic than the politicians in the national assembly. For instance, when the constitution (both the 1993 and the 1995 versions) gives to the president the right to appoint some members of the national assembly, this has been seen as a mechanism enabling the president to correct possible imbalances in the representation and influence of various ethnic groups.[53] The president's handpicked people in the Mazhilis have, however, frequently proven themselves at least as nationalistic as the popularly elected representatives. On one occasion in 1994, almost 45 percent of the members of the national assembly voted to remove the reference to the "statehood of the [ethnic] Kazakh nation" from the constitution; among the presidentially appointed members only 20 percent supported this antinationalistic motion.[54]

An analysis of the composition of the presidential and government apparatus in 1993 and 1994 revealed a considerable overrepresentation of ethnic Kazakhs (see Table 6.9). These figures indicate two things: that there was a marked Kazakh preponderance in the most important political organs of the republic and that this was growing. Within the presidential apparatus, this increase amounted to 6 percentage points in the course of a single year.

The Kazakh scholars behind these statistics explained the ethnopolitical discrepancies on the basis of demographic developments in the coun-

TABLE 6.9   Ethnic Distribution in Top Positions in the Government and
Presidential Apparatus of Kazakhstan, 1993 and 1994 (in percentages)

	1993			1994		
	Slavs	*Kazakhs*	*Minorities*	*Slavs*	*Kazakhs*	*Minorities*
Government	24.9	73.1	6.5	22.8	74.3	3.3
Presidential apparatus	25.8	67.7	6.5	22.8[a]	74.3[a]	3.1[a]
Share of total population				43.0	44.3	12.7

[a] First six months.

SOURCES: A. B. Galiev, E. Babakumarov, Z. Zhansugurova and A. Peruashev, *Mezhnatsional'nye otnosheniya v Kazakhstane. Etnicheskiy aspekt kadrovoy politiki* (Interethnic relations in Kazakhstan: The ethnic aspect of cadre policy) (Almaty: Institut Razvitiya Kazakhstana, 1994), 43; *O demograficheskoy situatsii v 1995 godu* (On the demographic situation in 1995) (Almaty: Pravitel'stvo Respubliki Kazakhstan, 1996), 66.

try: They admitted that "the major ethnic groups have differing degrees of representation" but added that this does not provide grounds for concern, since "the dynamics in ethnic representation are headed . . . in the same direction as are ethnodemographic developments in the country."[55]

In recent years the Kazakhs have definitely increased their share of the total population, whereas the Russophone population has decreased in both relative and absolute terms. A stream of Russians and other Russian-speaking groups has been leaving Kazakhstan, headed for Russia, Germany, and other countries. At the same time, the Kazakhstani authorities have been actively encouraging Kazakhs living outside the country to return.[56] Between 1991 and 1993, some 100,000 Kazakhs moved to Kazakhstan from Mongolia, Russia, and Iran.

In addition there are considerable differences in the birthrates of the various ethnic groups in Kazakhstan. Rural Kazakh families tend to have far more children than do Russians living in the towns and cities. As an overall result of natural growth and migration, the Kazakh share of the population of the republic increased from approximately 40 percent in 1989 to some 46 percent in 1995, whereas the Russian share during the same period fell from approximately 38 percent to less than 35 percent.[57]

Demographic developments may at most be a small part of the explanation of the ethnic disparities in the distribution of political posts and top-level administrative jobs. After all, such positions are held not by newborn babies but by fully grown adults. Thus, changes in ethnic composition of the population should not be expected to make their mark at this level until at least one full generation after they appear in population statistics. In Kazakhstan, however, the reverse seems to be the case: The pronounced overrepresentation of Kazakhs in top political posts comes not as a result of changes in the ethnic composition of the population but rather in advance of them.

Demography has become a central topic in the Kazakh nation-building discourse. A leading Kazakh demographer, M. Tatimov, sees the high proportion of children and young people in the Kazakh nation as indicating that this is a "young" nation. By the same token, the large share of pensioners and middle-aged among the Russians shows that the Russian nation is "old."[58] According to Tatimov's typology, the Ukrainian and Baltic peoples are also "old."

Tatimov goes on to say that when two "old" groups dominate on one and the same territory, there will often be a "psychological cold war" for control. The ethnic tensions in Estonia and Latvia, according to Tatimov, are expressions of this. In Kazakhstan, however, the situation is fundamentally different. Here one of the two dominant groups, the Kazakhs, is a young nation. This means that the Kazakhs will be able to defeat the Russians without challenging them to open battle, quite simply because time is on their side. In Kazakhstan the ethnic rivalry is thus a struggle fought in the bedrooms of the nation—so to speak—and here the Kazakhs cannot but win. By 2002 Kazakhs will make up over 55 percent of the total population, whereas the Russian share will have fallen to less than 30 percent, concludes Tatimov.

In fact, it is not so certain that he will be proven correct. The exodus of Russophones reached a high-water mark in 1994—two years later than the same development in Latvia. Since that time it has lessened. Perhaps most of the Russians and Germans who wished to leave the country— and who had possibilities for so doing—have already departed. In 1996 the total loss in population due to out-migration was only half the corresponding figure for 1994: 179,000 as against 411,000.[59] In addition there are reports indicating that even the ethnic Kazakhs are beginning to have fewer children. This has long been in evidence in the urban areas, where Kazakh residents have a lifestyle and family structure not so unlike that of the Russians. What is new is that the drop in population growth is spreading to the countryside, partly as a result of falling standards of living and poorer health services. This also means that the tendency may reverse itself when (or if) Kazakhstan gets a better grip on its economy. It might also be a more permanent trend.

Lack of Russian Mobilization

On several occasions the Russian authorities have delivered harsh criticism of the treatment of Kazakhstan's Russian population. And even though today's Russia is not the superpower that the USSR once was, it is undeniably the most powerful regional actor in this part of the world.

Russia has considerable economic muscle to underpin its demands, since Kazakhstan is far more dependent on its trade with Russia than vice versa.

Seen as a group, the Russophones of Kazakhstan must be considered to be resource-strong. They have a high average level of education and are particularly well represented among the technical intelligentsia. In this respect they differ somewhat from the Russophones of the Baltic states, far more of whom are industrial workers. The Russians of Kazakhstan might be assumed to have in their midst strong potential leaders and to be able to organize in defense of their interests. On several occasions political parties and movements in Kazakhstan have emerged with the interests of the Russophones as their particular focus. Some of these are now permanently or temporarily banned for having broken the laws of the country, as has been the case with various Cossack leagues that have been hit by the prohibition against paramilitary movements. Some Russian activists have also announced that they do not recognize the legitimacy of the Kazakhstani state and have openly declared that all or parts of the country should be annexed to Russia. A few Russophones have received prison sentences for such statements, which has in turn unleashed sharp protest from Moscow.

The largest and most representative Russophone organization in Kazakhstan is the Slavic league Lad (Harmony). In 1993 Lad had a membership of some 10,000, an impressive figure for Kazakhstan.[60] In elections to Kazakhstan's Supreme Soviet in 1994, the league gained four seats; however, representation in the new Mazhilis after the 1995 election was reduced to a single representative, and a rather disillusioned one at that.[61] Today it seems safe to conclude that Lad no longer has a role to play.

Lad is not an extremist organization: It is willing to take part in the political life of Kazakhstan on the premises defined by the powers of the state. All the same, on some occasions Lad has been subjected to bans on its activities, for instance, when it has participated in joint arrangements with other, more right-wing organizations. There are also other ways in which Lad and similarly law-abiding Russian-speaking groups have been countered, openly or more discreetly, by the authorities. This is probably an important part of the explanation behind the weak degree of political mobilization found among the Russophones of Kazakhstan.

The authorities have deliberately sought to split up the Russophone population into small, more manageable groups that are also politically weaker. Ukrainians, Belarusians, Germans, Jews, and other Europeans are encouraged to rediscover their more or less forgotten ethnic identities. In 1995 President Nazarbayev established the Assembly of the Peoples of Kazakhstan as an advisory organ under the presidency. This assembly has subdivisions in all counties of the republic and has at its disposal a

certain amount of means for supporting organizational work among ethnic minority groups. The precondition is that such work be strictly apo-
litical and purely cultural. As one of its duties, the assembly administers
admission quotas for minority students applying for higher studies. The
quota represents 10 percent of all admissions throughout the country; in
1995–1996 some 2,500 students benefited from its provisions.[62] Young
people from all the non-Kazakh ethnic groups—except Russians—are entitled to apply. Surely this is a clear signal to non-Russian minorities that
they should seek their futures outside the Russian-language fellowship.

There are also some indications that this divide-and-rule strategy is
bearing fruit. In April 1995 Nazarbayev prolonged his tenancy as president until the year 2000 by means of a referendum—in other words, the
presidential elections scheduled for 1996 were canceled. Prior to this referendum, one Lad leader urged the electorate to vote against what she
saw as a step in the direction of a more authoritarian regime. Kazakh
commentators noted with satisfaction, however, that certain Polish, Belarusian, and Ukrainian spokespersons supported the proposal; this was
taken as a sign that the Poles, Belarusians, and Ukrainians are more loyal
than the Russians, not only toward the president but indeed toward the
Republic of Kazakhstan.[63] Incidentally, the motion was passed with over
90 percent of the vote in favor.

•   •   •

As we saw in Chapter 2, as early as the 1960s and 1970s the non-Russian
Soviet republics began increasingly to be viewed as the "property" of the
titular population, perhaps as a kind of compensation for the fact that
Russians and other Slavs monopolized so much of Soviet politics at the
central level. These ideas would seem to have been strengthened after the
dissolution of the USSR and today act as a brake on the political involvement of the Russophone populations. Even in those cases where they
enjoy the full formal range of civic rights, Russophones often appear to
see politics as a matter for the titular population.

To some extent we can explain the power relations between ethnic
groups in Latvia and in Kazakhstan as a result of shared Soviet experiences, such as institutionalized and objectified ethnicity, and ethnic rights
for members of the titular nations within their territory. But it appears
that power relations in these countries reflect a more universal pattern as
well. Outside the post-Soviet area there are bicultural states in which one
ethnic group has managed to achieve political hegemony, even if all citizens of the country have the same formal rights. R. Milne has undertaken
a comparative study of three such countries in the Third World: Fiji,
Malaysia, and Guyana.[64] On the Fiji islands, the Fijians have the upper
hand over the Indians; in Malaysia the Malays have gained a series of

special political rights even though the Chinese population is better educated and wealthier; and in Guyana parties that primarily represent the
Creole-black descendants of liberated African slaves have been in power
ever since independence in 1966, even though immigrants from India
constitute a numerically larger group.

Despite the many clear differences among these three states, they share
one important feature—which they also share with Latvia and Kazakhstan: In all these states, political power is in the hands of the most "native" ethnic group. In Fiji and Malaysia, this is the titular group: They
have (as is the case with Latvia and Kazakhstan) given their name to
their respective countries and view themselves as its rightful "owners."
In the case of Guyana, all of the present population are immigrants: The
Indians arrived voluntarily in the 1800s, whereas the Africans came
against their will many generations earlier. This means that the Africans
have lived there the longest, which may well explain the emergence of
a political constellation corresponding to that found in other bipolar
countries. According to Milne, this situation has made the nonnative
population groups in these countries "adopt, or acquiesce in, arrangements which limited participation but also limited the possibility of
violence."[65]

Since Milne wrote his comparative study in 1981, both Malaysia and
Fiji have taken long strides in the direction of ethnic hegemony of the
titular group. Since the early 1980s and the accession of Mahathir
Mohamad as prime minister, the Malaysian state has become more re-
pressive. "Accommodation has been marginalized, and ethnic relations
have deteriorated, although there have been no serious ethnic clashes."[66]
In Fiji military coup makers in 1987 oversaw the promulgation of a new
constitution that assigned disproportionately higher representation to
ethnic Fijians over other groups. "Further, in all major areas such as taxation, civil service appointments, recognition of religion, Fijians were accorded preferential treatment."[67] In this country, too, these changes were
brought about without bloodshed.

Thus, it would seem that ethnically bipolar states are *not* always as un-
stable as Horowitz assumed. The Horowitz thesis of sharp ethnic con-
frontations in those instances where two and only two groups are battling
for state power is often neutralized by what we might call the Milne effect. This is quite clearly the case in Latvia and Kazakhstan. Two groups
that are numerically similar will not necessarily be similar in other,
equally relevant respects—such as social structure, access to resources, or
in terms of collective ideas as to who is "entitled" to rule. And that in turn
means that we can once again discern the general ethnocentric pattern in
post-Soviet nation-building—where we might least expect to find it.

7

Two Romanias,
Two Moldovas

During the Communist period, it was generally believed in the West that
what Soviet sources termed "Moldovans" were actually Romanians.[1]
High politics had split the Romanian nation in two, forcing its members
to live as a divided nation, in two states. As soon as the totalitarian
regimes were out of the way and the people were allowed to decide for
themselves, they would unhesitatingly join together in a single state—or
so it was held. Any separate "Moldovan" nation-building project seemed
just as unthinkable as a separate East Germany without communism. As
we know, some East Germans did in fact try to find acceptance for such
a separate nation after the fall of the Berlin Wall. These efforts proved
short-lived, however, in the face of German reunification.

And yet there exist today two separate states where the titular populations are Romanian-speaking. Thus, some might doggedly insist that
there are two Romanias—Romania itself and Moldova. This is, however,
a moot question. Strong forces are at work fighting for the soul of
Moldova. The majority of the population today would say that Moldova
is not Romanian but simply "Moldovan." In addition we have yet another (quasi) state with pretensions to being Moldovan—the breakaway
republic east of the Dniester. It could be said, then, that there are not only
two Romanias but also two Moldovas. And finally, a separate national
area has been established for the 150,000 or so ethnic Gagauz in southern
Moldova who now have a constitution and a national assembly of their
own. There is certainly no dearth of nation-building projects in this
southwesterly corner of the former Soviet Union.

•   •   •

Under perestroika Moldovan mobilization against Soviet power was channeled into the Moldovan Popular Front, an organization clearly modeled on the Baltic pattern. It began by taking up very sensitive issues: the Ribbentrop-Molotov pact and the language situation in Moldova. The Soviet authorities, the front insisted, would have to concede that Moldova had been snatched from Romania in 1940 and annexed on the basis of the secret deal struck between the dictators Stalin and Hitler. Second, Moldovan must be accorded status as the state language in Moldova. Furthermore, the language should be written in the Latin and not the Cyrillic script—as is Romanian and indeed as was the case in Bessarabia when the area was part of Romania during the interwar years. (Until 1918, however, it was written in Cyrillic, as in Romania proper prior to the mid-nineteenth century.)

In Moscow these demands were interpreted as the first steps in a strategy that would gradually expand to include further demands—for secession from the USSR and reunification with Romania. Fears of this eventuality were rampant as well among the various minority groups in Moldova. As a counterforce to the Moldovan Popular Front, another movement was established: the United Council of Workers' Collectives (UCWC, or OSTK in Russian). UCWC had branches on both sides of the Dniester but was especially strong in the industrialized areas of eastern Moldova. It organized several large-scale demonstrations and strikes in protest against the draft language law. Despite its name, UCWC was not first and foremost a workers' union or a trade union but had been formed on the initiative of the factory management. The factories sited along the banks of the Dniester were under the direct control of the powerful ministries of industry in Moscow, and the local directors risked losing all their influence and power if these links with Moscow were broken. Thus, in what might appear as a purely cultural struggle for language and alphabet there were in reality more tangible and mundane interests at stake as well.

Opposition to the new Moldovan language law ran deep not only in the industrial centers of the Dniester region but also among impoverished Gagauz peasants in the villages of the south. The Turkic-speaking Gagauz had never enjoyed any autonomous status within the Soviet federation and thus lacked any institutionalized form of protection for their own language and culture. Actually, to call them Turkish- or Turkic-speaking is perhaps a bit of an exaggeration. Most of them use Russian for everyday communication and lack fluency in either Gagauz or Moldovan.[2] A small-scale popular front was formed, Gagauz Khalki (The Gagauz people), to fight for autonomy for the Gagauz.

This opposition from non-Moldovans did not deter the Moldovan Popular Front. To the contrary: The new language law was adopted to thunderous acclaim on 31 August 1989 by the Supreme Soviet of Moldova. This day was to mark a milestone in Moldovan history, and even today one of the main thoroughfares in Chișinău, the capital of Moldova, bears the name "31st of August Street." The letter of this new law was in fact very liberal: Bulgarian, Yiddish, Gagauz, Ukrainian, Romany, "and others" were all recognized as minority languages with cultural functions within their respective circles. Russian—alongside Moldovan—was defined as the "language of interethnic communication." At the same time, the law stipulated that the state language was Moldovan and that this was to be used in all public administration (with translation into Russian as necessary).[3] Many of the clauses and paragraphs, however, were either unclear or self-contradictory. This enabled rather arbitrary interpretation, and in many offices and institutions Russophones either lost their jobs or were not granted promotion, their employers pointing to the new language law.[4] Language tests for future job applicants, supposed to be held by 1995, never occurred.

In the school system, a pronounced Moldovization or Romanization also took place. The teaching of the history of the USSR was replaced by instruction in the history of the Romanians. Many Russian-medium schools were closed down or transformed into Moldovan-medium institutions. It is difficult to estimate the extent of the school campaign more precisely because Russian and Moldovan sources operate with noncomparable figures.[5] The Moldovan school authorities maintain that the medium of instruction was changed in line with the wishes of the parents, which may well have been correct in some cases. Most Moldovan parents who had previously sent their offspring to Russian-medium schools now wanted them to be instructed in the Moldovan tongue. Yet those schools that continued to teach in Russian soon became overfilled and even had to teach in shifts—which would indicate that the authorities were closing down the schools faster than the pupils were deserting them.

In the spring 1990 elections to the Moldovan Supreme Soviet, the popular front together with affiliated groups won a landslide victory, and one of the front leaders, Mircea Druc, formed the new government. The popular front saw its government as a purely transitional ministry: Its mission was to wind up the Moldovan Soviet Republic and join the country to Romania. In protest, on 19 August 1990 the Gagauz proclaimed their own autonomous republic, with the village of Komrat in southern Moldova as its capital. Only a fortnight later, a popular meeting was convened in Tiraspol on the Dniester, and the Dniester Moldavian Republic (DMR) was proclaimed.

No statues of Lenin have been torn down in Tiraspol, and the DMR state emblem features both the hammer and the sickle. In many ways this

Courtesy of Trond A. Svensson

tiny area would seem a museum of past history. But we should not exaggerate the importance of Communist ideology in the Dniester state. The number of former party bosses in the top administration is probably no higher than in most other post-Soviet states. The ideological differences between Tiraspol and Chişinău were rooted mainly in what the new leaders wanted to distance themselves from: For Chişinău, Moscow was the political Other, the opposite pole, so the new Moldovan ideology became anticommunism. In Tiraspol, however, the main opponent was Chişinău, so here the ideology became anti-anticommunism.

During the abortive August 1991 coup attempt in Moscow, an article was published in the UCWC newspaper in Tiraspol declaring support for the putschists. As a result, UCWC leader Igor Smirnov was kidnapped in Kiev (that is, in the territory of another country) by agents from the Moldovan security forces and taken to Chişinău, where he was incarcerated until court proceedings could be initiated. This action spurred a women's committee affiliated with the UCWC to organize a blockade in Tiraspol of the railway line linking Chişinău with Ukraine. Angry elderly women took up their places astride the railway tracks, armed with posters and knitting. As practically all Moldovan transport communication with the rest of the Soviet Union used to pass through Tiraspol-controlled territory, this effectively choked the Moldovan economy. Shortly thereafter, Smirnov was released without trial. He returned in triumph to Tiraspol and was elected president of the self-proclaimed Dniester Republic on 1 December 1991. On the same day, the independence of the republic was confirmed in a referendum by over 95 percent of the vote.[6] At this referendum the town of Bendery (Tighina) voted to join the DMR even though it is located on the western (right) bank of the Dniester.

In order to uphold its independent status, the Dniester Republic set about building up its own defense forces, the Republican Guard. These forces were, however, modest when compared with the enormous war machine represented by the Soviet Fourteenth Army. The latter was stationed outside Tiraspol as a kind of cold war leftover: The rationale had been that in case of a third world war, it would fight its way down the Balkans and take control of the Straits of Bosporus. With the collapse of the Soviet Union, these military divisions had lost their raison d'être. Nor was there anyone willing to assume responsibility for maintaining the officers and soldiers—until April 1992, when Boris Yeltsin signed a decree declaring that the Fourteenth Army was to be Russian.

A great many of the officers and soldiers of the Fourteenth came from the Dniester area and sympathized with the breakaway republic. For a long time, the army leaders sought to keep their divisions out of the increasingly frequent skirmishes between the Dniester Guard and Moldovan police forces. In spring 1992 these skirmishes were to take a toll of several human lives. In that way both sides got their first martyrs, and conflict lines hardened. In June Moldovan forces attempted to storm the Dniester Republic right bank bridgehead at Bendery. After hard fighting, they were about to take the town when tanks from the Fourteenth Army began rolling over the bridge from the opposite bank. The army recaptured Bendery within a few hours—in a matter of minutes, according to some.[7] The death toll was between 500 and 1,000, most of them soldiers but many civilians as well.[8]

On 21 July 1992, a cease-fire agreement was signed in Moscow between Yeltsin and Moldova's president, Mircea Snegur. By the terms of this agreement, Moldova was to remain a unified state, whereas the Dniester region was to be granted "special status." Just what that was supposed to mean was the subject of countless rounds of negotiations between Chișinău and Tiraspol in the ensuing years, negotiations in which the OSCE and Russia were also involved as mediators.

A security zone was drawn up between the two parties, and a joint peacekeeping force was stationed there consisting of three battalions from Moldova, three from the Dniester Republic, and six from Russia. Trade and free movement between the areas on both sides of the river were resumed.

In the shelter of the security zone, the leaders in Tiraspol could again concentrate on their state-building project. A separate DMR government moved into what had been the offices of the Tiraspol municipal administration. Special DMR laws were enacted, including a law on separate citizenship for the Dniester Republic. In deliberate contrast to the nationalizing regime in Chișinău, Tiraspol leaders opted for a nonnationalistic or even antinationalistic concept of the nation. The DMR has been given no less than three official languages—Moldovan, Ukrainian, and Russian. Note that the first of the three is Moldovan, not Romanian, and it is to be written using the Cyrillic alphabet. Fluency in Moldovan or Ukrainian is highly limited among the political elite of Tiraspol, however, and these languages are rarely employed in "state-level" public administration. (They are, though, used in Ukrainian-speaking villages in the north and Moldovan-speaking villages in the south.) When the republic had its own currency printed in Moscow in 1994, the Dniester ruble notes bore inscriptions in all three official languages, but the Ukrainian text contained an embarrassing spelling mistake that spoke volumes as to the linguistic proficiency of its authors.

Western media have often presented the DMR as a Russian minority regime where Moldovans suffer oppression.[9] The so-called school war that raged in 1994 provided fuel for these fires. When it was discovered that some Moldovan-medium schools had, in contravention of the new

DMR laws, started using the Latin alphabet, some teachers were dismissed. The parents of Moldovan-speaking children held demonstrations and a school strike. The Dniester government realized that this conflict was bad publicity and sought to downplay it as much as possible, whereas UCWC activists wanted to bring matters to a head.[10]

Moldovans who express pro-Romanian attitudes are indeed liable to harassment and even persecution in Dniestria. At the same time, many of the most vehement anti-Romanians in Tiraspol are Moldovans themselves. The Russianized Moldovans of Dniestria established their own association under the leadership of the head of Tiraspol State University, Valeriy Yakovlev. Whenever the Tiraspol government seemed to be revealing the slightest indications of accommodation toward Chişinău, members of this group would raise an outcry. Yet there have been several other ethnic Moldovans in the Dniester leadership accounted to be relatively moderate, among them the leader of the DMR Supreme Soviet, Grigore Marakutsa.

Turnabout in Moldovan Nation-Building

The defeat in the June war of 1992 dealt a hard blow to pro-Romanian unionists in the popular front. President Snegur, who had been loosely associated with the front, had never been an active advocate of unification and after the war came out as a strong antiunionist. If he were to have any chance of reuniting the eastern and western banks of his country, any and all plans of reunification with Romania would have to be shelved. Snegur then replaced the popular-front-dominated government with one formed on the basis of the Democratic Agrarian Party, which pursued an antireunification line. Having ended up in the opposition, the Moldovan Popular Front split. The more moderate elements formed the Congress of Intellectuals, whereas the rump front became fanatically obsessed with a single issue: reunification with Romania.[11] Demonstratively dropping the adjective *Moldovan* from its name, the organization termed itself the Christian Democratic Popular Front. It also tried to avoid, wherever possible, using *Moldova* as the name of the country, referring instead to *Bessarabia*.[12] In a kind of symbolic anticipation of the desired event, front leader Mircea Druc took up Romanian citizenship and stood for election to the Romanian presidency in autumn 1992, but he garnered less than 1 percent of the vote.

Throughout 1993 a hard tug-of-war was fought over formulation of the Moldovan constitution. A major bone of contention concerned what to call the state language. The Constitutional Commission proposed *Moldovan*, whereas the popular front launched a counterproposal: *Romanian*.[13] This might sound like splitting hairs, a mere semantic quibble, but we should recall that both sides saw the language issue as representing a direct preliminary skirmish to the decisive battle for the future of their state: If the state language were Romanian, then the Moldovans were to be considered Romanians, and Moldova, strictly speaking, was then a Romanian state. In that case reunification would be only natural. A compromise resolution was submitted by the parliamentary chairman, Petru Lucinschi, the future president: "Moldovan, which is identical with Romanian." In the end, *Moldovan*, without any qualificatory explanations, was the term adopted.

In March 1994 President Snegur called a referendum in which a full 95 percent of those voting supported the independence of the Moldovan state. The Christian Democratic Popular Front charged that the results were manipulated, but even if that were the case, this was an overwhelming vote of confidence to the nation-builders of Moldova.

Moldovan intellectuals within the Democratic Agrarian Party formed the association Pro Moldova and sought to develop a suitable ideology for an independent Moldovan state. Pro Moldova emphatically maintained that the Moldovans are a different ethnos than the Romanians and that the Moldovan language is significantly different from Romanian.[14] The historian Vasile Stati wrote *Moldovans in History*, in which he traced a separate Moldovan people and Moldovan identity all the way back to the 1300s.[15] The cover of the book featured a map of Greater Moldova from the time of Stephen the Great. Since about half of the realm of Stephen lies within the borders of present-day Romania, one might be forgiven for suspecting Pro Moldova of harboring irredentist or even imperialist ambitions.[16] This was in fact scarcely the case: It was more an expression of the view that attack is the best defense.

President Snegur wished to find a third way between Pro Moldova and the Christian Democratic Popular Front. He launched the motto "Politically Moldovan, Culturally Romanian" to describe the dual nature of the Moldovan state. But as Charles King has pointed out, Snegur's in-between position was far from pellucid. His statements were frequently opportunistic, tailored to suit the wishes of his audience. It is not clear how to reconcile the promises of retaining the state's Moldovan character Snegur offered to the national minorities and separatists in the Dniester Republic with the ethnic concept he bandied about in his bouts with the Pan-Romanians.[17]

In March 1995 the Moldovan Ministry of Education announced that the school subject "the history of the Romanians" was to be replaced by a new one, "Moldova's history." This decision triggered vehement protests among the pro-Romanian elements of the populace. Led by students, tens of thousands marched in the streets in Chişinău, demanding that "the history of the Romanians" be reinstated in the curriculum and that the state language be called Romanian. These demonstrations attracted as many as 60,000 on a single day.[18] That is a large number for such a small place as Chiçinau and was enough to make Snegur retreat. Meeting with student leaders, he promised to recommend to the national assembly that the state language change its official name. And this in turn unleashed an indignant outcry in the Democratic Agrarian Party, from whose ranks Snegur resigned in protest. At this point most of the Russians and other non-Moldovans who had hitherto supported Snegur in his struggles with the pro-Romanians of the Christian Democratic Popular Front now turned their backs on him.[19]

Moldovan Nation-Building and the Non-Moldovans

After 1992 the Moldovan concept of the "nation" developed in various directions. The idea of the ethnically defined nation-state was gradually replaced by other concepts—sometimes more multiethnic, at other times civic, at still other times binational. In August 1992 one of President Snegur's closest advisers on ethnic questions declared that Moldova was a Moldovan national state, not a multinational one.[20] From 1994, however, Moldova was increasingly referred to in official connections as a "multiethnic state."[21] In a conversation with me in 1996, that same adviser advocated that all information on ethnic background should be removed from Moldovan passports, since no ethnic distinctions should be made among people. At the same time, however, he stated that there were two national groups that were to enjoy special status in Moldova—Moldovans and Gagauz. This he explained by the fact that most members of these two groups live within the borders of Moldova, whereas all others—Russians, Ukrainians, Bulgarians, Jews—already have their own national states elsewhere in the world.[22]

The new special treatment accorded to the Gagauz in the Moldovan concept of the state was followed up by an agreement with the Gagauz leaders in December 1994. A new law gave autonomy to a separate Gagauz homeland, Gagauz Yeri, comprising the area around several villages in southern Moldova. This law has the status of the constitution of Gagauzia, next to the constitution of Moldova. Gagauz Yeri has three official languages: Gagauz, Moldovan, and Russian. The area also has its own symbol and its own popularly elected assembly—the latter, however, with little real power. If at some point in the future the status of Moldova as an independent state should be changed (by which is understood through reunification with Romania), the population of Gagauzia will be entitled to choose full independence.[23]

There were great expectations that the solution to the Gagauz problem would breathe new life into the sluggish negotiations between Chişinău and Tiraspol. At a meeting held between the parties in summer 1995, several important agreements were signed, including one on bank cooperation and a mutual pledge not to resort to violent means. But there was no real breakthrough. When fall arrived, the chill also descended upon the negotiating table.

The obstinacy of the Dniester leaders did not reflect their actual negotiating strength, which had been growing weaker and weaker. Since 1992 the Dniester Republic had experienced both severe economic decline and serious political shake-ups. In the midst of the June 1992 war, the Russian Fourteenth Army had been assigned a new commander, General Aleksandr Lebed. His rough Russian nationalistic rhetoric soon made him an especially popular person in the Dniester Republic, but he rapidly came to blows with the leadership. The head of the DMR secret police, Vadim Antufeyev, had formerly been among the leaders of the Soviet forces in Latvia and was a wanted man in that country because of his participation in the January 1991 bloodshed in Riga. He had been living in Tiraspol under the alias Shevtsov until Lebed's men made public his true identity. Shevtsov was one of several powerful Dniester politicians accused of corruption, contacts with the Russian mafia, and harsh persecution of opposition figures. Winter 1993–1994 found the Dniester Republic on the verge of a new civil war, this time not left bank versus right bank but various factions on the left pitted against each other. The Smirnov regime, however, managed to ride out the storm, and no violence occurred.

In October 1994 an agreement was signed between Moldova and Russia that provided for withdrawal of the Fourteenth Army over a three-year period, counting from the moment when the agreement was ratified. Russian ratification, however, was not forthcoming, and many doubted whether Russia would respect the agreement. Even so, the army was gradually diminishing in resources and size anyway, perhaps mainly because of the general problems affecting the entire Russian defense apparatus. In addition, Lebed found himself in trouble with his superior in Moscow, Defense Minister Pavel Grachev. In April 1995 Lebed resigned his command and embarked on a new career in Russian politics—with remarkable success in the July presidential elections. For Smirnov in Tiraspol, Lebed's departure was heaven-sent: It meant he was rid of his most dangerous critic. At the December 1995 elections to the new Supreme Soviet in the Dniester Republic, groups on Smirnov's side received even greater backing than they had garnered in the 1991 Dniester parliamentary elections.

But the economy of the DMR had ground to a halt. Scarcely any market reforms had been implemented. The value of the new Dniester ruble—which was not a currency but merely a payment voucher—plummeted. Notes with more and more zeros rolled off the presses. By summer 1995, average income in the DMR had fallen to the equivalent of $7 to $10 a month. This began to contrast increasingly with developments on the west bank of the Dniester. Not that people there were wealthy, but generous loans and guarantees from the International Monetary Fund (IMF) and the World Bank ensured stability for the Moldovan leu. People in the DMR began putting their savings into lei.

Against this backdrop it is not easy to understand how the Dniester Republic could still manage to exist and enjoy the support of much of the population. At a December 1995 referendum on the new Dniestrian constitution, over 80 percent of the voters supported the continued existence of the DMR as a "sovereign and independent state." Many observers will, of course, say that such figures are without interest. They see the Dniester Republic as a totalitarian (quasi) state where all elections are just as pro forma as those of the Soviet Union.[24] In order to explain the survival capacity of the DMR, we shall probably have to look at several factors and circumstances. The 1992 war left permanent scars, creating a sharp distinction between "us" (the DMR) and "them" (the Chişinău politicians) in the awareness of the Dniestrian populace. The fighting thus served to strengthen and give shape to what has been termed a specific "Dniestrian identity."[25] This is an identity linked to a whole series of factors: language, geography, culture, history. The Dniester region has never been part of Romania, except for the period under the terror regime of Ion Antonescu during World War II. All the ethnic groups are considerably Russified, socialized into a Soviet lifestyle. The river Dniester forms a natural border to the rest of Moldova.

In December 1993 the CSCE delegation in Chişinău presented a proposal for a solution to the Dniester conflict, the so-called report number 13. Here it was explicitly stated that there exists "a separate Dniestrian feeling of identity" shared by all ethnic groups of the region.[26] Leading Moldovan politicians in Chişinău have acknowledged that the area to the east of the river has "distinctive features that must be recognized in any agreement."[27] Petru Lucinschi, who was elected president of Moldova in December 1996, has said that it would not represent any concession if Moldova were to grant to the Dniester region a separate status, as this would only reflect the region's "peculiarities," and "one must be naive not to take them into account."[28]

All the same, this does not mean that disagreement concerning the Dniester Republic can be reduced to a question of culture policy pure and simple. Power politics are very much involved as well. The Russian industrial leaders in Tiraspol who took the initiative in the formation of the UCWC in 1989 did so because they feared—and not without reason—

that they would lose economic power if Moldova were to become an independent state. They joined hands with Moldovan leaders from the Dniester region who were already witness to the disappearance of much of their political power. In Soviet times the Dniester Moldovans had been clearly overrepresented among the Moldovan political elite.[29] The Kremlin had felt more comfortable with those Moldovans who had never lived in a foreign country and who spoke fluent Russian as well. Then, under Gorbachev, there came a change in power relations between the east and west banks of the river Dniester. Mircea Snegur and Petru Lucinschi both belonged to the first generation of Moldovan Communist leaders to grow up west of the Dniester.

Thus, we can say that the general feeling of a separate Dniestrian identity began to coincide with the desire of the Dniestrian elite for power and positions. A similar correspondence between cultural specificity and the power ambitions of the elite also help explain why the desire for reunification with Romania has been so weak west of the river Dniester. In Bessarabia as well, historical, geographical, and political factors contributed to the formation of a separate Moldovan identity different from that of the Romanians. With the exception of a twenty-year period in the interwar years, Moldovans and Romanians have lived in separate states and under different political systems ever since the early 1800s. In this case, too, a river—the Prut—marks a clear dividing line between groups of people.

All the same, during the Soviet period most Western scholars focused almost exclusively on the linguistic fellowship between the Romanians and the Moldovans, citing that as proof that they shared a common identity. Indeed, some persist in calling the Romanian-speaking population of Moldova "Romanians."[30] Others, however, have now changed their views. For instance, the U.S. political scientist Vladimir Socor, who in the 1980s insisted that Moldovans were Romanians pure and simple, in 1992 was the first Western expert to declare unequivocally that the Moldovans had no wish to be reunited with Romania.[31] This he explained first and foremost on the basis of pragmatic and situational factors: The development of democracy in Romania under Ion Iliescu had not been proceeding very smoothly, to put it mildly. Nor would reunification yield any particularly great economic benefits for Moldova: Romania was just as poor, and the industrial/commercial structures of the two countries are very similar, so that they have little to sell one another.

Furthermore, many Moldovans—and now Socor as well—remembered that the interwar years had not been any rose garden for the Moldovans. As long as Moldova was ruled from Bucharest, Romanian politics remained largely the province of elites from the Regate (the territory of the pre–World War I Romanian kingdom), who paid scant attention to Moldova. And finally, as Socor has remarked, the leaders in Chișinău had to take into account the anxieties of the non-Moldovan minorities. Since Romania—even after the fall of Nicolae Ceausescu—was notorious for its harsh, ethnically based nation-building, these groups were terrified at the prospect of ending up as minorities in a Greater Romanian state. Preferable by far would be to remain minorities within a separate Moldovan state.

Several other scholars have reached the same conclusion as Socor but tend to emphasize other aspects, especially that concerning identity. Charles King has interpreted the 1994 referendum on Moldovan independence as clearly expressing that the Moldovans have rejected an ethnic Romanian identity and have developed one of their own. That is only to be expected, he feels. "Indeed, the real surprise about Moldovan identity is not the fact that the Moldovans have rejected their ostensible Romanianness, but rather the fact that so many Western observers, both journalists and scholars, predicted that they would embrace it."[32]

Germany's Claus Neukirch also places great importance on the Moldovans' development of a separate cultural identity. Although this identity is partly rooted in older times, he sees it as primarily a product of the Soviet era. During that period, almost all contact between Romania and Moldova was broken, and the Moldovans underwent a process of modernization, Soviet-style. This modernization affected first of all those living in urban areas, who became strongly influenced by Soviet and Russian culture, but in the rural areas as well Neukirch finds a specifically Moldovan identity distinct from that of Romania. Here the peasants have kept to their own local, Moldovan version of the language, which the intelligentsia—in Bucharest but also partly in Chişinău—dismiss as uncultured.[33]

According to Neukirch, rather than comparing relations between Romania and Moldova with the two Germanies, it makes more sense to draw a parallel to relations between Germany and Austria. The Austrians of today have an unquestionably national identity of their own, even though it did take a good while to develop.[34]

Neukirch introduces yet another important variable: the Moldovan elite. Most of them would have had little to gain from reunification and all the more to lose.[35] A great many top civil servants and politicians in today's Moldova would risk becoming redundant if Moldova were to (re)join Romania, so they have a very real personal interest in preventing any such development. Moreover, there will always be more prestigious positions in an independent state than in a mere province. Who, for example, would gladly switch over from being the director of the national bank to heading a measly provincial branch?

The only groups within the Moldovan elite with any self-interest in reunification are those involved in the cultural establishment—journalists, writers, historians. After all, they are professional practitioners of the Moldovan language, in its "cultured," Romanian version. In case of re-unification, these Bessarabian culture workers would be able to stand their own in competition with their professional colleagues from the Re-gate. And just as important, in a common Romanian state they would have a clear competitive edge over the more Russified portions of the Moldovan elite in Bessarabia. These culture workers were the groups that predominated within the popular front.

Within modern research on nationalism, some theoreticians place the main emphasis on the role of the elites in the emergence of national movements.[36] But others have stressed that no nationalist, however de-termined, can make something out of nothing: There must be some kind of cultural raw material from which to weave the fabric of the nation.[37] As we have seen here, both cultural identities and the interests of the elite are important to an understanding of the current nation-building projects in Moldova. In my opinion the Moldovan material does not provide a basis for maintaining that one of the main lines of thought within na-tionalism studies hit the mark more accurately than the other.

8

BELARUS: THE DOG
THAT DIDN'T BARK

Throughout the postwar period, Belarus (White Russia, Belorussia) was one of the most Russified of the Soviet republics. In 1960 only one-third of all books published in the republic were written in the Belarusian language; the remainder were largely in Russian. That was a low figure for the titular language of a Union republic, but it was to fall even lower. New figures released in 1971 showed almost total stagnation in the number of Belarusian titles, whereas nearly twice as many books were being published in the Russian language in Belarus—or the Belorussian Soviet Socialist Republic, as it was then known.[1]

When it came to the daily press, the picture seemed somewhat different: In the 1970s and 1980s, more Belarusian than Russian newspapers were printed in the republic. But the Belarusian newspapers were mainly local papers with low circulation figures in small rural districts; almost all of the widely read papers in the towns and cities were written in the Russian language. The dividing line between Russian and Belarusian cultural areas was basically an urban-rural one—and it was the former culture that was both dominant and expanding.

At the all-Soviet census of 1989, some 80 percent of the ethnic Belarusians of the republic indicated Belarusian as their native tongue. This was the lowest figure among all the titular nations in a Union republic—and even then it is probably unrealistically high. Many gave Belarusian as their native language even if they used Russian in everyday speech. There may be various explanations for this: People could have reasoned that they were, after all, Belarusians—that was what it said in their passports. And at any rate, they were definitely not Russians, and they *did* know some of the Belarusian language. Or perhaps their mother or father had spoken Belarusian, and that would have made Belarusian into a sort of mother tongue for them. Especially among young Belarusians there was considerable mismatch between the officially reported native language and the language actually used. Many Western experts took this as an indication that Belarusians would be assimilated into the Russian nation at an ever-increasing pace.[2]

Young Belarusians living in the easterly parts of the republic often experience the distance between their local dialect and standard Belarusian as just as great as that between their spoken language and standard Russian. The difference between standard Russian and standard Belarusian is somewhat greater than between, say, Scots dialect and standard English or Norwegian and Swedish: A Russian must listen carefully to understand someone speaking Belarusian. Nor is everyone willing to go to all that trouble. Back in 1959, when Nikita Khrushchev visited a Communist Party meeting in Minsk, the local party head gave his speech in Belarusian. Afterward Khrushchev whispered furiously to the person next to him, "I couldn't understand a damned thing!"[3]

The relationship between Russian and Belarusian in Belarus is not only a question of numerical ratios but also of prestige. The Khrushchev episode illustrates how Russian—like any other language—is spoken by all kinds of people, uncultured as well as cultured individuals. All the same, in Belarus the Belarusian language was generally considered an uncultured, peasant tongue, low in status, even by those who used it every day. It was Russian that stood for high culture. The Russian language was associated with modernization and a better standard of living. Until well into the 1950s, Belarus had been largely agricultural, with few large towns or cities and with a low standard of living. Then in the 1960s and 1970s, industries were established, especially within machinery construction. Belarus now became a major manufacturer of precision instruments, synthetic fibers, plastics, trucks, and tractors. By the 1980s the republic was the world's third largest in the manufacture of tractors. The brand name "Belarus" could be found on tractors the length and width of the Soviet Union. Such manufacturing industry was well paid in Soviet times, and the standard of living in Belarus rose, in the course of the 1980s even surpassing that of Russia.[4]

Belarusian peasant sons and daughters who moved to the towns and started working in the new factories earned far more than their mothers and fathers who kept on hoeing potatoes back on the farm. When they went to visit their children in their new Soviet-style apartments, they could admire the fridges and the television sets—and they would notice

154

Courtesy of Trond A. Svensson

that their children were speaking Russian. The blocks of flats were probably located in gigantic anonymous suburbs of the kind found throughout the Soviet Union. And yet such living quarters carried far greater prestige within the Soviet hierarchy of values than did the *izby* (peasant cottages) of the countryside.

Why precisely was Belarus selected for industrialization in the 1950s, 1960s, and 1970s? One important reason concerned the aftermath of World War II. Belarus was probably the Union republic that suffered the greatest material damages: According to official figures, 209 towns and cities were totally destroyed. In cities like Minsk and Vitebsk, perhaps 5–20 percent of the buildings remained; the need for reconstruction was enormous. And whereas this damage had been inflicted on the republic by foreign invaders, reconstruction could be carried out thanks to help and support from the Russian "brotherly people"—a point repeated time and again in official propaganda. Nor did the propaganda fail to point out that those Belarusian nationalists who had collaborated with the German forces of occupation had employed the national symbols of the Belarusian People's Republic of 1918 together with the Nazi SS emblem.[5]

Under Brezhnev there existed no Belarusian dissident movement akin to those found in Moscow, Leningrad, Kiev, and the Baltic republics.[6] At the same time, however, it is clear that in Belarus there existed a cultural intelligentsia who tended the national language and waited for the opportunity to stage a national renaissance: In the 1920s considerable progress had been made toward Belarusification, and afterwards it might still not have been too late. And then with perestroika it seemed that the time had finally come.

Perestroika and Belarusian Nationalism

A Belarusian Popular Front with a national democratic program was formed in June 1989. Its focus was directed primarily toward three main issues: rescuing the Belarusian language from oblivion, revealing the crimes committed under Stalin against the Belarusian people, and the Chernobyl disaster. As to this final point, it is true that Chernobyl itself is located in Ukraine. But it was Belarus that came to bear the brunt of the April 1986 disaster because of the prevailing winds that deposited as much as 70 percent of all the radioactive fallout on its territory. The despair and fury of the populace was directed not so much against the Ukrainian authorities as against Moscow, against the leaders in the Kremlin who had approved the construction of that unsafe nuclear plant and then shown so little will or capacity to help the victims after the accident there. No logical direct linkage, however, could be made between the popular Belarusian mobilization against nuclear power and the

struggle for national independence. After all, people who succeed in getting a state of their own, with control over their own territory, can manage to close the borders to other people, to goods, and perhaps even to
ideas—but not to radioactive fallout.

In order to mobilize the people around the idea of the "nation," it was
more important to bring out the real story of the Stalinist terror regime.
Excavations in the Kuropaty Forest outside Minsk revealed that the Belarusians had indeed fallen prey to the dictator's full wrath. Here were
more than 500 mass graves of some 200,000 Belarusian peasants who had
been shot during the forced collectivization of the 1930s. On the Orthodox All Souls' Day in 1988, 3 October, the independent movement
Martyrolog arranged a memorial ceremony for these victims. The police
intervened, attacking the peaceable demonstrators with dogs and water
hoses. But these traditional means of repression no longer worked: Almost immediately, news of the treatment accorded the demonstrators
was featured on the front pages of the liberal glasnost newspapers in
Moscow. (In Minsk, by contrast, such publications scarcely existed.)

It was the leader of Martyrolog, the archeologist Zyanon Paznyak, who
took the initiative in establishing the Belarusian Popular Front. The
founding meeting took place in Vilnius in neighboring Lithuania: In
Belarus the Communists were still in full control and would not permit
any such activity. In February 1989 the popular front arranged a mass
gathering in Minsk; over 40,000 people took part. In the course of that
one year, membership increased to over 100,000.[7] It seemed as if the
Belarusian opposition had finally managed to mobilize past the decisive
threshold after which a chain reaction of new recruitment sets in.

The winds of nationalism blowing across the wide plains of Belarus also
swept into the Supreme Soviet of the republic. In January 1990 this assembly—which had always been content to murmur a docile yes and amen to
each and every decree from Moscow—passed a new law making Belarusian the official language of the republic. This language law proclaimed, in
rather high-flown rhetoric, that "a language is not merely a medium of
communication; no, it is also the soul of the people. It forms the foundation
for the most essential part of the culture of a people. As long as the language lives, so will the people."[8] The various provisions of the language
law were to take effect in three to ten years. September 1990 saw the adoption of a detailed program of action for the development of the Belarusian
language and other languages used in the republic. Among the points on
the program was that within five years at the latest all correspondence and
written work within the public administration was to be in the Belarusian
language; likewise for teacher training within the republic.[9]

In March 1990 elections were held to the Supreme Soviets of all the Soviet republics. Although a multiparty system had not yet been introduced,

the popular front, together with other pro-reform forces, managed to gain a majority in all of the western republics—Estonia, Latvia, Lithuania, Moldova—except one: Belarus. The Belarusian Popular Front emerged with less than 10 percent of the mandates: only twenty-seven out of 345. Most of those who were elected came from the old *nomenklatura* elite. A political outsider was chosen as head of the Belarusian Supreme Soviet: Stanislau Shushkevich, former vice rector of the state university. Shushkevich and his supporters were democrats and moderate nationalists. Then, in July 1990, the Supreme Soviet of the republic adopted a formal declaration of sovereignty for Belarus—some time after similar declarations had been issued in most of the other Union republics. This document proclaimed that the Republic of Belarus was to be nuclear-free and nonaligned yet remain a component part of the Soviet Union.

In March 1991 Mikhail Gorbachev called a referendum on the future of the Soviet Union. Of the Belarusian populace, some 83 percent voted in favor of his proposal for a continued, renewed union—a higher figure than the results in any of the neighboring republics, including Russia. The mood was to change dramatically, however, after the failed Moscow coup attempt of August that year, not only among the general population but also among the leaders. Acting on motives of their own, many members of the Belarusian *nomenklatura* now proclaimed themselves keen advocates of an independent Belarusian state. Many of them had supported the putschists directly or indirectly and now feared that the new strongman in the Kremlin, Boris Yeltsin, would take revenge on them. If, however, Belarus and Russia were two independent states, that would make it harder for the democrats in Moscow to reach them. On 25 August 1991, the Supreme Soviet in Minsk declared Belarus an independent state. On 8 December, as speaker of the Belarusian national assembly, Shushkevich acted as host to the signing of the Belavezha agreement, which established the CIS.

The White Knight Stumbles, Then Falls

It would appear that a political atmosphere had been created that would make it possible to imbue the action program for Belarusification with more specific meaning. The number of books published in the Belarusian language was on the rise, and fewer and fewer books were being published in Russian. In the school year 1990–1991, less than 30 percent of all first-grade pupils had been taught in Belarusian; according to official sources, only two years later this figure had more than doubled, to 68.5 percent.

But these dramatic figures were misleading. Not enough teachers or textbooks in Belarusian were available for all these classes, and in practice Russian was frequently used as an auxiliary language, even in classes (ostensibly) instructed in Belarusian.[10] And at any rate, it would take decades before these young first-graders would be able to make their mark on a new Belarusian consciousness. An opinion poll conducted in summer 1992 in Minsk yielded some thought-provoking results. To the question of what they counted as their native tongue, 34 percent responded "Belarusian." This was clearly lower than at the census of 1989 (when 45 percent of those queried in Minsk had given Belarusian as their first language) but still far higher than the percentage of those who said that they actually had a *command* of Belarusian: only 18 percent. To this question 14 percent responded in the negative, whereas 68 percent said that they could understand the language without being able to express themselves in it. Only 3 percent said that they used Belarusian as their everyday language. Of those who did not have a command of Belarusian, 23 percent said that they intended to learn the language, whereas 77 percent had no such plans. Furthermore, 33 percent said that they supported the ongoing campaign of Belarusification, whereas 29 percent were opposed to it—and 21 percent said that they had not noticed that there was a Belarusification campaign under way at all.[11] Figures like that ought to be enough to discourage even the most dedicated nation-builder.

It soon became clear that no extensive legal settlement would be instigated in Moscow after the August coup attempt, whereupon the need of Belarusian politicians to distance themselves from Moscow dwindled rapidly. Early on, the conservative majority in the Belarusian national assembly began instead to work for close cooperation with their powerful neighbor. Parliamentary speaker Shushkevich was somewhat reluctant, however, refusing in May 1992, for instance, to sign the Tashkent Treaty, in which many CIS states pledged close security policy cooperation. Such cooperation, in his view, would be contrary to the nonaligned status Belarus had adopted. But the majority in the Belarusian Supreme Soviet put pressure on Shushkevich, who finally signed in April 1993, thereby putting an end to the country's brief flirtation with nonalignment.

In September 1993 Belarus entered into an agreement with Russia on a new type of common currency union to replace the ruble zone that had been dissolved earlier in the year. Then, in April 1994, came an agreement of intent for further economic integration between Belarus and Russia. All trade restriction and toll tariffs between the two countries were to be removed in the long run, and the Central Bank of Russia was to have full control over the issuing of currency in both countries.

In January 1994 Shushkevich was deposed by the Belarusian Supreme Soviet by 209 to thirty-six votes. The popular front also supported the vote of no confidence against him, although for different reasons from those of the Communists: Whereas the latter found Shushkevich too nationalistic, the popular front thought he had been too accommodating toward the *nomenklatura*.

In March 1994 a new Belarusian constitution was adopted. One of the main elements was the establishment of a strong presidency. At the presidential elections held in summer 1994, both Shushkevich and popular front leader Paznyak were among the candidates, but they received only 10 percent and 13 percent, respectively, of the total vote. The battle for this important post came to be fought between the prime minister, Vyacheslav Kebich, and the challenger, Alyaksandr Lukashenka. Lukashenka, who had been the foreman of a collective farm, had been a tabula rasa as far as politics went until he was voted into the Supreme Soviet on the Communist Party list in 1990. In autumn 1991 he had been the sole member of the Belarusian national assembly to vote against the CIS treaty that led to the disintegration of the USSR. Even then he had stood out as an uncompromising antinationalist.

In the Supreme Soviet, he was made head of the anticorruption committee, where he became known for harsh accusations against most of the political leaders in the country. In Lukashenka's eyes, almost every single Belarusian politician—including Shushkevich and Kebich—was corrupt. If he were elected president, vowed Lukashenka, he would send off the entire lot of them to the Himalayas.[12]

Prime Minister Kebich was backed up by the whole old party apparatus. From Moscow came clear signals that Kebich was the preferred candidate over the unpredictable Lukashenka. Still, Lukashenka won a landslide victory in the elections, garnering almost 85 percent of the vote in the second round. Both Lukashenka and Kebich had stood out as firm friends of Russia. Some Western commentators saw the presidential elections as a strange sort of contest of the highest bidder, with each of the main candidates trying to show himself more pro-Russian than the other.[13] But there were clear differences in nuance between the two. Kebich sought to appeal to pronationalist opinion as well; on one occasion he stated, "The fact that currently many Belarusians cannot even read Belarusian, are ashamed to speak in their mother-tongue, and cannot overcome their shame does confirm, once again, how we have destroyed our national mentality and why any efforts, state and public initiatives to revive our national history are so necessary and valuable."[14]

Statements like the above probably did not enhance Kebich's chances of victory. Few people like to be reminded of their shame or told that their mentality has been destroyed. Lukashenka, however, saw nothing shameful whatsoever in a weakly developed Belarusian consciousness. In February 1995 he stated, "Nothing great can be expressed in Belorussian. The Belorussian language is an impoverished one. There are only two great languages in the world—Russian and English."[15]

From his very first days as president, Lukashenka undertook serious attempts to limit democracy and freedom of expression in Belarus. A series of newspapers were temporarily closed down, editors were dismissed, and the postal system was forbidden to distribute certain foreign newspapers. In December 1994 several newspapers appeared with gaping white spaces showing where the censors had been at work. The reason? The papers had sought to print a parliamentary report that indicated that the Lukashenka administration was at least as corrupt as its predecessor had been.

On 14 May 1995, elections were held to the Supreme Soviet of Belarus. The president urged voters to boycott the polls, dismissing the parliamentarians as an incompetent and querulous lot not worth their salt. The people apparently heeded this advice: As a result of low voter turnout, only 119 of the 260 seats in the national assembly were filled; this was too little to constitute a quorum. Many observers presumed that Lukashenka wanted to use this situation as an excuse for getting rid of the entire popularly elected assembly and introducing a presidential dictatorship instead. At this point, however, the Belarusian Supreme Court declared that the president had no authority to dissolve the parliament on such grounds: By-elections would have to be held.

In the run-up to the December 1995 by-elections, there was practically no election campaigning, since the candidates were permitted to spend no more than the equivalent of $50 each on their election campaigns. Neither were they allowed slots on television, since TV appearances might influence the voters. This time, however, there was sufficient voter turnout—62 percent—to enable a quorum to be elected. Of the 260 members of the new national assembly, the Communists were the single largest group, with forty-two representatives. The majoritarian election system favored independent candidates, however, and as many as ninety-six of the new representatives were not affiliated with any political party.

Lukashenka had managed to ensure that on the same day as the parliamentary elections a referendum would be held. He himself had formulated the questions. The people were asked to give their support to four measures:

- abolish the new Belarusian symbols of state and reintroduce a variant of the country's old flag and coat of arms from the Soviet period
- introduce Russian as the second official language, next to Belarusian
- strengthen economic cooperation with Russia
- give the president the right to dissolve the Supreme Soviet

On all four of these points, Lukashenka received a clear mandate to do as he wished. A full 83.3 percent supported giving Russian the status of official language, and just as many favored stronger integration with Russia. Slightly fewer—75.1 percent—agreed that the white-red-white flag should be abolished and the white knight removed from the state coat of arms.[16] (Immediately prior to the referendum a film was shown on Belarusian television featuring pro-Nazi Belarusians during the war wearing uniforms with precisely the symbols that Lukashenka wanted to forbid.)

On a visit to Moscow in October 1995, Lukashenka talked about establishing an integrated state or confederation with Russia, with himself and Yeltsin alternating at the top.[17] But further integration between Belarus and Russia progressed slowly. It takes two to tango, and in Moscow leading politicians worried that full economic integration with Belarus could prove a highly costly affair for Russia. Very few market reforms had been implemented in Belarus, and the country was lagging further and further behind Russia in economic development.

It was not until the campaign prior to the 1996 Russian presidential elections that efforts toward integration really got under way. In the course of that spring, Yeltsin came to realize that the Communist challenger, Gennadiy Zyuganov, was breathing down his neck. Since Zyuganov was a keen advocate of greater integration among the CIS states, Yeltsin decided on some moves intended to take the wind out of the Communist sails. In late March 1996, Russia, Belarus, Kazakhstan, and Kyrgyzstan signed an agreement on closer economic cooperation. Only four days later, on the heels of this quadrilateral collaboration, came bilateral cooperation: On 2 April 1996, Lukashenka and Yeltsin signed a new, even more comprehensive union agreement between Russia and Belarus. This agreement includes both economic and political components and has been compared to the ties that linked together the republics of the former USSR. This new cooperation is officially termed the "Union of Sovereign Republics"—with an acronym, USR, perhaps more than coincidentally reminiscent of USSR. The Belarus-Russian union was deepened in April 1997, once more in April 1998, and then again in December 1999. But neither side has as yet ceded any sovereignty, and Russian spokespersons have tended to downplay the importance of the union. For his part, Lukashenka refers to it as a major step toward full state reunification.

This interpretation of the USR agreement is fully shared by the Belarusian opposition in the popular front. But whereas the president of the republic sees this as a step toward the Promised Land, to the popular front it means one step closer to ruin.[18] In the days prior to and after the signing of the first agreement in April 1996, large demonstrations involving up to 40,000 persons were held in Minsk.[19] These were the biggest mass gatherings in Belarus in many years. For a brief moment, it seemed as if Lukashenka had pressed his luck too far and had unleashed powerful nationalistic sentiment. The authoritarian president retained full control of the means of power, however, and had no qualms about using them. The demonstrations were dispersed by force, and arrest warrants issued for the organizers as well as several foreign journalists. Paznyak fled to Poland and was finally granted political asylum in the United States. Although the popular front still exists, it has been reduced to a mere shadow of its former self.

The power struggle with the Communist-dominated Belarusian Supreme Soviet continued until November 1996, when the parliamentary majority produced a draft constitution that would have abolished the presidency. Lukashenka, however, parried this challenge by presenting his own draft based on the Russian counterpart that granted him further powers. His version of a new Belarusian constitution was adopted after a referendum that Lukashenka, in contravention of Belarusian law, announced would be legally binding.[20]

Within the school system, the new political climate is reflected in a pronounced transition from Belarusian to Russian as the medium of instruction. For the school year 1995–1996, the number of first-grade classes in Belarusian-medium schools had sunk back to 25 percent.[21]

Perhaps Lukashenka's various moves on the Belarusification issue can be interpreted as expressions of a civic nation-building concept. The introduction of Russian as the second official language could be cited as evidence of this: Efforts to promote the Belarusian language at the expense of Russian could invite the risk of splitting the political nation into two camps. Decoupling the language issue from the project of nation-building was necessary to allow Lukashenka to forge ahead toward full noncultural nation-building. Or he might have done that had he so wished: He has not. On the contrary, many of his moves indicate that he is also opposed to political, nonethnic nation-building. In civic nation-building it is important to rally support around the country's own symbols of state and to ensure good control of the national economy. As we have seen, Lukashenka would prefer to get rid of all this as well. That is why I would say that his is *not* a program of civic nation-building: Instead, it is more an expression of skewed ethnic nationalism, a kind of distorted reflection of the views held by the popular front.

It can often seem as if Belarusian nationalists and antinationalists are thinking along the same lines—only they draw different conclusions from the same shared reasoning. The chain of thought consists of two components: (1) no language, no people; (2) no people, no state. As the

Belarusian language law puts it: "As long as the language lives, so will the people." More and more Belarusians came to register that in their circles the Belarusian language was *not* alive, so that must have led to the antithetical conclusion that the Belarusian people no longer existed either.

In 1993 the presidential candidate Vyacheslav Kebich had maintained that the Belarusian national mentality was "destroyed." Therefore, in his view, all conceivable efforts should be made at reawakening it. Many other Belarusians, however, have obviously drawn the opposite conclusion: What is destroyed is gone forever. Why bother trying to resuscitate it? Belarusian newspapers have run statements claiming that the Belarusian "idea of a national state . . . is simply absurd because it is based on a nation that does not exist. All that exists is a very small stratum of the population that, for certain reasons, has a need for the so-called Belorussian language." According to Russian scholars Dmitriy Furman and Oleg Bukhovets, these are views shared by the Belarusian president as well.[22]

This analysis seeks to reconstruct the reasons behind a series of choices made by the Belarusian elite as well as average Belarusian citizens. Together these choices have pushed Belarus further and further away from the kind of nation-building so often found in new states. One apparent weakness of this analysis is that it assumes a high degree of conscious choice among the actors. Terms like *reasoning* and *antithetical conclusion* presuppose rationality and a coolheaded balancing of alternatives. In reality, however, many of those who support Lukashenka on the Belarusification/Russification issue do so on the basis of a far vaguer, more emotionally laden foundation. Nor need they have any conscious feeling of deliberately undertaking a choice of identity: They simply avoid choosing one way or the other, between a Russian and a Belarusian identity, because the elimination of either seems equally unreasonable. But even if in many cases we should perhaps replace the expression *reasoning* with *gut feeling* or *sheer reflex*, that does not change my basic assumptions here.

Who Killed the Belarusian National Movement? Three Explanatory Models

Writing in 1996, George Sanford maintained that "Belarus has embarked on nation-building and is developing a national identity."[23] In view of the results of the May 1995 referendum, such a statement may seem odd indeed. But the tendency toward active nation-building is generally very strong in new states the world over, so we should not dismiss Sanford's conclusion out of hand. For instance, it might be that Lukashenka will gradually find himself a prisoner of what we may term "institutional logic." After all, he is the president of the independent state of Belarus and will necessarily identify his role with the institutions of that state.[24] Symbols are power, so Lukashenka may fall prey to the temptation to bolster up his personal power with more and more nation-state ornamentation. And if the day comes when he concludes that he and his people are no longer wanted in Russia, then Belarusian nation-building can become his fallback strategy. Then again, he could also be overthrown and replaced by more nationalist-oriented leaders.

At the moment this is mere speculation. Today's challenge is to explain why the Belarusian nation-building project seems to have missed its mark. Several explanations could be offered; we might divide them into three broad categories: To use rather rough and colorful analogies, the Belarusian national movement either was murdered, shot itself in the foot and then died of the injuries, or died on its sickbed. These three metaphors may be mutually exclusive, but I would not say the same of the real-life situation of Belarus. All three point up important aspects of the dynamics and the political processes that were to lead to the fiasco of Belarusian nationalism.

Murder Theory

According to this explanation, the old party elite of Belarus have managed, by nondemocratic means, to suppress the nationalist opposition. If the people were allowed to express their views freely, they would give full support to the project of nation-building. In 1994 the leaders of the popular front maintained that they would be able to win an election that was free and fair, conducted in line with a just electoral system and where all candidates were allowed access to the media.[25]

Beyond any doubt the old *nomenklatura* elite have retained firm control of most positions of power in Belarus. On various occasions they have put this power to active use in suppressing the nationalists. For example, in spring 1992 the popular front collected over 440,000 signatures on a petition demanding a referendum on new elections to the Supreme Soviet—far more than prescribed by law to force the authorities to hold the referendum. But the *nomenklatura*-dominated parliament did not want a referendum and quite simply refused to hold one.[26]

Yet this cannot be the whole explanation for why nation-building in Belarus has foundered. This so-called party of power was shown to be less than omnipotent when the outsider Alyaksandr Lukashenka managed a landslide victory over the *nomenklatura* candidate in the 1994 presidential elections. If an outsider can win over the establishment, then there seems every reason to account the elections as free and fair. Prior to the elections Lukashenka had profiled himself as more strongly pro-Russian than any of his opponents. This, however, need not have been what ensured his victory at the polls. It might equally have been his extreme populist version of anticorruption policy that went to the hearts of the voters. At any rate, we can certainly say that lack of Belarusian patriotism has not been a drawback in any elections since Belarus proclaimed its independence.

Self-Inflicted Wounds

It seems clear that the nationalists of the popular front have not made maximum use of the possibilities that have emerged since independence. Several observers have pointed out how the movement underwent a major radicalization in 1992–1993 and how this sharper profile cost them many adherents.[27] As the Belarusian Popular Front found itself losing influence, it reacted, like its Moldovan counterpart, by sharpening its demands rather than softening them. Instead of collaborating with the more moderate nationalists in the circle around parliamentary speaker Shushkevich, they turned against him. In the 1994 presidential election, Paznyak and Shushkevich faced one another as rival candidates rather than working together.

Shushkevich had taken pains to stress that his form of Belarusian patriotism was untainted by anti-Russian leanings. He insisted that "Russians and Belarusians are like two fingers on the same hand"—a type of rhetoric rarely found among the popular front.[28] Although the front has maintained that its policies have not been directed against the Russian minority of Belarus, many of its leaders have distinguished themselves through unrelentingly anti-Russian rhetoric.[29]

In April 1993 a Belarusian historian with popular front links claimed that Belarus and Russia have historically been poles apart: "They were two worlds and two separate civilizations. The one was characterized by feudalism, democracy, and freedom; the other by totalitarianism and despotism."[30] In early 1994 Zyanon Paznyak himself issued a scathing broadside against "Russian imperialism and its dangers."[31] In this article the popular front leader denounced Russia as an imperial state with an imperial public consciousness and an imperialist, expansionist policy. This imperial Russian tradition had, he maintained, prevented the emergence of a "fully developed European Russian nation and a fully developed European Russian consciousness. This is a patchwork of a people with no clearly demarcated national territory, speckled with Finno-Ugric, Turkic, Mongol, and other enclaves."

Although Paznyak accused the Russians of imperialism, he laid himself wide open to charges of Belarusian expansionism and irredentism:

> As a result of Russian Communist policy (the Ribbentrop-Molotov pact, the decrees of Stalin and Lenin, etc.) Belarus (the Belorussian People's Republic) lost one-third of its ancient territory with an indigenous Belarusian population, including the capital of Vilnius and the cities of Bialystok, Smolensk, Bryansk, Nevel, Sebezh, Novozybkov, Dorogobuzh, and vast areas to the east right up to Vyazma.[32]

With these words Paznyak implied that not only large areas of Russia but also portions of Poland and Lithuania (including the capital itself!) rightfully belonged to Belarus.

To the pro-Russian forces in Belarus, Paznyak's article was manna from heaven. The major Russian-language newspapers in Minsk and Moscow reprinted the most glaring passages again and again.[33] The Belarusian movement Belaya Rus', which holds that Belarusians, Ukrainians, and Great Russians are indeed three of a kind, were among those to profit from the publication of Paznyak's article. It enabled them to stand forth as the counterforce capable of preventing such popular front provocations from stirring up ethnic conflict in the peaceable society of Belarus. Two Russian scholars have noted how the Belarusian Popular Front "was caught in a kind of vicious circle: the more it compensated for its weakness with aggressive Russophobia . . . the more it frightened people away."[34] Paznyak, the unchallenged leader of the popular front and highly respected by the nationalists, soon became, in the words of David Marples, "the most intensely disliked of any individual politician in Belarus."[35]

Sickbed Hypothesis

Today a great many Western observers would hold that for historical and structural reasons Belarusian nationalism is doomed to remain too weak to catch on. Even if Belarusian nationalists had managed to avoid making so many tactical and strategic blunders, they would still never have stood a chance of winning the populace over to their cause. A thoroughgoing, sophisticated analysis based mainly on this line of thought has been presented by the Swedish scholar Barbara Törnquist Plewa.[36] Of decisive importance in her analysis are the historical and cultural factors mentioned earlier here: Belarus lacks a separate state tradition. Religion has not been able to serve as a national rallying point, since Catholicism has been seen as Polish, whereas the other dominant creed, Orthodoxy, is a source of Russification. Moreover, the Belarusian language finds itself squeezed between Polish and Russian, both of them with long traditions as literary languages.

Törnquist Plewa includes not only cultural but also socioeconomic factors in explaining why Belarusian nationalism has been so weak. A widely held view among scholars of nationalism is that periods of rapid modernization are particularly favorable for the growth of nationalist movements.[37] Young people from minority groups that receive higher education will often feel that the dominant society denies them career possibilities to which their abilities and degrees should entitle them. They then seek to create a somewhat smaller "dominant society" in their own image, one in which *their* language and cultural background give competitive advantages. When modernization finally came to Belarus after World War II, however, it failed to unleash any such dynamics. According to Törnquist Plewa, this was because it came too late: Belarusians never managed to develop an intelligentsia strong enough to create a viable national culture as an alternative to Russian culture.

Some of the factors that Törnquist Plewa adduces to explain the absence of Belarusian nationalism can also be found in societies that have nevertheless managed to create strong national movements in this century. In Lithuania, for example, the traditional economic structure has resembled that of Belarus. Lithuanians were drawn into the process of modernization at about the same time as the Belarusians—in the 1960s and 1970s. How, then, can Lithuanian nationalism be so strong today? Törnquist Plewa believes that it has been able to build on many other important sources that Belarusians have lacked: a clearly defined language, a state tradition that the people feel is "theirs," and affiliation to the Catholic Church as a sharp demarcation against the Russian Orthodox culture.[38]

These observations are both correct and important. All the same, Törnquist Plewa is perhaps making the task of explaining the absence of Belarusian nationalism too easy for herself. The point is not so much the different ways followed by Belarusians and Lithuanians. Far more remarkable is that the nation-builders of Ukraine have managed to convince their populace of the importance of an independent nation project, and the Belarusians have not. On the face of it, the objective conditions for successful nation-building in both Ukraine and Belarus would appear similar indeed. Both the Ukrainians and the Belarusians dwell in the borderlands between Russia and Poland and have throughout the centuries been subjected to considerable cultural pressures from both sides. And as to language, Ukrainian is even closer to Russian than is Belarusian.

In a comparative nation-building perspective, then, it is the contrast between Belarus and Ukraine that is the most interesting. Whereas the Belarusian dog has quietly lain down to sleep, his Ukrainian counterpart is standing nearby, barking away like mad. How has this come about? In the next chapter we will try to find some answers.

9

UKRAINE: BUILDING A NATION ON MARGINAL DIFFERENCES

In czarist times and during the Soviet epoch as well, Ukrainians and Belarusians were frequently accorded the same treatment. Prior to the Russian Revolution, they had been viewed as two lesser branches of the common Russian tree, dwarfed by the main—Great Russian—branch. After the revolution the Ukrainians and the Belarusians found themselves among that select group of Soviet nationalities who were able to make a career on an equal footing with Russians even outside their own republics.[1]

In his oft-cited 1965 survey of Soviet nationalities, John Armstrong spoke of the Ukrainians and Belarusians as "the younger brothers"—culturally close to the Russians but socially and economically far less modernized. Gradually, as Belarusians and Ukrainians left the countryside and moved into the towns and cities, said Armstrong, they would either become Russified or develop a strong separate ethnic identity of their own. Noting indications pointing in both directions, he concluded, "The question of the ultimate assimilation of the younger brothers therefore hangs in the balance." [2] Today it would appear that the balance is going to tilt one way for the Belarusians and the other way for the Ukrainians.

Ukrainian Regionalism and Nation-Building

Ukrainian society today is marked by strong regions and deep regional contrasts. This has presented Ukrainian nation-builders with special challenges. One modern presentation of Ukrainian nationalism concludes by saying that "historical and regional differences have combined to make nationalist political mobilization much more difficult than in many other parts of the former communist world, such as Transcaucasia and the Baltic states."[3]

As mentioned in Chapter 1, strong regional identities need not be a barrier to successful nation-building. Problems arise only when these identities become politicized and set themselves up as rivals to the pan-national project. In Ukraine there is no dearth of politicized regionalism: Galicia, Transcarpathia, northern Bukovina, Novorossia, the Crimea, and the Donbass areas are all examples of this. On most scores, however, these regionalisms are very different: In some areas it has an ethnic basis, in others not. Moreover, not all these instances of regionalism are equally strong and effective. Some are better seen as minor curiosities, whereas others represent true centers of power.

Finally, not all of these regionalisms are basically anti-Ukrainian, rival state projects. In only a few places is the regional force headed in a centrifugal direction, with regionalists wanting secession from the state. Elsewhere the force is centripetal: regionalists seeking to gain control of the center and mold the unitary state in their image. If, however, they do not succeed in this, they may do a quick about-face and emerge as adherents of separatism or regional autonomy.

Galicia

Ukrainian politics is often represented as split in two: eastern Ukraine on the one hand, western Ukraine on the other. The eastern regions are Russian-dominated and Soviet-nostalgic, whereas the western ones are heavily influenced by Ukrainian culture. Such a picture is painted with far too broad a brush, however. True, the river Dnieper does flow through Ukraine from north to south, dividing the country into two, almost equally large geographical areas, but it should not be seen as marking a firm cultural boundary. On the contrary: Both in the center and in the north there are large ethnoculturally "neutral" areas heavily influenced by both Ukrainian and Russian culture. Kiev, the capital, situated on the banks of the river, may be Russified as far as language goes, but in politics its denizens have tended to sympathize with Ukrainian national demands. (Indeed, much of the same duality is also typical of Minsk, the capital of Belarus.)

Strictly speaking, *western Ukraine* refers only to the three westernmost counties, L'viv, Ternopil, and Ivano-Frankivsk. From the late 1700s until World War I, these were part of the Habsburg empire and were ruled from Vienna. They formed the easterly portion of the province of Galicia, whose capital, Krakow, lies in what is now Poland.[4]

The major population groups in Galicia were Poles, Ukrainians (as the Habsburgs called the Ruthenians), Germans, and Jews. Ukrainians were the largest group in the east and Poles in the west, but in political matters Poles predominated throughout. This the Habsburgs accepted, albeit not without fears that the Poles might become too self-willed—which was why they encouraged a limited degree of national mobilization among the Ukrainians, as a counterweight.

During the first half of the nineteenth century, the Ukrainian movement in Galicia remained basically nonpolitical and oriented toward Russia. Its leaders saw the Ruthenians as a variant of the Russian ethnic group, which thus became a group with not three subgroups but four: Belarusians ("White Russians"), Ukrainians ("Little Russians"), Great Russians, and Ruthenians. Toward the end of the century, however, a new generation of Ukrainian-Galicians came to the fore: Far more politically radical, these were the "young Ruthenians" or the "Ukrainophiles." To them the Galicians were a part of the Ukrainian people, and eastern Galicia was the nucleus of a future Pan-Ukrainian state. In their view this state-to-be would have to include all the ethnographically Ukrainian areas under the Russian czar.[5]

Political repression in Russia led some Ukrainian nationalists to leave the Russian-controlled areas and take refuge in Habsburg Galicia. Among their number was Mykhaylo Khrushevskyy, known as the father of Ukrainian historiography. He was later to return as the president of the independent Ukrainian Central Rada Republic in 1917–1918. At the time, Galicia was spoken of as "the Ukrainian Piedmont," the reference being to the small Italian duchy that became the driving force behind the unification of Italy.

After the fall of the Habsburg empire during World War I, Galicia ended up under Poland. All signs of budding Ukrainian nationalism were repressed, and the dream of an independent Pan-Ukrainian state seemed more remote than ever before. And then, after World War II, the dream was to be fulfilled—in a way that turned it into a nightmare. The Ribbentrop-Molotov pact made possible a Soviet territorial expansion that brought all Ukrainians under the same roof, the Ukrainian Soviet Socialist Republic. Stalin viewed all his "new compatriots" in the Baltics and in western Ukraine with deep suspicion. After all, they had lived under non-Communist rule and were thus not to be trusted. Stalin's deep skepticism toward the western Ukrainians was further bolstered by the undeniable fact of the Galician partisan movement, which continued its struggle against the Soviet forces right up until the early 1950s.

For some reason, few Russians moved to Galicia after the war. Whereas hundreds of thousands of Russians and other Soviet citizens streamed to the Baltic republics—another recently annexed Soviet region full of unrest—the Russification of Galicia remained weak in the extreme, demographically, linguistically, and in terms of identity. The Galicians were allowed to retain Ukrainian as the language of administration and the schools; indeed, in the course of the 1970s and 1980s the Ukrainian influence gradually became stronger, not weaker. More and more Ukrainian-language newspapers were printed in the region, and some of the ethnic Russians living there began to move out again.[6] The advent of perestroika found the Galicians mentally prepared to implement a program for the establishment of a unified and separate Ukrainian state. This program, while subversive toward the unity of the Soviet state, represented no threat to the territorial unity of Ukraine.

Transcarpathia

Directly to the west of Galicia, on the other side of the Carpathian range, lies Transcarpathia, or Carpato-Ruthenia. This area, too, had been under Habsburg rule until World War I, but as part of the Hungarian portion of the Austro-Hungarian empire and with a history totally different from that of Galicia. Not the Poles but the Hungarians were politically dominant in Transcarpathia, and their subjects had to toe a straight and narrow line indeed. In these parts there was no encouraging any kind of Ukrainian nationalism, however limited.

In socioeconomic terms Transcarpathia was poorly developed, and its Slavic-speaking peasantry had not fostered any strong protonational intelligentsia. All the same some did develop a separate identity as Rusyns (Ruthenians)—an identity they maintained even after their territory had been annexed by the USSR after World War II. In contrast to the Galicians, many Transcarpathian Rusyns do *not* see themselves as part of the Ukrainian nation but as a distinct ethnic group with Catholic (Uniate) faith and their own East Slavic language. Today's Ukrainian authorities in Kiev have refused to acknowledge this identity, insisting, as did the Soviet authorities, that the Transcarpathian Rusyns are simply Ukrainians.[7]

Rusynian activists in Transcarpathia issue their own newspaper (somewhat irregularly) but are otherwise not particularly noticeable. Most of them are retired people who explain that members of the younger generation do not dare risk their careers by supporting them. They go on to say the entire population of Transcarpathia are Rusyns deep down in their hearts. A few members of the Transcarpathian County Council are said to be "closet Rusyns" who lack the courage to declare their support openly—hardly the elements with which to build an effective movement.[8]

Northern Bukovina

A fifth county in today's Ukraine, Chernivtsi, used to be part of the Habsburg empire. Chernivtsi is the northernmost portion of the former

Austrian crownland of Bukovina, which was joined to Romania after World War I. In line with the provisions of the Ribbentrop-Molotov pact, it was ceded to the USSR in 1940. The population is mixed Ukrainian-Romanian.

There are in Chernivtsi some strongly anti-Ukrainian Romanian activists, but they are few in number and are under strict political control.[9] I had the opportunity of speaking with one of them in the Romanian Cultural Center in May 1996. In the course of our conversation, the telephone rang. It was a high-level civil servant in the local administration, calling to warn me not to believe everything these Romanians said. The authorities obviously had a mole in the cultural center who had immediately informed the higher-ups that his or her boss was consorting with a foreigner. No attempt was made to conceal this stool pigeon activity.

Novorossia

From the Middle Ages until the late 1700s, the southern Ukrainian steppes north of the Black Sea were controlled by Turkic-speaking Muslim nomads. Very few Slavic peasants dared settle there. When the generals of Catherine the Great conquered the area around 1790, it was almost uninhabited. In order to consolidate the new territories, which were called Novorossia, "the new Russia," the czarist authorities organized large-scale colonization projects involving Germans, Serbs, Bulgarians, Jews, Moldovans, Russians, and Ukrainians. In this way these fertile lands got a populace of highly mixed ethnic origins—with, it is said, a unique mentality. The main city, Odessa, was called "the Marseilles of Russia": Its denizens are known for their sanguinity, their lighthearted sense of humor, and their ever-ready smiles. Little Ukrainian is spoken here: People manage very well with Russian.

Occasionally articles will be written in the newspapers of Odessa about the need to reestablish Novorossia as a separate region, perhaps with a certain degree of autonomy within Ukraine.[10] But the Odessans themselves do not appear very interested one way or the other. When I asked passersby in the streets of Odessa whether they were not afraid of becoming Ukrainianized, the usual response was just a shrug of the shoulders. The danger is not seen as particularly imminent.

Crimea

The relaxed atmosphere of Odessa stands in stark contrast to the strong feelings that have been aroused on the nearby Crimean peninsula. Leading political activists of Crimea maintain that the danger of Ukrainization is real, even though they also have to admit there have been few signs of it as yet.[11] The peninsula is almost totally Russian in culture and language. Over two-thirds of the population are ethnic Russians; in addition, even those whose passports identify them as Ukrainian have become thoroughly Russified after decades of all-Russian schooling. Up until 1954 Crimea was part of the Russian Soviet Socialist Republic, and since 1991 several strong movements on the peninsula have fought for reunification with Russia. Others have wanted to establish a sovereign republic within or outside the confines of Ukraine.

As early as February 1991, before the actual dissolution of the Soviet Union, the Ukrainian authorities granted autonomous status to Crimea within the Ukrainian SSR. In April 1992 the new autonomous status of Crimea was to be defined by means of a special law prepared by the Ukrainian parliament. The first draft was quite liberal, but the final version, adopted a few days later, was far more restrictive.[12] Crimea's parliament reacted by adopting its own constitution as well as a declaration of Crimean independence on 6 May 1992. Although the next day the Crimeans did tack on a sentence to the effect that Crimea was to remain part of Ukraine, Ukrainian parliamentarians in Kiev were furious. The Ukrainian Supreme Soviet countered by adopting a proclamation to the Crimean population warning that "the situation now developing in the Crimea can have unpredictable consequences. It may lead to social tragedy, ruining the lives of hundreds of thousands of people."[13] This proclamation went on to remind the Crimeans of the civil wars in the Caucasus and the Dniester region. The message was clear: Ukraine was prepared to go to war in order to keep the Crimean peninsula.[14]

Crimean politicians took this threat seriously and shelved their declaration of independence, temporarily at least. The most important independence movement on the peninsula, however, the Republican Movement of Crimea (RMC, or RDK in Russian) did not give up. At the January 1994 Crimean presidential elections, they managed to get their leader, Yuriy Meshkov, elected. Later in the year, Meshkov and his adherents won a landslide victory at the elections to the Crimean Supreme Soviet. Meshkov then took the declaration of independence out of mothballs. In addition he introduced some symbolic legislation tailor-made to provoke the Ukrainian authorities. For one thing, clocks on the peninsula were to be set back one hour, in line with Moscow rather than Kiev time. (In exactly the same manner, Ukraine had marked independence from the USSR a few years earlier by moving the clocks forward one hour.) The stage seemed set for new and harrowing conflicts between Kiev and Crimea.

The Ukrainian authorities may not have managed to put an end to the Crimean independence movement, but its own members did. In September 1994 President Meshkov fell out with his own supporters in the

174

Courtesy of Trond A. Svensson

Crimean parliament when they sought to restrict his broad presidential powers. This was the same type of conflict that had unleashed the October 1993 bloodbath in the White House in Moscow, where the Supreme Soviet held sway. At this point, however, history repeated itself according to the Marxist scheme of things: first as tragedy, then as farce. Meshkov barricaded himself inside his own office but fell prey to the cholera epidemic that had erupted on the peninsula. In the end he had to be evacuated in an ambulance. And that was for all practical purposes the end of the Crimean fight for independence.

In the early phases of the conflict, Crimea had received a certain degree of support from Moscow (from the Supreme Soviet more than from President Yeltsin). But after war broke out in Chechnya in December 1995, Russian support gradually dried up.[15] Russia had its hands full with internal conflicts of its own, and the leadership had come to realize that separatism was really not such a good thing after all.

In March 1995 the Ukrainian authorities abolished the Crimean presidency and rescinded the constitution of the peninsula. Since then, disagreement on the status of Crimea has continued with ups and downs, at a lower level of intensity. In October 1997 the Crimean parliament declared Russian the official language of the peninsula, with 6 May as Constitution Day—in memory of the now invalid constitution.[16] These were fairly toothless gestures: No longer did the Crimea represent a threat to the territorial unity of Ukraine.[17]

Donbass

The industrialized counties of eastern Ukraine are by far the most populous in the whole country. Whereas some 5 million people live in the three Galician counties, there are altogether almost 12 million in Donetsk, Luhansk, and Dnipropetrovsk. This area has long represented a center of gravity—in demographic, economic, and political terms—not only in Ukraine but indeed for the entire Soviet Union. Yuzhmash in Dnipropetrovsk was the largest missile factory in the world. A great many of the top Soviet leaders of the 1970s and 1980s came from this area—including Politburo members Andrey Kirilenko, Vladimir Shcherbytskyy, and Leonid Brezhnev.[18] Their network of protégés was often known as the "Dnipropetrovsk clan."

During perestroika Donbass and Dnipropetrovsk represented the one pole within Ukrainian politics, the other being western Ukraine. It is because of the contrasts between these two regions that Ukrainian politics is often seen as polarized along an east-west axis. Regional unrest in Transcarpathia, Chernivtsi, and Odessa may at most be minor irritants to the nation-builders of Kiev. The Crimean conflict could have developed into a serious threat, but even if the peninsula had managed to secede, this would scarcely have had any repercussions for the other portions of Ukraine. In legal, historical, and cultural terms, the situation of Crimea is seen as unique and thus hardly likely to set a precedent. But if the inhabitants of Donbass should want to break out of the unitary Ukrainian state, then danger would indeed be afoot.

As we have seen, the contrasts between Galicia and Donbass are based on historical and cultural conditions. Even though most of the inhabitants of eastern Ukraine are ethnic Ukrainians according to their passports, culturally they are almost indistinguishable from the Russians living in the area. Mixed Ukrainian-Russian marriages are common; in fact, hardly anyone would consider them to be ethnically mixed marriages at all. The Ukrainians of the Donbass area are perhaps somewhat better at speaking Ukrainian than are their Russian neighbors, but the Ukrainian they speak bears a strong resemblance to southern Russian dialects. There also exists a mixed language, *surzhik,* with low status, a patois spoken primarily by rural peasants and first-generation urban immigrants.[19] A Ukrainian from Donbass may have considerable difficulty understanding a Ukrainian from Galicia, even if they both speak what is officially the same language.

In the 1970s and 1980s, the cultural gap between western and eastern Ukraine gradually widened.[20] Whereas Galicia became increasingly Ukrainian-speaking, more and more of those living in Donbass took to speaking Russian. And whereas many Ukrainian nationalists from Galicia had had to serve long sentences in the gulag, there was no underground independence movement in the eastern portions of the country.

Ukrainian Independence Policy

The first initiative to the formation of a Ukrainian popular front, known as Rukh, meaning "the movement," came in October 1988. In the course of one year, Rukh gained strong support, but only in the capital and western Ukraine. In January 1990 Rukh arranged its first mass gathering: a human chain several hundred kilometers long, stretching from L'viv to Kiev. This was an idea borrowed from the three Baltic republics, where the sixtieth anniversary of the Ribbentrop-Molotov pact had been marked on 23 August 1989 with a show of solidarity, a human chain extending all the way from Vilnius to Tallinn. The Baltic demonstration had had a major impact on public opinion, but the Ukrainian copy was not quite as effective. Even though distances in Ukraine are on a far vaster scale than in the Baltics, it was not a terribly convincing manifestation of solidarity to connect two points on the western bank of the Dnieper, as there were no signs of mobilization on the other side of the river. Quite the contrary: It served to underline how Ukrainian nationalism was a western Ukrainian phenomenon.

Eastern Ukraine, however, was also marked by unrest among the population and increasing discontent with Moscow. Here the grievances were economic, not nationalist issues. In summer 1989 the miners of Donbass joined with their fellow workers in Siberia and northern Russia in a series of strikes demanding better working conditions and higher wages. The Nikolay Ryzhkov government in Moscow finally acceded to their demands, even though it could by no means afford to. When it became apparent that the Kremlin was not able to honor its promises, the Donbass workers became furious and instigated new strikes.

On 16 July 1990 the Ukrainian Supreme Soviet adopted a proclamation of sovereignty for Ukraine—a few weeks after the corresponding declaration from Russia and eleven days prior to the Belarusian declaration. At this point the Communist Party was still in full control in Kiev, and the Ukrainian proclamation was seen as remarkably radical. Among other points, it declared that even if Ukraine were to remain a part of the USSR, the republic would retain the right to issue its own currency and to maintain its own armed forces. Sovereignty was proclaimed on behalf of "the Ukrainian people."[21] The key word *people (narod)* was ambiguous: It could be given both an ethnic and a political, civic interpretation. In that particular context, however, it was clear that the "nation" concept of the Ukrainian legislators was far less ethnic and less exclusive than the case in many of the other republics.

When Gorbachev held his referendum on the future of the Soviet Union in March 1991, he received support from a full 70 percent of the people of Ukraine.[22] But the Ukrainian authorities managed to get an additional question on the ballot, concerning support for the Ukrainian declaration of sovereignty. Over 90 percent in Galicia and two-thirds in Donbass answered affirmatively to this as well.[23]

In spring 1991 a remarkable fusion took place between the western and eastern Ukrainian mass movements. As one political commentator remarked, "It is well known that the miners have been indifferent, if not directly opposed, to the more extreme manifestations of the Ukrainian nationalist movement. And now, in the course of one political season, they have suddenly joined ranks with them."[24] At the political rallies in the main street of Kiev, the yellow and blue nationalist flag fluttered in the breeze above the orange miners' helmets. Nor was the language from the podium necessarily Ukrainian any longer. A certain degree of Russianization of the Ukrainian national idea had taken place. Within the Ukrainian Communist Party leadership, discord had begun to erupt. Whereas the party chairman stuck to traditional Soviet communism, the party secretary for ideological matters, Leonid Kravchuk, introduced more and more nationalist rhetoric into his speeches. In 1990 Kravchuk had been elected speaker of the Ukrainian Supreme Soviet.

In Kiev, as in the capitals of the other Soviet republics, the August 1991 coup attempt by old-line Communists in Moscow resulted in a totally new situation. On the first day of the coup, Kravchuk had appeared on Moscow television and announced his conditional support. When the coup failed, that should have marked the end of his life as a politician— but no, he arose to a new life as a non-Communist Ukrainian nationalist. On 24 August, one day before its neighbor Belarus, the Ukrainian national assembly voted for full independence. At the same time, it was decided that this independence was to be confirmed through a referendum to be held on 1 December of that year.

In Russia people began to get used to the idea that the days of the Soviet Union were numbered. Russian politicians were prepared to cede control over Central Asia and the Caucasus. But Ukraine and Belarus— that was a different story. These were not foreign territories but integral portions of Rus' itself. Losing them would be like having an arm or a leg amputated. And if my language here seems melodramatic, rest assured that it is moderate in comparison with many of the expressions used in Moscow at the time.[25]

Yeltsin's press secretary declared that if Ukraine were to secede from the union, Russia would reserve the right to reopen the question of boundary revisions.[26] He was apparently thinking first and foremost of Crimea, though perhaps of Donbass as well. At any rate this statement provoked violent outcries from Kiev, further inflamed by rumors that Yeltsin had had a secret meeting with the Russian general staff to discuss (but also dismiss) the use of nuclear weapons against Ukraine.[27] These rumors were probably sheer fabrication, but at the time they further fueled the anti-Russian mood in Ukraine.

Several Russian politicians and prominent cultural figures held that the results of the forthcoming December referendum in Ukraine should be tallied by county. Those counties not voting for independence ought to be given the opportunity to remain within the Soviet Union.[28] Not unexpectedly, Kiev brusquely rejected that demand. As it happened, this would have made no difference: In all the counties of Ukraine, a clear majority supported independence—83 percent in Donetsk and Luhansk, 90 percent in Dnipropetrovsk.[29] Only in Crimea was there any pronounced opposition to an independent Ukrainian state, but also there over 50 percent of those voting gave their support. (Voter turnout in Crimea, however, was very low: barely above 50 percent.)

For many denizens of Ukraine, a vote in support of Ukrainian independence in this referendum was primarily a vote against Moscow and against communism. Not least, it was a protest against President

Gorbachev, who by this time had managed to become surprisingly unpopular throughout most of the Soviet Union. In addition, economic motives clearly played an important role in Ukraine. Western experts had long held that Ukraine had a considerable potential for economic growth. These prognoses were exploited—indeed, exaggerated out of all proportion—in Rukh's pre-referendum campaign. Rukh proclaimed that in a number of ways Ukraine was "actually" economically better off than Britain, Italy, France, or Germany. Why, then, did the average Ukrainian not see any of this? Because the country was an "internal colony" of the USSR, prevented from reaping the benefits of its enormous potential. For example, Ukraine produced over 2 tons of iron ore per capita each year, whereas the corresponding figures for the UK and Germany were a measly 4 kilograms and 2 kilograms, respectively.[30] In a broader socio-economic perspective, such comparisons were not particularly relevant, but they struck a chord in the Ukrainian population, not least among the miners of Donbass. Rukh was simply providing confirmation of what they had maintained all along: The ore they dug out of the earth was the true wealth of Ukraine.

Nation-Building After Independence

It is not surprising that it was the Ukrainian referendum that sealed the fate of the Soviet Union. Only one week afterward, the presidents of Russia, Ukraine, and Belarus met outside Minsk, where they proclaimed the establishment of the Commonwealth of Independent States. Whereas Russian politicians hoped that the CIS would be able to develop into a powerful organization for cooperation, their Ukrainian colleagues made it clear from the start that they saw it as a means of achieving a peaceable, orderly divorce among the Soviet republics.

The Ukrainian referendum had been a formidable victory for the Ukrainian nationalists; what now remained was to consolidate that victory. A strong, viable nation-state would have to be created—a far more difficult task. A major problem was the economy. Sky-high expectations as to what independence would bring in terms of rubles and kopecks—or, preferably, dollars and cents—stood no chance of being fully realized. Indeed, with the economic policy that Ukraine was to pursue in the years to come, they never even came close. The country began sinking ever deeper into an economic quagmire, to which eastern Ukrainians responded by withdrawing the support they had, under erroneous assumptions, given to the Ukrainian nation project.

On the same day as the referendum on independence, Ukraine also held presidential elections. The Rukh leader, Vyacheslav Chornovil, ran on a pro-West ticket specifically aimed at a rapid transition to a market economy. But Chornovil was a Galician, and he received votes almost exclusively in his home region. Elsewhere the preferred candidate was Leonid Kravchuk, who was seen as much more of a unifying figure.[31]

It emerged, however, that President Kravchuk was not able (or not willing) to get firm control of the economy, the basic building block of the new, independent Ukraine. He let his old comrades of the *nomenklatura* elite line their pockets by dubious transactions through which they suddenly became the "owners" of the factories where they had previously been directors. Ukraine lagged further and further behind Russia in economic development. In 1992, key economic figures for Ukraine and Russia had been fairly similar: Annual inflation stood at 1,145 percent in Ukraine and 1,350 percent in Russia. In that year the drop in production was greater in Russia—18 percent as against 14 percent for Ukraine. One year later the gap had widened: Russian inflation was now a "mere" 940 percent, whereas in Ukraine it had soared to a staggering 3,300 percent. For several months in 1993, Ukraine experienced hyperinflation, that is, over 50 percent; for December 1993 it was a full 90 percent. At the same time as the Ukrainian karbovanets (ruble) plummeted, production fell—according to official figures, by nearly 36 percent in 1993. Ukraine thus experienced the particularly harmful combination of inflation and negative growth known as stagflation.

The citizenry of eastern Ukraine saw the dissolution of the Soviet Union as a major cause of their country's financial straits. In an opinion poll conducted in spring 1994, only 24 percent of those asked in the eastern and southern regions of the country replied that they would have voted for national independence if a new referendum were to be held.[32] In another survey 40 percent said that Russia and Ukraine should join together to form one state.[33] Although workers in the Donbass area wanted stronger ties to Russia, they were also demanding that the government in Kiev step in and save their unproductive mines by granting hefty subsidies. In other words, what they wanted was not more market economy, as Rukh did, but less of it.

In summer 1993 the miners instigated a new series of strikes. They demanded a new referendum, this time on confidence in the new Ukrainian president and national assembly, the Supreme Rada. No longer did they parade Ukrainian flags and other symbols of state in their demonstrations. In the words of the liberal Moscow newspaper *Moskovskie novosti* (Moscow news): "The idea of the nation-state has suffered defeat in Ukraine."[34] Demands for a new referendum were not met. Instead, elections were moved forward, to March–April 1994 for the Supreme Council and June–July for presidential elections.

The Kravchuk administration may have evinced minimal capabilities in economic policy, but it was certainly active when it came to political and symbolic nation-building. The *nomenklatura* elite seized upon the nation project originally launched by the Galicia-dominated cultural intelligentsia and made it their own.

Two important elements in any nation-building project are cultural and educational policy on the one hand and foreign policy on the other. Under Kravchuk, Ukrainian nation-building tended in two separate directions: It was ethnocentric in culture but state-oriented in foreign policy.

Russia was far and away the most important state on the Ukrainian horizon. After independence, conflicts between the two states were many and serious. There were the questions of the status of the Crimean peninsula, the fate of the Black Sea fleet, the conditions for Ukraine's delivery of nuclear weapons to Russia for destruction, rent for Russian gas pipelines to Western Europe crossing Ukrainian territory, and the whole issue of Ukraine's balance of payments.[35] These were tough questions, with strong feelings on both sides—especially when power politics became linked to more emotionally laden politics of symbolism. The most explosive mixture was found in connection with the fate of the Black Sea fleet. For both states, this was far more than merely a matter of the distribution of vessels—they were in fact often old and in bad shape—it was a question of national prestige. After all, any coastal nation worth its salt must have a proper fleet. Moreover, that very fleet had, some 140 years earlier, played a central role in the Crimean War and, only fifty years before, in World War II. Western observers, keenly aware that both Russia and Ukraine were still nuclear powers, feared the very worst.[36]

The fleet crisis peaked time and again but also subsided. This may have been sheer luck, but it seems equally probable that both sides knew where the line was and took care to back off in time. Why, then, did the conflict continue as long as it did? One reason may be that the parties did not see it as entirely destructive, even though it certainly was in many ways. Both sides may have felt there were also certain advantages in nurturing the flames of conflict.

One American scholar has held that the Kravchuk regime exploited the fleet crisis to strengthen its own power:

> The first generation of independent Ukrainian leaders needed the specter of a Russian threat for domestic political mobilization. The perceived ability to stand up to Russian bullying and to rebut the challenge of Russian "neo-imperialism" was an important element of Kravchuk's domestic political position and crucial to his image as father and protector of Ukrainian independence. . . . If Russia didn't exist, it would have to be invented.

This analysis makes a lot of sense. The sharp verbal battles with Russia served to rally the Ukrainian nation against an outside enemy and helped to give the Ukrainian state an identity of its own.

This form of nation-building concerned the Ukrainian state—its interests and need to make its mark—and in theory this should affect each and every citizen. In a political confrontation between Ukraine and Russia, ethnic Russians and to some extent Russified Ukrainians living in Ukraine could certainly feel that they were placed between the hammer and the anvil. Even so, I would maintain that most of the Russian-Ukrainian state-level conflicts have developed in such a way as to stimulate the unification of the Ukrainian political nation rather than splitting it.

What of cultural policies? Here we find a different picture. Even though perhaps over half the citizenry of Ukraine speak Russian as their daily language, Ukrainian has been proclaimed the sole official state language. In clear contrast to the situation in Belarus, the Ukrainian state authorities have implemented clearly targeted, energetic measures to get the people to speak the titular language. In the central regions of the country, parents are put under considerable pressure to choose Ukrainian as the medium of instruction for their children's schooling.[38] In some other regions as well, there are signs of a language shift. But not in the schools of Donbass or Crimea: There Russian still reigns supreme.

The development of pupils' identity is influenced not only by the medium of instruction but also by the content of this instruction. In Chapter 3 I showed how the curriculum on the history of Kievan Rus' is utilized for nation-building. The teaching of literature has also been revamped in Ukrainian schools. Many Russians in Ukraine are angered that Russian literature is no longer a separate subject but has been subsumed under world literature. By 1995 Russian fiction still composed about one-fourth of the required reading in foreign literature, but this was a transitional arrangement: If this percentage share were cut too drastically and too quickly, thousands of Russian teachers would find themselves out of work. As these teachers gradually leave the school system through natural attrition, the teaching of Russian literature will be further reduced, officials explain.[39]

Some Ukrainian politicians have maintained that Russian is a foreign language on a par with, say, English and French, and should be treated accordingly.[40] Such attitudes explain why important literary figures of international renown like Nikolay Gogol (in Ukrainian, Mykola Hohol) and Vladimir (Volodymyr) Korolenko have been relegated to the curriculum for foreign literature.[41] Both of these authors were born and grew up in Ukraine and often focused on Ukrainian conditions in their literary works—though they wrote in Russian.

All over the world, the usual practice among nation-builders has been to incorporate into the "national cultural heritage" every famous figure who can somehow be linked to the country. Norway, for example, was joined to Denmark for centuries and can boast very few all-Norwegian cultural eminences from the 1700s. But without so much as a blush, Norwegians have taken the dramatist Ludvig Holberg to their hearts and made a Norwegian of him, even though he lived his entire adult life in royal Copenhagen. Because he happened to be born in Bergen, on the west coast of Norway, and spent his childhood years there, today he stands on his pedestal in the center of Bergen, gazing with bronze eyes on the fish market below.

Why has the same thing not happened in Ukraine? A world-famous author like Gogol could surely be put to good use in the Ukrainian nation-building project.[42] There is no clear-cut answer to this, but part of the explanation may lie in deep-rooted feelings of insecurity vis-à-vis "Big Brother" Russia.[43]

Ukrainian Ethnonationalism and Ethnic Consolidation

By now the reader should be quite aware that the East Slavic cultural area is a continuum with no sharply defined boundaries between the Russian, Belarusian, and Ukrainian areas. To make possible the creation of separate Belarusian and Ukrainian ethnic identities, more or less arbitrary dividing lines have to be drawn. Elsewhere in the world, in cases where cultural boundaries are not particularly sharp, political and geographical markers can sometimes do the job—in Scandinavia, for example, there are bodies of water and mountains. In the East Slavic areas, however, physical barriers are notoriously lacking between countries, and ethnic boundaries fail to coincide with state borders. Over 13 percent of the population of Belarus is Russian; in Ukraine the Russian demographic element is even stronger: More than 11 million of Ukraine's 50-odd million inhabitants are ethnic Russians (and this figure does not include the Russian-speaking Ukrainians). In a situation like that, "ethnos-builders" may well find themselves forced to undertake the oddest maneuvers in order to construct that necessary modicum of cultural distance to everything Russian.

We have already seen how Zyanon Paznyak and other members of the Belarusian Popular Front sought to brand the Russian people as imperialists and worse. In this case, however, the Belarusian citizenry proved an unwilling audience, and the plan backfired on the popular front. Among Ukrainian ethnonationalists we may also note some tendencies toward hyperbolical contrasts between the "Russian" and the native Slavic culture. When visiting Rukh headquarters in Kiev in September 1994, I was informed that there exists no other European nation more different from the Ukrainians than precisely the Russians. This rather surprising statement was backed up by examples of what were held to be linguistic contrasts: The word for "leader" in Ukrainian is *holova,* which actually means "head" or "head figure." A common Russian word for the same concept is *predsedatel',* derived from the Russian verb "to sit." This was—according to my host—a clear indication of the most important parts of the body for a Ukrainian and for a Russian leader, respectively.[44] And in the same vein, Ukrainians say that they are going "to work" *(na pratsyu),* whereas Russians often say they are going *na prisutstvie.* As this means literally "in order to be present," the implication is clear: For Russians, it is enough merely to show up at work; they need not actually *do* anything as long as they are "present."[45] The same contrast between activity and passivity, my Rukh host pointed out, could be seen in the words for "cafeteria": In Ukrainian the term is derived from the verb "to eat," whereas in Russian it comes from the word for "table." Whether or not there happens to be any food in a Russian cafeteria or whether or not people actually eat there is clearly less important to the Russian soul. *Quod erat demonstrandum.*

The point of departure for this thumbnail character analysis of two peoples was that not only the Ukrainians but also the Russians are after all a European people. Not all Ukrainian nationalists would agree to that. Even many center-right politicians in Kiev, not to mention the extreme right-wing nationalist parties—Congress of Ukrainian Nationalists (CUN, or KUN in Ukrainian), State Independence for Ukraine (SIU, or DSU in Ukrainian), and the Ukrainian National Assembly (UNA)—insist that Ukrainians are Europeans—but not Russians. All these groups claim to follow in the footsteps of Dmytro Dontsov (1883–1973), a leading right-wing radical Ukrainian ideologue of the interwar years. Dontsov emphatically maintained that the Russians are not Europeans but Asiatics.[46]

Even if CUN, SIU, and UNA share a common ideological foundation in the tradition of Dontsov, their messages today are highly disparate. The SIU is headed by what we may term "romantic ethnocrats" under the slogan "Ukraine for Ukrainians." Their organization was established by a former gulag inmate, Ivan Kandyba, who has since been replaced by a young doctor, Roman Koval', whose program is unashamedly racist.[47] The various leaflets and pamphlets issued by the SIU are bursting with crude attacks on the Russians.

The members of SIU's rival, UNA, wear uniforms and are highly militant. The organization has its own paramilitary forces with battle experience through participation in several armed conflicts in the former Soviet Union.[48] UNA activists would appear to have conquered any minority complex they might have had toward the Russians. They seek to appear as Pan-Slavists and advocate unification of all the East Slavic peoples—under Ukrainian leadership. True enough, there are more Russians than

Ukrainians in the world, but the Russians have such a weakly developed, wishy-washy identity that it would be easy and natural for them to submit to Ukrainian leadership and let themselves be assimilated into the Ukrainian nation, says UNA leader Dmytro Korchynskyy.[49]

Yet the UNA claims that it is impossible to find objective criteria for determining who actually should be counted as part of the "Ukrainian nation." Physiological criteria are no good, since Ukrainians living east of the Dnieper are brachycephalic (or round headed), whereas those west of the river are dolichocephalic (long headed). Nor are official passport entries any use, since a large number of Jews are registered as Ukrainians. And even the linguistic criterion must be rejected, as so many Ukrainians are Russian-speaking. The conclusion drawn by Korchynskyy is logical enough but still totally unexpected: The Ukrainian nation does not exist. Or more correctly, it does not yet exist. It is in the process of being created—by the UNA. People become Ukrainian by joining this organization. It was in just this way, explains Korchynskyy, that an Italian nation was created by the fascist movement of Benito Mussolini.

Many Western presentations of modern Ukrainian nationalism have focused on CUN, UNA, and the SIU. According to some observers, in the hopeless economic quandary Ukraine now finds itself such movements represent a real danger.[50] Indeed, it is undeniably disturbing that UNA gained three seats in the Ukrainian Supreme Council in 1994. But it lost these seats again in the 1998 elections, and as far as I can ascertain all these organizations remain relatively marginal groups with only limited growth potential. There would seem greater grounds for concern when elements of such ethnocratic thinking turn up elsewhere, among more respectable, center-oriented nationalists in Ukraine.

From Kravchuk to Kuchma: Political Nation-Building and Back Again?

Leonid Kravchuk won the presidential elections in 1991 not least because he gave the appearance of being an all-inclusive, nonethnic nation-builder. During summer 1991 he told *Pravda*, "The Russians in Ukraine should not be compared with the Russians in the Baltic republics. Here they are indigenous residents; they have lived on this land for hundreds of years."[51] Kravchuk has since changed the way in which he speaks about the Russians. Andrew Wilson has documented that after 1991 Kravchuk's political rhetoric underwent a pronounced development, away from a politically based idea of the nation and in the direction of a more ethnically founded one. In his 1994 memoirs, Kravchuk placed himself more or less on the same line as my Rukh host: "The Ukrainian people in their culture, form of life, and outlook on life differ from the Russians."[52] Here it is not quite clear whether Kravchuk is comparing the

Russians with the Ukrainians the way they ought to be or as he actually sees them. In a speech to the Ukrainian Supreme Council in December 1991, he claimed that "Ukrainian culture, language, national self-consciousness, and historical memory have been subject to so much damage for so long that we must apply enormous force in order to revive them."[53] This statement is not very far from Kebich's declaration that the national consciousness of the Belarusians is "destroyed." In his memoirs Kravchuk sets forth another proclamation that we can recognize from the language law of Belarus: "Without a language, there can be no people." Through such statements, says Wilson, Kravchuk and his colleagues were sending out political messages that undermined the credibility of their commitment to a multiethnic civic state.[54]

By the time of the spring 1994 presidential election, Kravchuk had managed to make himself mightily unpopular in the eastern and southern portions of the country yet had gained support in western Ukraine. Factory director Leonid Kuchma from Dnipropetrovsk, who had served as prime minister for a time in 1992–1993, ran as the eastern Ukrainian candidate, defeating Kravchuk by a narrow margin. The distribution of votes followed clear geographical lines and provided strong confirmation of the political importance of regional differences in Ukrainian politics.[55] Kuchma emerged victorious in all thirteen counties in the east and south; Kravchuk gained a majority in all thirteen counties of the center and west. Indeed, in L'viv, where Kravchuk had garnered less than 15 percent of the vote in 1991, he boasted a full 94 percent of the vote in 1994.[56] Since the eastern counties are much more populous than the Western ones, however, they secured victory for Kuchma.

Kuchma is a Russian-speaking Ukrainian. In his inaugural speech, he pledged support to changing the national language law: Whereas Ukrainian would remain the sole "state language" of the country, Russian would be given the status of an "official language."[57] Some commentators saw this as a judgment of Solomon applied to an intricate issue; others dismissed it as sheer verbiage: After all, in most countries "official language" and "state language" are two terms for one and the same thing. Such a decision would, it was feared, provide the coup de grâce to the entire Ukrainization campaign.

In September 1994, Mykhaylo Kosiv, leader of the Committee on Cultural Affairs of the Ukrainian Supreme Rada, attacked Kuchma's proposal in a sharply worded article tellingly entitled, "No Language—No People: No People—No State." With this he made himself the spokesperson for a rigid interlinking of language and nation:

> Ukraine is the fatherland of the Ukrainian people. This is a people that has realized its sacred right to self-determination and has created the Ukrainian state, in which there also live some national minorities. . . . The Russian

people live in Russia, whereas lesser portions of this people live as national minorities in Ukraine (as they also do in Estonia, Latvia, Lithuania, Moldova, Belarus, etc.).[58]

If the Russians of Ukraine had not been quite sure as to whether they should consider themselves members of the Ukrainian or the Russian nation, this certainly gave them an unequivocal answer.

In a 1994 research report from the Ukrainian Academy of Sciences, a well-known Ukrainian social scientist expressed an understanding of the "nation" very close to that of Kosiv. Yevhen Kamynskyy regarded himself as a firm opponent of Ukrainian nationalism—understood as the ideology of the SIU and UNA—but still maintained:

> Ukraine is the state of the indigenous Ukrainian nation. In this state there live various national minorities side by side with the Ukrainians. At the same time, they constitute ethnic groups within their own respective nations. The nuclear groups of these nations live in other states. In view of the tragic fate suffered by Ukrainian culture and the Ukrainian language, I feel that the question of introducing multiculturalism and two state languages in Ukraine should not be raised at all.[59]

Kuchma had indeed raised that question, but he did not go on to do much about it. In June 1996 the Ukrainian Supreme Rada adopted a new constitution, as the last of all the Soviet successor states to do so. After a hard tug-of-war between the president and the parliament, Kuchma largely got his way—and official bilingualism was not included in this way. The new constitution mentions only one state language: Ukrainian.

Instead of keeping his election pledge, Kuchma set about learning better Ukrainian; today this is almost always the language the Ukrainian president uses when speaking in public. Whereas Minsk has functioned as a school for Russification, it is obvious that Kiev exerts a different influence on those who move there and join the political elite in the Ukrainian capital: They become more or less Ukrainianized. But why? The reason cannot be that they would otherwise have problems making themselves understood. In the 1989 census, some 40 percent of the city's inhabitants said Russian was their native tongue, and there is reason to believe that this was a very conservative figure. Here as elsewhere many Ukrainians gave Ukrainian as their native language even though they used Russian every day. To judge from what is heard on the streets, Kiev has remained very much a Russian-speaking city.

The Ukrainianizing effect that Kiev exerts on the Ukrainian political elite is not so easy to explain. My own hypothesis is that the members of this elite have already made up their minds: Ukraine is to remain inde-

pendent of Russia. They nurture no illusions that this can be possible unless the country has a cultural identity distinct from that of Russia. And
the clearest, most obvious cultural marker at their disposal? Language, of
course.

And thus in Ukraine we see again the same close linkages connecting
language, (titular) nation, and state that we noted in Belarus—but now
with the opposite result. Let us have a look at the different lines of reasoning involved here:

Lukashenka's reasoning:
[– language] → [– nation] → [– state]

Kosiv's reasoning:
[+ language] → [+ nation] → [+ state]

Kuchma's reasoning:
[+ language] ← [+ nation] ← [+ state]

In this model Kosiv and Kuchma represent two ideal-typic positions in
Ukrainian nation-building, the ethnonational and the state-national.
Kuchma's line of reasoning begins where Kosiv's ends, but that is not the
main point. What is decisive is that this line of reasoning has led the
Ukrainian president to give his support to the basic cultural premise of
the ethnonationalists: a separate state must have its own language.

The logic of this model is not foolproof. After all, all over the world
there exist a great many states with the same language as their neighbors. Austria is one; the Arab states of the Middle East and the Spanish-
speaking countries of Latin America further extend the list.[60] In the case
of the latter, however, the ex-colonial power is situated safely on the
other side of the Atlantic and has made no attempt to regain control of
its former possessions. As long as there are strong Russian forces in
Moscow that continue to see Ukraine as ancient Russian ancestral territory, Ukrainian nationalists will feel the need to keep their distance from
everything Russian.

In summer 1996 the Ukrainian deputy prime minister for humanities
and the arts, Ivan Kuras, gave an interview to the leading Russian-
language newspaper in Kiev. Here he made it quite clear that the
Kuchma government had fully adopted Kosiv's tight linkages among
language, titular nation, and state. "Now that we have a sovereign, independent state, it would be ridiculous not to have a state language—
the language of the titular nation. Otherwise, it would simply not be a
state at all."[61] The Kravchuk administration may have left, but the ghost
of ethnonationalism lingers.

TABLE 9.1   Enrollment in Ukrainian-Language Educational Institutions and
Share of Ukrainians in the Regional Population (in percentages)

Region	Schools, 1988–1989	Schools, 1993–1994	Schools, 1996–1997	Higher Educ. Inst. 1993–1994	Ukrainians in Population
East	15.5	20.7	26.7	14.8	59.3
South	23.4	29.5	33.5	18.5	52.5
Center east	60.6	69.6	79.0	61.8	88.2
Center west	77.1	83.9	89.9	82.3	88.9
West	88.0	92.6	94.5	98.3	89.2
Kiev City	20.1	54.7	75.8	52.8	72.4
Total Ukraine	47.4	54.3	60.5	43.8	72.7

SOURCE: Germ Janmaat, "The Ukrainization of Education and the Response of the
Russians and Russian-Speaking Ukrainians in Four Cities," paper presented at the annual
convention of the Association for the Study of Nationalities, Columbia University, 16–19
April 10, 1998.

The policy of linguistic Ukrainization is yielding results—perhaps not
spectacular ones but noticeable all the same. In 1989, 73.6 percent of the
primary schools of Ukraine were Ukrainian-medium; four years later the
share had risen to 77.8 percent. For kindergartens, the figures were 49.8
percent in 1991 and 65.1 percent as of 1995.[62] Statistics on higher education show a similar pattern: In 1991 Ukrainian was the medium of instruction in 23.4 percent of all colleges and universities. Four years later
this figure had almost doubled, to 44.4 percent.[63]

There are, however, marked regional differences in this educational
shift. Although enrollment in Ukrainian-language educational institutions in the east has experienced only a modest increase—up from 15.5
percent to 26.7 percent in eight years—in Kiev the increase has been dramatic: from 20.1 percent in the 1988–1989 school year to 75.8 percent in
1996–1997 (see Table 9.1).

Russian-Speaking Ukrainians: Squeeze or Pivot?

The decisive factor in the Ukrainian-language nation project concerns the
Russian-speaking Ukrainians living in Ukraine. According to official statistics, they number about 4.5 million; the real figure may be three or four
times higher.[64] In terms of the identity criteria used in the Soviet Union,
their culture is neither fish nor fowl. Ukrainian Russophones who join
with ethnic Russians in defense of Russian language and culture are
branded "Janissaries" by Ukrainian nationalists—the reference being to
the young Christian boys from the Balkans who were taken to Istanbul in

Ottoman times and molded into fanatical Muslims: They are brain-washed, culturally warped renegades, traitors to their nation.[65]

Some studies have found that Russophone Ukrainians express differing attitudes and views from ethnic Russians who live in the same town. One opinion poll conducted in September 1992 showed that almost 80 percent of the Ukrainians but only 27 percent of the Russians in Simferopol (the Crimean capital) wanted Ukrainian citizenship. Further, 9 percent of the Russians there would prefer to have their children attend Ukrainian-medium schools, as against 43 percent of the ethnic Ukrainians. The U.S. scholar who undertook this survey saw in this the germ of harsh ethnic conflicts between Russians and Russophone Ukrainians in the Crimea.[66]

Other scholars, however, consider language more important than ethnicity in the formation of the identity and loyalty of the Russophone Ukrainians. Dominique Arel (1994) believes that most of them will join with the Russians against the western, Ukrainian-speaking elite.[67] Arel's analysis indicates the contours of a deep split in the Ukrainian populace—not between Russians and Ukrainians but between Russophones and Ukrainian speakers.

Some Russophone Ukrainians wish to locate themselves between the two poles and hope to create space for a separate Russophone Ukrainian culture.[68] In 1993 a professor from Dnipropetrovsk wrote, "There exists a unique, Russophone Ukrainian culture that can serve as a link between the Ukrainian and the Russian cultures."[69] The professor failed to point out the specifics of this unique culture, however, and as far as I can judge, his views have been taken up by few others. There is in Ukraine no organized movement fighting for the cause of a mixed or intermediate Russian-Ukrainian culture.

It may well be that it is in fact not necessary for Russophone Ukrainians to choose between Russian and Ukrainian. Their cultural and demographic position need not mean that they are squeezed between east and west. Instead, their elites may be in a pivotal position to tip the balance. It is, after all, to this group that both eastern and western Ukraine must appeal in order to gain support for their major causes.

The Galicians had a firm hold on Ukrainian politics in the immediate aftermath of perestroika, but this was a passing phenomenon. By the end of the 1990s, it was the populous eastern Ukraine that dominated both government offices and the Supreme Rada. Almost all the republic's prime ministers since independence—and there have been quite a few of them—have come from the east: Vitold Fokin, Leonid Kuchma, Yukhim Zvyagilskyy, Pavlo Lazarenko, Valeriy Pustovoytenko.[70] "The east" is in reality no coherent unit, and Ukrainian analysts increasingly distinguish between several rival power centers in the Russophone areas. Donetsk is the most populous, but it is the Dnipropetrovsk "clique" that has proven strongest in politics, now as in the days of communism.[71]

In 1994 over 70 percent of the eastern Ukrainian members of parliament represented the Communist, Socialist, or another left-leaning party. These were all antinationalist and pro-Russian. With ninety-one members in the Supreme Rada, the Ukrainian Communist Party was clearly the largest single party. A full seventy-four of these delegates came from eastern and southern Ukraine. After the April 1998 elections the Communists increased their parliamentary faction to a full 120 but still got the bulk of their vote in the industrial east. Rukh had hoped to tap into a potential reservoir of support in the east but garnered only about 2 percent in the Donbass. Although Rukh did increase its total number of seats from twenty-five to forty-three, this was almost entirely because of more western votes. A number of new parties hurriedly put together for the elections were formed around existing or past prime ministers, each with its own regional power base. Pavlo Lazarenko's Hromada, for instance, was almost exclusively Dnipropetrovskian. In fact, all major Ukrainian parties, in spite of their all-embracing names and platforms, are regionally based.[72]

The Ukrainian Communist Party has focused mainly on economic, political, and ideological issues. According to its platform, however, it also supports Russian as a state language for Ukraine.[73] That this is a popular item among the voters of the Donbass area was shown by a referendum the local authorities arranged in parallel with the 1994 parliamentary elections: A full 85 percent of the Donbass electorate supported the demand for making Russian the second state language of the republic. But eastern Ukrainian parliamentarians have not accorded this question much priority. Russian activists in the Donbass Intermovement have complained that as soon as these politicians settle down in Kiev, they forget how they promised the voters to fight for the Russian-language culture of Ukraine.[74]

Part of the explanation for this may lie in the Ukrainization effect that Kiev seems to exert on its political elites. Nor does the pressure from local voters to follow up cultural pledges made during the election campaign seem as great as the local referendum might indicate. The Ukrainization of the republic has been (at least thus far) limited to the state level and to the central and western areas. As long as Kiev does not pressure the populace in eastern and southern Ukraine to switch to the Ukrainian language, it is likely to remain difficult to mobilize them to fight for the Russian language. Ukraine has made greater concessions to the Russian-speaking regions than is the case in most of the other new states of the former USSR. Indeed, if the politicians of Kiev had not quietly made these concessions, it is doubtful whether they would have had a free hand to pursue Ukrainization at the state level.

Eastern Ukraine was after a while disappointed with the "new" Kuchma, whereas the western Ukrainians started liking him, as was the case with Kravchuk. Already in April 1995 a survey revealed that support for Kuchma in the east was down to 40–50 percent, while it had risen to 55–60 percent in the west.[75] It is likely that a new presidential challenger will emerge from the east to replace him. Petro Symenenko, leader of the Ukrainian Communist Party, tried just that in the November 1999 Ukrainian presidential elections and failed. But should another challenger from the east succeed next time, the new president may become entrapped in the logic of the Ukrainian nation-building project and gradually emerge as more and more Ukrainian.

•   •   •

We have seen that in both Belarus and Ukraine the conditions for post-Communist nation-building have been strikingly similar in many ways. Various theories have been launched to explain why the Belarusian project collapsed whereas the Ukrainian one seems here to stay. Stephen Burant has noted that Stalin found he had to use the Ukrainian language to implement the Sovietization of Galicia after World War II, whereas Russian could be used as the language of Sovietization in the Belarusian territories that were captured at the same time.[76] Even if this may explain much of what happened in Ukrainian politics under perestroika, it does not explain why Ukrainization has continued long after the Galicians were pushed out of most central positions and no longer set the political agenda in the republic.

Leonid Kuchma and Alyaksandr Lukashenka were both elected president at about the same time, summer 1994. Prior to their election, both had portrayed themselves as being more Russia-friendly than their competitors, and many observers drew parallels between the two men. But it was the commentators who focused on the differences that seem to have got the last word.[77] The differences between the semifascist dictator in Minsk and the pragmatic nation-builder in Kiev have become increasingly apparent.[78]

Ethnic romantics and the power elite in Belarus soon found themselves on a collision course. In Kiev, however, they have discovered that they have common interests on many questions. They have not concluded any formal alliances, but in practice they have ended up pulling in the same direction, despite their different starting points. Their shared goal has been to keep Ukraine outside the embrace of Russia and to give the populace a separate identity. To gain credibility the Ukrainian state project had to be imbued with a cultural content distinct from that of Russia. And the main pillar of this culture has been the Ukrainian language.

10

RUSSIA: THE OLD CENTER VERSUS THE NEW— VERSUS THE PERIPHERY

The post-Communist nation-building project of Russia is full of paradoxes. Here are a few:

- Russia is one of the countries of the former Soviet Union that can definitely lay claim to a long and well-recognized history as a separate state. And yet the country has in many ways not come as far in the nation-building process as most of its neighbors. Considerable disagreement still attends such central attributes of the state as the national flag, the coat of arms, and citizenship. There is no such thing as a generally accepted concept of the "Russian nation."
- Today's Russia is a continuation of the Russian Soviet Federated Socialist Republic (RSFSR). During the Soviet era, this republic was never—unlike the other Soviet republics—seen as part of the periphery. The capital of Russia, Moscow, was the capital of the entire Soviet Union. And yet the RSFSR was never really part of the center either. Rather, it seemed a kind of indeterminate residual category: What was left over when the ethnically defined republics had been subtracted.
- The circle of radical reformers around former Politburo member Boris Yeltsin utilized this residual category to create a politically

independent Russian state that they really did not desire. What they would have preferred would have been for the Soviet Union to continue to exist, without communism and in a highly decentralized form, but as *one* common state. Anticommunism rather than nationalism was the motive behind the establishment of today's Russian Federation.

- Russia is one of the most ethnically homogeneous states of the former Soviet Union. True, within its borders live more than 100 different ethnic groups, but most of these are small indeed. More than 83 percent of the total population are ethnic Russians, and Russian enjoys a sovereign position as the language of communication for all strata of society. All the same, ethnopolitical demands from the minorities have had greater impact in Russia than in any other former Soviet republic.

- Russia is unique among the Soviet successor states in being defined as an ethnic federation. Within the Russian Federation, some thirty different ethnic groups have been allocated their own "homelands" of varying types: republic, autonomous county (*oblast*), or autonomous district (*okrug*). Taken together, these homelands occupy more than half the territory of Russia, even though their ethnic groups represent only some 7 percent of the total population.

What Is Russia?

In 1922 Lenin and his followers established the Union of Soviet Socialist Republics. The name said nothing about where on the globe this state lay. Although it occupied largely the same territory as the czarist empire, its new leaders categorically denied that this was merely a case of the centuries-old Russian state in a new guise. During its first years of existence, the leaders of the USSR did not see it as the homeland of the Russian people, nor for that matter of the "Soviet" people. It was to be the homeland of the world revolution.

To the Bolsheviks, all nationalism was anathema, and great-power chauvinism was the worst of all. The Russians were the dominant population group within the USSR, and their nationalism was seen as great-power chauvinism. And thus, in those first years, priority was accorded to the struggle against Russian nationalism rather than against nationalism among small population groups.[1]

In the 1930s these attitudes changed. Stalin declared that the question of which nationalism came first—be it local or Great Russian—was an academic matter. In 1952 it was proclaimed that Great Russian chauvinism had finally been overcome.[2] This was after the Communist Party

196

Courtesy of Trond A. Svensson

1 Adygeya
2 Karachay-Cherkessia
3 Kabardino-Balkaria
4 North Ossetia
5 Ingushetia
6 Chechnya
7 Dagestan
8 Kalmykia
9 Karelia

10 Mordvinia
11 Chuvashia
12 Tatarstan
13 Mari El
14 Udmurtia
15 Bashkortostan
16 Nenets autonomous okrug
17 Khanty-Mansy autonomous okrug

itself had to an increasing degree become the exponent of exactly this Great Russian chauvinism. At the triumphant celebration in the Kremlin in May 1945, Stalin had proclaimed a toast for "the great Russian people" to whom the main share of the honor for the Soviet victory over Nazism was apparently due. After the death of Stalin, such blatant Russian ethnonationalism disappeared from the official propaganda, but still the expression "big brother of the Soviet peoples" could be heard, referring to the ethnic Russians.

And yet a great many Russians felt that their ethnic group was made invisible in the Soviet state. For example, there existed no separate Russian Communist Party like those found in the other republics. Likewise, whereas each Soviet republic had its own academy of sciences, a Russian academy of sciences was all the more conspicuous by its absence. Russian nationalists were also worried because Russian areas were receiving less than their fair share through the economic policy pursued by the Communist Party. Although many non-Russian peripheral areas could enjoy the benefits of an active regional policy that brought about a marked increase in welfare after World War II, many Russian villages in the so-called non-black-earth zone in the north (where rain, cold, and less fertile soil led to smaller harvests) were becoming ghost towns. This in turn meant, it was said, that the Russian cultural heritage was in danger, because it was in the villages that genuine Russian traditions had been maintained for generations.

That no separate Russian academy of sciences existed had, in fact, a mostly practical explanation: The Pan-Soviet Academy of Sciences had its main headquarters in Moscow and two important branches in Leningrad and Novosibirsk. Thus, all three institutions lay on Russian territory and were staffed mainly by Russians. To have a separate Russian academy of sciences in addition to the Soviet one would have been an unnecessary duplication of efforts. Similar reasoning applied to the nonexistence of a Russian Communist Party. Here, however, we should note another likely motive: The Soviet leaders probably feared that if there were a separate party organization for the Russian Republic, it might develop into an alternative power center and even a hotbed of opposition.

Be all this as it may, during the Communist era very few Russian nationalists were opponents of the Soviet state. Quite the contrary: They noted with satisfaction that the Bolsheviks had managed to gather most of the czarist empire into one realm again, after its dissolution during the Russian civil war. In 1919 Lenin moved the capital from Petrograd (St. Petersburg; after 1924, Leningrad) back to the ancient seat of the Muscovite sovereigns. This move was motivated largely by strategic concerns: Petrograd was too vulnerable to attack from the White generals.

But it was scarcely considerations of defense tactics alone that made Lenin move into the Kremlin, the centuries-old seat of the czarist powers. It was an act rich in symbolism, as the new Russian Communists thereby assumed the nation-building heritage of the czars of Old Russia.

During the Soviet era, a great many non-Russians identified themselves strongly with their titular Soviet republic. By contrast, the RSFSR derived its name not from the Russians as an ethnic group but from the territory of Russia. In general, we can say that the Russian people did not feel strongly linked to "their" republic. It would seem that Russians, to a greater degree than non-Russians, considered the entire Soviet Union their homeland.[3] A survey conducted in the late 1970s and early 1980s, for instance, found that 80 percent of Georgians and Uzbeks considered their titular republic as their "homeland," whereas Russians, regardless of where they lived, in most cases (70 percent or more) named the Soviet Union as their homeland.[4]

Perestroika, or Political One-upmanship

When the Soviet system began to crumble under perestroika, most Russian nationalists were conservative in a double sense: They wished to maintain the territorial unity of the state, and—as a result of this—they tended to support the Communist regime. They saw the Communist Party of the USSR as the sole organizational force capable of holding the Soviet Union together. And on this matter they were to be proven correct. When the Communist Party dissolved, so did the unitary state.

During the Soviet Congress of People's Deputies held in May 1989, the Russian author Valentin Rasputin declared that many of the republics were pursuing a highly anti-Russian policy line. Unless this could be stopped soon, he said, perhaps the Russian Soviet Republic should consider withdrawing from the Soviet Union.[5] Now this suggestion was not intended to be taken at face value. Rasputin's point was to unmask what he saw as the hypocrisy in the non-Russian nationalist movements: They wanted full control—economic and political—over their own republics while at the same time continuing to milk Russia for all it was worth.

Rasputin's words turned out to be prophetic. In 1988 and 1989, a strong anti-Communist movement emerged in Russia. Led by Andrey Sakharov and Boris Yeltsin, the movement was represented in the Congress of People's Deputies by several hundred deputies. In many cases these Russian radicals joined with anti-Communist nationalists from the other republics, not so much because they wanted to dissolve the Soviet Union as because they saw Soviet politics as primarily a struggle between authoritarian communism on the one hand and the forces of democracy on the other. This struggle was to coincide with the clash between centralism and decentralization.

It was Mikhail Gorbachev who had taken the initiative toward liberalizing the Soviet regime. From 1989 onward, though, Russian radicals saw him as an obstacle to the development of a democratic Russian society. The Yeltsin wing defined itself as a democratic counter-center to the more cautious reform regime of Gorbachev. More and more, Soviet policy was characterized by bitter opposition between the two former party colleagues, Gorbachev and Yeltsin. And as this conflict gradually intensified and matters came to a head, it became obvious that only one of them would be able to emerge victorious.

In spring 1989 Gorbachev was still entrenched in power, as leader of both the Soviet Communist Party and the Congress of People's Deputies. By contrast, Yeltsin lacked a formal institutional platform on which to stand. Then, in spring 1990, he got the chance to gain precisely such a platform: the RSFSR itself. No one, not even the most seasoned Sovietologists, had ever paid much attention to the elected organs of this Kremlin-overshadowed republic. True, the Supreme Soviet of the RSFSR had its own premises, a quite attractive white edifice on the banks of the river Moscow, but it lacked any real power until Yeltsin, with his undeniable political acumen, realized the potential. The campaign before the spring 1990 elections to the Russian Soviet saw the radicals in full mobilization, and the results were overwhelming: They captured about half of the seats. Finally, after a close battle, Yeltsin was chosen to lead the Supreme Soviet of Russia.

Russia's democracy movement thereby became territorialized, as an indirect result of the power struggle between Gorbachev and Yeltsin. "Where you stand depends on where you sit"—and Yeltsin was now sitting in the Russian national assembly, where he identified himself with the cause of Russia, the RSFSR. Thus came about a situation in which Russian nationalists were striving to maintain a multinational empire, whereas their ideological adversaries, the Russian democrats, began to construct out of Russia something that resembled a nation-state.[6]

With their new institutional interests, the pro-Yeltsin forces gradually took over some of the Russian nationalist rhetoric. Safely ensconced in the Moscow White House, they suddenly "discovered" that Russia was being economically exploited by the other republics. In June 1990 the Supreme Soviet of Russia adopted a declaration of sovereignty for its republic.

In spring 1990 Gorbachev was appointed to a newly created position, that of Soviet executive president. In response, Yeltsin was chosen president of the Russian Republic the following summer. Whereas Gorbachev had been elected indirectly, by the Soviet national assembly, there were direct presidential elections in Russia, a point that provided Yeltsin with a strong popular mandate. And after the failed old-line Communist coup of August that year, Yeltsin emerged as clearly the most popular politician in Russia. Most of the honor for thwarting the coup was directed toward the Russian president.

From Soviet Union to Russia

The attempted coup brought about a radical change in Soviet politics. The Pan-Soviet governmental structures, long ailing, suddenly found themselves paralyzed, with no aims, no leadership, and no legitimacy. In mid-September Yeltsin signed a series of presidential decrees granting Russia the ownership rights to all oil, gas, and other sources of energy on the territory of the republic. In November the RSFSR assumed control of the Soviet Ministry of Finance and the mint.[7] Russia took the initiative to establish an interrepublican commission, headed by former RSFSR prime minister Ivan Silayev, to regulate economic relations among the republics. Throughout the territory of the Soviet Union, there was a distinct feeling that this new Russia was poised to take over the role of authoritarian center: The Yeltsin clique was seen as seeking to dictate the policies of the other republics as well.

During the days of perestroika, there had existed a kind of alliance between Russia and several of the other republics, an alliance motivated largely by tactical concerns and directed against the common foe: the Soviet center. Now this same center was about to exit from the political scene, and other conflict lines, previously relegated to the wings, began to emerge more clearly.

In fall and winter 1991, all the other Soviet republics declared their political independence, seceding entirely from what had been the Soviet Union. Centrally placed politicians in the circles around Yeltsin urged that Russia should follow suit. Presidential adviser Sergey Stankevich maintained that after the August coup attempt the other republics had been behaving as if all the institutions and resources in their own republics belonged solely to themselves, while viewing everything on the territory of Russia as if it were common property: "Russia has in reality been left without any separate statehood. In my opinion, the country has no choice. In the present situation it would be self-destructive for Russia to cling to the attributes of the Soviet Union. The country must, as soon as possible, become a separate state and must adopt a declaration of full national independence."[8]

This, however, did not come to pass. Even though Yeltsin and his coterie certainly contributed actively toward the momentum behind the dissolution of the Soviet Union, the scenario described by Valentin Rasputin was never formally enacted. What happened was that Russia remained behind as a kind of leftover USSR, in its own eyes and in the eyes of others. Whereas all the other former Soviet republics could designate themselves "successor states" (*strana-naslednik* or *strana-pravopreem-nik*) to the Soviet Union, Russia was recognized as the "continuator state" (*strana-prodolzhatel'*) to the Soviet Union.[9]

The international community viewed all this as a nice, safe solution to a tricky problem. Many Western experts had feared that the dissolution of the gigantic Soviet empire would unleash a veritable judgment day. Back in 1988, the U.S. historian Paul Kennedy had written: "There is nothing in the character or tradition of the Russian state to suggest that it could ever accept imperial decline gracefully."[10] There seemed to be all reason to worry about what might happen once the Soviet army was no longer under firm, centralized political control. In Yugoslavia the people's army had resorted to massive use of arms in attempting to prevent dissenter republics from seceding from the unitary federal republic. The Yugoslav wars of succession were still at full throttle when the Soviet Union fell to pieces.

Once it had become obvious that the Soviet state could not be salvaged, Western leaders began a frantic search for solutions that could ensure the greatest possible degree of continuity and a controlled transition to a new state system. It was important that there be one state that could assume responsibility for the international obligations and treaties signed by the USSR, not least regarding disarmament and arms control. Russia's leaders, for their part, welcomed any opportunity to promote the image of Russia as a superpower akin to the now defunct Soviet Union. This was an important reason why Russia agreed to take over responsibility for the entire foreign debt of the Soviet Union. To begin with, of course, there was no chance that it could be repaid, but this was meant as a signal to the international community as well as to the country's own inhabitants. It also allowed Russia to "inherit" the foreign embassies of the Soviet Union as well as its seat in the UN Security Council.

This solution bears a certain resemblance to the case of Yugoslavia, where Serbia together with Montenegro clung to Pan-Yugoslav institutions and symbols. But the links to the old state were far less clear with Russia than in the Serbian case. Although the Russian Federation assumed much of the mantle of the old center, it also contributed actively to the final dissolution of the Soviet state in December 1991.

On 8 December 1991 Yeltsin and the Belarusian and Ukrainian heads of state met at the Belavezha Pushcha hunting lodge outside Minsk to agree to the establishment of a new international organization: the Commonwealth of Independent States. This took place while the Soviet Union still existed, on paper at least; a spokesperson for Soviet president Gorbachev denounced the Minsk agreement as a coup d'état.[11] Two days later, Gorbachev met with several Soviet generals, presumably to ask for armed assistance in halting the dissolution of the Soviet Union.

Nothing came of this, however. On 10 December the Minsk agreement was ratified by the Russian parliament by 188 votes to 6, without any attempt by the military to intervene. Some may explain this by noting that Soviet officers have no tradition of interference in politics. Others will point out that Yeltsin promised the officers a 90 percent pay raise and assured them that the Soviet army would remain as one entity under joint command in the new Commonwealth of Independent States.[12]

On 16 December Norway became the first Western country to recognize Russia as an independent state. At 7:35 P.M. on 25 December the red flag over the Kremlin was lowered, and ten minutes later the Russian flag was fluttering in its place. Yeltsin moved into Gorbachev's office even before this president without a country had had a chance to remove his belongings.

A Confused Giant

Like the other former Soviet republics, Russia faced enormous problems regarding its finances and its identity. But Russia's problems were often the reverse of those elsewhere. One important difference concerned state structures. Even though none of the other new states had to start from scratch in institution-building, in most cases the former governing organs from the Soviet era were too weak to function as the state apparatus for an independent state. In Russia, by contrast, the new leaders inherited an apparatus far too big for their needs. The Soviet Union had had a population almost twice the size of Russia's. Moreover, Russia now wanted to introduce a market economy where the role of the state would be mightily reduced. Thus, the first major challenge for the Russian state was to slim down. And anyone who has ever tried to lose weight will know how hard that can be.

Identity problems were another big challenge to post-Soviet Russia. Deep within leading political circles there was basic uncertainty as to the status and character of this new state. The fall of the Communist regime had created a situation where nothing could be taken for granted any longer. The very foundations for the life of the nation and the state had crumbled. The identity discussion concerned some very basic questions: Who or what is really the "nation"? How do we delimit the state? What of the relations between state and nation? Who are we, and where are we headed?

Newspaper articles with headings punctuated by question marks filled the political columns. Many of their writers asked questions like, "Will Russia survive the collapse of the empire?"[13] The human aspects were also a cause of great concern: "The empire has collapsed. Who is lying there, trapped in the rubble?" Others feared that ethnic and political unrest could spill over the borders and into Russia.[14] Still others saw other dangers. An MP from the Caucasus inquired, "Is Russia after the coup really nothing but the imperial Russia?"[15]

To these many questions came many different answers. Everyone from centrally placed decisionmakers to armchair politicians felt compelled to make a contribution to the debate, and no consensus seemed to crystallize. There were those who held that Russia was still an empire, whereas others maintained it was a nation-state. Most of those who cried, "Empire!" meant this as criticism and reproach, but there were some who felt that Russia *should* be an empire.[16]

But if Russia was a nation-state, *whose* nation-state was it? That of the Russians or of all its citizens?[17] After 1990, a new concept, *rossiyane*, gradually gained ground as an ethnically neutral common term for all the people of Russia. The word derived from the name of the country, *Rossiya*, and not from the adjective meaning "Russian," which is *russkie*. Taking as its starting point the difference between the vowels *u* and *o*, the Yeltsin administration sought to encourage a new common national identity for all citizens of the new republic. This identity was to be linked to unifying political symbols and institutions, not to specific and divisive ethnic traditions. These efforts met with heavy resistance from Russian nationalists, however. They feared that the Russians, in contrast to the titular nations in the other former Soviet republics, would thus be cheated out of their own ethnically defined nation-state. At the same time, the new *rossiyane* identity was attacked by leaders of various ethnic minorities, who held that nation-building of that ilk would become a tool for cultural homogenization and assimilation.

Even if the Soviet Union was gone, identification with the former state entity remained strong among much of the Russian populace. In many cases Soviet nostalgia was mingled with Communist convictions, but it could also be strong among non-Communists and anti-Communists. There existed no logical or necessary connection between the struggle against the Communist regime and the struggle against the Soviet unitary state. The philosopher Aleksandr Tsipko, who had been a pioneer figure in the theoretical crusade against Soviet ideology, openly admitted, "I personally will always remain a citizen of the old, great, now late, lamented Russia."[18] Opinion polls revealed that he was not alone in feeling this way. In a large-scale survey undertaken in November–December 1993, only 21 percent responded that they saw the dissolution of the Soviet Union as something "positive" or "more positive than negative," whereas 70 percent felt that this event was "negative" or "more negative than positive."[19] In another study undertaken in 1996, only 12 percent thought the dissolution was the right decision, whereas 68 percent took the opposite view.[20]

For most Soviet nostalgists, the loss of the unitary state was also marked by a feeling of resignation. They accepted the new state of affairs and had no plans for actively working to overthrow it. Yet at either end of the political spectrum in Russia, extreme right and extreme left, there was a firm belief that the dissolution of the Soviet Union was at most temporary. It was, they believed, based on a misunderstanding, a misunderstanding that would have to be cleared up as soon as possible, by force if need be. Every now and then these undercurrents in the Russian debate surfaced, at times featured in the news. This could be seen, for instance, in March 1996, when the Russian national assembly, by 250 votes to 98, adopted a resolution denouncing the dissolution of the Soviet Union. This resolution sent shock waves throughout the international diplomatic corps, who wondered just how the Russian parliamentarians intended to set about implementing it.

The Duma resolution was in turn heartily denounced in the other former Soviet republics, and Azerbaijan threatened to withdraw from the CIS in protest. Yeltsin then asked the Duma representatives to adopt a new resolution specifically stating that the former one was to have no effect on Russia's international obligations and that the Duma recognized the country's legal status as valid. This proposal was defeated by 186 to 65 votes. But the MPs did announce that their resolutions were meant as expressions of their political views and were not to have any consequences within international law.[21] All the same, this episode dramatically demonstrated that the Russian state had a frightening lack of legitimacy in the eyes of its own democratically elected representatives.

Visions, Scenarios, and Models

Since 1991 a wide-ranging and frequently confused debate on the Russian state and nation has blossomed in the Russian media. Most of the ideas that have been presented define Russia in such a way that the state borders fail to coincide with the borders of the Russian Federation. Visions have been put forth of a Greater Russia considerably larger than the Russian state of today. A few, however, seem to wish a Russia shrunk to encompass only the ethnic Russian core areas within today's Russian state. In their own ways, these macro- and microversions of the Russian state concept hinder the consolidation of an internationally recognized nation-state of Russia.

Empire, Ethnocracy, and the Great Mission

During the days of perestroika, the journalist Eduard Volodin established himself as a leading ideologue of Russian imperial thought.[22] In a hard-

hands full trying to maintain order in their individual zones, and there will be no time for them to develop conflicts with one another.

Ethnocultural Models

Not all Russian nationalists are imperialists. For many, the main point is not territorial expansion but maintaining the specific character of Russian national culture. What is important is not so much that the state is large but that it is truly Russian.

A typical representative of this line of thought is Kseniya Myalo. During the perestroika era, she was an active proponent of glasnost, but she gradually distanced herself from the Yeltsin circle and what she saw as its nihilism on the national question. Her message is not that the Russian people must have more land and power than other people but that they must at least get the same rights as the others. And this, she feels, has not been the case.

Myalo admits that during the Soviet period several of the republics were subjected to unwarranted Russification. Thus, it was hardly unreasonable for them to wish to break loose and form states of their own—as long as this was not to be at the expense of the Russian people. But that was precisely what happened. As a side effect of the other Soviet peoples' making use of their right to self-determination, the Russian people were rendered stateless.

Does that mean that the USSR was the state of the Russian people? Well, the position of Russians within the Soviet Union was ambiguous, according to Myalo. Politically speaking, ethnic Russians were indeed overrepresented in the central organs of power. But this was in itself of scant importance because these so-called Russian leaders were already thoroughly denationalized. In practical politics the Russians were in fact subjected to more discrimination than were other peoples.[31]

Today's Russia cannot, as Myalo sees it, be considered a Russian national state. First of all, there are more than 25 million ethnic Russians living outside its borders. Second, Russia is the sole Soviet successor state to define itself as a multinational rather than a national state. By contrast, the various autonomous areas on the territory of Russia are defined in ethnic terms.[32]

This line of thought is consistently ethnocultural. Whereas Lysenko, Zhirinovskiy, and Volodin are what Lenin would have characterized as typical representatives of Russian great-power chauvinism, Myalo is proof that what Lenin saw as typically small-nation nationalism—the desire to break loose and establish one's own, ethnically delimited state—has also found its exponents in Russian nationalism.

The first and best-known representative of this variant of Russian nationalism is Aleksandr Solzhenitsyn. In his 1973 *Letter to the Soviet Leaders*, Solzhenitsyn sought to remind Leonid Brezhnev and the other Soviet leaders that they, too, were ethnic Russians. What they were by birth they should also be in deeds. Solzhenitsyn therefore urged them to give back to the Soviet Union its identity as Russia. For that to be possible, the country would have to renounce its Asian possessions and direct its vision to the northeast, he held.[33]

Although Solzhenitsyn explicitly favored ceding territory, he still wished to retain far more of the Soviet state than that which makes up today's Russian Federation. He saw also Ukraine, Belarus, and northern Kazakhstan as good Russian core areas.[34] This is a theme to which he has returned again and again, regularly provoking the wrath of the nation-builders of Ukraine and Kazakhstan.

Given today's situation, many Russian ethnonationalists have lowered their sights. Not only do they consider Ukraine, Kazakhstan, and Belarus as lost causes, but some of them are even willing to define the non-Russian autonomous areas within the Russian Federation out of Russian statehood. As an absolute minimum, those portions of today's Russia that have not already been given to the various ethnic minorities as autonomous areas must be proclaimed a separate, ethnically defined Russian republic. If any groups are entitled to territories of their own, then this must also apply to the Russian people: everyone or no one.[35] This line of thought has received support from, among others, Viktor Kozlov, who was one of the Soviet Union's most prominent social anthropologists during the 1970s. Kozlov finds proof of the anti-Russian tendency in Leninist-Stalinist national policy in the fact that "the largest ethnic group in the country never got its own Russian republic."[36]

New Variants of Eurasianism

Many Russian cultural theoreticians and social scientists today are turning to the Russian writers in exile of the interwar years to find ideas for constructing a post-Communist Russia. The Russian émigré journals published in Prague, Sofia, Munich, and Paris featured long and often sophisticated debates on the "Russian idea" and the future of the Russian state. This is literature that Russians were not allowed to read during the Communist period and that they now devour eagerly. Often, however, they are disappointed. The ideas they find in these writings are outdated, or else those who promulgated them have become discredited because of their sympathies with the Soviets, with European fascism, or perhaps both.[37]

Still, some of the émigré writers do have disciples in today's Russia. This is particularly true of the so-called Eurasians, an intellectual movement that in the 1920s included a wide range of prominent experts and leading intellectuals.[38] They believed that Russia had a special mission and a unique historical path of development different from that of the West. Unlike most Russian nationalists of their time, these Eurasians deemphasized the linguistic element in the "Russian character." True, they said, Russian is a Slavic tongue, but the Russian people have little in common with the western and southern Slavic people. Instead, they saw the Russian people as being deeply influenced by the neighboring Finno-Ugric and Turkic groups. All those who live in Russia thus make up one common nation. This nation is both Russian and multinational at the same time. Neither European nor Asian, it lies at the crossroads of both cultural universes. It is Eurasian.[39]

As applied to modern Russian politics, this line of thought can assume different forms. It may easily serve as an ideological superstructure over attempts to reestablish the Soviet Union or perhaps the czarist empire. Indeed, many Russian imperialists and revanchists have adorned their programs with Eurasianist formulations.[40] Students of Neo-Eurasianism as a political movement in contemporary Russia generally see this as the most usual variant.[41] But the Eurasian vision of a vast European-Asiatic population mass can also be scaled down and translated into a program for ethnic solidarity among the many peoples of Russia. Former presidential adviser Sergey Stankevich and the economist Leonid Abalkin were among those who stood forth between 1992–1994 as advocates of this type of nation-building, nonimperialist Eurasianism.

Common to all variants of Eurasianism is a strong underlying distrust of the peoples of the West and Western culture. One of the founders of the movement, Nikolay Trubetskoy, maintained, "We ought to get used to the idea that the Romano-Germanic world and its culture is our worst enemy."[42] It would seem to be this aspect of Eurasianism that has made it attractive to ideologues within Russia's Communist Party. Indeed, the party leader, Gennadiy Zyuganov, has explicitly stated that Russia is a Eurasian country, where East meets West.[43] This, however, does not mean that Russia can or even should serve as a bridge-builder between Europe and Asia. Instead, Zyuganov portrays all influence from Europe as dangerous and subversive. By its very nature, the relationship between Russia and Europe is antagonistic.[44] Basic to Zyuganov's version of Russian nation-building are the ideals of isolationism and "state self-sufficiency."[45]

State Patriotism, Soviet-Style

Zyuganov has no desire to be seen as a "nationalist." He styles himself a "patriot," quite in line with the nation-building rhetoric of the Soviet era.

We can find a different type of Soviet-inspired Russian state patriotism in one of the most active participants in the national debate, Ramazan Abdulatipov, who from 1990–1993 was the leader of the Chamber of Nationalities in Russia's Supreme Soviet and later was appointed Russian minister of nationalities. Abdulatipov himself is an Avar, a member of a tiny ethnic group of northern Caucasus, and as such can hardly be accused of running the errands of Russian imperialists or great-power chauvinists. Yet he has clearly been socialized into a Soviet mindset.

According to Abdulatipov, relations among the various ethnic groups in Russia have always been good. As more and more new groups were incorporated into the czarist realm through its territorial expansion, they were treated with respect and tolerance. They were allowed to maintain their traditions and their ways of life. Indeed, says Abdulatipov, the Soviet powers also did much good for the small nations within the country.[46] And this is something Russia must continue to build on today as well.

Abdulatipov employs the terms *patriotism* and *nationalism* in precisely the same way as they were used in Soviet ideology. He sees patriotism as a healthy love of the state and brands nationalism as an exaggerated devotion to one's own ethnic group. Nationalism acts to subvert the state and is therefore to be rejected. For all the peoples of Russia, a strong common state provides the best protection for their interests and possibilities to develop. The tragedy of Russia today is that far too many of the inhabitants have transferred their patriotic sentiments down from the level of the state to that of the group, the region, or the ethnonation.

At the same time, any and every attempt by the state to undermine ethnic diversity by means of cultural standardization must also be condemned.[47] Abdulatipov terms his program for Russian nation-building "state patriotism as a shared national idea of unity and construction of the motherland." Patriotism of this kind is meant to bring the various individuals, ethnoses, and territories together to constitute one shared, multinational Russian people. It will obliterate the contradiction between *russkiy* and *rossiyskiy*, between what is ethnically Russian and what is politically Russian.[48]

Nation-Building, Western-Style

Abdulatipov is deeply skeptical of all Western nation-building models, which he sees as based on the ideal of assimilation and eradication of ethnic diversity. But another Russian professor, Valery Tishkov, is a wholehearted proponent of precisely the view that Russian nation-building should proceed along Western lines. Tishkov, who is director of the Institute of Ethnology and Anthropology of the Russian Academy of Sciences, has, like Abdulatipov, also been active in politics.[49] In 1992 he was minister of nationalities in Boris Yeltsin's government but resigned after realizing that his views were not being heard. Tishkov explains this lack of response in terms of opposition from Abdulatipov and from Yeltsin's presidential adviser on nationalities issues, Galina Starovoytova.[50] It is also obvious that despite some superficial similarities, the nation model advocated by Tishkov is qualitatively different from theirs.

Tishkov is influenced by the so-called modernists and constructivists—British historian Benedict Anderson and Norwegian anthropologists Fredrik Barth and Thomas Hylland Eriksen, to mention only a few. They see an ethnic group not as a naturally determined entity but as a modern social construction. Every community is a varied cultural mosaic. By focusing on some elements and ignoring others, we can bring certain ethnic dividing lines to the fore, but other divisions might have been equally possible. Cultural elites play a central role in the development of ethnic identity. Once an ethnic group has been established, this can lay the foundations for political demands, perhaps culminating in demands for a separate state. Pure self-interest—the dream of power and privilege—is an important driving force when the elite issue demands on behalf of "their" group.[51]

"Natural" states are just as nonexistent as "natural" ethnic groups. All state formations come about as the result of historical chance, and then, once a state has emerged, it begins to knead and shape its population into a national community. In a discussion with the Russian ethnonationalist Kseniya Myalo, Tishkov refers to a famous statement from the Italian freedom struggles of the 1800s: "We have created Italy—now we have to create Italians."[52] In the same way, says Tishkov, today's Russian authorities should give priority to creating a Russian nation with a shared, supraethnic identity. Active, citizenship-oriented nation-building is necessary to counter the ethnic and ethnocratic national ideas found throughout Russian society.

Russia is and must remain a nation-state but not a *russkiy* nation-state. No, it is a *rossiyskiy* or what Tishkov calls a *"Rossian"* nation-state, one shared by all its citizens. Tishkov has proposed introducing into English and other Western languages the distinction already present in Russian, between *Russian* in the ethnic sense and *Rossian* to denote the political aspect.[53]

The "Rossian" identity is upheld not only by political institutions. but also strong cultural bonds, not least the Russian language, which is understood by all the country's inhabitants. "Russia is more culturally homogeneous than many other large and even small countries considered to be nation-states."[54] The nation-builders of Russia are thus not starting from scratch: There exists a considerable shared cultural heritage on which to build. Opinion surveys have shown that more and more of the population see Russia as their homeland, Tishkov reports. In 1987 over two-thirds of those interviewed in Moscow had stated that the Soviet Union was their homeland, whereas less than 15 percent mentioned the Russian Federation. Only five years later, in 1992, the results were markedly different: 27 percent named the USSR and 54 percent Russia.[55]

The Official View

Tishkov notes with some satisfaction that after he resigned as minister of nationalities, several of his ideas gained acceptance within the Russian nation-building doctrine. He sees some of them reflected in the document "Ob ukrepleniy Rossiyskogo gosudarstva" (On strengthening the Russian state), which President Yeltsin presented in February 1994.[56] Here the nation (*natsiya*) is defined in strictly supraethnic terms, as "common citizenship" (*sograzhdanstvo*). The concept of the "nation" is thus decoupled from ethnicity and explicitly linked to territory and political community.

Yet the new Russian constitution, adopted by referendum on 12–13 December 1993, defines Russia as a "multinational" state. Here the term *nation* is used in the traditional Soviet sense as synonymous with ethnocultural group. The sum of the many different ethnic nations in the country composes, according to the constitution, the multinational "people" of Russia. Between these two official Russian documents, made public within months of each other, there exist considerable differences in terminology as well as content.

Eduard Bagramov, once a prominent Soviet nationalities expert, was quick to attack the concept of the nation as "common citizenship": "Proponents of this concept believe that by proclaiming the existence of one shared nation in Russia they have also ensured the unity of the state and the indivisibility of the country. The right of nations to self-determination, a principle which they characterize as 'the greatest folly of the 20th century' is thereby—or so they would say—discredited with a single blow."[57] To the extent that the term *the people of Russia (narod Rossii)* is used in official documents in the singular, it cannot but help to sow doubt as to whether the new nationalities policy is honestly meant and has a democratic content, says Bagramov. It could be taken as a new version of the Leninist ideal of the "merger of nations." And the first ones who would react negatively would be the Russians: "Almost every single Russian sees himself as a representative of a great nation and not merely as a member of an ethnic group or tribe."

Who is right, then—Tishkov or Bagramov? Is the idea of "nation" as the average Russian sees it based on ethnicity or on citizenship? In a survey conducted in several Russian cities immediately before Bagramov's article was published, over 1,000 persons were asked who could in their opinion be considered a Russian *(russkiy)*. The results were in part surprising, but neither Tishkov nor Bagramov should automatically see in them support for their views. About half of those interviewed chose an ethnic or genetic criterion: 29 percent said that in order to be considered Russian, both one's parents should be Russian, whereas 15 percent opined it was enough if one parent was Russian. Further, 6 percent replied that only those whose passports proclaimed them as Russian should be counted. In contrast, 17 percent felt that all those who live in Russia should be considered Russian. And finally, 25 percent opted for the purely subjective response category: A Russian is someone who considers him- or herself to be one.[58]

Unitary State and Ethnic Federation

The strongest opposition to the citizenship-based concept of nation comes not from the average person in the street but from the elite in Russia's ethnically defined republics. For these elites, the principle of the right of the nation to self-determination has been a potent weapon in the struggle for power and resources. During the Soviet period, there were sixteen autonomous republics, five autonomous counties *(oblasti),* and ten autonomous districts *(okruga)* within the RSFSR. These had had only a highly limited degree of autonomy and rights, but with perestroika came hopes of totally new possibilities for greater power.

When Russia's new political elite challenged the regime of Gorbachev at the union level in 1990, this unleashed a political mobilization throughout the lower levels of the federation structure of the USSR. National elites in the autonomous republics and *oblasti* felt that if the union republics were to be granted greater sovereignty, then there was no reason why this should not apply to their own units as well. In August 1990 Karelia was the first autonomous republic in the RSFSR to adopt a declaration of sovereignty, two months after Russia had done so. In the ensuing weeks and months, the other autonomous units followed like pearls on a string: Komi and Tatarstan on 30 August; Yakutia on 17 September; Udmurtia on 19 September; Buryatia on 8 October; and Bashkortostan on 11 October—to mention only the first ones.[59] The main points in these declarations were that relations with the USSR and the Russian Federation were to be based on treaties and agreements and that within the territory of each republic the constitution and other laws of that republic were to take precedence over Soviet law. Finally, the natural resources of each republic were to belong to the local population.

Not all these declarations were promulgated with equal power and conviction. In some cases the local politicians seemed to see this as a headlong rush to get on the bandwagon while they could. They had no idea where the bandwagon was headed, but neither had they any wish to be left on the sidelines when the others paraded jubilantly past. In other cases the declaration of sovereignty remained an isolated incident, with the leaders doing little in the way of follow-up. Karelia would seem to be a case in point. Nor is this so strange, since Karelia has become one of the most Russified of the republics: Only one-tenth of the population are ethnic Karelians, and of these less than half can speak their Finno-Ugric native tongue.

Two republics were soon to take the lead: Chechnya and Tatarstan. They were far from forming a couple; even though they found themselves united in opposition to the center on several occasions, the methods, course of events, and results were very different indeed for these two republics.

Chechnya

The Chechens can look back on a long history of revolts against the Russians. As early as the eighteenth century, the armies of the czar began their offensives into the Caucasian mountains. In contrast to some of their neighbors, the Chechens offered fierce resistance. Their legendary leader Imam Mansur was captured in 1791, but the fight continued. In the nineteenth century, it was led by the no less legendary figure of Sheikh Shamil, who warded off the advancing Russian armies for twenty-five years, from 1834 to 1859, before he was defeated. An Avar himself, Shamil recruited most of his guerrilla fighters among the Chechens.

In 1920–1921 the Chechens made another desperate attempt to regain their freedom, and yet another rebellion took place during World War II. Stalin accused the entire Chechen nation collectively of collaboration with the Nazis and deported them en bloc to Central Asia. Tens of thousands died en route to exile. This act of punishment strengthened rather than weakened the Chechens' will to resist.

Chechnya joined the sovereignty bandwagon rather late, not until 27 November 1990. The republic was led by a relatively conservative regime that had supported the August 1991 coup attempt in Moscow. This Chechen regime was overthrown in October 1991 by Chechen nationalists, with the blessings of the central Russian authorities. An air force general, Dzhokhar Dudayev, became president. Dudayev was, to all appearances, thoroughly Sovietized: He was married to a Russian and had lived most of his adult life outside Chechnya.[60]

Very soon, however, the Chechen revolution took a highly radical turn. In November 1991 the republic declared itself fully independent of Russia, to which Yeltsin responded by decreeing a state of emergency for the republic on 7 November and sending a small contingent of Russian soldiers to the capital town of Grozny. But the Russian Supreme Soviet lifted the state of emergency a few days later, and the soldiers were withdrawn. Chechnya was thus in most respects de facto politically independent, but its economy remained highly dependent on Russia. The central authorities in Moscow continued to view the republic as a part of the Russian Federation, including it in all annual budgets.

President Dudayev soon found himself at odds with the Chechen politicians who had brought him to power. In June 1992 he dissolved the Chechen parliament by force of arms and introduced direct presidential rule. To Moscow it gradually appeared that there might be a chance to exploit the ever-deepening splits in Chechnya. Chechen oppositional politicians (or indeed, exile politicians) in Moscow were provided with weapons and sent home to topple Dudayev. A brief civil war erupted in Chechnya in autumn 1994 in which the Dudayev faction prevailed. Because it had collaborated with the Russian authorities, the Chechen opposition was now thoroughly discredited, and support for Dudayev rose markedly again in Chechnya.[61]

Yeltsin's security council determined that Dudayev was to be removed by force of Russian arms. Defense Minister Pavel Grachev assured them that Grozny would surrender in three hours and one week would suffice for the entire operation.[62] Over 40,000 soldiers poured over the borders of the republic in December 1994; two months and several bloody battles later, Grozny was taken.[63] The remainder of the country, however, was never properly pacified. Dudayev and his adherents withdrew to mountain strongholds to continue the struggle from there. On several occasions Russian soldiers were massacred in ambushes. The Russian troops responded by bombing civilian targets. More and more the pattern of battle began to resemble the Vietnam War. Two dramatic hostage dramas in southern Russian towns in 1995 demonstrated that the Chechens were also capable of moving the violence into Russian territory.

Even after Dudayev was killed in a Russian rocket attack in May 1996 the Chechen resistance was not broken. Finally, the popular Russian general Aleksandr Lebed was given the task of finding a negotiated solution. The so-called Khazavyurt agreement of 31 August 1996, named after the small town where it was concluded, brought the hostilities to an end. In a peace agreement signed in May 1997, the parties decided to postpone a resolution to the republic's status until 2001. In the meantime Moscow's writ did not run in Chechnya, and the republic had for all practical purposes achieved independence. The price was about 90,000 human lives.

Toward a Separate Tatarstan

For Chechnya, the struggle for independence became a *danse macabre*. By contrast, Tatarstan managed to gain acceptance for existence as a separate state entity without any bloodshed. There has been no civil war nor indeed any signs of one, even though many had feared that this would be the outcome.[64] The leaders have carried through a whole series of quite breathtaking political acrobatics and legalistic pirouettes, each time landing safely on the ground again.

The Tatars represent the second largest ethnic group in Russia, some 5.5 million. On the basis of most historical, geographical, and demographical conditions, however, it should have been impossible to form a separate state of Tatarstan. Tatarstan lies in the very heart of Russia, surrounded on all sides by Russian-dominated territories. In addition, not more than about 1.8 million of the 5.5 million Tatars in Russia live within the borders of the Republic of Tatarstan itself. The remainder are to be found partly in neighboring republics like Bashkortostan and Chuvashia, partly in Siberia, Moscow, and St. Petersburg. Moreover, almost 2 million non-Tatars live in Tatarstan, most of them Russians. Ethnic Tatars thus make up only slightly over half the total population of the republic.

Tatarstan was the first non-Russian area to be incorporated into the Russian empire. In 1552 the forces of Ivan the Terrible conquered Kazan, capital of the Volga Tatars. Throughout more than 400 years of coexistence with the Russians, the Tatars have been exposed to considerable Russian cultural influence. All the same, in 1990 there arose several popular movements in the republic demanding political independence for Tatarstan as well as the reestablishment of the old Tatar khanate. The most radical of these movements was Ittifak, the Tatar Party for National Independence. According to its party platform:

> In today's Tatar territories by the Urals and the Volga, the ancestors of the Tatar people had had their own statehood for over one thousand years. When they lost this statehood as a result of the expansionist drive of the Muscovy Empire, this was a national catastrophe. It brought the people to the brink of annihilation as a separate ethnos.[65]

Ittifak's program is a maximalist one. The party rejects the concept of "limited independence," that is, of Tatarstan as a state within another state. Independent Tatarstan must have its own professional army, its own security forces and police. The Tatar language must be the sole official language. Its territory must also be extended to include all areas along the Volga and in Siberia in which Tatars live.[66] Several of the points on the party program are clearly aimed against the Russian population in Tatarstan, like the denunciation of ethnically mixed marriages and the demand that the "genetic pool" of the Tatar people be reestablished.[67]

Another ethnonationalist movement in Tatarstan, the Tatar Public Center (TPC, or TOTs in Russian), has presented many of the same demands and viewpoints as Ittifak but in somewhat less radical form, and it has attracted a larger following. Together these two movements took the initiative to summon a Tatar people's assembly, Milli Mejlis. It was intended to become the new national assembly, replacing the Tatarstani Supreme Soviet.[68]

Had this power shift succeeded, Tatarstan might easily have followed the same path as Chechnya. In Kazan, however, the old Soviet power elite managed to retain control, not least because of the president, Mintimer Shaymiev, who proved himself a very able politician. He, too, promulgated a Tatar nationalistic program, but without expansionism and anti-Russian facets. Quite the contrary: Shaymiev received considerable support among the non-Tatar population in the republic, who saw in him a moderate alternative to Ittifak and TPC. Further assistance came, albeit inadvertently, from the Russian authorities in Moscow, who through various contradictory and clumsy maneuvers strengthened support for the Tatarstani independence struggle.

During the 1990 power struggles with Yeltsin, Gorbachev attempted to play the Yeltsin regime and the leaders of the Russian autonomous republics off against each other. Yeltsin should not, warned Gorbachev, believe that he would be able to keep Russia unified if he withdrew the country from the Soviet Union. That could unleash a chain reaction that might well dissolve the unity of Russia as well. To remove some of the sting from this statement, Yeltsin responded by saying that the autonomous republics in Russia should take as much sovereignty as they could stomach.[69] This presumably off-the-cuff remark was made during a visit to Tatarstan in August 1990. The Russian leaders were anxious to be seen as more democratic than the Gorbachev regime, which refused to accept that Lithuania had seceded from the Soviet Union. At the same time, Yeltsin had indicated that the Tatars and leaders of the other republics ought not gulp down so much sovereignty that they ended up with a stomachache. In fact, however, they managed to demonstrate appetites and cast-iron stomachs of impressive dimensions.

Only a few weeks after Yeltsin's speech in Kazan, the Tatarstan declaration of sovereignty was adopted.[70] It differed from most other similar declarations on one vital point: There was no mention whatsoever of Tatarstan's being part of the Russian Federation. Instead, the leaders wished to conclude an agreement directly with the USSR, thereby getting the status of their republic elevated to Union republic on a par with—and apart from—Russia. When the Soviet Union disintegrated, this was no longer a viable option. Now Tatarstan would either have to become a totally independent state or remain within Russia—or so one might think. The leaders of Tatarstan, however, held other views. They kept on battling for international legal recognition as an independent state with a seat in the UN, while at the same time insisting that they had no wish to secede from Russia.[71]

Reactions from the Russian leaders were varied. President Yeltsin's adviser on nationalities issues, Galina Starovoytova, insisted that the autonomous republics in Russia should be granted as much sovereignty as they wished: "I maintain that Russia cannot have a dual standard, one for its foreign policy and another for domestic policy. We have recognized the right of the Estonian, Moldovan, and Georgian people to self-determination. Thus we must also recognize that the Chechen people have the same right."[72] This line of argument was formulated in such a way as to apply not only to the Chechens but also to the Tatars and other groups wishing to break free of the state.

The head of the Russian Supreme Soviet, Ruslan Khasbulatov, himself a Chechen saw things differently, however. "The position of Russia," he said, "is that those republics that compose the Russian Federation are part of a unitary Russian state."[73] This view was also supported by Vice President Aleksandr Rutskoy, who expressed in down-to-earth terms the fear of dissolution felt by many a Russian: "I have no desire to live in a banana republic." As he put it, "On the territory of Russia there live more than 130 different nations and nationalities. If all of these were to realize their [right to self-determination], we might get more than a hundred 'banana republics.' . . . We should be fully cognizant that if we destroy the Russian statehood, that can become the beginning of a frightening dissolution."[74]

But the Tatarstani leaders were not easily frightened. In February 1992 the Supreme Soviet of Tatarstan decided to hold a referendum in the republic on the status of Tatarstan. The question put to the electorate was as follows: "Do you agree that the Republic of Tatarstan is a sovereign state and a subject of international law that develops its relations with the Russian Federation and other republics on the basis of bilateral treaties?"[75]

Plans for this referendum triggered hectic activity in Moscow. In March the Russian Constitutional Court ruled that such a referendum would contravene the existing Russian constitution. That constitution, however, was in fact a remnant from Soviet days. True enough, it had been patched up a bit since 1990, but its general legitimacy was low. A committee in the Supreme Soviet had long since begun work on a completely new constitution, but as this had not been completed, Russia found itself in a constitutional interregnum as it were. And this was something that the leaders of Tatarstan exploited to their advantage.

Tatarstan held its referendum as planned on 21 March 1992. In the days immediately prior to the referendum, the local television repeatedly ran footage showing Yeltsin's now famous speech in Kazan where he had enjoined the republics to take as much sovereignty as they could "stomach."[76] Referendum turnout was an impressive 82 percent; around 61 percent voted for independence and some 37 percent against.[77] This revealed a deep split in the population: It meant that only 50.3 percent of the total electorate had in fact given their active support to the state-building project of Tatarstan.[78] But the leaders chose to interpret the results as a clear mandate to forge ahead with their policy of independence.

It would seem that in this tug-of-war for power and influence the Russian central authorities had greater weight on their side. The international community had made it clear that it did not support separatism in Russia. The central authorities also had at their disposal considerable means of force, both economic and military, that they could bring to bear against insurgent republics.

But to the leaders of the republics it was obvious that the center was divided. As we have seen, prominent figures in presidential circles had been sending out widely divergent signals. Even worse was that Yeltsin became embroiled in a bitter struggle with the national legislative assembly, the Supreme Soviet, concerning the new constitution. The bone of contention concerned top power at the central level: Was it to be vested in the president or in the national assembly? But center-periphery relations were another highly important issue that was to be regulated by means of this new constitution.

Yeltsin and the leaders of the Supreme Soviet alike had started by wanting a strong and centralized state, but in 1992 and 1993 the clash between them commanded almost all their attention. Little time remained to devote to the challenges from the most vociferous of the republics. Occasionally both Yeltsin and the parliamentary leaders would try to bribe the republics by holding out promises of increased sovereignty to those willing to support them.

The draft federation treaty that Yeltsin tabled in March 1992 gave the republics many new rights. According to a commentator in the liberal newspaper *Nezavisimaya gazeta* (Independent gazette), it would in fact create an entirely new Russia:

> We would find ourselves in a totally new state, in reality a "federation of fatherlands." This treaty gives to the republics full control over their natural resources; it allows them to pursue an independent foreign policy and to establish international economic relations. They can even determine their own border regimes, something that the former union republics could never even dream of doing as long as they remained union republics.[79]

These were far more comprehensive rights than what the regular, territorially defined *oblasti* were given. All the same, leaders of the republics were in no hurry to sign. Tatarstan and Chechnya never signed at all, whereas the leaders of Bashkortostan, Karelia, and Sakha procrastinated, finally signing only after they had gained acceptance for a series of additional clauses, inter alia one granting to the republics the right to decide their own budgets.[80]

In November 1992 the Supreme Soviet of Tatarstan adopted a constitution for the republic that stipulated, "The Republic of Tatarstan is a sovereign state in international law and is associated with the Russian Federation on the basis of a treaty for the mutual delegating of powers and jurisdiction."[81] At this point no such treaty actually existed, and the Russian authorities averred that they certainly would not sign one either. Before long, however, they sat down to negotiate bilateral agreements with several obstreperous republics. In 1992–1993 not only Bashkortostan but also the nonsignatory Tatarstan entered into a whole series of favorable economic agreements with Russia. This did not pass unnoticed: Other republics noted how the most stubborn republics managed to end up with particularly favorable conditions. The signing of the new federation treaty thus became only one staging post on the way to developing a new state system for Russia, not the final destination of the debate.

Tatarstan's Secession Ideology

Tatarstan's struggle for state independence was underpinned by ideological and theoretical argumentation. Prominent in the ideological struggle on the Tatar side stood Rafael Khakim, a close coworker of President Shaymiev. His *Sumerki imperii. K voprosu o natsii i gosudarstve* (Twilight of an empire: About the nation and the state), published in 1993, is a good example of the line of argumentation pursued by the intellectual elites in the separatist republics.

> Every state is created by, and reflects, the interests of a certain people. It is the language of this nation, its culture and its traditions that are dominant. The civil service and administration are recruited from this nation and are called to defend its values and ideals. France is the nation of the French, Turkey the nation of the Turks, Japan of the Japanese, and Russia—the nation of the Russians.

According to Khakim, it would thus be naive to believe that the Russian authorities were set to protect the rights of the Tatars: The leaders of that country do not know so much as one word of the Tatar language. Just as the Soviet Union was an empire, so is today's Russia. The only way to ensure the rights of non-Russians is for them to get states of their own.

At the same time, Khakim admits that ethnic Russians did not enjoy any special privileges in the USSR or in the RSFSR. This makes it highly unclear exactly what he means in saying that Russia is the "state of the Russians." Khakim's practical conclusion, however, is clear enough: "Since Russia does not—neither in its foreign nor in its domestic policy— stand as guarantor of the rights of the Russians, the Russians will have to seek support locally, in the republics."[83]

Khakim's use of the terms *Russians* and *Tatars* is unconditionally ethnic. It is on the basis of their collective rights as an ethnic group that the Tatars should be granted a state of their own. At times, however, Khakim also operates with a concept of "nation" very similar to that of Tishkov. He claims, for instance, that "a nation consists of the citizens of a country who are linked together in a state community, independently of their ethnic origins."[84] With this definition, it is not easy to understand why all the people living in Russia cannot constitute a common Russian/Rossian nation.

Furthermore, Khakim repeatedly cites ethnocultural arguments in his defense of Tatarstan's political independence—for example, when he discusses the principle of national self-determination. This right is, according to Khakim, a right primarily for the indigenous population, not for all who live in a country. The size of this indigenous population is not important: "Only with the most oversimplistic concepts of society is it possible to arrive at a theory that requires that the indigenous population must make up a majority of the population in its historical homeland in order to be entitled to the right to form its own sovereign state—in other words, that it should have a chance to survive."[85]

The question of majority versus minority in a republic can be discussed only after portions of the population have been defined out of "the nation." Khakim has clearly switched back to an ethnically based concept of nation here. If the independence of Tatarstan had depended on the logical force of arguments alone, it would never have got off the ground.

New Constitution

The power struggle between President Yeltsin and the Supreme Soviet culminated in a violent confrontation. On 21 September Yeltsin declared the dissolution of the Supreme Soviet by force, and the parliamentary building in Moscow, the White House, was surrounded by a military cordon. The legislators responded by deposing Yeltsin and agitating for an overthrow of his regime. When paramilitary units in sympathy with the Supreme Soviet tried to occupy the mayoral offices and the state television center on 4 October, troops loyal to Yeltsin shelled the White House, and about 150 people were killed. This left Yeltsin virtually free to formulate the principles for the new Russian constitution as he wished. His variant, adopted by the new legislative body, the Duma, following a referendum held on 12–13 December 1993, provides the basis for today's Russian state system.

The federation treaty of 1992 was not incorporated into the new constitution as originally announced. Instead, the constitution stipulates that in cases of disagreement between the constitution and the federation treaty, the former is to apply. On several points the constitution grants to the republics fewer rights than does the federation treaty. According to the constitution, all *oblasti* and *okruga* enjoy the same formal status as the republics: They are all "subjects of the federation." And all subjects of the federation are represented in the same manner in the new upper chamber of the national assembly, the Federation Council: two deputies for each unit. No subject of the federation may unilaterally alter its status within the federation. Several important areas are specified as being within the exclusive competence of the federal authorities, whereas many other matters—including the exploitation of natural resources—are to be decided jointly by the federation and the subjects of the federation. For all areas not specifically mentioned in the constitution, subjects of the federation are entitled to adopt their own legislation, as long as it does not contravene the Russian constitution or other Russian legislation.[86]

Even though the constitution explicitly states that all subjects of the federation are to be equal in their relations to the federation, it still gives the republics more rights than other units. Only republics may adopt their own constitutions, whereas matters of domestic policy in the *oblasti* and *okruga* are to be regulated by means of statutes. The central authorities can appoint key administrative personnel in the regular *oblasti* but not in the republics.

In article 5 the republics are referred to as "states," whatever that may indicate. During the negotiations several republican leaders had insisted on the term *sovereign national states,* but the central authorities did not accept this.[87] They feared that the strong ethnic connotations linked to the word *nation* in Russia might give the titular populations a disproportionately strong status in "national state" republics. The noun *state,* however, was retained.

All the same, the idea that the republics belong especially to their titular nationalities is very much alive and well today. In a great many republics, the titular group is heavily overrepresented in political life. For instance, almost twice as many Russians as Bashkirs live in Bashkortostan, yet as of March 1995 the legislative assembly of the republic was composed of 55 percent Bashkirs and only 21 percent Russians.[88] Similarly, in 1995 in the Republic of Tatarstan 73 percent Tatars and 25 percent

Russians were elected to the State Council, although both groups are about equal in size.[89]

Neither the federation treaty nor the new constitution has managed to put an end to debate and disagreement concerning the Russian Federation. A great many of the republics have adopted their own constitutions that contravene the Russian constitution on one or more points. The authorities in some republics have permitted themselves the right to issue their own currency, whereas others have decided that they can regulate their boundaries with other republics and even with other states without asking the permission of the Russian federal authorities. By November 1996, according to figures from the Yeltsin administration, nineteen of the twenty-one republics had what could be termed "anti-Constitutional constitutional paragraphs."[90]

To an increasing extent, relations between the center and the republics are regulated by means of bilateral agreements. By 1998 the Kremlin has signed bilateral power-sharing treaties with more than half of Russia's eighty-nine regions. The first agreement of this type was signed between Russia and Tatarstan in February 1994. (Thus, the Tatars finally got what they had been demanding ever since 1992.) According to the terms of this agreement, the Russian Federation and the Republic of Tatarstan are linked on the basis of the constitutions of both countries and the bilateral agreement. The Tatar side had agreed to drop the demand that Tatarstan was to be referred to as a "subject of international law."[91] Tatar nationalists saw this as treason to the cause of Tatar independence and therefore denounced the agreement.[92] Still, there can be no doubt that the Tatars managed to secure an excellent result from their negotiations.

The conclusion of such bilateral agreements has meant that the Russian Federation, which according to the constitution was to have a symmetrical structure, has developed in a more asymmetrical direction instead.[93] Just how many rights and powers the various federation subjects have been granted depends on the negotiation results. This in turn depends partly on what others before them have achieved, on their skill and flexibility at the negotiating table, and not least on how strong an economic hand has been dealt to them. Those republics with the greatest wealth in natural resources have frequently managed to get bilateral agreements with terms that more impoverished republics can only dream about. Thus, for instance, the richest of them all, the Siberian republic of Sakha (formerly called Yakutia), with its fabulous deposits of gold and diamonds, has been granted full tax exemption. The republics of Tatarstan and Bashkortostan must transfer only about 10–15 percent of their tax revenues to Moscow; the remainder they can keep to use locally as they see fit.

At the same time, Russia continues to transfer considerable sums from the central state treasury to subjects of the federation, including the

republics. In fact, several of the republics that contribute least to the treasury receive the most back in the form of various subsidy arrangements.
From forty-seven of the forty-nine regular *oblasti*, however, more goes to
the center in the form of taxes and duties than goes the other way.[94] The
economic circuit in Russia would thus appear to be organized largely according to the so-called St. Matthew principle: "For unto every one that
hath shall be given, and he shall have abundance: but from him that hath
not shall be taken away even that which he hath" (Matthew 25: 29).

Many of the *oblast* leaders considered this deeply unfair, so they decided to do something about it. If the word *republic* was the open sesame
of the Moscow treasury, well, then, republics they would be. In summer
1993 the *oblasti* of Primor'e, Amur, Sakhalin, and Sverdlovsk demanded
status as republics. Sverdlovsk, in the southern Urals, is not only the
home *oblast* of Boris Yeltsin, but it also has considerable natural resources, especially in the form of iron ore and magnesium. Moreover,
Sverdlovsk also had a dynamic and very popular governor, Eduard
Rossel, who in autumn 1993 managed to convince four other *oblasti* in the
Urals to join together to form the Ural Republic. Isn't a territory supposed to have a separate identity in order to qualify as a republic? Well
then, came the reply, hasn't everyone heard of the special Ural tempera-
ment and folk character? And why should this identity be any less valuable than that of the Bashkirs or the Tatars?

Yeltsin, however, was not impressed. In November 1993, having won
the power struggle against the Supreme Soviet, he promptly dissolved
the Ural Republic and deposed Rossel. But Rossel was reelected governor of Sverdlovsk in August 1995, and in 1996 Sverdlovsk became the
first *oblast* to sign a power-sharing agreement with the center. By that
time Rossel had given up trying to play the republic card.[95]

At the same time, the *oblasti* would seem to be winning a different important battle with regard to resources and status in the Russian Federation. All ten autonomous districts, or *okruga,* mentioned in the new constitution are located within the territories of these regular *oblasti*. These
okruga are ethnically defined, but their titular groups are too small for
their lands to be entitled to the status of republics: In Khanty-Mansy
okruga in Tyumen *oblast,* for instance, there live 12,000 Khanty and 6,000
Mansy (of a total population of approximately 1.3 million); in the Nenets
okruga in Arkhangelsk *oblast* live some 6,000 Nenets (corresponding to
about 12 percent of the total population). Within both these *okruga* lie
enormous petroleum reserves. The local populations have attempted to
gain control over these by withdrawing their *okruga* from the *oblasti* in
question, in a struggle led primarily by nonindigenous leaders. They
have unabashedly utilized ethnic arguments in what is first and foremost
a battle for economic power. Moreover, they have had good legal cards in

their hands: When it comes to the relationship between the *okruga* and their "host" *oblasti*, the Russian constitution is simply self-contradictory. It states both that the *okruga* "are part of them" *(vkhodit v sostav)* and that the *okruga* are independent subjects of the federation on a par with the *oblasti*.[96] Several of the *okruga* have refused to participate in *oblast* elections, seeking thereby gradually to weaken *oblast* competence in the *okruga*. The message is clear: "We don't interfere in your domestic affairs, so please keep your hands off ours—and that includes our natural resources."

These competence battles have proven a tough nut for the Russian authorities to crack. In July 1996 the matter was dealt with by the Russian Constitutional Court, without success. Then in July 1997 the struggle was once again taken up in the court, and this time the verdict went against the secession plans of the *okruga*.[97]

Quo Vadis, Russia?

On several occasions Russian politicians have demanded that the ethnofederal structure of the country be scrapped. As early as 1991, Vladimir Zhirinovskiy was calling for a reintroduction of the old gubernatorial system of the czarist epoch.[98] The idea is linked with the wish to reestablish the prerevolutionary Russian unitary state. Thus, Zhirinovskiy wants to have separate governors-general for Central Asia (Turkestan) and for the Baltics (Kurland and Livland). In the Zhirinovskiy version, criticism of the ethnic autonomies thereby becomes a further link in a Great Russian project of empire-building.

Russia's ethnofederalism can also be criticized from the standpoint of democratic ideals of equal treatment and nondiscrimination.[99] Among Russian liberal thinkers, skepticism about the federational structure has grown as the leaders of the republics have managed to use it as an effective weapon in the struggle for power and resources.[100] The party Forward Russia, led by former minister of finance Boris Fyodorov, made the abolition of differential treatment of federation subjects one of its main issues.[101]

Some antifederalists have launched the concept of national-cultural autonomy as an alternative way of ensuring ethnocultural diversity within a unitary state. The focus is on ethnic rights, but instead of being linked to specific territories, the idea is to link them to the individual person.[102] According to this line of thought, ethnic groups may certainly have protection for their distinctive culture and language—as long as this protection is not bound up in territorial rights.

In April 1994 the social anthropologist Georgiy Sitnyanskiy sketched out how a regime for national-cultural autonomy might be shaped in

Russia.[103] In this view, each nation would be entitled to its own state attributes, president, parliament, flag, coat of arms, and national anthem. What they would not have would be autonomous national territories. Instead of, say, the "president of Tatarstan," there would be the "president of the Tatars," and this person would be "head of state" for *all* of Russia's Tatars, no matter where in the country they happened to live. An important proviso: Any Tatars who might desire not to join this national-cultural autonomy would have full rights to remain outside and be direct citizens of Russia instead.

Sitnyanskiy's model also illustrates clearly the many problems that a regime of national-cultural autonomy might pose to Russian nation-building. Sitnyanskiy considers it necessary that the various autonomous groupings be allowed to adopt their own laws and establish their own courts of justice. If, for instance, a Tatar robs or kills another Tatar, punishment should be an internal affair for the Tatar community, according to Sitnyanskiy. Only in cases where victim and perpetrator come from different ethnic groups should the central authorities become involved. But a system like that would establish nearly watertight social barriers between ethnic groups. If such a system could be established at all, it would probably hinder, to an even greater degree than an ethnoterritorial federation, the evolution of a shared nation-state identity among the peoples of Russia.

In 1998 the leaders of Tatarstan began sniffing at the possibility of introducing a variant of national-cultural autonomy, not as an alternative to territorial autonomy but in addition to it. In February 1998 they discussed a citizenship bill for the republic, a bill that, if adopted, would give ethnic Tatars living outside the republic the right to Tatarstani citizenship. Whereas separate Tatarstani citizenship had previously been little more than a fancy kind of residence permit, it was now imbued with ethnic meaning and detached from Russian citizenship. It would serve to increase the power of the republic in its relations with the center: With such an arrangement, Mintimer Shaymiev would become both the president of Tatarstan and the president of the Tatars.

At the same time, however, the central Russian authorities have been attempting to delink Russian citizenship and ethnicity. In 1997 it was made known that the new Russian passports, long in preparation, were not to contain a separate category for nationality. The Russian authorities argued that most Western countries make no distinction between citizenship and nationality, and they referred to the fact that article 26 of the new Russian constitution stipulates that national affiliation cannot be forced upon anyone.

Yet the constitution does affirm that every citizen is entitled to a national affiliation if he or she so wishes. Opponents of the new regulations held that this right would become illusory without a separate entry in Russian passports (this had formerly been the famous "point 5" in the Soviet passports) for such national affiliation. In the national assembly of Tatarstan, the abolition of point 5 was denounced as "the greatest provocation in the history of Russia."[104] Indeed, some Tatar leaders went so far as to maintain that this opened the gates to genocide: If non-Russians were no longer to be distinguished as a separate category in official documents, they would become assimilated and lose their identity.

In the debate around point 5, we see how the various threads in the Russian nation-building debate cross and interweave. Traditional allies suddenly find themselves standing on separate sides of the barricades, whereas bitter enemies are equally surprised to be rubbing shoulders. Both Russian liberals like Grigoriy Yavlinskiy and reactionary nationalists like Vladimir Zhirinovskiy have opposed demands for retaining point 5. Although Yavlinskiy's ideal is a modern, citizenship-based nation-state, he cannot help noticing that arguments resembling his own are adduced to promote the establishment of an ethnocratic Russian empire. Similarly, we can find warm defenders of point 5 both within the Russian Communist Party and among anti-Communist nationalists in the various republics.[105]

Russia appears destined to remain a federal state for the foreseeable future. Can it manage also to become a "national state" in any reasonable sense of the term? The ethnic aspect of the Russian federational structure will certainly complicate the task of nation-building, but it need not represent an insurmountable barrier.

As Valery Tishkov has indicated, Russia is culturally more homogeneous than a great many other nation-states. But—as Tishkov would be the first to acknowledge—identity is not determined by culture alone. The subjective experience of the country's culture and history among the populace in general and among the elite in particular is the decisive factor. Only to the extent to which the inhabitants actually see their country as their homeland, as their *patria*, as the unit to which they connect their own identity—only to that extent will the state be able to assume the nation-state mantle. That is why the most serious obstacle to Russian nation-state consolidation is that so few of Russia's politicians contribute to it, whereas so many actively work against the entire project.

11

COMPARISONS AND CONCLUSIONS

It is tempting to compare the possibilities now available to social scientists in connection with the demise of the Soviet Union to the unique opportunities provided to natural scientists three decades earlier, when a series of volcanic eruptions off the coast of Iceland gave birth to a new island, Surtsey. Immediately after the eruptions, there was no organic life whatsoever on the island. For researchers, it was almost as if a time machine had suddenly transported them back to the first days of creation, where they could witness a biological system come into being out of nothing.

This comparison is, of course, far from perfect. Human behavior is not determined by the laws of nature in the same rigid way as other forms of life are. Nor is nation-building in the former Soviet republics something that is starting from scratch—on the contrary, each and every one of these republics has its own heavy burden of earlier experiences and attitudes. All the same, the former Soviet republics represent a wealth of opportunities for the social scientist. Processes that elsewhere have taken decades, even centuries, are being compressed into the framework of a few years. What direction will developments take? A great many paths are open. Much is at stake, and little can be taken for granted. Scholars accustomed to studying minuscule changes, differences of a few percentage points or less, have the chance to study politics in the making, and on a scale hitherto undreamed-of.

This concluding chapter offers a synoptic overview of the nation-building processes of the Soviet successor states, focusing on certain important topics. Why and how was the nationalities issue in the Soviet Union given a territorial treatment, and what are the lasting consequences of this decision in the successor states? Will they opt for a similar territorial approach, or will they settle on other models? Can nation-building and minority protection go together at all, or are these two goals basically incompatible? What can the symbolic expression of nationhood in the new and newly independent countries tell us about the priorities and strategies of the nation-builders? And finally, will the nationalizing states ever become true nation-states, or are they doomed to sink back into oblivion?

The Soviet Legacy: The Importance of Being Territorial

Nation-building requires a construction site, a politically defined and delineated territory. In order to press a claim for ownership of a certain territory, nation-builders will insist that they have a higher degree of attachment to it than rival groups. Other groups may live there, but they may not claim ownership of the land and should not be allowed to influence the nation-building strategies.

The degree of territoriality or territorial attachment of various ethnic groups in a polity can be a highly charged political question: Territoriality is not a given; it is determined not only by geography, demography, and history but also by such intangibles as perceptions and ideas. The members of a numerical minority group may see themselves as clearly rooted in the land, whereas the members of the majority culture will refuse to accept this claim. Thus, for instance, Ossetians in South Ossetia regard themselves as native to the region they inhabit in northern Georgia, having lived there for more than 200 years. This claim, however, is generally rejected by ethnic Georgians, who insist that the home territory of the Ossetians is in North Ossetia, on the other side of the Caucasus mountains, from which they migrated in the eighteenth century.[1] The Bolsheviks decided in favor of the Ossetians, granting them two autonomous territories, one north and one south of the mountain range. Many Georgian nationalists never accepted this, and after the dissolution of the USSR the independent Georgian state scrapped the South Ossetian autonomous *oblast* in 1992. Civil war ensued.

From the very beginning of the Soviet Union, the link between ethnicity and territoriality was both strong and institutionalized. Even though the various peoples of the Russian empire had lived intermingled for centuries, the Bolsheviks made strenuous efforts to attach each group to one specific "home" territory. This initial territorialization laid the groundwork for the current pattern of nationalizing states.

In 1913 the future people's commissar for nationalities, Joseph Stalin, wrote a treatise called *Marxism and the National Question*, presenting for the first time what was to become the Stalinist model of nationality. A nation, Stalin explained, "is an historically formed, stable community of people, which has arisen on the basis of a common language, common territory, common economic life, and common psychological cast of mind, which is manifested in a common culture."[2] Thus, Stalin emphasized territoriality as an essential element of nationhood. He used this point to explain why the Americans and English do not constitute one common nation, even though they speak the same language. "Nations are formed only on the basis of protracted and regular contacts as a result of a community of life over generations. And a protracted community of life is impossible without a common territory."[3] A side effect of this definition is that it denied Jews the status of a nation, but on this score Stalin was hardly breaking new ground. Back in 1903 his mentor Vladimir Lenin had written, "The Jews have ceased to be a nation, for a nation without a territory is unthinkable."[4] Lenin's statement is highly indicative not only of his ideas on Jewishness but also his view of nationhood. From the very beginning, territorial thinking was thoroughly ingrained in the minds of Russia's Communists.

Lenin had described the Russian empire as "a prison-house of the peoples," and he promised that if only the non-Russians would help him topple the autocratic regime, he would grant them complete freedom of self-determination, up to and including the right to secede altogether from the state. Only territories can secede, not individuals, so this right presupposed the existence of separate, nationally defined territories for all major ethnic groups in the country.

After the October Revolution, this right to secession soon proved illusory, but the territorial thinking remained, reflected in the very structure of the Soviet socialist state. The USSR was established in 1922 as a federation in which most of the federal units were ethnically defined. After Stalin's death it gradually became filled with a certain amount of real content, and increasingly so as the grip of the Brezhnevite regime slipped in the 1980s. In many cases the ethnically defined autonomous units provided the elites of the titular nation with the means to influence political life locally, far beyond what their share of the total population in the area would lead us to expect.

Many ethnic groups in the USSR were so small that establishing a separate autonomy for them was out of the question. More important, some larger groups had to make do without a homeland of their own: These were the diasporas of Poles, Koreans, Bulgarians, Greeks, and other groups. There seem to have been two reasons for this exclusion. In most cases these diaspora groups did not live on a compact territory but were widely dispersed. Even if some did have their own distinct settlements in the interwar period, this was no longer the case after the forced deportations to Central Asia during World War II.[5] The other reason was that these groups belonged to nations that had their own separate nation-states elsewhere: Poland, Korea, Bulgaria, Greece. People could hardly be expected to have more than one territorial unit, could they? In a similar way, Ukrainians living outside Ukraine and Tatars living outside Tataria, for instance, enjoyed no cultural protection or linguistic rights. This was an egregious case of collectivist thinking: It is groups, not individuals, that have rights.

The other important exception to the rule that major national groups in the Soviet Union should be entitled to their own socialist territory was the Russians themselves. The Russian Soviet Federated Socialist Republic was not named after the Russian nation but took its name from the supraethnic title Peter the Great had given his empire, Rossiya. In any case, it was held that Russian language and culture dominated throughout the entire Soviet state. The Russians were in no need of special territorial protection since they, as Paul Goble has expressed it, enjoyed "extraterritorial status."[6]

Glasnost opened up formerly unheard-of possibilities to express grievances of all kinds in the Soviet press, including ethnic grievances. The Russian researcher V. K. Malkova has shown how the concept of the ethnically understood "us" changed in the non-Russian press during perestroika. The "we" was associated with the group's national history—with its language, culture, and economy—and with its territory.[7]

The political exploitation of territoriality in the Soviet Union during perestroika passed through several phases, Malkova points out. First, the damage the Communist regime had caused to the ecology and environment of the national homelands was exposed and decried. In the next phase, praise for the beauty of nature was crowded out by calls for political and economic independence for the national territory. In the third stage, territoriality was turned into a weapon against "alien" ethnic elements living in the national territory, the "migrants," "the newcomers," and—in some republics—"the occupants." This third stage set in at somewhat different times in the various republics, but generally around 1989–1990.

Even so, when the Soviet republics were proclaimed as independent states during the second half of 1991, no formal distinctions were made among their citizens on ethnic criteria. With two exceptions—Latvia and Estonia—all former Soviet republics granted the status as original citizens to all persons residing permanently in their territory at the time when independence was proclaimed (or alternatively, when the new citizenship law was adopted or entered into force). But even in Latvia and Estonia no formal distinctions were made among the permanent residents along ethnic lines in the constitutions or the citizenship laws.

It is necessary to underline the word *formal* here. Although all new and newly independent states make strenuous efforts to live up to Western ideas about civic statehood in their legislative practices, the ethnicity-neutral formulations in their legal acts often amount to grandstanding. A good example is the revision of the Latvian language law in March 1992, severely restricting the rights of Russophones (see Chapter 6). The preamble to this law gave the following official justification for the changes: "Latvia is the sole ethnic territory in the world populated by the Latvian nation. The Latvian language is one of the most important preconditions for the survival of the Latvian nation and for the preservation and development of its culture."[8] This was an unequivocal expression of an ethno-territorial understanding of the nation.

In 1996 the new *Kontseptsiya formirovaniya gosudarstvennoy identichnosti respubliki Kazakhstan* (Concept for the shaping of the state identity of Kazakhstan) proclaimed Kazakhstan to be the "ethnic center" of the Kazakhs. Nowhere else in the world, it said, is there a state concerned with preserving the Kazakh people as an ethnic group or developing the culture, language, traditions, and lifestyle of the Kazakhs. "When we define Kazakhstan as a national state, it is first and foremost this aspect of the state that we should have in mind." At the same time, the authors declared that Kazakhstan is also undeniably a multiethnic state—but then went on to say that ethnic groups other than the Kazakhs are not entitled to equal claims to belonging to the country: "Changes in the national composition of Kazakhstan are solely the result of immigration of non-Kazakh ethnic groups, most of whom have their own statehood [elsewhere]."[9]

As several chapters of this book have demonstrated, the struggle for and against certain formulas in the constitutions, laws, and other official documents of the Soviet successor states is not an academic game of words for philologists but rather the symbolic expression of hard-nosed power politics. In most of the new states, the titulars have been able to dominate political life even more than in the Soviet period and far out of proportion to their demographic strength.

In most cases the reactions of the minorities to this ethnocentric nation-building have been muted. The nontitulars have generally accepted the titulars' claim to a special role in society and national politics. Some have reacted by migrating to Russia or to some other putative "historical homeland," implicitly accepting that this is where they "belong." But there have been times and places when minority leaders in the nationalizing states have challenged the titulars' exclusive claim to "indigenousness."

In 1992 a Russian historian from Ust-Kamenogorsk, a compactly Slavic city in the northeastern Altay region of Kazakhstan, wrote a small treatise on Russians, Kazakhs, and Altay. His message was that ethnic Kazakhs had no right to claim Kazakhstan as their exclusive ancient homeland—at least not in northeastern Kazakhstan: "The terms 'indigenous people' and 'indigenous inhabitants' . . . are *incorrect*."[10] Surveys in Kazakhstan indicate that the clear majority of the Slavic inhabitants have either been born in the country or have lived there for more than ten years. The local organizer of one of these surveys concluded that "the nontitular persons interviewed have struck rather deep roots in the soil of Kazakhstan. They have life traditions here stretching several generations back, and their dear ones are buried here."[11] Similar observations have been made in the Baltics. Having conducted a series of surveys in Lithuania, Latvia, and Estonia, Richard Rose concluded that a large majority of the Russophones in these countries have dual identities, as Russians and as residents of a city or region within a Baltic state: "Significantly, a majority put their local identity before their national identity; they are Rigans and then Russians, or Vilnians and then Russians."[12]

Local territoriality, however, does not automatically translate into political loyalty. Integration is a two-way street, and if the nontitulars conclude that their integrative endeavors are not reciprocated, strong feelings of local attachment may galvanize them into determined opposition toward a nationalizing regime that refuses to accept them as full-fledged members of the "nation." This can give rise to secessionism, as in the case of the Dniester republic in eastern Moldova. An official memorial book commemorating the more than 400 victims on the Dniestrian side in the Moldovan civil war in 1992 thus explained the outbreak of the war: The inhabitants of Moldova had been inhumanely divided into two categories: the Moldovans, who were regarded as the *korennoy* population, the "masters of the land," versus the "newcomers," the "migrants," and "occupants." Although Western observers tend to describe the Russian population in the Dniester as late arrivals, they themselves insist that they are living on "ancient Slavic land."[13]

Nation-Building, Cultural Diversity, and Democracy: Some Models

The political leaders of the new and newly independent states of the former Soviet Union are single-mindedly pursuing policies of nation-building and national consolidation. But they have also solemnly pledged to respect the political and cultural rights of the nontitular populations. Are these goals compatible? Can nation-building in the new states be combined with the safeguarding of democracy and cultural diversity? Will a liberal minority regime strengthen the state by ensuring greater support for it among the nontitular population, or will extensive minority rights jeopardize the unity and stability of the new states?

In the wake of the collapse of communism in Eastern Europe, minority rights rose to the top of the political agenda in Pan-European institutions. The Copenhagen Meeting of the Conference on the Human Dimension of the CSCE in 1990 stated that persons belonging to national minorities have the right freely to express, preserve, and develop their ethnic, cultural, linguistic, and religious identities and to maintain and develop their cultures in all aspects. The meeting further affirmed that "respect for the rights of persons belonging to national minorities . . . is an essential factor for peace, justice, stability and democracy in the participating states."[14] Thus, not only democracy but also social stability, it was claimed, flows from good minority regimes. This view was based on the premise that inequitable relations between cultural groups will be a smoldering source of resentment and anger that will remain until all groups in society are granted their due share of goods and influence.

Others have had their doubts. Some have argued that cultural diversity may go together with political stability or with democracy but not with both at the same time. And they go on to argue that if you cannot have it both ways, then political stability and avoiding civil war must be preferable to political pluralism and democracy. A societal system that is quintessentially democratic but unsustainable is, after all, of little lasting value to its members. If cultural diversity enhances democracy but contributes to the breakdown of states, this may mean too high a price tag on democracy. This is a favorite argument of political leaders in many illiberal states, including the former Soviet Union, but it can be found among political scientists as well.

In his 1969 study of pluralism in Africa, Leo Kuper argued in general terms that cultural diversity and democracy are an impossible combination: "Cultural diversity or pluralism automatically imposes the strictest necessity for domination by one of the cultural sections. It excludes the possibility of consensus, or of institutional integration, or of structural balance between the different sections, and necessitates non-democratic regulation of group relationships."[15]

Probably few researchers today would subscribe to such bombastic determinism, but many will lean toward similar positions.[16] The American expert on democracy Robert A. Dahl, for one, has remarked that democracy is "significantly less frequent in countries with marked subcultural pluralism."[17] One might perhaps argue that even if this was true in the past, the development toward greater liberalism and tolerance in the modern world has increased the scope for a combination of democracy and cultural pluralism. In the postindustrial "permissive society," one would think, state authorities are less concerned about the cultural life of the citizens than they used to be. It is worth noting, however, that one of the most influential theoreticians of nationalism in the last decades,

Ernest Gellner, saw the historical development as headed in the opposite direction. He pointed out that cultural diversity had worked well in the past, in traditional societies, and indeed had sometimes been invented where it was previously lacking. In Gellner's view, though, such diversity was no longer an option under the conditions of modern nationalism and nation-building. Nowadays people can live only in units defined by a shared culture, internally mobile and fluid. Genuine cultural pluralism ceases to be viable under current conditions.[18]

Classical nation-building theory had noted how the European states that had pioneered the development of democratic institutions had also pursued a consistent and conscious policy of cultural homogenization of their populations. Charles Tilly explicitly remarked that increased homogeneity followed almost without exception as an important result of nation-building:

> Almost all European governments eventually took steps which homogenized their populations: the adoption of state religions, expulsion of minorities like the Moors and the Jews, institution of a national language, eventually the organization of mass public instruction. . . . The failure to homogenize increased the likelihood that a state existing at a given point in time would fragment into its cultural subdivisions at some time in the future.[19]

In this perspective, cultural homogenization is not only a concomitant effect of nation-building: It is a precondition for the very survival of the nation-state.

Thus, some Western researchers tended to take for granted the cultural pluralism of the societies they studied and rejected the viability of democracy under such plural conditions. Others, focusing on changes in the cultural landscape toward greater homogeneity, saw these as steps in the direction of stable democracies. Both of these research traditions were implicitly premised on the assumption that in the long run cultural pluralism, democracy, and stability would prove to be an impossible combination.

Consociationalism

This premise was forcefully challenged by the theory of consociationalism, which sprang up in the 1960s and 1970s. In his pioneering works *The Politics of Accommodation* and *Democracy in Plural Societies*, Arend Lijphart studied four states—the Netherlands, Belgium, Switzerland, and Austria—that are both democratic and marked by clear cultural divisions in society. These states have traditionally had strong, distinct subcultures in society organized along ideological and religious lines, such as Catholicism and socialism. In one state, Austria, social peace broke down in the interwar period, resulting in a bloody civil war. After World War II, Austrian community leaders agreed upon several mutual concessions in order to avoid such catastrophes in the future. Although the other three states did not experience similar traumas, in these countries as well the elites opted for a series of self-imposed constraints that restricted the operations of democracy as this political model was understood in the classical, liberal sense. Lijphart divided the various accommodation devices into four categories: mutual veto, grand coalitions, an electoral system of proportional representation (with or without a quota system for distribution of high offices in the state), and finally, a high degree of autonomy for each cultural segment. Such autonomy could take the form of either territorial government or institutions that confer some self-government on the segments.[20]

In a consociated state, in Lijphart's interpretation, cultural diversity is neither an impediment to the development of democracy nor an extraneous or irrelevant factor. Rather, it is in a sense the very stuff of which this variety of democracy is made: Culture is the structuring element of society. At the same time, the state as such is not associated with any of its constituent cultural groups but is elevated above all ethnic divisions in society.[21]

Consociationalism is a model in two different senses of the word. On the one hand, it is a theoretical model distilled from a large empirical material, designed to give a better understanding of the workings of democracy in certain types of societies. On the other hand, it is also offered by its proponents as a normative model to be emulated by the leaders of other states with marked cultural cleavages who want to promote the development of stable democracy in their countries.

Lijphart himself discussed at length the potential of consociationalism in Third World countries. He identified several conditions under which consociated democracy was most likely to develop, one being that the cultural segments in society should preferably be clearly delineated and identifiable. Already according to this criterion, the Slavic states of the former Soviet Union are not well suited. As I argued in Chapters 8 and 9, the cultural differences between the dominant ethnic and linguistic groups in Belarus and Ukraine are very small. Moldova, where there is a high degree of intermarriage and a shared religion for all major ethnic groups, may likewise be regarded as a cultural continuum rather than a segmented society. This leaves the new states in the Baltics and Central Asia as the more likely candidates for consociated democracy. In these regions the titulars and the Russophones represent clearly different cultural communities. In some parts of these regions, however, the Russophones are too few to constitute a politically relevant group. Only in four states—Latvia, Estonia, Kazakhstan, and Kyrgyzstan—do they represent more than 25 percent of the population.

But if the preconditions for consociationalism might seem in place in these countries, the new state leaders in most cases ignore the toolbox of social conflict regulation proffered by Lijphart and his school. For instance, in February 1996 the first deputy prime minister in the Kazakhstani government remarked that "if we make an attempt to fill up the parliament on the basis of proportional ethnic representation, then we would have to do the same with regard to social groups as well."[22] Without discussing the validity of this argument, we may observe that it is based on an implicit rejection of consociationalism as a conflict-reducing mechanism in plural societies.

To be sure, a handful of Russophones and other nontitulars are indeed members of the presidential apparatus in Kazakhstan and Kyrgyzstan, and official spokespersons in these countries are wont to point to them to disprove charges that their countries are run as ethnocracies. The nontitulars, however, are not included in the political power structures as representatives of their cultural groups; moreover, many locals tend to regard these appointments as sheer tokenism. All political parties that set out to represent the Russophones of Kazakhstan or the Uzbeks of Kyrgyzstan have been systematically marginalized.

In Latvia certain policy measures undertaken by the state authorities may perhaps be seen as an instinctive recognition of the merits of consociational democracy. For instance, the reluctance to mix Latvian and non-Latvian pupils in the same schools will have the effect of isolating the main cultural segments in society from each other and may strengthen their distinctiveness. Such arrangements will perpetuate and reinforce the plural structure of Latvian society. The same is true with regard to the retention of an ascriptive nationality entry in Latvian passports.

In Estonia, too, some elements of the ethnopolitical arrangement seem to conform to the consociational model. To a much larger degree than, for instance, Russophones in Latvia, Russophones in Estonia have mobilized around specifically Russian or Russophone parties.[23] Estonia's restrictive citizenship legislation, however, ensures that even when the Russophones band together they can at most make a slight dent in the political monopoly of the titulars. Although the nontitulars constitute approximately one-third of the total population in Estonia, the Russophone parties taken together in 1998 had only six representatives in the 100-member parliament, the Riigikogu.

Partly in order to compensate for the underrepresentation of minorities in the legislative and executive bodies of the country, Estonian president Lennart Meri in 1993 established the Presidendi Ümarlaud (Roundtable), a consultative organ for nontitular groups. With this, it might seem that a channel had been opened through which the leaders of the non-Estonian communities could influence minority-related aspects of Estonian politics. But many members of the roundtable increasingly felt that they were being held hostage to policies highly detrimental to the nontitular parts of the population. The Estonian authorities made a show of listening to their recommendations but habitually ignored them when decisions were made. In February 1999, for example, despite vociferous protests from the roundtable (as well as the international community), the Riigikogu adopted amendments to Estonia's language and election laws requiring all parliamentary and local government members as well as those in the service sector to be proficient in the Estonian language. Four Russophone members left the roundtable, concluding that the organ was "no longer a forum for dialogue but . . . a decorative body of 'collective approval.'"[24]

Latvia and Estonia no more than Kazakhstan or Kyrgyzstan may be regarded as countries moving toward consociationalism or even semi-consociationalism. The crucial factor of power sharing and mutual accommodation is conspicuously lacking in these countries. Rather than neutral zones of cooperation among the various cultural groups, the Latvian and Estonian states are clearly identified with and set to serve first and foremost the interests of one cultural segment, the titular nation. As David Laitin has dryly remarked, "Consociation was ruled out because the titulars, by moving first and decisively, successfully negated that opportunity."[25]

Federalism and Territorial Autonomy

Federalism is the only minority protection scheme with which the post-Soviet nationalities have had any real-life experience. Several of the nationalizing new states have within their borders ethnically defined autonomous territories that are left over from the Soviet federal system. Besides the plethora of territorial units in Russia, these territories are Karakalpakia in Uzbekistan; Gorno-Badakhshan in Tajikistan; Nagorno-Karabakh in Azerbaijan; and Ajaria, South Ossetia, and Abkhazia in Georgia.

In the Western world, more and more states are evolving toward an ethnofederal model—the prime examples being Spain, Belgium, and most recently the United Kingdom.[26] In the assessment of one Western researcher, "Federalism offers innumerable possibilities for addressing the absolute complexity of ethnic demands in deeply divided societies within a democratic framework."[27] In a similar vein, Russian authors have maintained that "the federalization of several of the CIS countries

(Ukraine, Moldova, Kazakhstan, Georgia, and the Transcaucasus in general) might be a highly effective instrument in the resolution of local and ethnic conflicts."[28]

It should be pointed out that federalization as such does not contradict the national principle. Several states widely recognized as viable nation-states, such as Germany and Austria, are also federations. In some such states—such as Switzerland and Canada—the federal structure also has a cultural (ethnic or linguistic) component.

In the 1990s two new autonomous territories were established in the Soviet and post-Soviet space: the Crimean republic in Ukraine in 1990 and the Gagauz Yeri territorial administrative unit for the Turkic-speaking Gagauz in southern Moldova in 1994. The Gagauz autonomy has been hailed as one of the most liberal minority arrangements in the new Europe. Indeed, some Western leaders have criticized the arrangement for going too far in setting a potential precedent for ethnic-territorial autonomy in other (read: their own) countries.[29] This is particularly true of leaders of countries where the imperatives of civic nation-building have taken precedence over the protection of minority rights protection, as in France.

One of the motives behind the liberal conditions granted to the Gagauz by the Moldovan authorities has clearly been to convince the leaders in the breakaway Dniester Moldavian Republic on the left bank of the Dniester that they will be allowed to enjoy real powers if they, too, accept a federal arrangement within a common Moldovan state. The offer held out by Chişinău to the Dniestrians in fact contains even more extensive powers and formal sovereignty than the Gagauz have been granted. Dniestria has been proffered "legal status as a state" (*gosudarstvenno-pravovoy*) within the framework of a single and indivisible Moldova, whereas the Gagauz have had to be content with "territorial" self-determination.[30]

Even so, no agreement has been reached on the Dniestrian issue. Various models of "special status," federation, and confederation have been suggested and rejected. The DMR leadership now wants "associate membership" of the kind the Åland archipelago enjoys in Finland. While remaining an integral part of the Finnish state, Swedish-speaking Åland is also free to conclude international agreements. Formally, Åland is a Finnish *län* (county) but with a very high degree of autonomy and even its own flag. It is a separate member of the Nordic Council, not a part of the Finnish delegation.[31] In a similar manner, DMR leaders insist, Dniestria should be allowed to be a separate member of the CIS and other international organizations, and not necessarily the same ones as Moldova has joined.

Moldovan authorities, however, cannot accept a settlement on such terms, which they regard as simply a perpetuation of Dniestria's de facto separatism. Fears of separatism are very strong not only in Chişinău but in all the new capitals throughout the former Soviet Union. Federalism and territorial arrangements for cultural minorities may work in stable, Western societies, it is argued, but not in newly established post-Soviet states where all political authority is still shaky. Give the minorities an inch and they will take a mile. This expectation has been reinforced by the demise of Yugoslavia and Czechoslovakia—not to mention the currently de facto independence of the former Soviet autonomies of Abkhazia, South Ossetia, DMR, and Nagorno-Karabakh—as well as their own successful breakaway from the Soviet Union.

And so the post-Soviet state leaders are fighting tooth and nail to keep their new states together. All former Soviet republics have adopted constitutions that proclaim the state as "one and indivisible," and a good number of them also lay down the principle of unitary (unitarnyy) statehood.[32] It is somewhat surprising that the latter formula is used even by Azerbaijan, with its disputed Karabakh autonomous oblast.[33] The neighboring state of Armenia, by contrast, which hopes to see this enclave turned into an Armenian exclave, is one of the few former Soviet republics that does not specify in its constitution whether the type of the state structure is unitary, federal, or something else.

In July 1993 the municipal authorities in two compactly Russophone cities in northeast Estonia, Narva and Sillamäe, organized local referendums on "national-territorial autonomy" for their region. Support for this proposal was above 95 percent in both places (with a turnout of 54 percent and 60 percent, respectively).[34] The Estonian authorities, however, were unwilling to accept any kind of territorial autonomy for Russian-speaking regions, and the referendums were declared illegal by the Estonian state court. As only some 30 percent of the population of Narva were Estonian citizens in 1998, this region continues to have less real local government than do other cities, towns, and counties in Estonia.

Several observers have remarked that Ukraine has given its eastern counties such a high degree of self-rule that it amounts to de facto autonomy.[35] President Kuchma does favor greater economic autonomy for the regions, but—presumably for the kind of reasons discussed above—he is opposed to federalism.[36] The Ukrainian constitution adopted under Kuchma proclaims the country as a unitary state, the existence of the autonomous Republic of Crimea notwithstanding.

This leaves Russia as the sole federal republic in the post-Soviet state— as the situation was in the Soviet period as well. The Russian federal structure has several peculiarities: It is multilayered in that it includes several varieties of "subjects of federation" with differing degrees of autonomy—republics, national districts, kraya (a term used for some oblasti in border areas), and oblasti, in addition to one autonomous oblast (that is, an ethnically defined unit distinct from a regular oblast). Further, it is incomplete in the sense that the *kraya* and *oblasti* are treated as regular administrative units, not federal elements proper. Third, it is asymmetrical: Even units that formally belong to the same level in the federal hierarchy may have very different rights and privileges, as reflected in bilateral agreements concluded with the center.[37] And last, the structure of the Russian federation is still not settled. Years after the adoption of the Russian constitution, the exact relationship between the center and federation subjects, as well as among the various subjects of the federation, remains to be finalized.

Some observers have indicated that the tendency seems to be toward greater differentiation in the Russian Federation, whereas others see trends toward tighter structures and a strengthening of central power.[38] Graham Smith has pointed out that the various bilateral agreements reached between the republics and the central authorities have been characterized by increasingly cautious use of language: In the February 1994 agreement with Russia, Tatarstan was called "a state joined with the Russian Federation"; in the agreements with Bashkortostan and Kabardino-Balkaria concluded later that year, the republic was referred to as "a sovereign state within the Russian Federation" and "a state within the Russian Federation," respectively. In the October 1995 Udmurtia agreement, this was further reduced to "republic."[39]

Other observers, however, hold that by 1996 the republican and regional leaders had begun to increase their powers at the expense of the center. In 1996 Yeltsin once more needed to lean on them for support in his electoral campaign. The authority of the regional governors was boosted by the wave of gubernatorial elections in late 1996; prior to that, most of them had been directly appointed by Yeltsin.[40] When the Russian presidency became further weakened in 1998 as a result of economic collapse and a renewed power struggle with the Duma, this trend seemed to gain strength.

On the basis of its complex and unsettled character, it might be tempting to call the Russian federation unique in world history. We should, however, bear in mind that most other federations in the world today also have some unique elements reflecting their specific histories and preconditions. In these arrangements the structures and the power relations among the various component parts are continuously changing as well—albeit perhaps not at the same speed and in the same erratic pattern as in present-day Russia.

Ethnic Democracy

Having rejected such minority-protecting arrangements as consociationalism and federalism, can the new states in the post-Soviet space still become democracies? The question is a huge one and cannot be given comprehensive treatment here.[41] I limit myself to a brief discussion of the "ethnic democracy" model, which, according to some authors, represents a combination of democracy and the political domination of one ethnic group.

The term *ethnic democracy* was first coined to describe the political system of Israel, in particular the relationship between the Jewish majority and the Arab minority in that state. Sammy Smooha maintains that the Israeli case demonstrates the viability of ethnic democracy as "a distinct type of plural society. In such states the dominance of a certain ethnic group is institutionalized along with democratic procedures."[42] All state symbols in Israel are drawn from Jewish history and Jewish traditions. The Arab minority enjoys full political rights, but there has never been an Arab cabinet minister or even a director general of a government office. Unlike the Orthodox Jews, which constitute another distinct cultural segment of Israeli society, the Arabs have never been invited to join a coalition government.

In a comparative study of conflict regulation, Sammy Smooha and Theodor Hanf argue that ethnic democracy may serve not only as a descriptive model but also a normative one, "a viable option for nondemocratic, deeply divided societies."[43] They acknowledge, however, that compared with other varieties of democracy, such as liberalism and consociationalism, ethnic democracy must be regarded as "least democratic." Smooha and Hanf also indicate that ethnic democracy will not be applicable to all kinds of societies. As they see it, an ethnic democracy arrangement will be most likely to succeed if the dominant group has certain specific characteristics: It is strongly influenced by integral, exclusive nationalism; it has sufficient control of the state to curb the resistance of the minority; and it constitutes a clear-cut demographic majority.

A leading expert on Baltic ethnic politics, Graham Smith, suggests that the model of "ethnic democracy" fits the political landscape in Latvia and Estonia better than any rival model, and this view seems to be gaining acceptance among Western observers.[44] There are nevertheless considerable differences between the Israeli and Baltic cases. The titular ethnic groups in Estonia and Latvia do not enjoy the same solid demographic predominance as do the Jews in Israel. Moreover, all Arab permanent residents of Israel (within the 1948 borders) enjoy full formal citizenship rights, whereas large groups of nontitular permanent residents in Estonia and Latvia do not. Thus, both the preconditions for and the instruments of building ethnic democracy differ. What is shared, then, is that both Estonia and Latvia as well as Israel manage to fulfill the minimum criteria of democracy and at the same time clearly favor the titular ethnic group.

Can the ethnic democracy model be extended to the political system of other Soviet successor states as well? To be sure, all Central Asian states have granted their minority populations citizenship rights on far more generous terms than have Latvia and Estonia. The question, however, is whether their political systems may be described as "democratic" in any meaningful sense. Although all of them have popularly elected bodies such as parliaments and organs of local government, elections are frequently manipulated, often to the point of becoming just as pro forma as in the Soviet period. Even more important, these organs are rarely the real loci of politics. Much of the political power and decisionmaking processes in the former Soviet south run outside of these institutions, being invested instead in the presidential apparatus centrally and in the traditional clan and tribe structures locally.

Symbolic Nation-Building, with Mixed Results

The choice of flag and other state emblems often reveals important priorities and tendencies in nation-building strategies. Likewise, their reception or rejection by the populace may tell us whether these strategies will succeed or fail.

Alexander Motyl has remarked that the post-Soviet elites cannot rely exclusively on a refashioning of neglected ethnic identities. They must also "forge thoroughly new national ones involving popular allegiance to myths and symbols that are neither narrowly ethnic, nor conceptually vapid. Drawing on the folklore of only one ethnic group, no matter how rich and meaningful it may be, is not acceptable."[45] The new state symbols of the former Soviet republics differ with respect to their ability to serve as rallying points for the entire nation. Some fail by appealing to one part of the population only, others by being "conceptually vapid," incapable of stirring up strong emotions of any kind. Yet others seem to succeed on both counts.

During perestroika the flags of the three Baltic states held a strong emotive power for two interrelated reasons: They had been actively used in the interwar period of independence, and they had been actively suppressed in the Soviet period. Large parts of the Estonian population associated their lost independence with the colors white, blue, and black; in Lithuania with yellow, red, and green; and in Latvia with deep red and white. Thus, for instance, the very first seeds of the Latvian *atmoda*, or national awakening, were planted on 23 August 1987—the anniversary of the Ribbentrop-Molotov pact—when Latvian dissidents laid down red and white flowers at the foot of the monument of Liberty (another powerful symbol of independent Latvian statehood, which had miraculously been left in place during the Soviet era).[46] Two and a half years later, the replacement of the Soviet flag and state insignia in the Lithuanian Supreme Soviet building to the singing of the old national anthem marked the symbolic departure of the first Soviet republic from the union.[47]

Albeit central to the struggle against Soviet power, the Baltic flags and state symbols have not been similarly controversial in the ensuing struggles between the titular nations and the Russophone populations. Once in place, these emblems seem to have been widely accepted as symbols of the state rather than of one particular ethnic group. The Estonian coat of arms, for instance, depicts the same three lions as does the Danish state emblem, a relic of the time when Estonia was a Danish crown colony in the thirteenth century. With regard to the sharp ethnopolitical conflicts between Estonians and Russians in contemporary Estonian society, this symbol is, strictly speaking, a neutral one.

A very different effect is produced by the Moldovan flag, adopted in 1991. Apart from the center figure, which depicts the bull of Stephan the Great's sixteenth-century Moldovan principality, the flag is identical to the flag of the contemporary Romanian state. This circumstance could not but reinforce Russian fears of imminent unification of Moldova with Romania.

Post-Communist Ukraine would seem to have managed to find unifying rather than divisive state symbols. The light blue and yellow flag symbolizes the open sky over Ukrainian grainfields, and the state emblem, the trident (the *trizub*), is taken from the heraldry of Kievan Rus'. The Ukrainian state has chosen symbols drawn from geography and history, not ethnicity. But just as important as the origin of the state symbols is their later history. The trident was used not only by Yaroslav the Wise in the eleventh century and by the first Ukrainian republic in 1918 but also by the odious Organization of Ukrainian Nationalists in the 1940s. For this reason, many Russians and antinationalist Ukrainians protested loudly in 1992–1993 when they were required to report to the passport authorities and have the trident stamped in their old Soviet passports to confirm their acceptance of their status as Ukrainian citizens.[48]

In Central Asia, in the words of one Western expert, the new state symbols incorporate "carefully selected symbols specific to the titular nation's culture."[49] In both Uzbekistan and Turkmenistan, the flag displays the Islamic crescent moon. The Turkmenistani flag also bears a representation of various traditional carpet designs, each of which is associated with a specific tribe. Non-Muslims and nontitulars are left without any symbolic representation.[50]

The national flag day in Turkmenistan is celebrated on the birthday of President Saparmurad Niyazov, thus adding to the glory of the national leader. As Annette Bohr has remarked, "Many aspects of nation-building [in Turkmenistan] have been condensed into the distorted embodiment of the nation in the form of its leader."[51] Niyazov is officially referred to as "Turkmenbashi," meaning "father of the nation" or "chief of all Turkmens." The presidential portrait is ubiquitous, smiling at his subjects from everywhere, even from the obverse side of the national banknotes, and practically every town and city is adorned with a statue of him. Similar cults of personality of the state leader are central to the nation-building strategies in most of the former Soviet south, although usually in less hyperbolic forms than in Turkmenistan.

Even in Central Asian countries with large European settler communities, it is almost exclusively the traditional culture of the titular ethnic group that the new national symbolism celebrates. Thus, the Kyrgyzstani flag depicts a sun with forty rays, representing the forty Kyrgyz tribes. In the center of the sun is a stylized representation of the Kyrgyz nomadic tent, the yurt. In a similar way, the central features of the Kazakhstani coat of arms are the winged horse of Kazakh myth and the smoke wheel of the nomadic yurt—symbols that scarcely exert a strong emotional pull on the European residents of Kazakhstan.[52]

The state symbols of the Russian Federation hark back to the prerevolutionary past. Post-Communist Russia has adopted the coat of arms of the czars, the double-headed eagle, and even left in place the crowns adorning the bird's two heads. This emblem was imported into Muscovy from Byzantium by Ivan III in the fifteenth century, to signal the Russian grand duke's aspiration to make Russia a new Orthodox universal monarchy. The imperial connotations of this emblem are unmistakable, but the non-Russian population groups do not seem to resent them much. Like the Baltic coats of arms, the Russian state emblem does not draw specifically on the titular ethnic culture.

It is the new Russian flag—the white-blue-red tricolor—that has provoked far greater agitation. The antagonism it has generated has not so much pitted Russians against non-Russians as it has led to clashes between various political camps among the Russians. Whereas this tricolor was used under the Romanovs, primarily by the merchant fleet, it was not directly associated with the czarist regime, whose colors were white, black, and gold. During the Russian Revolution, however, the white-blue-red banner was used by the provisional government of Aleksandr Kerenskiy, and primarily for that reason it is rejected by contemporary Russian right-wing nationalists. At their gatherings they fly the white, black, and gold, together with other Orthodox and czarist symbols. At the same time, Russian Communists and nationalists with left-wing leanings continue to use the Soviet red flag, with its hammer and sickle. This means that any Russian can easily signal which of the three main camps of Russian politics he or she sympathizes with—right-wing imperialist, centrist nation-builders, or left-wing Soviet patriots—simply by hoisting the appropriate flag.

An attempt to cut through this confusion in January 1998 ended in utter failure. The Duma was asked to pass into law the new state symbols currently in use—flag, state coat of arms, and national anthem.[53] Less than one-fourth of the 450 members of the Duma voted in favor of these; the majority wished to retain the symbols of the Soviet era. Several representatives had brought with them enormous red flags, which they waved demonstratively before the TV cameras in the Duma chamber.[54]

A proposal to reintroduce the Soviet anthem that had been composed during World War II was, however, also defeated—as the proposal to bring back the hammer and sickle had been voted down during an earlier session of the Duma. It seemed that an impasse had been reached, with no proposal likely to gain the necessary majority. Finally, Yeltsin decided to take the questions of state symbols off the political agenda.[55] And thus it is that today's Russia is a state without unifying, generally recognized national symbols.

Russian citizens who wish to link their devotion and their very identity to the existing Russian state, it would seem, lack any generally agreed-on symbols and state attributes on which to pin this loyalty. And yet there is a Russian flag in daily use, and likewise a Russian national anthem. As long as the athletes of Russia keep on winning Olympic medals, and the population of Russia keeps up an interest in sports and watches TV, these state symbols will imprint themselves on the audience as picture and sound, becoming deeply embedded in the memory as recollections of times when the Russian nation accomplished something positive. In this way Russian national identity can be strengthened from one Olympiad to the next—not least since Russia is a gold-medal specialist, summer and winter: In Lillehammer, Norway, Russia won eleven gold medals; in Atlanta in the United States, twenty-six; in Nagano, Japan, nine. The politicians may bicker and the economy may seem to be heading downhill, but for a few precious weeks Russians can feel that it is typically Russian to excel.

Among the new states, the smaller ones lack the same chances for showers of gold at international sports events, but many have made considerable achievements: Ukraine took an impressive nine gold medals in Atlanta, for example. And at the Lillehammer winter Olympics, figure skating champion Oksana Bayul became an instant idol. Kazakhstan managed three medals on this occasion—all won by the popular skier Vladimir Smirnov.

Smirnov is an ethnic Russian from northern Kazakhstan. But when he mounts the winners' block, he is not first and foremost a Russian but a Kazakhstani. His sports achievements should thus contribute to civic rather than ethnic nation-building. And yet many in these new states are having a hard time adjusting to this way of thinking. As a journalist in the Kazakh-language newspaper *Ana Tili* put it after Kazakhstan had won ten medals in Atlanta, "It is sad to realize that there were no representatives of the titular nation among Kazakhstan's winners."[56] But that same journalist did go on to say, "No matter which nationality they belong to, we should thank them a thousand times over. We have one and the same Fatherland."

When I was in Kiev in 1994, I attended a soccer match between the home team, Dynamo Kiev, and the top Russian team, Spartak Moskva. Dynamo stadium was crowded, and the fans were cheering lustily. Very few bothered to think about whether members of their team had *Ukrainian* or *Russian* written in their passports. No, there was only one thing that counted just then: getting those goals.

At halftime the score was 2–0, with Russia in the lead, and I feared the worst: Would it all end in anti-Russian riots? Then Ukraine suddenly scored two goals in the space of a few minutes, and—miracle of miracles—twenty seconds before the end a final goal brought the score to 3–2 for the Ukrainians. It seemed that the jubilation would never end. Here indeed was confirmation of the opening lines of the Ukrainian national anthem, played at the start of the match: "Ukraine has not yet perished." Such a victory over the archrival could even compensate for the humiliating concessions being made at that time in the conflict over the Black Sea fleet. That well-worn cliché about "peaceable competition" on the athletic field was given new meaning.

Postage stamps, insignificant as they may seem, are another important tool in civic nation-building. Postage stamps honor the heroes of the nation-state, not least those from the world of sports. In 1992 Ukraine issued a special minisheet to celebrate the achievements of Ukrainian athletes at the Olympics in Barcelona, indicating exactly how many medals they had won, and Kazakhstan did likewise in celebrating its gold medal in the Atlanta games in wrestling. In 1991 Russia issued three postage stamps to commemorate the young men killed during the unsuccessful coup attempt in August that year. They are the martyrs in what has become the mythology of the renewal of the Russian state: the tale of how the Russian state awakened to new life after the Communist sojourn in the valley of the shadow of death.

Postage stamps can also be utilized to mark historical events. In 1993 Latvia celebrated the seventy-fifth anniversary of the founding of the first independent Latvian state, and Moldova issued a series of pictorials with portraits of Moldovan princes of the 1300s. In the same year, the Ukrainian postal authorities commemorated the fiftieth anniversary of the liberation of Kiev from the Nazis and issued a mourning stamp in memory of the great famine of 1933.

States that lack international recognition probably feel an even greater need to signal their presence than other new states. Postage stamps have been used actively in marketing the breakaway Dniester republic: These stamps are not valid for international correspondence but are used for internal mail and are sold to philatelists around the world. The first attempts, printed on paper normally used for wine labels, were not particularly impressive. More recently, however, the DMR has issued a series of beautiful collectors' items. Stamps for everyday use feature a map of the country, as well as the coat of arms, with its sickle and hammer.

In Belarus the white knight is found on the most usual series of everyday stamps. In 1993 and 1994, the average Belarusian citizen could hardly avoid this omnipresent gentleman, as inflation drove up postage costs and more and more stamps were needed to ensure that letters reached their destinations. One registered letter sent to me from Minsk in 1994 sported no less than 113 stamps, each with its white knight. Although philatelists may rejoice, in terms of nation-building this stepped-up use of stamps is probably counterproductive: It leads to a close association between the supposed prime symbol of the nation and an economy in free fall.

Europeans traveling in the Third World are often surprised to see that small, destitute countries unable to pay their debts to foreign lenders nevertheless maintain such an expensive institution as a national airline. An important part of the explanation for this is simply that to have one's very own national aviation company is widely regarded as an indispensable attribute of nationhood. By acquiring the equivalent of British Airways, Air France, and Lufthansa, the aspiring nation-states hope to become the equivalent of the United Kingdom, France, and Germany.

The same kind of thinking is clearly afoot in the former Soviet Union. In the early 1990s, Baltic state leaders received advice from their Scandinavian counterparts, who tried to convince them about the cost-cutting advantages of regional cooperation in the air, indicating that they might want to emulate the Scandinavian Airlines Systems (SAS) model. These suggestions, however, fell on deaf ears, and the national principle prevailed. Estonian Air, Lithuanian Air, and the Riga-based Baltic Air Corporation now compete for passengers in the Baltic market.

Often the national airline was one of the earliest national attributes to be put into place in the former Soviet republics. In 1991–1992, while their citizens were still carrying Soviet passports and their national postal services had to make do with their old Soviet stamps, paintbrushes had already worked wonders on old Aeroflot carriers, transforming them into different fleets of national jets. Thus, for instance, when I traveled from Moscow to Chişinău in September 1992, a full year after the proclamation of Moldova's state independence, there were still no border guards, passport inspections, or customs controls at Chişinău airport. Passengers might have been led to believe that the Soviet Union still existed and the flight they arrived on was domestic—were it not for the fact that an airplane from Air Moldova was parked on the tarmac.

Once again, however, Russia is different. Rather than one national airline, post-Communist Russia sports a wide variety of competing aviation companies. All the major republics have their own—Bashkortostan Airlines, Tatarstan Air, and so on—and in addition a good many planes carry the name of one of the *oblasti*: Orenburg Air, Samara Air, and so on. This proliferation of airlines may be seen as evidence of the stronger centrifugal tendencies in Russian nation-building. Nation-building takes place on the ethnorepublican and regional levels just as much as on the national level.

Will the Nationalizing States Ever Become Nation-States?

Political developments in Europe in the 1990s have been characterized by earnest moves toward integration in the West—and equally earnest moves toward disintegration in the East. By an irony of fate, the Minsk meeting that established the Commonwealth of Independent States started only one day prior to the Maastricht meeting that established the European Union (replacing the European Community)—on 8 and 9 December 1991, respectively. Maastricht marked the start of a program of increasingly ambitious plans for European integration; Minsk marked the beginning of the end of the Soviet Union.

In Western Europe an intense debate is under way as to the future of the nation-state. Challenges are coming both from "below"—from self-assertive subnational regions like Catalonia in Spain, Flanders in Belgium, and Lombardy in northern Italy—and from "above"—from supranational bodies like the EU. The question increasingly being asked is, "Has the nation-state exhausted its role?" In the former Soviet Union, however, the question is quite a different one. Here there is little point in asking whether the nation-state has exhausted its role because it has scarcely had any role to play whatsoever. It makes more sense to ask, "Are these new nation-states capable of surviving? Have the nation-building processes of the new countries reached the point of no return?"

Three different scenarios would lead to a negative answer to this question: (1) if the new states (or some of them) were reabsorbed by a resurgent, neoimperialistic Russia; (2) if the new states (or some of them) voluntarily gave up their new sovereignty and rejoined Russia in a new common state; (3) if the new states continued to exist as independent and

internationally recognized subjects of international law but their populations nevertheless did not acquire a common identity as a "nation."

But there is a fourth scenario that would lead to a positive answer:
Nation-building may be an uphill struggle, but the nationalizing states
may muddle through and gradually acquire many or most of the same
attributes and characteristics as other nation-states in the world.

Reabsorption

Most of the new states in the former Soviet Union had some experience
with independent statehood earlier in the twentieth century, usually
ephemeral but in the Baltic cases for a protracted period of time. They
acquired this statehood primarily as a result of one contingent circumstance, World War I, which led to a historically unique situation: The
traditionally dominant states in Eastern and Central Europe—Russia,
Germany, and Austria-Hungary—were all severely weakened simultaneously. In this power vacuum, many of the lands between either were able
to proclaim independence or felt compelled to do so in order to shield
themselves from the ensuing political and social chaos in the decaying
empires. As soon as social order had been reestablished in Russia proper,
however, a process of regathering of lost territories began, culminating
with the annexation of the Baltics, Bessarabia, and eastern Poland in
1939–1940. Can the same thing happen again?

In my view, of the scenarios sketched above, this is the least probable.
For this to happen, the victim countries must fail to establish credible security arrangements for themselves; the outside world must sit idly by
allowing this to happen; and Russia must acquire both the will and the
capacity for aggressive expansionism. The simultaneous confluence of all
these factors is highly unlikely. Although many Russian political forces
today express open nostalgia for the Soviet state and/or the Russian empire, only Zhirinovskiy's Liberal Democratic Party plus some fringe
groups advocate reunification by forceful means. The Communists, who
in March 1996 pushed through the Duma vote denouncing the Belavezha
agreement and the dissolution of the USSR, insist that what they want is
peaceful and voluntary reunification.

In any case strong political support for aggressive state expansion is
not sufficient: The aggressor must also have the capacity to carry through
this program. At present Russia is decades removed from such a capacity.
The Russian army has been reduced to a shadow of its former formidable self; indeed, when the Russian Communists tried to initiate impeach-
ment procedures against President Yeltsin in May 1999, one of the
charges against him was that he had "ruined" the army and the country's
defense capacity. It can even be argued that the stronger Moscow's will

for territorial aggression, the weaker Russia's capacity for such a policy will become. Any attempt to rebuild the Russian armed forces to previous levels will all too easily siphon off resources that are badly needed for economic recovery and thus inadvertently delay the day when it will be possible to carry out an expansionist policy.[57]

Voluntary Reintegration

In this scenario the leaders of the new states will become convinced that it is in their own interest to mend their severed ties and huddle together again in some kind of a common state. So far, however, evidence of such a development is meager indeed. Although some politicians in Moscow in the early 1990s hoped that the CIS could become a vehicle of close regional integration, this organization has failed to live up to even the most modest expectations. Of the close to 1,000 agreements signed within its framework, only a handful are really working.

CIS integration reached a high-water mark in 1994 and has since then been in decline. For a while, security cooperation was one of its main pillars, but in spring 1999 Georgia, Azerbaijan, and Uzbekistan allowed their membership in the Tashkent treaty of mutual security to lapse.[58] Even though the CIS has achieved status as a UN-recognized organization of subregional cooperation, it has become a byword for failed or fake integration.

Some Russian analysts and politicians argue that one should not judge the potential for subregional integration in the post-Soviet space by the yardstick of the CIS and its deficiencies. The CIS got off on the wrong foot, trying to cover too many countries and too many areas of cooperation in one stride. They point out that the EU as we know it today is the mature result of a long and tortuous integration process, with many setbacks and false starts. The initial spurts of this organization back in the 1950s were highly practical and limited in scope: a union of coal and mining industries in two countries only, the German Federal Republic and France. A similar partnership of two is now taking shape in the former Soviet Union, between Russia and Belarus. It is here and not in the CIS as such that one should look for the new beginnings of voluntary post-Soviet integration, some claim.[59]

This upbeat scenario, however, seems less than convincing. The parallelism between the German-French axis and the Russian-Belarusian axis is spurious. There is a balance and equality in the former that is completely lacking in the latter. In any integration arrangement in the post-Soviet space, Russia is bound to be the hub, leaving the other participants to be the spokes. This remains true even if Ukraine should some day decide to reorient its foreign policy and become an active and enthusiastic partner in such an arrangement. The relative weight of Russia in Eurasia will remain immeasurably greater than Germany's dominance in the EU, even after German reunification. As Russian sociologist Dmitriy Furman has expressed it, "The only kind of integration that may take place here is the reestablishment of Russia's role as kernel and center, as the leader of the unification, as 'the master of the space.' It will be a unification 'around Russia,' the weak gathering around the strong, the periphery around the center."[60] For these very reasons, the leaders in the national-izing states—with a few notable exceptions—have remained extremely wary of any such integration.

The major exception is Kazakhstan. Frustrated by the lack of progress in CIS cooperation, Kazakhstan's president Nazarbayev in March 1994 launched the idea of a Eurasian union for states that wanted to move ahead with faster and deeper regional integration than the CIS laggards. The conclusion of the "union of four"—Russia, Kazakhstan, Kyrgyzstan, and Belarus—two years later, in April 1996, was hailed by Nazarbayev as the fruition of his vision.[61] The union has been renewed several times and in spring 1999 turned into a union of five when Tajikistan joined. The scope and breadth of integration in this organization, however, is only marginally more impressive than in the CIS. None of the member states is prepared to invest it with any kind of supranational structures similar to those of the EU.

The Ukrainian and Moldovan elections in 1994 brought to power regimes that were less Russophobic than the ones they replaced, but even the new power holders were determined to keep Russia at arm's length. In 1997 these two countries, together with Georgia and Azerbaijan, launched the quadripartite organization GUAM, clearly an attempt to build regional integration structures from which Russia was excluded. The fact that Uzbekistan joined GUAM—or GUUAM as it was hence-forth known—in April 1999 reinforced suspicions in Moscow that this was primarily an anti-CIS, anti-Russian organization.[62] Although GUUAM members indignantly deny this, it seems obvious that their pre-ferred form of regional cooperation is designed to safeguard their own national sovereignty, not to divest themselves of it.

Quasi States

The above discussion leads to the conclusion that in the foreseeable fu-ture we will continue to see a plurality of states in the post-Soviet space. But will these states be "nation-states" in any meaningful sense of the word? Western political scientists have maintained that the nation-state is the exception rather than the norm in the contemporary world. Failure has marked the nation-building efforts of most former European colonies that gained independence in the 1960s and early 1970s. Even though they have been independent for more than a generation, neither the institutional nor the cultural preconditions are yet in place. Robert Jackson has called such Third World states "quasi-states": "Their populations do not enjoy many of the advantages traditionally associated with independent statehood. Their governments are often deficient in the political will, institutional authority, and organized power to protect human rights or provide socioeconomic welfare."[63]

The quasi-states of earlier centuries were eventually swallowed up by stronger states, but in the postwar period the rules of the international system were changed to ensure that there would be no return to European overseas colonialism. As a result, the quasi-states enjoy *negative* sovereignty, Jackson maintains. They are propped up from without by the rules of nonintervention, with very little support from within:

> It is no longer a positive right of national self-determination—very few new states are "nations" either by long history or common ethnicity or successful constitutional integration. Instead it is the negative right of ex-European colonies—which usually contain different peoples but are not peoples themselves—to constitutional independence regardless of conditions or circumstances.[64]

Does this description fit the new states created in the northern part of the Eurasian landmass after the collapse of the Soviet Union? The parallels are many and compelling. Most of the former Soviet republics, especially the southern ones, are certainly deficient in institutional authority as well as organized power and the will to protect human rights or provide socioeconomic welfare. Thus, in a study of transition policies after the fall of communism in Transcaucasia, Shireen Hunter flatly concludes that nation-building in Armenia, Georgia, and Azerbaijan has been a failure. In her view six factors have served as impediments to successful nation-building, some of which the former European colonies in Africa were spared:[65]

- *Years of struggle:* Unlike many Third World countries, the former Soviet republics did not achieve independent statehood through protracted conflict against an imperial power. Those struggles, though materially damaging, helped the colonial peoples forge a sense of unity and purpose. The nation-builders in the post-Soviet states cannot benefit from a similar experience.
- *External state actors:* Other states have manipulated the existing internal divisions of the Transcaucasian countries, thus contributing to their fragmentation.

- *Political leadership:* The Transcaucasian states have suffered from a lack of individuals with adequate commitment and sufficient political skills to govern, people who could also act as a unifying force.
- *Ideology:* The Transcaucasian states have failed to develop a new ideational framework for the organization of their societies.
- *Economics:* The three Transcaucasian countries have failed to implement reforms to revitalize their economies and improve the living conditions of their peoples.
- *Foreign policy:* The Transcaucasian states have had great difficulties in developing balanced relations with each other and with other countries.

Many of these problems are common to CIS countries outside the Transcaucasian region as well. Tajikistan, torn apart by a civil war that has caused tens of thousands of deaths, is perhaps the most saddening example of failed nation-building in the former Soviet Union, but it is not the only one. Even without similar bloodletting and even though blessed with important revenue sources in the form of enormous gas reserves, neighboring Turkmenistan remains as indigent and fragmented as ever.

What about Russia, then? As I pointed out in Chapter 10, the preconditions for nation-building in Russia are in many respects very different from those of the other Soviet successor states. Russia is not a "new" or newly independent state: It is the remnant of a former empire. The British expert on nationalism Anthony Smith has discussed the possibilities of transforming such empires—like Russia, China, Japan, Persia, Ottoman Turkey, and Ethiopia—into "territorial nations." Although the historical record is mixed, these processes are, under certain circumstances, quite feasible, he believes. One facilitating condition is that the dominant ethnic group and its rulers divest themselves of their imperial heritage, usually by redrawing their borders. Second, the transition will be smoother to the extent that the old ruling aristocracy is replaced (not necessarily by violence) by the middle and lower classes, while simultaneously preserving and adapting their ethnic cultural heritage.[66]

Smith was writing before the breakup of the Soviet Union—before Russia and the Russians had divested themselves of their non-Russian borderlands. According to the criteria he sets up, the preconditions for successful nation-building in Russia after 1991 would seem to be more or less in place. The pre-Communist Russian cultural heritage has been polished up and reinvigorated. The collapse of communism resulted in a certain amount of replacement within the elite, although not a complete overhaul. And the territory of the country has now been reduced and is basically composed of its ethnic core areas.

Addressing the same question as Smith, Igor Zevelev has adopted a different perspective. He maintains that nation-building on the rubble of an empire is usually an endeavor of ethnonationalists. He points to the evidence of Kemalist Turkey, which started its experiment with a nation-state by subjecting its Armenian, Greek, and Kurdish minorities to genocide and expulsion. Zevelev strongly fears that nation-building in Russia, if vigorously pursued, might lead to a similar appalling outcome:

> No longer hidden under an imperial veil, ethnic identity has become more salient to Russians after the collapse of the Soviet Union. Although ethnonationalism is not politically well organized in Russia, it might emerge ascendant, especially if a goal of nation-state building is introduced into contemporary political discourse, since the term "nation" has had a strong ethnic, not civic connotation in Soviet and post-Soviet academia, public opinion, and politics.[67]

As Zevelev acknowledges, however, as yet nation-building in Russia has *not* followed the ethnic pattern. It is a remarkable fact that Russia has used extremely few resources and no physical force in including the territories inhabited by Russian diaspora groups in the neighboring states into a Russian nation-state. By contrast, the country has been willing to sacrifice the lives of tens of thousands of its citizens and wreak material devastation worth billions of dollars in order to keep a territory inhabited by independence-seeking non-Russians—the Chechens—within a common Russian state. This contrast indicates that Russian nation-building elites have already adjusted to territorial rather than ethnic nation-building—although with no less deplorable results.

Muddling Through

As this book has tried to show, we should be extremely wary of treating all the former Soviet republics as one homogeneous group. The preconditions for national development vary enormously from the Baltics in the northwest to Central Asia in the southeast, from huge Russia to tiny Moldova. Few general conclusions about the prospects for successful nation-building could apply equally to all of these states. There is, however, good reason to expect that at least some of them will join the international community of nation-states. Even if they may qualify only as quasi-states today, that does not mean they are doomed to remain in this category forever. Quasi-states are separated from nation-states not by a chasm but by a continuum of shades and nuances. It may also be argued that Jackson's criteria for membership in the club of genuine nation-states are overly stringent. As we have seen, he believes that a true nation-state should be able to provide socioeconomic welfare to its citizens. But this is, strictly speaking, an attribute of the welfare state, not of the nation-state.

Political scientists have spoken of the "normative force of what actually is."[68] By this they mean that the alternatives that actually exist have a kind of ontological upper hand over hypothetical alternatives. This can serve as an important source of institutional and state legitimacy. The "normative force of what actually is" is clearly part of the explanation why the Soviet state continued to exist as long as it did, even when it lacked most of the sources of legitimacy deemed essential in Western democracies.

Immediately after a new state has been founded, other alternatives will be seen not as hypothetical but as highly real possibilities. Time is needed for this "normative force" to grow strong. How much time? Classical nation-building theory, as we saw, operates with a 400-year period for European nation-building. Any scenario, however, that stipulates a similar time span for the new nationalizing states is irrelevant. What may happen in the twenty-fifth century must necessarily remain a purely speculative question, and far beyond the scope of our discussion.

Present-day nation-builders do not sit idly back, waiting for history to run its own slow course. Nation-building processes are actively compressed into much shorter periods and proceed at a much faster pace. As Stein Rokkan observed,

> The great majority of the political systems of Latin America, Eastern Europe, Asia, and Africa have been faced with a critical cumulation of nation-building challenges over very short spans of time. By contrast to the older, slowly developing nation-states of Western Europe, [they] have had to cope with issues of national-cultural identity, issues of participation, and issues of economic inequality all in one.[69]

These are indeed formidable tasks, and although some of the nation-builders in the post-Soviet space may well be up to them, most likely not all of them will.

NOTES

Chapter 1

1. By *titular nation* I mean the ethnic group that has given the state its name—the Swedes in Sweden, Germans in Germany, and the like.

2. Claes Arvidsson and Lars Erik Blomqvist, *Symbols of Power: The Esthetics of Political Legitimation in the Soviet Union and Eastern Europe* (Stockholm: Almqvist & Wiksell, 1987).

3. Georgi Smirnov, *Soviet Man: The Making of a Socialist Type of Personality* (Moscow: Progress, 1973).

4. The most important exception is the Serbs, the Croats, and the Bosnian Muslims, who speak practically the same language but profess different religions.

5. Ernest Gellner, *Nations and Nationalism* (Oxford: Blackwell, 1990), 43.

6. Some other Soviet successor states—Uzbekistan, Tajikistan, and Azerbaijan—as part of the Soviet legacy have also ethnically defined autonomous units on their territories. The political authorities in these countries, however, do not see their states as ethnic federations. See Chapter 11.

7. Eric J. Hobsbawm, *Nations and Nationalism Since 1780* (Cambridge: Cambridge University Press, 1990), 182.

Chapter 2

1. Carl J. Friedrich, "Nation-Building?" in Karl Deutsch and William Foltz, eds., *Nationbuilding* (New York: Atherton, 1963), 28; Charles Tilly, ed., *The Formation of National States in Western Europe* (Princeton, N.J.: Princeton University Press, 1975).

2. Øyvind Østerud, *Utviklingsteori og historisk endring* (Development theory and historical change) (Oslo: Gyldendal, 1978), 117ff.

3. Stein Rokkan, "Dimensions of State Formation and Nationbuilding: A Possible Paradigm for Research on Variations Within Europe," in Tilly, *The Formation of National States*, 570ff.

4. Walker Connor, *Ethnonationalism: The Quest for Understanding* (Princeton, N.J.: Princeton University Press, 1994), 2–66.

5. Ibid.

6. Benedict Anderson, *Imagined Communities* (London: Verso, 1994), 6.

7. Anthony D. Smith, "Nationalism and the Historians," in Anthony D. Smith, ed., *Ethnicity and Nationalism* (Leiden: E. J. Brill, 1992), 74.

8. Anthony D. Smith, *The Ethnic Origins of Nations* (Oxford: Blackwell, 1986), 147.

9. John Stuart Mill, *On Liberty and Considerations on Representative Government* (1861; reprint, Oxford: Blackwell, 1946), 294–295.

10. John Emerich Edward Acton, *Essays in the Liberal Interpretation of History* (1862; reprint, Chicago: University of Chicago Press, 1967), 149.

11. Ibid., 150.

12. On the one hand, he saw the multinational character of Austria as one of the assets of this state. In the Habsburg domains, no single nation was so predominant as to be able to overcome and absorb the others. One the other hand, Acton accepted the idea that in the course of time "a State may produce a nationality." Acton, *Essays*, 152 and 156.

13. Karl Deutsch, "Nation-Building and National Development: Some Issues for Political Research," in Deutsch and Foltz, *Nationbuilding*, 7–8.

14. Connor pointed out that there were some vacillations and inner inconsistencies in Deutsch's writings on the subject. Connor, *Ethnonationalism*, 30–35. Deutsch's basic optimism was at times interrupted by fits of pessimism. The upbeat mood prevailed, however, and resonated in a number of scholarly works on ethnic integration in the 1970s.

15. He described it as "succumbing to foreign cultural inroads." Connor, *Ethnonationalism*, 139.

16. Ibid., 21.

17. Ibid., 37, 171.

18. Arend Lijphart, *Democracy in Plural Societies* (New Haven, Conn.: Yale University Press, 1977), 88.

19. Anthony H. Birch, *Nationalism and National Integration* (London: Unwin Hyman, 1989), 70.

20. Ernest Gellner, *Nations and Nationalism* (Oxford: Blackwell, 1990), 63.

21. Ibid., 71.

22. Friedrich, "Nation-Building?" 32.

23. Joseph R. Strayer, "The Historical Experience of Nationbuilding in Europe," in Deutsch and Foltz, *Nationbuilding*, 25.

24. Rokkan, "Dimensions," 600.

25. Hans Kohn, *The Idea of Nationalism* (New York: Macmillan, 1946); André Liebich, "Nations, States, Minorities: Why Is Eastern Europe Different?" *Dissent* 42 (Summer 1995): 313–317.

26. Peter F. Sugar and Ivo Lederer, eds., *Nationalism in Eastern Europe* (Seattle: University of Washington Press, 1994); Richard Pipes, *Russia Under the Old Regime* (Harmondsworth, England: Penguin, 1979), 191–221.

27. Raymond Pearson, *National Minorities in Eastern Europe* (London: Macmillan, 1983).

28. Theodor Shanin, *Russia as a "Developing Society"* (London: Macmillan, 1985), 58.

29. Andreas Kappeler, *Russland als Vielvölkerreich* (Russia as multiethnic state) (Munich: Beck, 1993).

30. Yuriy Slezkine, "The USSR as a Communal Apartment, or How a Socialist State Promoted Ethnic Particularism," *Slavic Review* 53, 2 (1994): 414–452; Ronald Grigor Suny, *The Revenge of the Past: Nationalism, Revolution and the Collapse of the Soviet Union* (Stanford: Stanford University Press, 1993).

31. Hélène Carrère d'Encausse, *The Great Challenge: Nationalities and the Bolshevik State, 1917–1930* (London: Holmes and Meier, 1992).

32. Gerhard Simon, *Nationalism and Policy Toward the Nationalities in the Soviet Union* (Boulder, Colo.: Westview, 1991). By this term Simon was referring, on the one hand, to the purposeful policy of the party and the state to consolidate or create nations and, on the other, to the internal processes of change that convert an ethnic community into a nation.

33. Gregory Gleason, *Federalism and Nationalism: The Struggle for Republican Rights in the USSR* (Boulder, Colo.: Westview, 1990); Viktor Zaslavsky, "The Soviet Union," in Karen Barkey and Mark von Hagen, eds., *After Empire: Multiethnic Societies and Nation-Building. The Soviet Union and the Russian, Ottoman, and Habsburg Empires* (Boulder, Colo.: Westview, 1997).

34. Hélène Carrère d'Encausse, *Decline of an Empire: The Soviet Socialist Republics in Revolt* (New York: Newsweek, 1979).

35. Bohdan Nahaylo and Victor Swoboda, *Soviet Disunion: A History of the Nationalities Problems in the USSR* (London: Hamish Hamilton, 1990).

36. I. V. Stalin, "Marksizm i natsional'nyy vopros" (Marxism and the national question), in *Sochineniya* (Works) (1913; reprint, Moscow: Ogiz, 1946), 320–332.

37. Robert A. Lewis, Richard H. Rowland, and Ralph Clem, *Nationality and Population Change in Russia and the USSR* (New York: Praeger, 1976); Mikk Titma and Nancy B. Tuma, *Migration in the Former Soviet Union* (Cologne: Bundesinstitut für Ostwissenschaftliche und Internationale Studien, 1992).

38. Rogers Brubaker, *Nationalism Reframed: Nationhood and the National Question in the New Europe* (Cambridge: Cambridge University Press, 1996), 57.

39. Anthony D. Smith, *The Ethnic Origins of Nations* (Oxford: Blackwell, 1986).

40. Ernest Renan, *Qu'est-ce qu'une nation? et autres essais politiques* (What is a nation? and other political essays) (1882; reprint, Paris: Presses Pocket, 1992).

41. Brubaker, *Nationalism Reframed,* 104–105.

42. Alexander J. Motyl, *Dilemmas of Independence: Ukraine After Totalitarianism* (New York: Council of Foreign Relations Press, 1993), 80.

43. Jack Snyder, "Nationalism and the Crisis of the Post-Soviet State," *Survival* 35, 1 (1993): 12.

44. Brubaker, *Nationalism Reframed,* 105.

45. S. Sabikenov, "Natsional'nyy i narodnyy suverenitet. V chem ikh razlichie?" (National and popular sovereignty: How do they differ from each other?) *Mysl'* (Almaty) 4 (1994): 9.

46. Elmars Vebers, *Latvijas Valsts un etniskas minoritates* (The Latvian state and ethnic minorities) (Riga: Latvijas Zinatnu Akademijas, 1997), 158.

47. Klara Hallik, "On the International Context of the Interethnic Relations in Estonia," paper presented at the conference "Democracy and Ethnopolitics," Riga, 9–11 March 1994, 9–10.

48. Reinhard Bendix, *Nationbuilding and Citizenship* (Berkeley: University of California Press, 1977).

Chapter 3

1. John Stuart Mill, *On Liberty and Considerations on Representative Government* (1861; reprint, Oxford: Blackwell, 1946), 291.

2. Ottar Dahl, *Norsk Historieforskning i 19. and 20. århundre* (Norwegian historical research in the nineteenth and twentieth centuries) (Oslo: Universitetsfor-
laget, 1970).

3. Henrik Wergeland "Til Forfædrenes Minde" (To the memory of our ancestors), 1834, quoted here from Arne Bergsgård, *Norsk Historie 1814–1880* (Norwegian history, 1814–1880) (Oslo: Det Norske Samlaget, 1975), 107.

4. Arne Kommisrud, "'Historiske' og 'historieløse folk.' En historisk-sosiolo-
gisk teori om nasjonalitetskonflikter i Sentral-Europa" ("Historical" and "ahistorical" peoples: A historico-sociological theory of nationality conflicts in Central
Europe), *Sosiologi i dag* (Sociology today) 22, 3 (1992): 52–53.

5. Rein Taagepera, *Estonia: Return to Independence* (Boulder, Colo.: Westview,
1993), 23.

6. Mikhas Tkachov, "Ob istoricheskom gerbe 'Pogonya'" (On the historical
coat of arms "Pohonia"), *Veter Baltiki* (The wind of the Baltic Sea) 1 (September
1990): 4.

7. See, for example, Alfred Erich Senn, "Lithuania: Rights and Responsibilities
of Independence," in Ian Bremmer and Ray Taras, eds., *New States, New Politics:
Building the Post-Soviet Nations* (Cambridge: Cambridge University Press, 1997).

8. Romuald J. Misiunas, "National Identity and Foreign Policy in the Baltic
States," in S. Frederick Starr, ed., *The Legacy of History in Russia and the New States
of Eurasia* (Armonk, N.Y.: M. E. Sharpe, 1994), 96; Mette Skak, *From Empire to An-
archy: Postcommunist Foreign Policy and International Relations* (London: C. Hurst,
1996), 196.

9. Ole Nørgaard, ed., *De baltiske land efter uafhængigheden. Hvorfor så forskellige?*
(The Baltic countries since independence: Why are they so different?) (Aarhus,
Denmark: Politica, 1994), 44.

10. Andrew Wilson, *Ukrainian Nationalism in the 1990s* (Cambridge: Cambridge
University Press, 1997), 158.

11. "National historiographies always have the tendency to project the modern
nation back in time. . . . Kievan Rus' was neither Russian nor Ukrainian, just as
that of Charlemagne was neither French nor German." Andreas Kappeler,
"Ukrainian History from a German Perspective," *Slavic Review* 54, 3 (1995): 698.

12. Germ Janmaat, "Ivan Mazepa and Stepan Bandera, Heroes or Traitors?"
paper presented at the fourth annual convention of the Association for the Study
of Nationalities, Columbia University, 15–17 April 1999, 4–5.

13. Wilson, *Ukrainian Nationalism,* 160.

14. Orest Subtelny, *Ukraine: A History,* 2d ed. (Toronto: University of Toronto
Press, 1993).

15. Serhiy M. Plokhy, "Historical Debates and Territorial Claims: Cossack
Mythology in the Russian-Ukrainian Border Dispute," in Starr, *The Legacy of History,* 147–170.

16. Zenon Kohut, "History as a Battleground: Russian-Ukrainian Relations and
Historical Consciousness in Contemporary Ukraine," in Starr, *The Legacy of History,* 133.

17. Ibid.

18. *Novye konstitutsii stran SNG i Baltii. Sbornik dokumentov* (New constitutions
in the CIS countries and the Baltics: A collection of documents) (Moscow:
Manuskript, 1994), 84.

19. The following account is based mainly on Jan Zaprudnik, *Belarus: At a Crossroads in History* (Boulder, Colo.: Westview, 1993).

20. Rainer Lindner, "Nationsbildung durch Nationalgeschichte. Probleme der aktuellen Geschichtsdiskussion in Weissrussland" (Nation-building through national history. Problems of the current historical debate in Belarus), *Osteuropa* 44, 6 (1994): 585.

21. Barbara Törnquist Plewa, *Språk och identitet in Vitryssland* (Language and identity in Belarus) (Lund, Sweden: Lunds Universitet, 1997), 57.

22. Nicholas P. Vakar, *Belorussia: The Making of a Nation* (Cambridge: Harvard University Press, 1956), 139.

23. Lindner, "Nationsbildung," 579.

24. "Deklaratsiya o nezavisimosti Respubliki Moldova" (Declaration of independence of the Republic of Moldova), Chişinău, 27 August 1991.

25. Wim van Meurs, "Carving a Moldovan Identity Out of History," *Nationalities Papers* 26, 1 (1998): 39–56.

26. V. I. Kozlov, *Natsional'nosti SSSR, Etnodemograficheskiy obzor* (The nationalities of the USSR: An ethnodemographic overview) (Moscow: Finansy i Statistika, 1982), 15.

27. Lee Schwartz, "Regional Population Redistribution and National Homelands in the USSR," in Henry R. Huttenbach, ed., *Soviet Nationality Policies: Ruling Ethnic Groups in the USSR* (London: Mansell, 1990), 121–161.

28. Pål Kolstø, "Anticipating Demographic Superiority: Kazakh Thinking on Integration and Nation-Building," *Europe-Asia Studies* 50, 1 (1998): 51–69.

29. Raisa Dobraya, "Gosudarstvo—eto my?" (The state—that is us?), *Kazakhstanskaya pravda* (Kazakhstan's truth), 12 April 1996.

30. Martha Brill Olcott, *The Kazakhs*, 2d ed. (Stanford, Calif.: Hoover Institution Press, 1995), passim; and Steven Sabol's review of Olcott's book in *Nationalities Papers* 25, 2 (June 1997): 361–362.

31. Martha Brill Olcott, "Kazakhstan: Pushing for Eurasia," in Bremmer and Taras, *New States, New Politics*, 550.

32. Grey Hodnett, *Leadership in the Soviet National Republics* (Oakville, Ontario: Mosaic Press, 1979), 94–98; Rasma Karklins, "Ethnic Politics and Access to Higher Education: The Soviet Case," *Comparative Politics* 16, 3 (April 1984): 284; Rasma Karklins, *Ethnic Relations in the USSR: The Perspective from Below* (Boston: Unwin Hyman, 1989), 82ff.

33. See Abish Kekilbayev's long commemorative article, "Surovoe ispytanie nakanune peremen" (A harsh ordeal on the eve of the changes), *Kazakhstanskaya pravda*, 12 November 1996, 1–2. Kekilbayev was state secretary of Kazakhstan and a close coworker of President Nursultan Nazarbayev.

34. Ernest Renan, *Qu'est-ce qu'une nation? et autres essais politiques* (What is a nation? and other political essays) (1882; reprint, Paris: Presses Pocket, 1992).

35. Mark von Hagen, "Does Ukraine Have a History?" *Slavic Review* 54, 3 (1995): 665.

Chapter 4

1. Andrew Greeley, "A Religious Revival in Russia?" *Journal for the Scientific Study of Religion* 33, 3 (1994): 253–272.

2. Sergey Filatov and Dmitriy Furman, "Religiya i politika v massovom soznanii" (Religion and politics in mass consciousness), *Sotsiologicheskie issledovaniya* (Sociological research), 7 (1992): 5.

3. David D. Laitin, *Identity in Formation: The Russian-Speaking Populations in the Near Abroad* (Ithaca, N.Y.: Cornell University Press, 1998), 319.

4. Svein Mønnesland, *Før Jugoslavia og etter* (Before and after Yugoslavia) (Oslo: Sypress, 1995), 213.

5. See, for example, Ernest Gellner, *Nations and Nationalism* (Oxford: Blackwell, 1990), 69–70.

6. The principle was first formulated in the Treaty of Augsburg in 1555, but at that time it was not implemented.

7. Norman Davies, *God's Playground: A History of Poland*, vol. 2, *1795 to the Present* (Oxford: Clarendon Press, 1982), 131.

8. Alfred Erich Senn, "Lithuania: Rights and Responsibilities of Independence," in Ian Bremmer and Ray Taras, eds., *New States, New Politics: Building the Post-Soviet Nations* (Cambridge: Cambridge University Press, 1997).

9. Patriarch Filaret (Romanov) was the father of Czar Mikhail. He had been one of the most powerful boyars in Russia but in 1601 was forced by Czar Boris Godunov to take holy orders and sent to a remote monastery. When his son was chosen as the new czar in 1613, he returned to Moscow to a position of honor and dignity.

10. John Anderson, *Religion, State and Politics in the Soviet Union and the Successor States* (Cambridge: Cambridge University Press, 1994), 138–144; John B. Dunlop, "Gorbachev and Russian Orthodoxy," *Problems of Communism* 38, 4 (1989): 96–116.

11. John B. Dunlop, "The Russian Orthodox Church as an 'Empire-Saving' Institution," in Michael Bourdeaux, ed., *The Politics of Religion in Russia and the New States of Eurasia* (Armonk, N.Y.: M. E. Sharpe, 1995), 15ff.

12. Author's interviews in Kazan, the capital of Tatarstan, October 1991.

13. Radio Free Europe/Radio Liberty Newsline, 28 August 1997.

14. Ibid., 23 July 1997.

15. Dimitry V. Pospielovsky, "The Russian Orthodox Church in the Postcommunist CIS," in Bourdeaux, *Politics of Religion*, 41–74.

16. Carsten Riis, "Jugoslavisk kirkepolitik i Makedonien" (Yugoslavian church politics in Macedonia), *Nordisk Østforum* 11, 3 (1997): 79–90.

17. "That is why there cannot be any other principle of Church order except a local, a territorial one. Any other principle would mean that the grace-endowed unity in Christ is replaced by some natural sign, national or racial." Filaret, metropolitan of Kiev and Galich, "The Local Church and the Universal Church," *Journal of the Moscow Patriarchate* 4 (1981): 74.

18. Stefan Zankov, *Nation, Staat, Welt und Kirche im Ortodoxen Osten* (Nation, state, world, and church in the Orthodox East) (Sofia: n.p., 1937), 14.

19. Peter F. Sugar and Ivo Lederer, eds., *Nationalism in Eastern Europe* (Seattle: University of Washington Press, 1994), 113ff.

20. See, for example, Yevgraph Kovalevsky, "The Universality of Orthodoxy and the Russian-Orthodox Church," *Journal of the Moscow Patriarchate* 10 (1946); P. Uzhrumtsev, "Christianity and the Nationality Question," *Journal of the Moscow Patriarchate* 4 (1962).

21. One survey indicates that there are some fifteen different Orthodox denominations in the United States. See Frank S. Mead, *Handbook of Denominations in the United States* (Nashville, Tenn.: Abingdon Press, 1970).

22. Hans-Dieter Döpmann, *Die Russische Orthodoxe Kirche in Geschichte und Gegenwart* (The Russian Orthodox Church in history and the present) (Berlin: Union Verlag, 1981), 283.

23. S. Troitsky, "On Ecclesiastical Autocephaly," *Journal of the Moscow Patriarchate* 7 (1948): 7.

24. Robert F. Goeckel, "The Baltic Churches and the Democratization Process," in Bourdeaux, *Politics of Religion,* 206.

25. Samuel P. Huntington, "The Clash of Civilizations?" *Foreign Affairs* 72, 3 (1993): 25.

26. See, for instance, the special issue on Estonia in *Nationalities Papers* 23, 1 (Spring 1995): 16 passim; Marju Lauristin and Peeter Vihalemm, with Karl Erik Rosengren and Lennart Weibull, eds., *Return to the Western World: Cultural and Political Perspectives on the Estonian Post-Communist Transition* (Tartu: Tartu University Press, 1997), 24–29, 130–132 passim.

27. The patriarch of Moscow, Aleksiy II, is in fact from Estonia and was formerly the bishop of Tallinn.

28. *Open Media Research Institute (OMRI) Daily Digest,* 16 January, 18 March, and 20 May 1996.

29. Dunlop, "The Russian Orthodox Church," 21.

30. Jan Zaprudnik, *Belarus: At a Crossroads in History* (Boulder, Colo.: Westview, 1993), 45. At that time terms like *Belarusian* or *White Russian* were not in use. The population tended to call itself *tuteyshie,* which simply means "we who come from this place" or "the locals."

31. V. Polikarpov, "Gosudarstvo i grazhdanin, puti sblizheniya" (The state and the citizen: Avenues toward their rapprochement), *Evropeyskoe vremya* (Minsk) 2, 1992.

32. Georg Seide, "Die Russische Orthodoxe Kirche in den Nachfolgestaaten der Sowjetunion" (The Russian Orthodox Church in the successor states of the Soviet Union), *Osteuropa* 44, 1 (1994): 71.

33. Radio Free Europe/Radio Liberty Newsline, 7, 14, 20, and 28 August 1997.

34. "On the 35th Anniversary of the Reunion of the Greek Catholic Church with the Russian Orthodox Church," *Journal of the Moscow Patriarchate* 6 (1981): 65–71.

35. Bohdan Bociurkiw, "Politics and Religion in Ukraine: The Orthodox and the Greek Catholics," in Bourdeaux, *Politics of Religion,* 131–162.

36. Gretchen Knudson Gee, "Geography, Nationality, and Religion in Ukraine: A Research Note," *Journal for the Scientific Study of Religion* 34, 3 (1995): 387. In Galicia support was almost equally divided between the Orthodox and the Uniate Churches. The proportion of believers in this region was far higher than the national average: Approximately three-quarters of the population of L'viv answered that they considered themselves to be believers.

37. "Doklad Patriarshego Mestoblyustitelya Filareta, Metropolita Kievskogo i Galitskogo, Eksarkha vseya Ukrainy" (Report from Metropolitan Filaret of Kiev and Galicia, exarch of Ukraine, patriarchal deputy), *Zhurnal Moskovskoy patriarkhii* 9 (1990): 17.

38. Frank E. Sysyn, "The Third Rebirth of the Ukrainian Autocephalous Ortho-dox Church and the Religious Situation in Ukraine, 1989–1991," in Stephen K. Batalden, ed., *Seeking God: The Recovery of Religious Identity in Orthodox Russia, Ukraine, and Georgia* (De Kalb: Northern Illinois University Press, 1993), 191–219.

39. Anderson, *Religion, State and Politics*, 189ff.

40. Vladimr Skachko, "Tserkvi ob 'edinilis', no ikh chislo ne umen'shilos'" (The churches have merged, but their numbers remain the same), *Nezavisimaya gazeta* (Independent gazette), 27 June 1992.

41. See Bociurkiw, "The Orthodox"; Vasyl Markus, "Politics and Religion in Ukraine," in Bourdeaux, *Politics of Religion*, 163–181; Christyna Lapychak, "Rifts Among Ukraine's Orthodox Churches Inflame Public Passions," *Transition* 2, 7 (5 April 1996): 6–10.

42. Fairy von Lilienfeld, "Reflections on the Current State of the Georgian Church and Nation," in Batalden, *Seeking God*, 224.

43. The Ethiopian, Egyptian Coptic, and Syrian Churches are Monophysite as well, but they have scant contact with the Armenian Church.

44. Tadeusz Swietochowski, "Islam and the Growth of National Identity in So-viet Azerbaijan," in Andreas Kappeler, Gerhard Simon, Georg Brunner, and Ed-ward Allworth, eds., *Muslim Communities Reemerge: Historical Perspectives on Na-tionality, Politics, and Opposition in the Former Soviet Union and Yugoslavia* (Durham, N.C.: Duke University Press, 1994), 446.

45. Anatoly M. Khazanov, *After the USSR: Ethnicity, Nationalism, and Politics in the Commonwealth of Independent States* (Madison: University of Wisconsin Press, 1995), 145. "Turkmenbashi," meaning "the father of the Turkmen," is the new name Niyazov has adopted.

46. Shirin Akiner, "Melting Pot, Salad Bowl—Cauldron? Manipulation and Mobilization of Ethnic and Religious Identities in Central Asia," *Ethnic and Racial Studies* 20, 2 (April 1997): 362–398.

47. Guy G. Imart, "Kirgizia-Kazakhstan: A Hinge or a Fault-Line?" *Problems of Communism* 39 (September–October 1990): 1–13.

48. Khazanov, *After the USSR*, 130ff.

49. Alexandre Bennigsen and S. Enders Wimbush, *Muslims of the Soviet Empire* (London: C. Hurst, 1985).

50. Roald Sagdeyev and William E. Sanford, "War, Peace, and Peacekeeping in Tajikistan," *Analysis of Current Events* 10, 3–4 (March–April 1998): 6.

51. See, for example, Alan Hetmanek, "Religion and Politics in the Former So-viet Union," *Central Asia Monitor* 2 (1994): 28–30.

52. Arkadiy Dubnov, "'Prodam BTR, kuplyu dom v Rossii'" ("We'll sell an ar-mored personnel carrier and buy a house in Russia"), *Novoe vremya* (New times) 43 (1992): 8–11; Bess Brown, "Tajikistan: The Conservatives Triumph," *Radio Free Europe/Radio Liberty Research Report* 2, 7 (1993): 9–12.

53. Khazanov, *After the USSR*, 145.

54. K. E. Kusherbaev, E. Z. Nazarbaev, and N. M. Sadykov, *Uroven' religioznosti i konfessional'nye orientatsii naseleniya Respubliki Kazakhstan* (The level of religiosity and the confessional orientations of the population of the Republic of Kaza-khstan) (Almaty: Institut Razvitiya Kazakhstana, 1996), 7.

55. Ibid.

56. Reef Altoma, "The Influence of Islam in Post-Soviet Kazakhstan," in Beatrice F. Manz, ed., *Central Asia in Historical Perspective* (Boulder, Colo.: Westview, 1994), 172.

57. Ibid.

58. Yuriy Mikhalkov, "Pravoslavnye v Kazakhstane" (The Orthodox in Kazakhstan), *Moskovskie novosti* (Moscow news) 33 (1991).

59. Kusherbaev, Nazarbaev, and Sadykov, *Uroven' religioznosti*, 19.

Chapter 5

1. Robert A. Lewis, Richard H. Rowland, and Ralph Clem, *Nationality and Population Change in Russia and the USSR* (New York: Praeger, 1976), 202–214; Pål Kolstø, *Russians in the Former Soviet Republics* (Bloomington: Indiana University Press; London: C. Hurst, 1995), 13–70.

2. Chauncy D. Harris, "The New Russian Minorities: A Statistical Overview," *Post-Soviet Geography* 34, 1 (1993): 1–27.

3. By *diaspora* in this context, I mean an ethnic group living outside the state that it regards, or is regarded, as its historical homeland.

4. For a general treatment of this triangular relationship, see Rogers Brubaker, *Nationalism Reframed: Nationhood and the National Question in the New Europe* (Cambridge: Cambridge University Press, 1996), 55–78.

5. See, for example, Andrew Maley, "Does Russia Speak for the Baltic Russians?" *World Today* 51, 1 (1995): 14–16.

6. See, for instance, a statement of Deputy Prime Minister Aleksandr Shokhin, "Na ugrozy sdelat' zalozhnikami russkikh b blizhnem zarubezh'e u nas est' adekvatnye otvety" (We have adequate replies to all threats to turn the Russians in the near abroad into hostages), *Izvestiya* (News), 16 November 1993, 2.

7. For more details, see Kolstø, *Russians*, and Pål Kolstø, "The New Russian Diaspora—an Identity of Its Own? Possible Identity Trajectories for Russians in the Former Soviet Republics," *Ethnic and Racial Studies* 9, 3 (1996): 609–639.

8. Ian Bremmer, "The Politics of Ethnicity: Russians in the New Ukraine," *Europe-Asia Studies* 46, 2 (1994); Nadezhda Lebedeva, "Russkaya diaspora ili chast' russkogo naroda? (K probleme samoopredeleniya russkikh na Ukraine)" (A Russian diaspora or a part of the Russian people? [On the problem of the self-identification of Russians in Ukraine]), in V. I. Kozlov and E. A. Shervud, eds., *Russkie v blizhnem zarubezh'e* (Russians in the near abroad) (Moscow: Institut Etnologii i Antropologii, 1994), 53–59.

9. Anatol Lieven, *The Baltic Revolution: Estonia, Latvia, Lithuania and the Path to Independence* (New Haven, Conn.: Yale University Press, 1993), 175–180. A survey conducted in 1993 showed that perceptions and attitudes among the Russians and the titular groups in the Baltic states were in fact surprisingly similar, indicating that the culture gap is smaller than many Balts are inclined to believe. See Richard Rose and William Maley, *Nationalities in the Baltic States: A Survey Study* (Glasgow: University of Strathclyde, 1994), esp. iv–v.

10. Aadne Aasland, "Russians Outside Russia: The New Russian Diaspora," in Graham Smith, ed., *The Nationalities Question in the Post-Soviet States* (London: Longman, 1996), 483.

11. William Fierman, "Problems of Language Implementation in Uzbekistan," *Nationalities Papers* 23, 3 (1995): 591; author's interviews in Tashkent and Bishkek, May 1993.

12. Martin Malek, "Sprachenpolitik im Baltikum" (Language politics in the Baltics), *Osteuropa* 44, 10 (1994): 926–937; Angelita Kamenska, *The State Language in Latvia: Achievements, Problems and Prospects* (Riga: Latvian Center for Human Rights and Ethnic Studies, 1995).

13. Asbjørn Eide, *Human Rights Aspects of the Citizenship Issues in Estonia and Latvia* (London: European Bank for Reconstruction and Development, 1992); Helsinki Watch, *New Citizenship Laws in the Republics of the Former Soviet Union* (New York: Helsinki Watch, 1992).

14. Helsinki Watch, *Violations by the Latvian Department of Citizenship and Immigration* (New York: Helsinki Watch, 1993); Max van der Stoel, "Letter from the OSCE High Commissioner on National Minorities to V. Birkavs, Minister of Foreign Affairs of the Republic of Latvia," 14 March 1996, reprinted in Hanne-Margret Birckenbach, *Preventive Diplomacy Through Fact-Finding: How International Organisations Review the Conflict over Citizenship in Estonia and Latvia* (Hamburg: Lit, 1997), 377–381.

15. Magda Opalski, Boris Tsilevich, and Piotr Dutkiewicz, *Ethnic Conflict in the Baltic States: The Case of Latvia* (Kingston, Ontario: Kashtan Press, 1994).

16. *Res publica* (Bishkek), 15 May 1993, 3; Anatoly M. Khazanov, *After the USSR: Ethnicity, Nationalism, and Politics in the Commonwealth of Independent States* (Madison: University of Wisconsin Press, 1995), 124ff.

17. See, for example, Gerhard Simon, *Nationalism and Policy Toward the Nationalities in the Soviet Union* (Boulder, Colo.: Westview, 1991); Victor Zaslavsky, "Nationalism and Democratic Transition in Postcommunist Societies," *Daedalus* 121, 2 (1992): 97–121.

18. Donald L. Horowitz, *Ethnic Groups in Conflict* (Berkeley: University of California Press, 1985), 291–332.

19. Robert J. Kaiser and Jeff Chinn, "Russian-Kazakh Relations in Kazakhstan," *Post-Soviet Geography* 36, 5 (1995): 257–273.

20. Y. V. Arutyunyan and L. M. Drobizheva, "Russkie v raspadayushchemsya soyuze" (Russians in a collapsing Union), *Otechestvennaya istoriya* (History of the fatherland) 3 (1992): 3–15.

21. Ilmars Mezs, Edmunds Bunkse, and Kaspars Rasa, "The Ethno-Demographic Status of the Baltic States," *GeoJournal* 33, 1 (1994): 21.

22. Hélène Carrère d'Encausse, *The End of the Soviet Empire: The Triumph of the Nations* (New York: Basic Books, 1993).

23. According to figures from the International Organization for Migration (IOM), upward of 2 million Russians left Central Asia between 1990 and 1996. See *CIS Migration Report (1996)* (Geneva: International Organization for Migration, 1997).

24. "Zakon o grazhdanstve" (Law on citizenship), *Vedomosti s"ezda narodnykh deputatov Rossiyskoy Federatsii i Verkhovnogo Soveta Rossiyskoy Federatsii* (Register of the Congress of People's Deputies of the Russian Federation and the Supreme Soviet of the Russian Federation), 6 (1992).

25. Pål Kolstø, "Territorialising Diasporas: The Case of the Russians in the Former Soviet Republics," *Millennium* 28, 3 (1999): 607–631.

26. Vello Pettai, "Political Stability Through Disenfrachisement," *Transition* 3, 6 (4 April 1997): 23.

27. Mette Skak, "Ungarns and Ruslands politik over for hhv. den ungarske og den russiske diaspora in nabolandene" (The policy of Hungary and Russian vis-à-vis the Hungarian and Russian diasporas in the neighboring countries), in Jørgen Kühl, ed., *Mindretalspolitik* (Minority policy) (Copenhagen: Dansk Udenrigspolitisk Institut, 1996), 149.

28. Constitution of the Russian Federation, article 61, section 2. The text of the constitution appears in *Novye konstitutsii stran SNG i Baltii. Sbornik dokumentov* (New constitutions in the CIS and the Baltics: A collection of documents) (Moscow: Manuskript, 1994), 365.

29. *Federal'nyy zakon o gosudarstvennoy politike Rossiyskoy Federatsii v otnoshenii sootechestvennikov za rubezhem* (Federal law on the state policy of the Russian Federation on relations with compatriots abroad), adopted 13 November 1998.

30. Kolstø, *Russians*, 259–262.

31. "Dmitriy Rogozin: 'Rossiya budet shire'" (Dmitriy Rogozin: "Russia will expand"), *Moskovskie novosti* (Moscow news), 8 May 1994; Sakala Center (Tallinn), "Second World Congress of Russian Communities: Declaration of Compatriots' Rights," *Survey of Baltic and Post-Soviet Politics*, February 1994, 18–22. See also the CRC's Website, available at: http//www.kro.ru.

32. Eide, *Human Rights Aspects*.

33. S. A. Karaganov, "Problemy zashchity interesov rossiysko orientirovannogo naseleniya v 'blizhnem' zarubezh'e" (The problems of protecting the interests of the Russia-oriented part of the population in the "near abroad"), in *Diplomaticheskiy vestnik* (Diplomatic bulletin) 15, 11 (1992).

34. *Nezavisimaya gazeta* (Independent gazette), 28 March 1992.

35. Vladimir Simonov, "Moskva gotova primenit' silu dlya zashchitu russkoy diaspory" (Moscow is prepared to use force to protect the Russian diaspora), *Delovoy mir* (Business world), 21 April 1995. For reactions to Kozyrev's remark, see, for example, *Diena* (Riga), 18 May 1995.

36. Zevelev, "Russia and the Russian Diasporas"; Neil J. Melvin, "The Russians: Diaspora and the End of Empire," in Charles King and Neil J. Melvin, eds., *Nations Abroad: Diaspora Politics and International Relations in the Former Soviet Union* (Boulder, Colo.: Westview, 1998), 41.

37. Anthony Hyman, "Russians Outside Russia," *World Today* 49 (1993): 205–208.

38. Pavel Baev, *The Russian Army in a Time of Troubles* (London: Sage, 1996), 39–40 and 104–112.

39. "Osnovnye napravleniya gosudarstvennoy politiki Rossiyskoy Federatsii v otnoshenii sootechestvennikov, prozhivayushchikh za rubezhem" (Main directions of the state policy of the Russian Federation toward compatriots living abroad), Postanovlenie Pravitel'stva Rossiyskoy Federatsii (Resolution of the government of the Russian Federation), 31 August 1994, no. 1064.

40. Nadezhda Lebedeva, *Novaya russkaya diaspora, Sotsial'no-psikhologicheskiy analiz* (The new Russian diaspora: A sociopsychological analysis) (Moscow: Institut Etnologii i Antropologii, 1995); David D. Laitin, *Identity in Formation: The Russian-Speaking Populations in the Near Abroad* (Ithaca, N.Y.: Cornell University Press, 1998).

41. Natal'ya Kosmarskaya, "'Ya nikuda ne khochu uyezzhat'.' Zhizn' v post-sovetskoy Kirgizii glazami russkikh" ("I don't want to go anywhere": Life in post-Soviet Kyrgyzstan in the eyes of Russians), *Vestnik Yevrazii* (Eurasian bulletin) 1–2, 4–5 (1998): 95–97.

42. "Second World Congress," 19.

43. Allen Buchanan, *Secession: The Morality of Political Divorce from Fort Sumter to Lithuania and Quebec* (Boulder, Colo.: Westview, 1991), 18–22.

44. "Second World Congress," 20.

45. *Rossiyskaya gazeta,* 27 May 1995.

46. *Federal'nyy zakon.*

47. Author's interviews in Moldova in 1992 and 1996 and in Kyrgyzstan in 1993.

48. *Vechernyaya Odessa,* 18 September 1992.

49. V. V. Vishnevskiy, president of the Slavonic Foundation of Kyrgyzstan, in *Chuyskie izvestiya* (Bishkek), 1–7 May 1993, 5.

50. See, for example, statements by the chairman of the Ukrainian Parliament Committee on Questions of Culture and Religious Affairs, Mykhailo Kosiv, "Bez movy, nemae narodu, bez narodu, nemae derzhavy" (Without a language, we have no people; without a people, we have no state), *Holos Ukrainy* (Voice of Ukraine), 16 September 1994, and the chairman of the Kazakh language association Kazak Tili (literally, "the Kazakh language"), A. Kaydarov, "Esli ischeznet yazyk . . . " (If the language disappears . . .), *Kazakhstanskaya pravda* (Kazakhstan's truth), 15 October 1992. Kaydarov also wanted to have the reference to Russian as the language of interethnic communication removed from the Kazakhstani constitution.

51. Vladimir Alpatov, "Yazyki v sovetskom i postsovetskom prostranstve" (Languages in the Soviet and post-Soviet space), *Svobodnaya mysl'* (Free thought), 4 (1995): 87–98.

52. Dominique Arel, "Language Politics in Independent Ukraine: Towards One or Two State Languages?" *Nationalities Papers* 23, 3 (1995): 603. In Russia, in contrast, the Belarusian and Ukrainian minorities are already so linguistically Russified and the Russians so reluctant to study the languages of their neighbors that Russian will no doubt remain the sole language of communication.

53. See, for example, an appeal from the Slavonic Foundation in Kyrgyzstan to the Kyrgyzstani president in *Slavyanskie vesti* (Bishkek) 9 (May 1992): 2, and "Second World Congress," 19–20.

54. I. P. Blishchenko, A. K. Abashidze, and E. V. Martynenko, "Problemy gosudarstvennoy politiki rossiyskoy federatsii v otnoshenii k sootechestvennikam" (The problems of the state policy of the Russian Federation vis-à-vis the compatriots), *Gosudarstvo i pravo* (State and law) 2 (1994): 3–14.

55. *Inostranets,* 24 November 1993; Khronid Lyubarskiy, "Grazhdane i 'sootechestvenniki'" (Citizens and compatriots), *Novoe vremya* (New times), 5 (1993): 40–43.

56. Rogers Brubaker, "East European, Soviet, and Post-Soviet Nationalisms: A Framework for Analysis," *Research on Democracy and Society* 1 (1993): 353–378; Melvin, "The Russians."

57. Andreas Kappeler, *Russland als Vielvölkerreich* (Russia as multiethnic state) (Munich: Beck, 1992), 233–267.

58. Y. V. Arutyunyan, ed., *Russkie. Etnosotsiologicheskie ocherki* (Russians: Ethnosociological sketches) (Moscow: Nauka, 1992); Valery Tishkov, "What Is Rossia? Prospects for Nation-Building," *Security Dialogue* 26, 1 (1995): 41–54.

59. See, for instance, the contributions of William Boris Kory and Robert Lewis in Edward Allworth, ed., *Ethnic Russia in the USSR: The Dilemma of Dominance* (New York: Pergamon, 1980). For a general theory of ethnicity that emphasizes the importance of contrast, see, for example, Thomas Hylland Eriksen, *Ethnicity and Nationalism: Anthropological Perspectives* (London: Pluto Press, 1993), 18–35.

60. David D. Laitin, "Identity in Formation: The Russian-Speaking Nationality in the Post-Soviet Diaspora," *Archives européennes de sociologie* 36, 2 (1995): 281–316.

61. V. Uleev, "'Slavyanskaya diaspora' . . . " (Slavonic diaspora), *Res Publica* (Bishkek), 15 May 1993.

62. Pål Kolstø, ed., *Nation-Building and Ethnic Integration in Post-Soviet Societies: An Investigation of Latvia and Kazakstan* (Boulder, Colo.: Westview, 1999).

Chapter 6

1. Donald L. Horowitz, *Ethnic Groups in Conflict* (Berkeley: University of California Press, 1985), 36ff.

2. Adolfs Silde, "The Role of Russian-Latvians in the Sovietization of Latvia," *Journal of Baltic Studies* 18, 2 (1987): 191–208.

3. The Latvian minister for nationalities, Vladimir Steshenko, protested against this counterlegal practice to no avail. Steshenko himself is a (Russified) Ukrainian and served as spokesperson for the Russophone populace in the Latvian government. He had, however, no real power. From author's conversation with Steshenko, Riga, May 1992.

4. "Chelovek vybiraet natsional'nost', ili kak rabotaet novyy zakon?" (A person chooses his nationality; or, How is the new law functioning?), *Diena* (Riga), 23 July 1997.

5. O. D. Komarova, "Ethnically Mixed Marriages in the Soviet Union," *Geo-Journal Supplementary Issue* 1 (1980): 3.

6. Information provided by Frank Aarebrot of the University of Bergen, who led the Scandinavian Helsinki group's observer corps in Latvia during the referendum.

7. See, for example, the interview with popular front leader Andrejs Pantelejevs: Zalman Kats, "Andrejs Pantelejevs: 'Sotvorenie Latviyskogo gosudarstva est' usilie obeikh storon'" (Andrejs Pantelejevs: "The establishment of a Latvian state is an effort of both sides"), *Subbotniy den'*, 20 July 1991, 1.

8. Pål Kolstø, *Russians in the Former Soviet Republics* (Bloomington: Indiana University Press; London: C. Hurst, 1995), 118–120.

9. See, for example, Eric Rudenschiold, "Ethnic Dimensions in Contemporary Latvian Politics: Focusing Forces for Change," *Soviet Studies* 44, 4 (1992).

10. Helsinki Watch, *Violations by the Latvian Department of Citizenship and Immigration* (New York: Helsinki Watch, 1993).

11. Another reason for the result was that proportionally more seats were allocated to rural districts, where ethnic Latvians are concentrated.

12. Pål Kolstø and Boris Tsilevich, "Patterns of Nation Building and Political Integration in a Bifurcated Postcommunist State: Ethnic Aspects of Parliamentary Elections in Latvia," *East European Politics and Societies* 11, 2 (Spring 1997): 372–374. As pointed out in Chapter 5, the non-Latvians reached a near proportional representation in the Saeima only in 1998. There seem to have been several reasons for this breakthrough. The four main antinationalist parties—Concord, For Equal Rights, the Socialists, and the Russian Party—this time put aside their disagreements and formed a common list. Fourteen out of the sixteen members of its combined faction were non-Latvians. In addition, some Latvians who were elected from other parties were appointed ministers in the new government and were replaced in the national assembly by the next person on their party's ballot, who were nontitulars. I am indebted to Boris Tsilevich for this information.

13. Angelita Kamenska, *The State Language in Latvia: Achievements, Problems and Prospects* (Riga: Latvian Center for Human Rights and Ethnic Studies, 1995), 25–26.

14. Ina Druviete, ed., *The Language Situation in Latvia and Lithuania* (London: Macmillan, 1996), 25.

15. For instance, at Riga Polytechnic Hospital in December 1992 and Daugavpils College of Music in August 1995.

16. Anton Steen, *Between Past and Future: Elites, Democracy and the State in Post-Communist Countries. A Comparison of Estonia, Latvia and Lithuania* (Aldershot, England: Ashgate, 1997), 48 and 54.

17. During the 1993 election campaign, this goal was set out in the party platform of the MNIL and the Latvian Farmers' Union.

18. Aina Antane and Boris Tsilevich, "Nation-Building and Ethnic Integration in Latvia," in Pål Kolstø, ed., *Nation-Building and Ethnic Integration in Post-Soviet Societies: An Investigation of Latvia and Kazakstan* (Boulder, Colo.: Westview, 1999), 73.

19. *SM-segodnya,* 30 December 1993, as cited in ibid 72.

20. Antane and Tsilevich, "Nation-Building and Ethnic Integration in Latvia," 91.

21. Boris Tsilevich, "Majority-Minority Integration in Latvia: Prospects and Comparisons," updated version of paper presented at the seminar "Minorities and Majorities in Estonia: Problems of Integration at the Threshold of the EU," Flensburg, Germany, 22–25 May 1998, 5.

22. David D. Laitin, *Identity in Formation: The Russian-Speaking Populations in the Near Abroad* (Ithaca, N.Y.: Cornell University Press, 1998), 256.

23. Irina Malkova, Pål Kolstø, and Hans O. Melberg, "Attitudinal and Linguistic Integration in Kazakstan and Latvia," in Kolstø, *Nation-Building,* 247.

24. Author's interviews in Riga, May 1995.

25. Maris Ginblats in *Latvijas vestnesis,* 13 June 1996; quoted in Antane and Tsilevich, "Nation-Building," 129.

26. Magda Opalski, Boris Tsilevich, and Piotr Dutkiewicz, *Ethnic Conflict in the Baltic States: The Case of Latvia* (Kingston, Ontario: Kashtan Press, 1994), appendix. According to various laws, noncitizens are not entitled to work as land surveyors, private detectives, head pharmacists, or crew on Latvian vessels or airlines.

27. Author's interview with Maris Grinblats, leader of the Party for the Fatherland and Freedom, Riga, May 1995.

28. MINELRES (Minorities Electronic Resource), 12 March 1998, available at: http://www.riga.lv/minelres/archive.htm.

29. Jan Cleave, "End Note: Latvia to Hold Referendum on Citizenship Law Amendments," Radio Free Europe/Radio Liberty Newsline 2, 163, part 1 (25 August 1998) (available at: newsline@list.rferl.org).

30. Kolstø, *Nation-Building*.

31. B. Abdygaliev, "Yazykovaya politika v Kazakhstane: Sostoyanie i perspektivy" (The language policy in Kazakhstan: Current situation and future perspectives), *Sayasat* 5 (May 1996): 31–38.

32. A. T. Peruashev, *Politicheskie aspekty mezhetnicheskoy konkurentsii v Kazakhstane* (Political aspects of interethnic competition in Kazakhstan) (Almaty: Institut Razvitiya Kazakhstana, 1994), 4.

33. Igor Rotar, ed., "Natsional'noe stroitel'stvo v Kazakhstane" (Nation-building in Kazakhstan), *Nezavisimaya gazeta* (Independent gazette), 8 April 1994.

34. Shirin Akiner, *The Formation of Kazakh Identity: From Tribe to Nation-State* (London: Royal Institute of International Affairs, 1995), 75–77.

35. A. Kaydarov, "Esli ischeznet yazyk . . . " (If the language disappears . . .), *Kazakhstanskaya pravda* (Kazakhstan's truth), 15 October 1992; Saulesh Esenova, "The Outflow of Minorities from the Post-Soviet State: The Case of Kazakhstan," *Nationalities Papers* 24, 4 (1996): 692.

36. "N. Nazarbaev: Esli my razrushim nyneshnyuyu stabil'nuyu obshchestvenno-politicheskuyu obstanovku, to o dal'neyshey sud'be respubliki govorit' budet problematichno'" (N. Nazarbaev: If we destroy the present stable sociopolitical situation, then it will be problematic to talk about the future fate of the republic), *Kazakhstanskaya pravda*, 28 November 1992.

37. Martha Brill Olcott, "Kazakhstan: A Republic of Minorities," in Ian Bremmer and Ray Taras, eds., *Nations and Politics in the Soviet Successor States* (Cambridge: Cambridge University Press, 1993), 315; Robert J. Kaiser and Jeff Chinn, "Russian-Kazakh Relations in Kazakhstan," *Post-Soviet Geography* 36, 5 (1995): 257–273; Ian Bremmer and Cory Welt, "The Trouble with Democracy in Kazakhstan," *Central Asian Survey* 15, 2 (1996): 179–200.

38. "Nursultan Nazarbaev: 'Nashi orientiry—konsolidatsiya, obshchestvenniy progress i sotsial' noe partnerstvo'" (Nursultan Nazarbaev: "Our guiding lines are consolidation, social progress, and social partnership"), *Sovety Kazakhstana,* 13 May 1993; *Znamya truda*, 13 May 1993, 1–2.

39. See, for example, "Postanovlenie prezidiuma Verkhovnogo Soveta respubliki Kazakhstan o pereimenovanii i uporyadochenii transkribirovaniya na russkom yazyke naimenovaniy otdel'nykh administrativno-territorial'nykh edinits Respubliki Kazakhstan" (A resolution of the Presidium of the Supreme Soviet of the Republic of Kazakhstan on the renaming of certain administrative-territorial units of the Republic of Kazakhstan and on the regulation of their transcription into Russian), *Kazakhstanskaya pravda,* 17 September 1992; Andrey Mikhaylov, "Eshche raz o 'neobdumannykh pereimenovaniyakh' ulits i gorodov" (Once more on the "precipitate renaming" of streets and towns), *Karavan,* 10 February 1996, 4.

40. "Konstitutsiya respubliki Kazakhstan" (Constitution of the Republic of Kazakhstan), *Mysl'* (Almaty) 4, 1993, article 4. This provision was dropped in the 1995 constitution.

41. See, for example, an article by V. Moyseyev in *Rossiyskaya gazeta,* 27 August 1993.

42. "Konstitutsiya respubliki Kazakhstan" (Constitution of the Republic of Kazakhstan), *Mysl'* (Almaty) 10, (1995), 322.

43. Shirin Akiner even maintains that the 1995 constitution has in fact moved more in the direction of Kazakh ethnocracy than that of 1993. See Akiner, *The Formation,* 69.

44. See Pål Kolstø, "Anticipating Demographic Superiority. Kazakh Thinking on Integration and Nation-Building," *Europe-Asia Studies* 50, 1 (1998): 51–68.

45. N. D. Baytenova, "Mezhetnicheskaya integratsiya v Kazakhstane: sostoyanie i perspektivy" (Interethnic integration in Kazakhstan: current situation and prospects for the future), *Sayasat* 3 (1995): 27–33.

46. For further examples of this ethnically based line of thought among Kazakh scholars, see Kolstø, "Anticipating."

47. Olcott, "Kazakhstan," 320.

48. "Kontseptsiya yazykovoy politiki Respubliki Kazakhstan" (Concept for the language policy of the Republic of Kazakhstan), *Kazakhstanskaya pravda,* 6 November 1996.

49. Pål Kolstø and Irina Malkova, "Is Kazakhstan Being Kazakhified?" *Analysis of Current Events* 9, 11 (1997): 1, 3–4.

50. Malkova, Kolstø, and Melberg, "Attitudinal," 246.

51. Askhat Abdrakhmanuly, as quoted in "Po stranitsam kazakhskoy pressy" (Excerpts from the Kazakh-language press), *Kazakhstanskaya pravda,* 20 March 1996; *Yeremen Kazakhstan,* 3 September 1996, as quoted in O. Kudaybaev, "Bednyy moy yazyk . . . " (My poor language . . .), *Karavan,* 6 September 1996; *Karavan,* 1 November 1996.

52. Bhavna Dave, "A New Parliament Consolidates Presidential Authority," *Transition* 2, 6 (1996): 33–37.

53. See, for example, Z. K. Dzhunusova, *Respublika Kazakhstan: Prezident. Instituty Demokratii* (The Republic of Kazakhstan: The president, the institutions of democracy) (Almaty: Zheti Zhargy, 1996), 179.

54. Nurbulat Masanov, "Reitingovoe golosovanie v parlamente" (Voting patterns in the parliament), in Valeriy Tishkov, ed., *Uregulirovanie etnopoliticheskikh konfliktov v postsovetskikh gosudarstvakh* (The regulation of ethnic conflicts in the post-Soviet states) (Moscow: Institut Etnologii i Antropologii RAN, 1995), 26–28.

55. A. B. Galiev, E. Babakumarov, Z. Zhansugurova, and A. Peruashev, *Mezhnatsional'nye otnosheniya v Kazakhstane. Etnicheskiy aspekt kadrovoy politiki* (Interethnic relations in Kazakhstan: The ethnic aspect of the cadre policy) (Almaty: Institut Razvitiya Kazakhstana, 1994), 43.

56. According to Kazakhstan's immigration law, all ethnic Kazakhs are entitled to move to Kazakhstan, whereas strict quotas apply to all other ethnic groups. "Zakon Respubliki Kazakhstan ob immigratsii" (The Republic of Kazakhstan's law on immigration), *Sovety Kazakhstana,* 23 August 1992, 2.

57. *O demograficheskoy situatsii v 1995 godu* (On the demographic situation in 1995) (Almaty: Pravitel'stvo Respubliki Kazakhstan [Government of the Republic of Kazakhstan], 1996), 66; "Kazakstan: Forced Migration and Nation-Building—a Special Report by the Forced Migration Projects," available at: http://www.soor.org/fm2/html/kazakstan.html.

58. M. Tatimov, "Vliyanie demograficheskikh i migratsionnykh protsessov na vnutripoliticheskuyu stabil'nost respubliki Kazakhstan" (The influence of demographic and migratory processes on the domestic political stability of the Republic of Kazakhstan), *Sayasat* 5 (1995), 18–23.

59. *CIS Migration Report (1996)* (Geneva: International Organization for Migration, 1997), 56. In 1997, however, the out-migration picked up speed again and reached a total of almost 300,000. Radio Free Europe/Radio Liberty Newsline, 19 March 1998.

60. *Politicheskie partii i obshchestvennye dvizheniya sovremmenogo Kazakhstana. Spravochnik* (Political parties and social movements in contemporary Kazakhstan: A handbook) (Almaty: Ministerstvo Pechati i Massovoy Informatsii, 1994), vol. 1, 9.

61. Author's interview with Mikhail Golovkov, Almaty, September 1996.

62. "Doklad Nursultana Nazarbayeva na IV Sessii Assamblei Narodov Kazakhstana 6 yunya 1997, Akmola" (Nursultan Nazarbayev's report to the fourth session of the Assembly of the Peoples of Kazakhstan, 6 June 1997, in Akmola), *Mysl'* (Almaty) 7, 1997, 10; author's interview with the local leader of the Assembly of the Peoples of Kazakhstan, Semipalatinsk, September 1996.

63. Baytenova, "Mezhetnicheskaya integratsiya," 29.

64. R. S. Milne, *Politics in Ethnically Bipolar States* (Vancouver: University of British Columbia Press, 1981).

65. Ibid., 10. Of the three states studied by Milne, Guyana has in fact experienced more ethnic violence than the others. This may be because the Africans of Guyana have gained less acceptance for their status as "sons of the soil" than have the Fijians and Malayans.

66. Diane Mauzy, "Malaysia: Malay Political Hegemony and 'Coercive Consociationalism,'" in John McGarry and Brendan O'Leary, eds., *The Politics of Ethnic Conflict Regulation* (London: Routledge, 1997), 113.

67. Ralph R. Premdas, "Balance and Ethnic Conflict in Fiji," in McGarry and O'Leary, *Politics*, 251.

Chapter 7

1. Nicholas Dima, "Moldavians or Romanians?" in Ralph Clem, ed., *The Soviet West—Interplay Between Nationality and Social Organization* (New York: Praeger, 1978), 41.

2. In 1996 I attended the May Day celebration in Komrat, the capital of Gagauzia. A girls' choir sang Gagauz songs—each of which was, however, introduced by the master of ceremonies in Russian.

3. *Zakonodatel'nye akty Moldavskoy SSR o pridanii moldavskomu yazyku statusa gosudarstvennogo i vozvrate emu latinskoy grafiki* (Legal acts by the Moldovan SSR to

make Moldovan a state language and return to the use of the Latin alphabet) (Chişinău: Cartea Moldoveneasca, 1990).

4. Alla Skvortsova, "Russkie Moldovy: aspekty istorii i sovremennaya etnopoliticheskaya situatsiya" (Russians in Moldova: Aspects of history and the contemporary ethnopolitical situation), in *Russkie Moldovy: Istoriya, yazyk, kul'tura* (Russians in Moldova: History, language, culture) (Chişinău: Inkonkom, 1994), 41–44.

5. See Pål Kolstø, *Russians in the Former Soviet Republics* (Bloomington: Indiana University Press; London: C. Hurst, 1995), 150–151.

6. So overwhelming are the figures given that one immediately suspects fraud or manipulation. Yet a corresponding referendum on Ukrainian independence held on the same day yielded approximately the same results. See Pål Kolstø and Andrei Edemsky, with Natalya Kalashnikova, "The Dniester Conflict: Between Irredentism and Separatism," *Europe-Asia Studies* 45, 6 (1993): 985. Likewise, the referendum on Moldovan independence, arranged by the authorities in Chişinău three years later, produced similarly high figures.

7. Suzanne Crow, Alexander Rahr, and Roman Solchanyk, eds., "Weekly Review," *Radio Free Europe/Radio Liberty Research Report* 1, 27 (1992): 70.

8. Pål Kolstø and Andrei Malgin, "The Transnistrian Republic—a Case of Politicized Regionalism," *Nationalities Papers* 26, 1 (1998): 103–127.

9. See, for example, Vladimir Socor, "Creeping Putsch in Eastern Moldova," *Radio Free Europe/Radio Liberty Research Report* 1, 3 (1992): 8–13; Vladimir Socor, "Moldova's 'Dniester' Ulcer," *Radio Free Europe/Radio Liberty Research Report* 2, 1 (1993): 12–16.

10. *Trudovoy Tiraspol'*, 2–9 February 1994, 2; 23–30 March 1994, 1.

11. The Congress of Intellectuals was later renamed the Party of Democratic Forces.

12. A rather ironic point here is that "Bessarabia" was the name the Russian imperialists had in their day bestowed upon the area in question.

13. *Novye konstitutsii stran SNG i Baltii. Sbornik dokumentov* (New constitutions in the CIS and the Baltics: A collection of documents) (Moscow: Manuskript, 1994), 305.

14. Vladimir Pelin, "Fal'sifitsirovat' istoriyu—prestupno" (It is criminal to falsify history), *Dreptate* (Justice) (Chişinău), December 1995, 8.

15. Petre P. Moldovan [Vasile Stati], *Moldovenii in istorie* (Chişinău: Poligraf, 1994).

16. Igor Munteanu, "'Moldovanism' as a Political Weapon," *Transition* 2, 4 (1996): 47–49.

17. Charles King, "Moldovan Identity and the Politics of Pan-Romanianism," *Slavic Review* 53, 2 (1994): 363.

18. Dan Ionescu, "Back to Romanian?" *Transition* 1, 15 (1995): 54. During the student demonstrations, economic grievances were increasingly added to the slogans. Thus, the high rate of mobilization was sustained in part by the dire economic situation in the country, for which the Agrarian Party-dominated government was held responsible.

19. Author's interviews in Chişinău, May 1996.

20. Author's interview with Victor Grebenscicov, director of the Ministry of Nationalities, Chişinău, May 1992. Grebenscicov is a Russian.

21. Vladimir Socor, "Moldova," *Radio Free Europe/Radio Liberty Research Report* 3, 16 (1994): 17.

22. Author's interview with Victor Grebenscicov, May 1996. In the interval since our previous conversation, four years earlier, Grebenscicov's pronouncements had become even more authoritative as he had since been promoted to presidential adviser.

23. *Law on the Special Juridical Status on Gagauzia (Gagauz-Yeri)*, adopted 23 December 1994; Charles King, "Gagauz Yeri and the Dilemmas of Self-Determination," *Transition* 1, 19 (1995): 21–25.

24. Socor, "Creeping"; Dan Ionescu, "Media in the 'Dniester Moldovan Republic': A Communist-Era Memento," *Transition* 1, 19 (1995): 16–20.

25. Author's interview with opposition leader Andrey Safonov, Tiraspol, May 1996.

26. The text of the report is printed in *Ot etnopoliticheskogo konflikta k mezhnatsional'nomu soglasiyu v Moldove. Materialy nauchnogo-prakticheskogo seminara* (From ethnopolitical conflict to interethnic harmony in Moldova: Materials from a scholarly-practical seminar) (Chişinau: Moldovan State University, 1998), 56–74.

27. Presidential adviser Nicolae Chirtoace, cited in Jeff Chinn and Steven D. Roper, "Ethnic Mobilization and Reactive Nationalism: The Case of Moldova," *Nationalities Papers* 23, 2 (1995): 318.

28. Radio Free Europe/Radio Liberty Newsline, 22 August 1997 (available at: newsline@list.rferl.org).

29. Charles King, "Eurasian Letter: Moldova with a Russian Face," *Foreign Policy* 97 (Winter 1994–1995): 108.

30. See, for example, Anneli Ute Gabanyi, "Moldova Between Russia, Romania and the Ukraine," *Aussenpolitik* (Foreign policy) 1 (1993): 98–107.

31. Vladimir Socor, "Why Moldova Does Not Seek Reunification with Romania," *Radio Free Europe/Radio Liberty Research Report* 1, 5 (1992): 27–33.

32. King, "Moldovan Identity," 366.

33. Claus Neukirch, *Die Republik Moldau. Nations- und Staatsbildung in Osteuropa* (The republic of Moldova: Nation- and state-building in Eastern Europe) (Münster: Lit, 1996), 103–107.

34. And, says Neukirch, even if we stick to the West German-East German parallel, the contrast to Moldova is not fully as great as one might believe at first glance. The differences in identity between *Ossies* (former East Germans) and *Wessies* (West Germans) are still an important reality. The wall may have fallen long ago, but many Germans still go about with a "wall in the mind" (Neukirch, *Die Republik Moldau,* 134).

35. Ibid., 108–110.

36. Ernest Gellner, *Nations and Nationalism* (Oxford: Blackwell, 1990); Eric J. Hobsbawm, *Nations and Nationalism Since 1780* (Cambridge: Cambridge University Press, 1990); Benedict Anderson, *Imagined Communities* (London: Verso, 1994).

37. Perhaps the best representative of this line of thought is Anthony Smith. See Anthony D. Smith, *The Ethnic Origins of Nations* (Oxford: Blackwell, 1986), and Anthony D. Smith, *National Identity* (Harmondsworth, England: Penguin, 1991).

Chapter 8

1. Jan Zaprudnik, "Belorussia and the Belorussians," in Zev Katz, Rosemarie Rogers, and Frederic Harned, eds., *Handbook of Major Soviet Nationalities* (New York: Free Press, 1975), 59.

2. Ralph Clem, "Belorussians," in Graham Smith, ed., *The Nationalities Question in the Soviet Union* (London: Longman, 1992), 115.

3. In Russian, "Ni cherta ne ponyatno!" Quoted in Jan Zaprudnik, *Belarus: At a Crossroads in History* (Boulder, Colo.: Westview, 1993), 106.

4. Jan Zaprudnik and Michael Urban, "Belarus: From Statehood to Empire?" in Ian Bremmer and Ray Taras, eds., *New States, New Politics: Building the Post-Soviet Nations* (Cambridge: Cambridge University Press, 1997), 285; Dmitriy Furman and Oleg Bukhovets, "Belorussian Self-Awareness and Belorussian Politics," *Russian Politics and Law* 34, 6 (1996): 11–12.

5. Barbara Törnquist Plewa, *Språk och identitet in Vitryssland* (Language and identity in Belarus) (Lund Sweden: Lunds Universitet, 1997), 65.

6. Mikhail Kukabaka, who spent seventeen years in a gulag, was apparently the sole Soviet prisoner of conscience from Belarus.

7. Zaprudnik, and Urban, "Belarus," 289.

8. Mikhail Guboglo, *Perelomnye gody,* vol. 2: *Yazykovaya reforma—1989. Dokumenty i materialy* (Years of upheaval, vol. 2: The language reform of 1989: Documents and material) (Moscow: Institut Etnologii i Antropologii, 1994), 91–92.

9. Ibid., 200–213.

10. Törnquist Plewa, *Språk och identitet,* 75.

11. Ales' Knyazyuk, "Velikiy nemoy" (The great, dumb people), *Dobryy vecher Minsk,* 24 June 1992.

12. Ustina Markus, "Belarus Elects Its First President," *Radio Free Europe/Radio Liberty Research Report* 3, 30 (29 June 1994): 5.

13. Ibid., 6.

14. Quoted from George Sanford, "Belarus on the Road to Nationhood," *Survival* 38, 1 (1996): 137.

15. *Narodnaya hazieta,* 1 February 1995, quoted here from Furman and Bukhovets, "Belorussian Self-Awareness," 5.

16. Törnquist Plewa, *Språk och identitet,* 78.

17. European Institute for the Media, *Monitoring the Media Coverage of the Belarussian Referendum in November 1996: Final Report, February 1997* (Düsseldorf: European Institute for the Media, 1997), 11.

18. I am not alone in using religious imagery in describing the politics of the Belarusian president; Lukashenka himself would seem to do so as well. When the Belarusian foreign minister visited Oslo in spring 1997, I was told by one member of the Belarusian delegation that Lukashenka considers himself a new messiah.

19. Ustina Markus, "Toothless Treaty with Russia Sparks Controversy," *Transition* 2, 9 (1996): 47.

20. *Monitoring the Media,* 13.

21. Ibid.

22. *Vitebskiy kur'er,* 13 February 1995, quoted in Furman and Bukhovets, "Belorussian Self-Awareness," 6.

23. Sanford, "Belarus on the Road," 132.

24. Furman and Bukhovets, "Belorussian Self-Awareness," 29.

25. Magdalene Hoff and Heinz Timmermann, "Belarus in der Krise. Die 'Partei der Macht' drängt auf Rückwendung nach Russland" (Belarus in crisis: The "party of power" pushes for return to Russia), *Osteuropa* 44, 8, (1994): 738.

26. Ustina Markus, "Belarus: You Can't Go Home Again," *Current History* 93 (October 1994): 338. The Shushkevich faction was also opposed to new elections—one important reason why they parted ways with the popular front.

27. Ibid.

28. "Doslovno: Russkie i belorusy—eto dva pal'tsa odnoy ruki, zayavil Stanislav Shushkevich v interv'yu 'Tokio simbun'" (Verbatim: Russians and Belarusians are two fingers on the same hand, declared Stanislav Shushkevich in an interview with "Tokyo Simbun"), *Respublika* (Minsk), 25 November 1993.

29. Hoff and Timmermann, "Belarus in der Krise," 736.

30. Henadz' Saganovich, "Russkiy vopros s tochki zreniya belorusa" (The Russian question, as seen by a Belarusian), *Narodnaya hazieta,* 30 April 1993, 7.

31. In Zyanon Paznyak, "O russkom imperializme i ego opasnosti" (On Russian imperialism and its danger), *Narodnaya hazieta,* 15–17 January 1994, 2.

32. The Western historian Jan Zaprudnik has pointed out that when Lithuania proclaimed its independence in 1990, it was the Belarusian Communists and not the Belarusian Popular Front who made territorial claims on parts of Lithuania. The intention was to foil the schemes of the Lithuanian nationalists like Vytautas Landsbergis, who pressed for secession from the USSR. At that time the popular front denounced such Belarusian territorial claims as political blackmail. See Zaprudnik, *Belarus,* 220. Seen in this light, Zyanon Paznyak's new message of 1994 would indicate a pronounced radicalization of the movement since independence.

33. Igor' Osinskiy, "Pisanie ot lukavogo" (The Scripture according to the evil one), *Sovetskaya Belorussia,* 18 January 1994, 1–2; Mikhail Shimanskiy, "Zenon Poznyak ob 'opasnosti russkogo imperializma'" (Zyanon Paznyak on the "danger of Russian imperialism"), *Izvestiya,* 21 January 1994; Yuriy Rostikov, "Antirusskiy aktsent Zenona Poznyaka" (Zyanon Paznyak's anti-Russian accent), *Rossiyskaya gazeta,* 16 June 1994.

34. Furman and Bukhovets, "Belorussian Self-Awareness," 13.

35. David R. Marples, *Belarus: From Soviet Rule to Nuclear Catastrophe* (New York: St. Martin, 1996).

36. Törnquist Plewa, *Språk och identitet,* 46–71.

37. See, for example, Karl Deutsch, "Nation-Building and National Development: Some Issues for Political Research," in Karl Deutsch and William Foltz, eds., *Nationbuilding* (New York: Atherton, 1963); Ernest Gellner, *Nations and Nationalism* (Oxford: Blackwell, 1990).

38. Törnquist Plewa, *Språk och identitet,* 70.

Chapter 9

1. David D. Laitin, "The National Uprisings in the Soviet Union," *World Politics* 44, 1 (1991): 139–177.

2. John Armstrong. "The Ethnic Scene in the Soviet Union: The View of the Dictatorship," in Rachel Denber, ed., *The Soviet Nationality Reader: The Disintegration in Context* (Boulder, Colo.: Westview, 1992), 239.

3. Andrew Wilson, *Ukrainian Nationalism in the 1990s* (Cambridge: Cambridge University Press, 1997), 198.

4. A somewhat broader definition includes Volhynia and Rivne as well. These formerly belonged to Poland but have never been part of the Habsburg empire.

5. Ivan L. Rudnytsky, "The Ukrainians in Galicia Under Austrian Rule," in Andrei S. Markovits and Frank E. Sysyn, eds., *Nationbuilding and the Politics of Nationalism: Essays on Austrian Galicia* (Cambridge: Harvard Ukrainian Research Institute, 1982), 46ff; Orest Subtelny, *Ukraine: A History*, 2d ed. (Toronto: University of Toronto Press, 1993).

6. Roman Szporluk, "The Strange Politics of Lviv: An Essay in Search of an Explanation," in Zvi Gitelman, ed., *The Politics of Nationality and the Erosion of the USSR* (London: Macmillan, 1992), 220ff.

7. Author's interview in the Ukrainian Ministry of Nationalities and Migration, Kiev, September 1995.

8. Author's interviews in Uzhgorod, May 1996.

9. Apropos of Chapter 8, let me add that they see themselves as Romanians, definitely not Moldovans.

10. Roman Solchanyk, "The Politics of Statebuilding: Centre-Periphery Relations in Post-Soviet Ukraine," *Europe-Asia Studies* 46, 1 (1994): 59–60. Historical Novorossia extended all the way to the banks of the Dniester and thus included the territory of what is today the self-proclaimed Dniester Republic in Moldova. Some Dniester activists see the possibility of attaching their republic to a Novorossia region, should such be established. Author's interviews in Tiraspol, September 1992.

11. Author's interview with leader of the Republican Movement of Crimea and later Crimean president Yuriy Meshkov, September 1992.

12. Roman Solchanyk, "The Crimean Imbroglio: Kiev and Simperopol," *Radio Free Europe/Radio Liberty Research Report* 1, 33 (1992): 14; "Konstitutsiya respubliki Krym" (Constitution of the Republic of Crimea), *Krymskie izvestiya*, 8 May 1992, 1.

13. *Pravda Ukrainy*, 19 May 1992.

14. Pål Kolstø, *Russians in the Former Soviet Republics* (Bloomington: Indiana University Press; London: C. Hurst, 1995), 190–199.

15. Tor Bukkvoll, "A Fall from Grace for Crimean Separatists," *Transition* 1, 21 (1995): 46–49.

16. Radio Free Europe/Radio Liberty Newsline, 16 November 1997 (available at: newsline@list.rferl.org).

17. In addition to the conflict between Kiev and the pro-Russian movements of Crimea, there is on the peninsula another conflict of nationalism, one I cannot describe in detail here: the question of the Crimean Tatars. The Tatars of Crimea had been forcibly deported to Central Asia during World War II. With perestroika they gradually began to return home; in the late 1990s they constituted about one-tenth of the total population. The Tatars consider themselves the indigenous population of the peninsula, which, they demand, should be recognized as *their* nation-state. This claim is accepted neither by the Ukrainian authorities in Kiev

nor by the peninsula's majority population. In 1994 the Tatars were nevertheless granted a special quota (of fourteen seats) in the Crimean Supreme Soviet in excess of their share of the total population. See Andrew Wilson, "Politics in and Around Crimea: A Difficult Homecoming," in Edward A. Allworth, ed., *The Tatars of the Crimea: Return to the Homeland* (Durham, N.C.: Duke University Press, 1998), 299–302. The quota system was abolished in 1998, as it satisfied no one.

18. Michael Voslensky, *Nomenklatura: The Soviet Ruling Class* (Garden City, N.Y.: Doubleday, 1984).

19. David D. Laitin, *Identity in Formation: The Russian-Speaking Populations in the Near Abroad* (Ithaca, N.Y.: Cornell University Press, 1998), 144–150.

20. Szporluk, "The Strange Politics."

21. "Deklaratsiya o gosudarstvennom suverenitete Ukrainy" (Declaration on the state sovereignty of Ukraine), *Argumenty i fakty* 29 (1990).

22. Roman Solchanyk, "The Referendum in Ukraine: Preliminary Results," *Report on the USSR* 3, 13 (1991): 5–6.

23. Wilson, *Ukrainian Nationalism*, 129.

24. Vadim Skuratovskiy, "Russkie na Ukraine—popytka prognoza" (Russians in Ukraine—a tentative prognosis), *Nezavisimaya gazeta* (Independent gazette), 6 March 1992, 5.

25. See, for example, Sergey Grigor'yev, "Ukrainskiy vopros v Rossiyskom kontekste," *Put'* 8 (1991): 14–15, as well as a whole series of other articles in the same newspaper (January 1991, 10; March 1991, 2; no. 4, 1992: 4–5). *Put'* was the party organ of the Russian Christian Democratic Movement. The amputation metaphor was used by, among others, the author Boris Mozhayev, "Rezat' po zhivomu? Otkrytoe pis'mo Ivanu Drachu" (Why cut into living flesh? An open letter to Ivan Drach), *Literaturnaya gazeta* (Literary gazette), 4 March 1992, 13. (Ivan Drach was a leading liberal Ukrainian nationalist at the time.) See also Zbigniew Brzezinski, "The Premature Partnership," *Foreign Affairs* 73, 2 (1994): 67–82.

26. *Report on the USSR* 3, 36 (6 September 1991): 81.

27. Roman Solchanyk, "Ukraine, the Kremlin, and the Russian White House," *Report on the USSR* 3, 10 (1991): 15; Stanislav Kondrashev, "Utki s yadernymi boegolovkami" (Canards with nuclear warheads), *Izvestiya*, 24 October 1994.

28. One advocate of this approach was Yeltsin's adviser on nationalities issues, Galina Starovoytova. Author's interview with Starovoytova in Moscow, November 1991. Aleksandr Solzhenitsyn went one step further and suggested that the vote should be tallied by *rayony* (the administrative unit below the county).

29. Bohdan Nahaylo, "The Birth of an Independent Ukraine," *Report on the USSR* 3 (13 December 1991).

30. Kolstø, *Russians*, 178–179.

31. Sven Holdar, "Torn Between East and West: The Regional Factor in Ukrainian Politics," *Post-Soviet Geography* 36, 2 (1995). In the three Galician counties, Chornovil garnered between 58 percent and 76 percent of the vote. In all other counties except for Chernivtsi, Kravchuk got over 50 percent. Kravchuk comes from Rivne, which is a westerly county but lies to the east of Galicia.

32. *Ukraina segodnya* 6 (1994): 63–64. See Tor Bukkvoll, *Ukraine and European Security* (London: Royal Institute of International Affairs, 1997), 26.

33. *Nezavisimaya gazeta,* 1 March 1994.

34. "'Chervona ruta'—emblema pechali: natsional'no-gosudarstvennaya ideya terpit krushenie na Ukraine" ("The red rue"—an emblem of sorrow: The idea of the nation-state has suffered defeat in Ukraine), *Moskovskie novosti* (Moscow news), 25 June 1993, 9–10.

35. Bukkvoll, *Ukraine,* gives a more detailed presentation of these conflicts.

36. See, for example, John J. Mearsheimer, "The Case for a Ukrainian Nuclear Deterrent," *Foreign Affairs* 72 (Summer 1993): 50–66; and Steven E. Miller, "The Case Against a Ukrainian Nuclear Deterrent," *Foreign Affairs* 72 (Summer 1993): 67–80. Mearsheimer held that there would be greater chances of avoiding war between Russia and Ukraine if the latter were allowed to keep its nuclear arms as weapons of deterrence, whereas Miller feared more what could happen if both states retained their nuclear status.

37. Eugene B. Rumer, "Eurasia Letter: Will Ukraine Return to Russia?" *Foreign Policy* 96 (Fall 1994): 135–136.

38. See, for example, Galina Remizovskaya, "Kak ya ustraivala rebenka v russkuyu shkolu," *Kievskie vedomosti,* 12 September 1992. As I pointed out in Chapter 5, many Russophones in Ukraine as well as in other non-Russian successor states will no doubt conclude that the future careers of their children will depend on proficiency in the state language and therefore send them to a Ukrainian-language school quite voluntarily.

39. Author's interviews in the Ukrainian Ministry of Education, Kiev, September 1994; A. Pogribnyy, "V iskazhennom svete" (In a distorted light), *Nezavisimost'* (Independence), 11 January 1993, 3.

40. "Ukraine Today," Radio Ukraina, 14 July 1992, *Radio Free Europe/Radio Liberty Media News and Features Digest.*

41. Vyacheslav Lashkul, "Chem prognevil ukraintsev Vladimir Galaktionovich Korolenko?" (In what way has Vladimir Galaktionovich Korolenko angered the Ukrainians?), *Emigratsiya* 9, March 1993.

42. Even though Gogol was linguistically Russified, his contemporaries considered him just as much of a Ukrainian. In 1845, when he visited Karlsbad/Karlovy Vary in today's Czech Republic, the local press referred to him as "Mr. Nicolas de Gogol, Ukrainien, établi à Moscou" (Mr. Nicolas Gogol, Ukrainian, resident of Moscow). Geir Kjetsaa, *Nikolaj Gogol. Den gåtefulle dikteren* (Nikolay Gogol: The enigmatic writer) (Oslo: Gyldendal, 1990), 300.

43. Christyna Lapychak, "Nation-Building in Ukraine: The Quest for a Common Destiny," *Transition* 2, 18 (6 September 1996): 7.

44. Incidentally, he had to ignore the fact that in Russian the word *glava* (a variant of *golova,* or "head") is also a common word for "leader."

45. Also here I should hasten to add that in Russian it is at least equally common to say that one "goes to work."

46. Dmytro Dontsov, *Rosiya chi Yevropa* (Russian or Europe) (1929; reprint, Kiev: Spilka Ukrainska Molod', 1992).

47. Author's interview with Roman Koval', Kiev, September 1994.

48. In the 1992 Dniester war, UNA soldiers fought side by side with local Russians against Moldovan forces. In the war in Abkhazia that same year, however, they fought on the Georgian side, *against* the Abkhazians and Russians.

49. Author's interview with Korchynskyy, Kiev, September 1994.

50. See, for example, Taras Kuzio, "Radical Nationalist Parties and Movements in Contemporary Ukraine Before and After Independence: The Right and Its Politics, 1989–1994," *Nationalities Papers* 25, 2 (1997): 211–242.

51. *Pravda*, 16 July 1991. Quoted from Roman Solchanyk, "Ukraine, the (Former) Center, Russia and 'Russia,'" *Studies in Comparative Communism* 25, 1 (1992): 38.

52. Leonid Kravchuk as quoted in Andrew Wilson, *Ukrainian Nationalism in the 1990s* (Cambridge: Cambridge University Press, 1997), 111. Wilson is citing Leonid Kravchuk and Serhii Kychyhin, *Leonid Kravchuk: ostanni dni imperii . . . pershi roky nadii* (Leonid Kravchuk: The last years of the empire . . . the first years of hope) (Kiev: Dovira, 1994), 120.

53. Ibid., 112. Here Wilson is citing *Holos Ukrainy* (The voice of Ukraine), 7 December 1991.

54. Ibid. (again quoting from Kravchuk and Kychyhin, *Leonid Kravchuk*).

55. David R. Marples, "Ukraine After the Presidential Election," *Radio Free Europe/Radio Liberty Research Report* 3, 31 (1994): 7–10; Adrian Karatnycky, "Ukraine at the Crossroads," *Journal of Democracy* 6, 1 (1995): 117–130.

56. Sven Holdar, "Torn Between East and West: The Regional Factor in Ukrainian Politics," *Post-Soviet Geography* 36, 2 (1995): 128–129.

57. "Leonid Kuchma prinyal prisyagu na vernost' narodu Ukrainy i pristupil k ispolneniyu svoikh obyazannostey" (Leonid Kuchma pledged allegiance to the people of Ukraine and began to carry out his duties), *Rabochaya gazeta Ukrainy* (Workers' paper of Ukraine), 21 July 1994, 1.

58. Mykhaylo Kosiv, "Bez movy, nemae narodu, bez narodu, nemae derzhavy" (No language—no people: No people—no state), *Holos Ukrainy*, 16 September 1994: 4–5.

59. Yevhen Kamynskyy, "Natsional'na polityka radyan'skoy derzhavy. Deukrainizatsya i rusifikatsya" (The nationality policy of the Soviet Union: De-Ukrainization and Russification), in *Ukrainian Experience in Human Minorities Rights/Dosvid Ukrainy v haluzi prav natsional'nykh menshin* (Kiev: Friedrich Ebert Stiftung, 1994), 21.

60. Those who would maintain that the states of Latin America are not nation-states but artificial products with no inner cohesion or identity should read Benedict Anderson, *Imagined Communities* (London: Verso, 1994). They should also try explaining how a sports event could unleash a war—the Soccer War—between Honduras and El Salvador in 1969.

61. Taras Marusyk, "Ivan Kuras: Prioritety gumanitarnoy politiki" (Ivan Kuras: The priorities of the politics of culture and education), *Zerkalo nedeli* (The mirror of the week), 10 August 1996, 14.

62. Russian-medium schools tend to be located in the major towns and cities and are generally larger than the Ukrainian-medium ones. If we look at total enrollment instead of number of schools, we find a somewhat lower figure for Ukrainian.

63. Marusyk, "Ivan Kuras."

64. Wilson, *Ukrainian Nationalism*, 198.

65. Author's conversations with Russophone Ukrainian members of the Donbass Intermovement Donetsk, September 1994.

66. Ian Bremmer, "The Politics of Ethnicity: Russians in the New Ukraine," *Europe-Asia Studies* 46, 2 (1994): 276–277.

67. Dominique Arel, "Language and Group Boundaries in the Two Ukraines," paper presented at the Research Planning Group on National Minorities, "Nationalizing State and External National Homelands in the New Europe," Los Angeles, 28–29 January 1994.

68. Stephen Shulman, "Competing Versus Complementary Identities: Ukrainian-Russian Relations and the Loyalties of Russians in Ukraine," *Nationalities Papers* 26, 4 (1998): 615–632.

69. V. Gordienko in *Rabochaya gazeta* (Kiev), 13 January 1993.

70. The only exceptions are Vitaliy Masol and Yevhen Marchuk, both from central Ukraine.

71. Taras Kuzio, "Ukraine: A Summer of Discontent," *Analysis of Current Events* 9, 9 (1997): 6, 9; Margarita Balmaceda, "Energy and the Rise and Fall of Pavlo Lazarenko," *Analysis of Current Events* 9, 9 (1997): 7–8. In political terms, Donetsk is definitely located to the left of Dnipropetrovsk. In 1994 Donetsk elected twenty-two Communists to the Ukrainian national assembly, whereas there was only one from Dnipropetrovsk.

72. Dominique Arel, "Ukraine: Renewed Paralysis at the Centre, and New Trouble in the Crimea?" *Analysis of Current Events* 10 (May 1998): 1, 3–4.

73. *Partiya kommunistov vozrozhdaetsya. Dokumenty i materialy* (The party of Communists is being reborn: Documents and materials) (N.p.: n.p., 1993), 69.

74. Author's interview with Dmitriy Kornilov, leader the Donbass Intermovement, Donetsk, September 1994.

75. Dominique Arel and Valeri Khmelko, "The Russian Factor and Territorial Polarization in Ukraine," in *Peoples, Nations, Identities: The Russian-Ukrainian Encounter*, special issue of *Harriman Review*, Spring 1996, 89.

76. Stephen R. Burant, "Foreign Policy and National Identity: A Comparison of Ukraine and Belarus," *Europe-Asia Studies* 47, 7 (1995): 1133.

77. *Economist*, 16 July 1994, 24–25; "Pochemu vybrali ikh? Ukrainskiy i belorusskiy prezidenty glazami rossiyskikh ekspertov" (Why were they elected? The Ukrainian and Belarusian president as viewed by Russian experts), *Literaturnaya gazeta*, 20 July 1994, 1–2.

78. During a visit to Germany in November 1995, Lukashenka spoke of Adolf Hitler in glowing terms. See, for instance, "Nash sosed fyurer. Vystuplenie prezidenta Belorussii" (Our neighbor the führer: The Belarusian president's speech), *Kommersant*, 5 December 1995, 17–19.

Chapter 10

1. Hélène Carrère d'Encausse, *The Great Challenge: Nationalities and the Bolshevik State, 1917–1930* (London: Holmes and Meier, 1992), 147–148, 152.

2. Robert Conquest, *Soviet Nationalities Policy in Practice* (London: Bodley Head, 1967), 55.

3. Paul Goble, "Three Faces of Nationalism in the Former Soviet Union," in Charles A. Kupchan, ed., *Nationalism and Nationalities in the New Europe* (Ithaca, N.Y.: Cornell University Press, 1995), 125; Vera Tolz, "Conflicting 'Homeland

Myths' and Nation-State Building in Postcommunist Russia," *Slavic Review* 57, 2 (1998): 267–294.

4. Rasma Karklins, *Ethnopolitics and Transition to Democracy: The Collapse of the USSR and Latvia.* (Baltimore, Md.: Johns Hopkins University Press, 1994), 48.

5. *Pervyy s"ezd narodnykh deputatov SSSR. Stenograficheskiy otchet 1989* (First Congress of People's Deputies of the USSR: Stenographical report 1989), 5 vols. (Moscow: Izdanie Verkhovnogo Soveta SSSR, 1990), vol. 2, 458.

6. George W. Breslauer and Catherine Dale, "Boris Yel'tsin and the Invention of a Russian Nation-State," *Post-Soviet Affairs* 13, 4 (1997): 303–332.

7. John B. Dunlop, *The Rise of Russia and the Fall of the Soviet Empire* (Princeton, N.J.: Princeton University Press, 1993), 269–270.

8. "Rossiya vyydet iz SSSR i chto dal'she?" (Russia secedes from the USSR and then what?), *Moskovskie vedomosti* (Moscow news), 20 October 1991, 6.

9. Interview with First Vice Foreign Minister Fedor Shelov-Kovedyayev in Aleksandr Sabov, "Rossiya i blizhnee zarubezh'e" (Russia and the near abroad), *Literaturnaya gazeta* (Literary gazette) 18, 29 April l992, 11.

10. Paul Kennedy, *The Rise and Fall of the Great Powers* (London: Fontana, 1988), 664.

11. Georgiy Shakhnazarov, referred to in Dunlop, *The Rise of Russia,* 272.

12. Ibid., 270–273.

13. Andranik Migranyan, "Mozhet li vyzhit' yel'tsinskaya Rossiya?" (Can Yeltsin's Russia survive?), *Moskovskie novosti* (Moscow news) 40, 6 October 1991, 9; Vladimir Ilyushenko, "Perezhivet li Rossiya krushenie imperii?" (Will Russia survive the collapse of the empire?), *Literaturnaya gazeta* 8, 19 February 1992, 11.

14. "Imperiya rukhnula. Kto obespechit stabil'nost'?" (The empire has collapsed: Who can provide stability?), *Demokraticheskaya Rossiya* (Democratic Russia) 31 (1991): 8.

15. Murat Sargishiev, "Neuzheli posleputchevskaya Rossiya est' Rossiya imperskaya?" (Is Russia after the coup really nothing but the imperial Russia?), *Nezavisimaya gazeta* (Independent gazette), 31 October 1991.

16. For instance, Konstantin Zatulin, former head of the Duma's Committee on Relations with CIS states. See Lina Tarkhova, "'Nepravda nam v ubytok'" ("Falsehood will damage us"), *Delovoy mir* (Business world), 15 June 1996.

17. Andrey Nazarov, "Gosudarstvo russkikh ili rossiyan?" (The state of the *russkie* or of the *rossiyane?*), *Literaturnaya gazeta* 31 (1992).

18. Aleksandr Tsipko, "Imperiya v ruinakh. Kto pod oblomkami?" (The empire is in ruins: Who lies under the debris?), *Literaturnaya gazeta* 44, 6 November 1991, 1, 3.

19. Valery Tishkov, *Ethnicity, Nationalism and Conflict in and After the Soviet Union: The Mind Aflame* (London: Sage, 1997), 252.

20. Tolz, "Conflicting 'Homeland Myths,'" 290.

21. *Open Media Research Institute (OMRI) Daily Digest,* 16, 17, and 21 March 1996.

22. Author's interview with Volodin, Moscow, October 1991. John Dunlop has characterized Volodin as "an ideologue of incipient Russian fascism." Dunlop, *The Rise of Russia,* 279.

23. Eduard Volodin, "Sud'ba russkoy natsii—sud'ba Rossii" (The fate of the Russian nation is the fate of Russia), *Molodaya gvardiya* (Young guard) 4 (1995): 10.

24. Ibid., 16. Emphasis in original.

25. Nikolay Lysenko, "Absolyutnaya ideya nashego budushchego" (The absolute idea of our future), *Molodaya gvardiya* (Young guard) 9 (1994): 38–39.

26. Ibid., 41.

27. Ibid., 39.

28. For an analysis of Russian imperialists and their relationship to European right-wing radicalism, see Walter Laqueur, *Black Hundred; The Rise of the Extreme Right in Russia* (New York: HarperCollins, 1993), 119–182.

29. Vladimir Zhirinovskiy, *Posledniy brosok na yug* (The last dash to the south) (Moscow: N.p., 1995).

30. Ibid., 50.

31. Kseniya Myalo, "Izgnannaya natsiya. Russkie kak inozemtsy" (The exiled nation: Russians as aliens), *Vek XX i mir* (Twentieth century and peace), 9–10 (1994); *Novoe vremya* 35 (1992): 9–12.

32. Kseniya Myalo, "Konets stoletiya: Russkiy vyzov" (The end of the century: The Russian challenge), *Nezavisimaya gazeta,* 12 April 1994.

33. Aleksandr Solzhenitsyn, *East and West,* trans. Alexis Klimoff (New York: Harper & Row, 1980), 101–108.

34. Alexander Solzhenitsyn, *Rebuilding Russia: Reflections and Tentative Proposals,* trans. Alexis Klimoff (New York: Farrar, Strauss and Giroux, 1991).

35. I. Voronina, "Obezdolennye" (The dispossessed), *Literaturnaya Rossiya,* 18 January 1991, 2–3.

36. V. I. Kozlov, "Glavnyy natsional'nyy vopros v Rossii vchera i segodnya" (The main national question in Russia yesterday and today), *Etnopoliticheskiy vestnik Rossii* (Ethnopolitical bulletin of Russia) 2 (1992): 102.

37. This is probably one reason why a name like Nikolay Berdyayev has made scant impact on the new Russian cultural debate.

38. Among them the linguist Nikolay Trubetskoy, the geographer Pyotr Savitskiy, the historian Georgiy Vernadskiy, the theologian Georgiy Florovskiy, and the literary historian Dmitriy Svyatopolk-Mirsky.

39. Lidiya Novikova and Irina Sizemskaya, "Dva lika evraziystva" (The two faces of Eurasianism), *Svobodnaya mysl'* (Free thought) 7 (1992); *Iskhod k vostoku. Predchuvstviya i sversheniya. Utverdzhenie evraziytsev* (Exit toward the east: Premonitions and achievements—a statement of the Eurasians) (Sofia: Russkoe Izdatel'stvo, 1921).

40. Author's interviews with Aleksandr Prokhanov, editor of the opposition newspaper *Den'* (The day—later renamed *Zavtra,* meaning "tomorrow"); Valeriy Skurlatov, a veteran Russian right-wing nationalist; and others, Moscow 1991.

41. Assen Ignatow, *Der "Eurasismus" und die Suche nach einer neuen russischen Kulturidentität. Die Neubelebung des "Evrazijstvo"-Mythos* (Eurasianism and the search for a new Russian cultural identity: The revival of the "Evraziystvo" myth) (Cologne: Bundesinstitut für Ostwissenschaftliche und Internationale Studien, 1992); Andrey Kolesnikov, "Zabludivshayasya Evraziya," (Eurasia gone astray), *Rossiyskie vesti* (Russian News), 22 January 1993; Laqueur, *Black Hundred,* 146–147 and 174–176.

42. Nikolay S. Trubetskoy, "Glubokie razdum'ya o sud'bakh Rossii" (Deep thoughts on the fate of Russia), *Delovoy mir*, 25 April–1 May 1994.

43. Gennadiy Zyuganov, *Rossiya i sovremennyy mir* (Russia and the contemporary world) (Moscow: Obozrevatel', 1995), 14f.

44. To underpin this, Zyuganov cites not only other Eurasians but also the apostle of Pan-Slavism, Nikolay Danilevskiy, and the U.S. political scientist Samuel Huntington.

45. Zyuganov, *Rossiya*, 20.

46. Ramazan Abdulatipov, "Smutnye vremena proidut" (Troubled times ahead), *Trud* (Labor), 27 February 1993; Ramazan Abdulatipov, "Silën tot, kto uvazhaet slabogo" (The strong one is the one who shows respect for the weak), *Rossiyskaya gazeta*, 15 September 1993.

47. Ramazan Abdulatipov, "O natsional'nom soglasii i segodnyashney deystvitel'nosti" (On national harmony and today's realities), *Zhizn' natsional'nostey* (The life of the nationalities), 1 (January 1993) 6–9; Ramazan Abdulatipov, "Vremya sobirat' Rossiyu" (The time has come to gather in Russia), *Rossiyskaya gazeta*, 25 June 1993.

48. Ramazan Abdulatipov, "Otvet kritikam Rossii, ili o natsional'noy gordosti rossiyan" (A reply to Russia's critics, or: on the national pride of the *rossiyane*), *Nezavisimaya gazeta*, 22 March 1994; Ramazan Abdulatipov, "National'naya ideya i natsionalizm" (The national idea and nationalism), *Nezavisimaya gazeta*, 28 April 1995.

49. After the breakup of the Soviet Union, all branches of the Soviet Academy of Sciences on Russian territory were reconstituted as the Russian Academy of Sciences (RAS, or RAN in Russian).

50. Tishkov, *Ethnicity*, 64.

51. Ibid., xi–xv and 1–82.

52. Marina Shakina, "Natsiya—to zhe plemya, no tol'ko s armiey" (A nation is a tribe that possesses an army), *Novoe vremya* 35 (1992): 9–12. These words were probably those of Massimo d'Azeglio. See Eric J. Hobsbawm, *Nations and Nationalism Since 1780* (Cambridge: Cambridge University Press, 1990), 44.

53. Valery Tishkov, "What Is Russia? Prospects for Nation-Building," *Security Dialogue* 26, 1 (1995): 41–54.

54. Tiskhov, *Ethnicity*, 261.

55. Ibid., 264. In another set of surveys conducted by the Public Opinion Foundation in Moscow in 1994 and 1995 the respondents were given three options of priorities in Russian state-building: restoration of the USSR, CIS integration, and strengthening of the Russian Federation. Of these, the last attracted the highest number of supporters, but the support nevertheless seemed to be weakening: 41 percent in 1994 and 35 percent in 1995. Quoted in Tolz, "Conflicting 'Homeland Myths,'" 291–292.

56. *Rossiyskaya gazeta*, 25 February 1994.

57. Eduard Bagramov, "Natsiya kak sograzhdanstvo? K otsenke novoy gosudarstvennoy kontseptsii" (The nation as common citizenship? An assessment of the new state concept), *Nezavisimaya gazeta*, 15 March 1994.

58. Tat'yana Kutkovets, "Russkiy vopros" (The Russian question), *Argumenty i fakty* 8, 1994.

59. Ann Sheehy, "Fact Sheet on Declaration of Sovereignty," *Report on the USSR* 2, 45 (9 November 1990).

60. Tishkov, *Ethnicity,* 200–202.

61. John Dunlop, *Russia Confronts Chechnya* (Cambridge: Cambridge University Press, 1998), 204–206.

62. Marie Bennigsen Broxup, "The Case for Chechen Independence," in Ole Høiris and Sefa Martin Yürükel, eds., *Contrasts and Solutions in the Caucasus* (Aarhus, Denmark: Aarhus University Press, 1998), 404.

63. Pavel Baev, *The Russian Army in a Time of Troubles* (London: Sage, 1996), 141–148.

64. See, for example, Andrey Nuykin, "My svoimi rukami sozdaem Karabakhi" (We are creating new Karabakhs with our own hands), *Komsomol'skaya pravda,* 20 March 1992; *Izvestiya,* 24 March 1992.

65. "Programma tatarskoy partii natsional'noy nezavisimosti ittifak" (Program of the Tatar party for national independence), *Panorama* (Kazan) 6 (1991): 15.

66. Fauziya Bayramova, "'Nastoyashchiy tatarin ispytivaetsya na ploshchadi,'" (The true Tatar is tested on the streets), *Vechernyaya Kazan',* 23 October 1991, 2.

67. "Programma tatarskoy partii," 21.

68. A. Tsyganov, "Tatarskiy vykhod" (The Tatar secession), *Moskovskie novosti,*15 March 1992.

69. *Literaturnaya gazeta,* 15 August 1990; Igor' Terekhov, "'Rasve ne Yel'tsin predlagal nam suverenitet?'" ("It was Yeltsin who offered us sovereignty, right?"), *Nezavisimaya gazeta,* 5 November 1991.

70. "Deklaratsiya o gosudarstvennom suverenitete Respubliki Tatarstan" (Declaration on state sovereignty of the Republic of Tatarstan), in *Belaya kniga Tatarstana. Put' k suverenitetu* (Tatarstan's white book: The path toward sovereignty) (Kazan: N.p., 1993), 4.

71. See, for example, Valentin Leksin, "Mintimer Shaymiev: Istinnaya politika ne terpit suety . . . " (Genuine politics does not brook any fuss . . .), in *Rossiya,* 18–24 March 1992, 4.

72. Margarita Belostotskaya, "Mir ili imperiya? Sovetnik prezidenta Rossii Galina Starovoytova otvechaet na voprosy" (Peace or empire? Presidential adviser Galina Starovoytova answers questions), *Vechernyaya Moskva,* 28 January 1992, 2; author's interview with Galina Starovoytova, Moscow, November 1991.

73. "Ne rvat' Rossiyu suverenitetami" (Don't tear Russia apart with declarations of sovereignty), *Izvestiya,* 13 March 1991, 4; and Ruslan Khasbulatov, "'Peredelyvat'sya ya ne khochu'" ("I don't want to be parceled out"), *Nezavisimaya gazeta,* 27 November 1991, 3.

74. "Aleksandr Rutskoy: Ne khochu zhit' v 'bananovoy respublike'" (Aleksandr Rutskoy: I don't want to live in a "banana republic"), *Komsomol'skaya pravda,* 17 January 1992, 1–2.

75. Vitaliy Marsov, "Tatarstan ne podpishet federativnogo dogovora s Rossiey" (Tatarstan will not sign the federal treaty with Russia), *Nezavisimaya gazeta,* 24 March 1992.

76. Ibid.

77. Vyacheslav Shepotkin, "Kogda na vesakh zhizn' giri brosat' opasno" (When life hangs in the balance, it is dangerous to drop the weights), *Izvestiya*, 24 March 1992.

78. Ann Sheehy, "Tatarstan Asserts Its Sovereignty," *Radio Free Europe/Radio Liberty Research Report* 1, 14 (1992): 23–35.

79. Vitaliy Portnikov, "I vse zhe—federatsiya otechestv" (And nevertheless it is a federation of fatherlands), *Nezavisimaya gazeta*, 17 March 1992. Yet the federation treaty did not grant the republics the right to secede from the federation; the Soviet Union republics had formally enjoyed this right.

80. Vera Kuznetsova, "Federativnyy dogovor ne yavlyaetsya takovym" (The federation treaty is not like this), *Nezavisimaya gazeta*, 31 March 1992.

81. *Konstitutsiya respubliki Tatarstan* (Constitution of the Republic of Tatarstan) (Kazan: Tatarskoe Knizhnoe Izdatel'stvo, 1995), 61.

82. Rafael Khakim(ov), *Sumerki imperii. K voprosu o natsii i gosudarstve* (Twilight of an empire: About the nation and the state) (Kazan: Tatarskoe Knizhnoe Izdatel'stvo, 1993), 11.

83. Ibid., 18.

84. Ibid., 21.

85. Ibid., 44.

86. *Konstitutsiya Rossiyskoy Federatsii* (Constitution of the Russian Federation) (Moscow: Yuridicheskaya Literatura, 1993).

87. Tishkov, *Ethnicity*, 65.

88. Il'dar Gabrafikov, *Respublika Bashkortostan. Model' etnopoliticheskogo monitoringa* (The Republic of Bashkortostan: A model of ethnopolitical monitoring) (Moscow: Institut Etnologii i Antropologii RAN, 1998), 35.

89. Tishkov, *Ethnicity*, 256–257.

90. Graham Smith, "Russia, Multiculturalism and Federal Justice," *Europe-Asia Studies* 50, 8 (December 1998): 1396.

91. Jens-Jørgen Jensen and Märta-Lisa Magnusson, *Rusland—samling eller sammenbrud* (Russia—consolidation or collapse?) (Esbjerg, Denmark: Esbjerg University Press, 1995), 131.

92. Marie Bennigsen Broxup, "Tatarstan and the Tatars," in Graham Smith, ed., *The Nationalities Question in the Post-Soviet States* (London: Longman, 1996), 86–88.

93. *Asimmetrichnaya federatsiya: Vglyad iz tsentra, respublik i oblastey* (Asymmetrical federation: The view from the center, from the republics, and from the *oblasti*) (Moscow: Izdatel'stvo Instituta Sotsiologii RAN, 1998).

94. Graham Smith, "Federalising Russia: The Uncertain Transition," paper delivered at the conference "Russian Regionalism and Centre-Periphery Relations," Norwegian Institute of Foreign Affairs, Oslo, 14 November 1996, 10.

95. Some other *oblasti* have merged into larger regional units in order to ensure a firm position vis-à-vis the central authorities, without, however, touching on the federal structure of the constitution. The most important of these is the Siberian Confederacy, established in 1990.

96. *Okrug* leaders can refer to Chukotskiy *okrug* in eastern Siberia, which in May 1993 successfully seceded from Magadan county. But this took place before the 1993 constitution entered into force and should thus be seen as a special case.

97. Mikhail Piskotin, "Federatsiya—eto yedinoe gosudarstvo" (Federation means a single state), *Nezavisimaya gazeta*, 27 November 1997.

98. See, for example, an interview with Zhirinovskiy: Vladimir Fomichev, "Pered russkim vzryvom" (Facing a Russian explosion), *Pu'ls Tushina* 22 (August 1991), 3. Similar views are held by A. Barkashov, extreme rightist leader of the party Russkoe Natsional'noe Edinstvo (Russian National Unity). See Sven Gunnar Simonsen, "Alexandr Barkashov and Russian National Unity: Blackshirt Friends of the Nation," *Nationalities Papers* 24, 4 (1996): 627.

99. Andrey Kibrik, "Protiv ellinov i yudeev v Rossii" (Against any distinctions between Greeks and Jews in Russia), *Moskovskie novosti*, 9 May 1993, 6.

100. *Izvestiya*, 6 October 1993.

101. Boris Fedorov, "Chechnya i razval rossiyskogo gosudarstva," (Chechnya and the collapse of the Russian state) *Izvestiya*, 13 September 1994.

102. This model for national-cultural autonomy was in fact elaborated by the so-called Austro-Marxists at the turn of the century. The idea seems to have been introduced in the modern Russian nationality debate by Viktor Kozlov in 1992, when he launched it as an alternative to a separate Russian republic. See Kozlov, "Glavnyy natsional'nyy vopros," 108.

103. Georgiy Sitnyanskiy, "Esli tatarin ograbil tatarina, zachem vmeshivat' sya tsentru?" (Why should the center interfere if a Tatar robs another Tatar?), *Nezavisimaya gazeta*, 30 April 1994.

104. Radio Free Europe/Radio Liberty Newsline, 21 October 1997 (available at: newsline@list.rferl.org).

105. Sven Gunnar Simonsen, "Inheriting the Soviet Policy Toolbox: Russia's Dilemma over Ascriptive Nationality," *Europe-Asia Studies* 51, 6 (September 1999): 1069–1088.

Chapter 11

1. Graham Smith, Vivien Law, Andrew Wilson, Annette Bohr, and Edward Allworth, *Nation-Building in the Post-Soviet Borderlands: The Politics of National Identities* (Cambridge: Cambridge University Press, 1998), 59–64.

2. I. V. Stalin, *"Marksizm i natsional'nyy vopros"* (Marxism and the national question) in *Sochineniya* (Works), vol. 2, (1913; reprint, Moscow: Ogiz, 1946).

3. Ibid., vol. 2, 294.

4. *Iskra*, 22 October 1903, as quoted in Zvi Gitelman, "The Jews: A Diaspora Within a Diaspora," in Charles King and Neil J. Melvin, eds., *Nations Abroad: Diaspora Politics and International Relations in the Former Soviet Union* (Boulder, Colo.: Westview, 1998), 62. In the Russian empire, the Jews had been designated not as a nation *(natsiya)* but as "allogenes" *(inorodtsy)*. This was a common designation for most Asian subjects of the czar, but the Jews were the only major European group included in this category.

5. The Germans had their own autonomous *oblast* on the Volga that was abolished in 1941 when its population was deported to Kazakhstan and Kirgizia on the suspicion that they might try to collaborate with the Nazi invaders if they got the chance.

6. Paul Goble, "Three Faces of Nationalism in the Former Soviet Union," in Charles A. Kupchan, ed., *Nationalism and Nationalities in the New Europe* (Ithaca, N.Y.: Cornell University Press, 1995), 125.

7. V. K. Malkova, *Obrazy etnosov v respublikanskikh gazetakh* (Images of the ethnoses in the republican press) (Moscow: Institut Etnologii i Antropologii, 1991), 56.

8. Mikhail Guboglo, *Perelomnye gody*, vol. 2: *Yazykovaya reforma—1989. Dokumenty i materialy* (Years of upheaval, vol. 2: The language reform of 1989: Documents and material) (Moscow: Institut Etnologii i Antropologii, 1994), 36.

9. *Kontseptsiya formirovaniya gosudarstvennoy identichnosti respubliki Kazakhstan* (Concept for the shaping of the state identity of Kazakhstan) (Almaty: Kazakhstan, 1996).

10. A. Feoktistov, *Russkie, kazakhi i Altay* (Russians, Kazakhs, and Altay) (Ust-Kamenogorsk: Alfa i Omega, 1992), 40. Emphasis in the original.

11. Irina Malkova, *Analiticheskiy otchet po rezul'tatam issledovaniya na temu 'Osobennosti natsional'nogo stroitel'stva i problemy sozdaniya yedinogo gosudarstva v bikul'turnykh obshchestvakh'* (Analytical report on the results of the research survey "Nation-building and ethnic integration in bicultural societies") (Almaty: Institut Gillera, 1996), 10.

12. Richard Rose, "Rights and Obligations of Individuals in the Baltic States," *East European Constitutional Review* 6, 7 (Winter 1997): 40.

13. *Kniga pamyati zashchitnikov Pridnestrov'ya* (Tribute to the defenders of the Dniester Republic) (Tiraspol: N.p., 1995), 16 and 20.

14. *The Document of the Copenhagen Meeting of the Conference of the Human Rights Dimension of the CSCE* (Copenhagen: CSCE, 1990), 40.

15. Leo Kuper, "Plural Societies: Perspectives and Problems," in Leo Kuper and M. G. Smith, eds., *Pluralism in Africa* (Berkeley: University of California Press, 1969), 14.

16. For an overview of some of these positions, see Arend Lijphart, "Cultural Diversity and Theories of Political Integration," *Canadian Journal of Political Science* 4, 1 (1971): 1–14.

17. Robert A. Dahl, *Democracy and Its Critics* (New Haven, Conn.: Yale University Press, 1989), 254f. Dahl uses the term *polyarchy* rather than *democracy*. In his vocabulary, however, this is not something different from democracy but his attempt to give democracy a precise and operationable content.

18. Ernest Gellner, *Nations and Nationalism* (Oxford: Blackwell, 1990), 54–55.

19. Charles Tilly, "Reflections on the History of European State-Making," in Charles Tilly, ed., *The Formation of National States in Europe* (Princeton, N.J.: Princeton University Press, 1975), 43–44.

20. Arend Lijphart, *Democracy in Plural Societies* (New Haven, Conn.: Yale University Press, 1977), 21–44.

21. Ibid., 55.

22. Nagashbay Shaykenov, as quoted in Yaroslav Razumov, "Primer Kazakhstana v razreshenii problemy mezhnatsional'nykh otnosheniy dostoin izucheniya sosedyam" (The example set by Kazakhstan in the solution of the problem of interethnic relations is worthy of being studied by the neighbors), *Panorama* (Almaty), 1 March 1996.

23. Pål Kolstø and Boris Tsilevich, "Patterns of Nation Building and Political Integration in a Bifurcated Postcommunist State: Ethnic Aspects of Parliamentary Elections in Latvia," *East European Politics and Societies* 11, 2 (Spring 1997): 366–391.

24. "Statement of Members of the Presidential Roundtable on National Minorities in Estonia," MINELRES (Minorities Electronic Resource), 19 February 1999, available at: http://www.riga.lv/minelres/archive.htm.

25. David D. Laitin, *Identity in Formation: The Russian-Speaking Populations in the Near Abroad* (Ithaca, N.Y.: Cornell University Press, 1998), 355.

26. Graham Smith, ed., *Federalism: The Multiethnic Challenge* (London: Longman, 1995), chapters 9 to 12; Liesbet Hooghe, "Belgium: From Regionalism to Federalism," in John Coakley, ed., *The Territorial Management of Ethnic Conflict* (London: Frank Cass, 1993), 44–68.

27. Timothy D. Sisk, *Power Sharing and International Mediation in Ethnic Conflicts* (Washington, D.C.: United States Institute of Peace, 1997), 53.

28. S. L. Tikhvinskiy, A. N. Sakharov, A. V. Zagorskiy, and V. I. Milyukova, *Rossiya i strany blizhnego zarubezh'ya* (Russia and the countries of the near abroad) (Moscow: Institut Rossiyskoy Istorii RAN, 1997), 31.

29. *Open Media Research Institute (OMRI) Daily Digest,* 10 November 1994; Vladimir Socor, as quoted by Paula Thompson, "The Gagauz in Moldova and Their Road to Autonomy," in Magda Opalski, ed., *Managing Diversity in Plural Societies: Minorities, Migration and Nation-Building in Post-Communist Europe* (Nepean, Ontario: Forum Eastern Europe, 1998), 138. The extremely limited financial resources at the disposal of the local Gagauz authorities, however, severely circumscribe their real political power.

30. *Nezavisimaya gazeta* (Independent gazette), 6 May and 9 June 1994. But later rounds of negotiations have shown that the Moldovan party is very unhappy about the state terminology of the April 1994 document and wants to have it removed or at least watered down. See Dan Ionescu, "Playing the 'Dniester Card' in and After the Russian Election," *Transition* 2, 17 (23 August 1996): 26–28.

31. Author's interview with DMR "foreign minister" Valeriy Litskay, Tiraspol, 2 May 1996.

32. Among them, Belarus, Kazakhstan, and Kyrgyzstan. See *Novye konstitutsii stran SNG i Baltii. Sbornik dokumentov* (New constitutions in the CIS and the Baltics: A collection of documents) (Moscow: Manuskript, 1994), 84, 215, 259; "Konstitutsiya respubliki Kazakhstan" (Constitution of the Republic of Kazakhstan), *Mysl'* (Almaty), 10 (1995): 3.

33. "Konstitutsiya Azerbaijanskoy respubliki" (Constitution of the Republic of Azerbaijan), *Azerbaijan* (Baku), 11 November 1995.

34. Neil J. Melvin, *Russians Beyond Russia: The Politics of National Identity* (London: Royal Institute of International Affairs, 1995), 49.

35. Dmitriy Kornilov, "Federatsiya—de fakto. A de yure?" (Federation—de facto: And what about de jure?), *Donetskiy kryazh*, 25 June–1 July 1993; Ivan Plyushch, "Rozumniy balans vlad—zaporuka stabil'nosti suspil'stva" (A sensible balance of powers is a guarantee of social stability), *Viche* 5 (1993), 3–14.

36. Marc Nordberg, "State and Institution Building in Ukraine," in Taras Kuzio, ed., *Contemporary Ukraine: The Dynamics of Post-Soviet Transformation* (Armonk, N.Y.: M. E. Sharpe, 1998), 46.

37. *Asimmetrichnaya federatsiya: Vglyad iz tsentra, respublik i oblastey* (Asymmetrical federation: The view from the center, from the republics, and from the *oblasti*) (Moscow: Izdatel'stvo Instituta Sotsiologii RAN, 1998).

38. For the former opinion, see Helge Blakkisrud, *Den russiske føderasjonen i støpeskjeen* (The Russian Federation in the melting pot) (Oslo: Spartakus, 1997), 40. The latter was expressed in an interview I conducted with former presidential adviser Emil Payn, Moscow, May 1999.

39. Graham Smith, "Russia, Multiculturalism and Federal Justice," *Europe-Asia Studies* 50, 8 (December 1998): 1397; Robert J. Kaiser, "Federalism in Russia: Present Trends and Future Currents," paper presented at the Fifth World Congress of Central and East European Studies, Warsaw, 6 August 1995.

40. Peter Rutland, "A Flawed Democracy," *Current History* 97, 621 (1998): 313–318.

41. Interested readers are advised to consult Will Kymlicka, ed., *The Rights of Minority Cultures* (Oxford: Oxford University Press, 1995).

42. Sammy Smooha, "Minority Status in an Ethnic Democracy: The Status of the Arab Minority in Israel," *Ethnic and Racial Studies* 13, 3 (July 1990): 410.

43. Sammy Smooha and Theodor Hanf, "The Diverse Modes of Conflict-Regulation in Deeply Divided Societies," in Anthony D. Smith, ed., *Ethnicity and Nationalism* (Leiden, Netherlands: E. J. Brill, 1992), 45.

44. Graham Smith, "The Ethnic Democracy Thesis and the Citizenship Question in Estonia and Latvia," *Nationalities Papers* 24, 2 (1996): 199–216. See also Anton Steen, *Between Past and Future: Elites, Democracy and the State in Post-Communist Countries. A Comparison of Estonia, Latvia and Lithuania* (Aldershot, England: Ashgate, 1997), 359–360; Kolstø and Tsilevich, "Patterns of Nation Building," 390–391; Aina Antane and Boris Tsilevich, "Nation-Building and Ethnic Integration in Latvia," in Pål Kolstø, ed., *Nation-Building and Ethnic Integration in Post-Soviet Societies: An Investigation of Latvia and Kazakstan* (Boulder, Colo.: Westview, 1999), 151.

45. Alexander J. Motyl, *Dilemmas of Independence: Ukraine After Totalitarianism* (New York: Council of Foreign Relations Press, 1993), 79.

46. *Russkaya mysl'*, 28 August 1987.

47. V. Stanley Vardys and Judith B. Sedaitis, *Lithuania: The Rebel Nation* (Boulder, Colo.: Westview, 1997), 156.

48. "O grazhdanstve Ukrainy" (On the citizenship of Ukraine), *Flag Rodiny* (Flag of the motherland), 19 September 1992; author's conversations in Crimea, 1992.

49. Annette Bohr, "The Central Asian States as Nationalising Regimes," in Smith et al., *Nation-Building in the Post-Soviet Borderlands*, 145.

50. By contrast, even the green flag of Pakistan—a state established as a homeland for the Muslim population of British India—contains a white column next to the staff, to symbolize the non-Muslim parts of the population.

51. Bohr, "The Central Asian States," 145.

52. Shirin Akiner, *The Formation of Kazakh Identity: From Tribe to Nation-State* (London: Royal Institute of International Affairs, 1995), 61.

53. The national anthem is taken from Mikhail Glinka's opera *A Life for the Tsar* (in the Soviet period known as *Ivan Susanin*, after its main hero), composed in 1836.

54. *Russia Today*, 26 January 1998. Available at: http://www.russiatoday.com today/news.

55. Radio Free Europe/Radio Liberty Newsline, 30 January 1998 (available at: newsline@list.rferl.org).

56. Saken Sabynbay in *Ana Tili*, 8 August 1996, as quoted in *Karavan*, 16 August 1996, 13.

57. Admittedly, the historical evidence is ambiguous on this point and does not allow the formulation of any social "law" of a reverse relationship of will to capacity. Both Germany under Hitler and Japan in the 1930s and 1940s managed to combine state expansion with an expanding economy, but Russia's experience is different: The architect behind Russia's limited economic miracle in the 1880s, Sergey Witte, was a pacifist, precisely as he did not want to squander the scarce resources of the czarist state on militaristic adventures (as nevertheless happened in 1904 and 1914). Many analysts have also argued that the enormous resources allocated to the upkeep of the hypertrophied Soviet army in the 1970s and 1980s were a major factor behind the final collapse of the Soviet state.

58. Roy Allison, "Subregionalism and Security in the CIS Space," in Renata Dwan and Aleksandr Parlink, eds., *Boundaries Without Barriers* (Armonk, N.Y.: M.E. Sharp forthcoming).

59. See, for example, O. Ziborov, "CIS Integration Potential," *International Affairs* (Moscow) 6 (1997): 106.

60. Dmitriy Furman, "O budushchem 'postsovetskogo prostranstva'" (On the future of the "post-Soviet space"), *Svobodnaya mysl* 6 (1996): 38–39.

61. "Nursultan Nazarbayev: Kak eto bylo" (Nursultan Nazarbayev: How it was), *Kazakhstanskaya pravda*, 12 April 1996.

62. Oleksandr Pavliuk, "GUUAM: The Spillover of Politics into Economics?" in Dwan and Parlink, *Boundaries*.

63. Robert H. Jackson, *Quasi-States: Sovereignty, International Relations and the Third World* (Cambridge: Cambridge University Press, 1996), 21.

64. Ibid., 41.

65. Shireen T. Hunter, *The Transcaucasus in Transition: Nation-Building and Conflict* (Washington, D.C.: Center for Strategic and International Studies, 1994), 179–186.

66. Anthony D. Smith, *National Identity* (Harmondsworth, England: Penguin, 1991), 102.

67. Igor A. Zevelev, "The Russian Quest for a New Identity: Implications for Security in Eurasia," in Sharyl Cross, Igor A. Zevelev, Victor A. Kremenyuk, and Vagan M. Gevorgian, eds., *Global Security Beyond the Millennium: American and Russian Perspectives* (London: Macmillan, 1999), 125.

68. Claes Arvidsson and Anders Fogelklou, "Kontinuitet och förändring" (Continuity and change), in Claes Arvidsson, ed., *Öststatstudier. Teori och metod* (Studies of Eastern states: Theory and method) (Stockholm: Leber, 1984), 34.

69. Stein Rokkan, "Dimensions of State Formation and Nationbuilding: A Possible Paradigm for Research on Variations Within Europe," in Charles Tilly, ed., *The Formation of National States in Western Europe* (Princeton, N.J.: Princeton University Press, 1975), 573–574.

Selected Bibliography

Acton, John Emerich Edward. [1862] 1967. *Essays in the Liberal Interpretation of History*. Chicago: University of Chicago Press.

Akiner, Shirin. 1995. *The Formation of Kazakh Identity: From Tribe to Nation-State*. London: Royal Institute of International Affairs.

_____. 1997. "Melting Pot, Salad Bowl—Cauldron? Manipulation and Mobilization of Ethnic and Religious Identities in Central Asia." *Ethnic and Racial Studies* 20, 2 (April): 362–398.

Allworth, Edward. 1980. *Ethnic Russia in the USSR: The Dilemma of Dominance*. New York: Pergamon.

Anderson, Benedict. 1994. *Imagined Communities*. London: Verso.

Anderson, John. 1994. *Religion, State and Politics in the Soviet Union and the Successor States*. Cambridge: Cambridge University Press.

Arel, Dominique. 1995. "Language Politics in Independent Ukraine: Towards One or Two State Languages?" *Nationalities Papers* 23, 3: 597–622.

Azrael, Jeremy R., ed. 1978. *Soviet Nationality Policies and Practices*. New York: Praeger.

Baev, Pavel. 1996. *The Russian Army in a Time of Troubles*. London: Sage.

Barkey, Karen, and Mark von Hagen, eds. 1997. *After Empire: Multiethnic Societies and Nation-Building. The Soviet Union and the Russian, Ottoman, and Habsburg Empires*. Boulder, Colo.: Westview.

Batalden, Stephen K., ed. 1993. *Seeking God: The Recovery of Religious Identity in Orthodox Russia, Ukraine, and Georgia*. De Kalb: Northern Illinois University Press.

Bennigsen, Alexandre, and S. Enders Wimbush. 1985. *Muslims of the Soviet Empire*. London: C. Hurst.

Bourdeaux, Michael, ed. 1995. *The Politics of Religion in Russia and the New States of Eurasia*. Armonk, N.Y.: M. E. Sharpe.

Bremmer, Ian, and Ray Taras, eds. 1997. *New States, New Politics: Building the Post-Soviet Nations*. Cambridge: Cambridge University Press.

Bremmer, Ian, and Cory Welt. 1996. "The Trouble with Democracy in Kazakhstan." *Central Asian Survey* 15, 2: 179–200.

Breslauer, George W., and Catherine Dale. 1997. "Boris Yel'tsin and the Invention of a Russian Nation-State." *Post-Soviet Affairs* 13, 4: 303–332.

Brubaker, Rogers. 1996. *Nationalism Reframed: Nationhood and the National Question in the New Europe*. Cambridge: Cambridge University Press.

293

Bukkvoll, Tor. 1997. *Ukraine and European Security*. London: Royal Institute of International Affairs.

Burant, Stephen R. 1995. "Foreign Policy and National Identity: A Comparison of Ukraine and Belarus." *Europe-Asia Studies* 47, 7: 1125–1144.

Carrère d'Encausse, Hélène. 1979. *Decline of an Empire: The Soviet Socialist Republics in Revolt*. New York: Newsweek.

_____. 1992. *The Great Challenge: Nationalities and the Bolshevik State, 1917–1930*. London: Holmes and Meier.

Chinn, Jeff, and Steven D. Roper. 1995, "Ethnic Mobilization and Reactive Nationalism: The Case of Moldova." *Nationalities Papers* 23, 2: 291–325.

CIS Migration Report (1996). 1997. Geneva: International Organization for Migration.

Connor, Walker. 1994. *Ethnonationalism: The Quest for Understanding*. Princeton, N.J.: Princeton University Press.

Dave, Bhavna. 1996. "National Revival in Kazakhstan: Language Shift and Identity Change." *Post-Soviet Affairs* 12, 1: 51–72.

Denber, Rachel, ed. 1992. *The Soviet Nationality Reader: The Disintegration in Context*. Boulder, Colo.: Westview.

Deutsch, Karl, and William Foltz, eds. 1963. *Nationbuilding*. New York: Atherton.

Dunlop, John B. 1993. *The Rise of Russia and the Fall of the Soviet Empire*. Princeton, N.J.: Princeton University Press.

Furman, Dmitriy, and Oleg Bukhovets. 1996. "Belorussian Self-Awareness and Belorussian Politics." *Russian Politics and Law* 34, 6: 5–29.

Gellner, Ernest. 1990. *Nations and Nationalism*. Oxford: Blackwell.

Gitelman, Zvi, ed. 1992. *The Politics of Nationality and the Erosion of the USSR*. London: Macmillan.

Glazer Nathan, and Daniel P. Moynihan, eds. 1975. *Ethnicity. Theory and Experience*. Cambridge: Harvard University Press.

Gleason, Gregory. 1990. *Federalism and Nationalism: The Struggle for Republican Rights in the USSR*. Boulder, Colo.: Westview.

Harris, Chauncy D. 1993. "The New Russian Minorities: A Statistical Overview." *Post-Soviet Geography* 34, 1: 1–27.

Hirsch, Francine. 1997. "The Soviet Union as a Work-in-Progress." *Slavic Review* 56, 2: 251–278.

Hobsbawm, Eric J. 1990. *Nations and Nationalism Since 1780*. Cambridge: Cambridge University Press.

Hodnett, Grey. 1979. *Leadership in the Soviet National Republics*. Oakville, Ontario: Mosaic Press.

Holdar, Sven. 1995. "Torn Between East and West: The Regional Factor in Ukrainian Politics." *Post-Soviet Geography* 36, 2: 112–132.

Horowitz, Donald L. 1985. *Ethnic Groups in Conflict*. Berkeley: University of California Press.

Huntington, Samuel P. 1993. "The Clash of Civilizations?" *Foreign Affairs* 72, 3: 22–49.

Hylland Eriksen, Thomas. 1993. *Ethnicity and Nationalism: Anthropological Perspectives*. London: Pluto Press.

Kaiser, Robert J. 1994. *The Geography of Nationalism in Russia and the USSR*. Princeton, N.J.: Princeton University Press.

Kaiser, Robert, and Jeff Chinn. 1995. "Russian-Kazakh Relations in Kazakhstan." *Post-Soviet Geography* 36, 5: 257–273.

Kappeler, Andreas, Gerhard Simon, Georg Brunner, and Edward Allworth, eds. 1994. *Muslim Communities Reemerge: Historical Perspectives on Nationality, Politics, and Opposition in the Former Soviet Union and Yugoslavia.* Durham, N.C.: Duke University Press.

Karatnycky, Adrian. 1995. "Ukraine at the Crossroads." *Journal of Democracy* 6, 1: 117–130.

Karklins, Rasma. 1989. *Ethnic Relations in the USSR: The Perspective from Below.* Boston: Unwin Hyman.

Katz, Zev, Rosemarie Rogers, and Frederic Harned, eds. 1975. *Handbook of Major Soviet Nationalities.* New York: Free Press.

Khakimov, Raphael S. 1996. "Prospects of Federalism in Russia: A View from Tatarstan." *Security Dialogue* 27, 1: 69–80.

Khazanov, Anatoly M. 1995. *After the USSR: Ethnicity, Nationalism, and Politics in the Commonwealth of Independent States.* Madison: University of Wisconsin Press.

King, Charles. 1994. "Moldovan Identity and the Politics of Pan-Romanianism." *Slavic Review* 53, 2: 344–368.

King, Charles, and Neil J. Melvin, eds. 1998. *Nations Abroad: Diaspora Politics and International Relations in the Former Soviet Union.* Boulder, Colo.: Westview.

Kolstø, Pål. 1995. *Russians in the Former Soviet Republics.* Bloomington: Indiana University Press; London: C. Hurst.

_____. 1996a. "Nation-Building in the Former USSR." *Journal of Democracy* 7, 1: 118–132.

_____. 1996b. "The New Russian Diaspora—an Identity of Its Own? Possible Identity Trajectories for Russians in the Former Soviet Republics." *Ethnic and Racial Studies* 9, 3: 609–639.

_____. 1998. "Anticipating Demographic Superiority: Kazakh Thinking on Integration and Nation-Building." *Europe-Asia Studies* 50, 1: 51–68.

_____, ed. 1999. *Nation-Building and Ethnic Integration in Post-Soviet Societies: An Investigation of Latvia and Kazakstan.* Boulder, Colo.: Westview.

Kolstø, Pål, and Andrei Edemsky, with Natalya Kalashnikova. 1993. "The Dniester Conflict: Between Irredentism and Separatism." *Europe-Asia Studies* 45, 6: 973–1000.

Kolstø, Pål, and Andrei Malgin. 1998. "The Transnistrian Republic—a Case of Politicized Regionalism." *Nationalities Papers* 26, 1: 103–127.

Kolstø, Pål, and Boris Tsilevich. 1997. "Bulletin of Electoral Statistics and Public Opinion Research Data: Patterns of Nation Building and Political Integration in a Bifurcated Postcommunist State: Ethnic Aspects of Parliamentary Elections in Latvia." *East European Politics and Societies* 11, 2: 366–391.

Kupchan, Charles A., ed. 1995. *Nationalism and Nationalities in the New Europe.* Ithaca, N.Y.: Cornell University Press.

Kuzio, Taras. 1997. "Radical Nationalist Parties and Movements in Contemporary Ukraine Before and After Independence: The Right and Its Politics, 1989–1994." *Nationalities Papers* 25, 2: 211–242.

_____, ed. 1998. *Contemporary Ukraine: The Dynamics of Post-Soviet Transformation.* Armonk, N.Y.: M. E. Sharpe.

Laitin, David D. 1991. "The National Uprisings in the Soviet Union." *World Politics* 44, 1: 139–177.

———. 1998. *Identity in Formation: The Russian-Speaking Populations in the Near Abroad.* Ithaca, N.Y.: Cornell University Press.

Lapychak, Christyna. 1996. "Nation-Building in Ukraine: The Quest for a Common Destiny." *Transition* 2, 18 (6 September): 6–8.

Laqueur, Walter. 1993. *Black Hundred: The Rise of the Extreme Right in Russia.* New York: HarperCollins.

Lewis, Robert A., Richard H. Rowland, and Ralph Clem. 1976. *Nationality and Population Change in Russia and the USSR.* New York: Praeger.

Lijphart, Arend. 1977. *Democracy in Plural Societies.* New Haven, Conn.: Yale University Press.

Manz, Beatrice F., ed. 1994. *Central Asia in Historical Perspective.* Boulder, Colo.: Westview.

Markus, Ustina. 1994. "Belarus: You Can't Go Home Again?" *Current History* 93 (October): 337–341.

Marples, David R. 1996. *Belarus: From Soviet Rule to Nuclear Catastrophe.* New York: St. Martin.

McGarry, John, and Brendan O'Leary, eds. 1997. *The Politics of Ethnic Conflict Regulation.* London: Routledge.

Melvin, Neil J. 1995. *Russians Beyond Russia: The Politics of National Identity.* London: Royal Institute of International Affairs.

Mill, John Stuart. [1861] 1946. *On Liberty and Considerations on Representative Government.* Oxford: Blackwell.

Motyl, Alexander J., ed. 1992. *The Post-Soviet Nationals: Perspectives on the Demise of the USSR.* New York: Columbia University Press.

———. 1993. *Dilemmas of Independence: Ukraine After Totalitarianism.* New York: Council of Foreign Relations Press.

Nahaylo, Bohdan, and Victor Swoboda. 1990. *Soviet Disunion: A History of the Nationalities Problems in the USSR.* London: Hamish Hamilton.

Olcott, Martha Brill. 1995. *The Kazakhs.* 2d ed. Stanford, Calif.: Hoover Institution Press.

Opalski, Magda, ed. 1998. *Managing Diversity in Plural Societies: Minorities, Migration and Nation-Building in Post-Communist Europe.* Nepean, Ontario: Forum Eastern Europe.

Opalski, Magda, Boris Tsilevich, and Piotr Dutkiewicz. 1994. *Ethnic Conflict in the Baltic States: The Case of Latvia.* Kingston, Ontario: Kashtan Press.

Pipes, Richard. 1997. *The Formation of the Soviet Union: Communism and Nationalism, 1917–1923.* Cambridge: Harvard University Press.

Ro'i, Yaacov. 1990. "The Islamic Influence on Nationalism in Soviet Central Asia." *Problems of Communism* 39 (July–August): 49–64.

Rubin, Barnett R., and Jack Snyder, eds. 1998. *Post-Soviet Political Order: Conflict and State Building.* London: Routledge.

Rumer, Eugene B. 1994. "Eurasia Letter: Will Ukraine Return to Russia?" *Foreign Policy* 96 (Fall): 129–144.

Sanford, George. 1996. "Belarus on the Road to Nationhood." *Survival* 38, 1: 131–153.

Silver, Brian D. 1978. "Ethnic Intermarriage and Ethnic Consciousness Among Soviet Nationalities." *Soviet Studies* 30, 1: 107–116.

Simon, Gerhard. 1991. *Nationalism and Policy Toward the Nationalities in the Soviet Union.* Boulder, Colo.: Westview.

Slezkine, Yuriy. 1994. "The USSR as a Communal Apartment, or How a Socialist State Promoted Ethnic Particularism." *Slavic Review* 53, 2: 414–452.

Smith, Anthony D. 1991. *National Identity.* Harmondsworth, England: Penguin.

_____, ed. 1992. *Ethnicity and Nationalism.* Leiden, Netherlands: E. J. Brill.

Smith, Graham, ed. 1996. *The Nationalities Question in the Post-Soviet States.* London: Longman.

Smith, Graham, Vivien Law, Andrew Wilson, Annette Bohr, and Edward Allworth. 1998. *Nation-Building in the Post-Soviet Borderlands: The Politics of National Identities.* Cambridge: Cambridge University Press.

Snyder, Jack. 1993. "Nationalism and the Crisis of the Post-Soviet State." *Survival* 35, 1: 5–26.

Solchanyk, Roman. 1992. "Ukraine, the (Former) Center, Russia and 'Russia.'" *Studies in Comparative Communism* 25, 1: 31–45.

_____. 1994. "The Politics of Statebuilding: Centre-Periphery Relations in Post-Soviet Ukraine." *Europe-Asia Studies* 46, 1: 47–68.

Starr, S. Frederick, ed. 1994. *The Legacy of History in Russia and the New States of Eurasia.* Armonk, N.Y.: M. E. Sharpe.

Suny, Ronald Grigor. 1993. *The Revenge of the Past: Nationalism, Revolution and the Collapse of the Soviet Union.* Stanford, Calif.: Stanford University Press.

Szporluk, Roman, ed. 1994. *National Identity and Ethnicity in Russia and the New States of Eurasia.* Armonk, N.Y.: M. E. Sharpe.

Tilly, Charles, ed. 1975. *The Formation of National States in Western Europe.* Princeton, N.J.: Princeton University Press.

Tishkov, Valery. 1995. "What Is Rossia? Prospects for Nation-Building." *Security Dialogue* 26, 1: 41–54.

_____. 1997. *Ethnicity, Nationalism and Conflict in and After the Soviet Union: The Mind Aflame.* London: Sage.

Tolz, Vera. 1998. "Conflicting 'Homeland Myths' and Nation-State Building in Postcommunist Russia." *Slavic Review* 57, 2: 267–294.

Wilson, Andrew. 1997. *Ukrainian Nationalism in the 1990s.* Cambridge: Cambridge University Press.

Zaprudnik, Jan. 1993. *Belarus: At a Crossroads in History.* Boulder, Colo.: Westview.

Zaslavsky, Victor. 1992. "Nationalism and Democratic Transition in Postcommunist Societies." *Daedalus* 121, 2: 97–121.

Zevelev, Igor. 1996. "Russia and the Russian Diasporas." *Post-Soviet Affairs* 12, 3: 262–284.

INDEX

Sakhalin, 224
Sakharov, Andrey, 198
Samara Air, 249
Samogitia, 40
Sanford, George, 163
SAS. *See* Scandinavian Airlines Systems
Saudi Arabia, 76
Scandinavian Airlines Systems (SAS), 248
Schools, 86–87
    Belarus, 157–158, 162
    Kazakhstan, 130–131
    Latvia, 119–120
    Moldova, 140, 145–146
    Ukraine, 183, 190(table)
Secession, 230
Shamil, Sheikh, 214
Shaymiev, Mintimer, 217, 226
Shcherbytskyy, Vladimir, 176
Shevardnadze, Eduard, 8, 70, 71
Shevchenko, Taras, 37
Shushkevich, Stanislau, 157, 158–159
Silayev, Ivan, 200
Sillamäe, 240
Sitnyanskiy, Georgiy, 225–226
SIU. *See* State Independence for Ukraine
Skak, Mette, 91
Skaryna, Franciåak, 41
Skoropadskyy, Pavlo, 37
Skrypnik, Mstyslav, 68
Slavic states, 83. *See also* Belarus; Ukraine
Slavophiles, 58
Smirnov, Igor, 142, 147
Smirnov, Vladimir, 246–247
Smith, Antony, 18–19, 27, 254
Smith, Graham, 241, 242
Smooha, Sammy, 242
Snegur, Mircea, 143, 145, 146, 149
Snegur, President, 144, 145
Snyder, Jack, 28
Social integration theory, 19–23
Socor, Vladimir, 149–150
Solzhenitsyn, Aleksandr, 208
South Ossetia, 7–8, 71, 229, 238, 240
Sovereign national states, 222
Soviet Congress of People's Deputies, 198
"Soviet man," 4–5
Soviet Marxism, 26
"Soviet values," 101
Spain, 238

Spartak Moskva, 247
Speranskiy, Mikhail, 48
Sports, 246–247
Stalin, Joseph, 11, 26, 39, 195–197, 229–230
    and Belarus, 155–156
    and Chechnya, 214
    and Kazakhstan, 49, 50
    and Moldova, 45, 139
    and religion, 58, 67
Stamps (postage), 247–248
Stankevich, Sergey, 92, 200, 209
Starovoytova, Galina, 211, 218
State Independence for Ukraine (SIU), 185–186
States (definition), 1–2, 16, 222. *See also* Nation-states
Steen, Anton, 116
Stephan the Great, 43, 244
Sterligov, Aleksandr, 59
Sufis, 75
Süleyman the Magnificent, 43
Sunni Islam, 76
Surtsey, 228
Svans, 8
Sverdlovsk, 224
Sweden, 32
Switzerland, 235–236, 239
Symbolic nation-building, 243–249. *See also* Flags; National anthems
Symenenko, Petro, 193

Tajikistan
    citizenship, 98–99
    clan antagonisms, 7
    ethnic discrimination, 90
    nation-building, 254
    religion, 75, 76–77
    voluntary reintegration, 252
Tajiks, 7
Tashkent Treaty, 158, 251
Tatar Public Center (TPC), 216–217
Tatars, 216
Tatarstan, 14, 213, 214, 215–222, 241
Tatarstan Air, 249
Tatimov, M., 134
Tbilsis, 71
Ternopil, 169
Territorial autonomy, 238–241
Territoriality, 229–233